SOCIOLOGY OF EDUCATION SERIES
Aaron M. Pallas, Series Editor

Advisory Board: Jomills Braddock, Sanford Dornbusch, Adam Gamoran, Marlaine Lockheed, Hugh Mehan, Mary Metz, Gary Natriello, Richard Rubinson

From the Series Editor

Manufacturing Hope and Despair is suffused with emotion: the emotional responses of Latino youth trapped in social webs they only partly understand, and the passion of author Ricardo Stanton-Salazar, who uses his considerable energy and skill to illuminate a social problem that demands a public response. The reader's outrage over the injustices of American schooling will certainly be incensed, but then gradually be transformed into a ray of hope as Stanton-Salazar's analysis comes into focus. Authors may think it unseemly to tout a book's merits, but series editors have no such compunctions. Ricardo Stanton-Salazar joins sociological and psychological theorizing to construct an extraordinarily rich account of the social ecology of adolescence. He describes the central role that social networks play in mediating the impact of social origins on educational success. The social webs in which students are embedded can either buffer them from the manifest and hidden injuries of class and race, or magnify these injuries.

Documenting the importance of adolescents' social networks in structuring school success is itself a major accomplishment. Stanton-Salazar's insights, however, extend to the social processes that produce these networks. Furthermore, he shows that while parents, school personnel, and others reading this account may feel that there is no shame in asking the help of others to overcome the difficulties arising from one's social background, doing so involves serious psychological risks for most adolescents. Thus, if students are reluctant to seek help, perhaps we can design schools in which help seeks them.

Manufacturing Hope and Despair is a worthy addition to the Sociology of Education Series, continuing the tradition of casting a distinctively sociological eye on an important problem of educational policy and practice. The result is a work that has much to say to social scientists, educators, and others concerned with the psychosocial development of the next generation of American youth.

Aaron M. Pallas

Manufacturing Hope and Despair

*The School and Kin Support Networks
of U.S.-Mexican Youth*

Ricardo D. Stanton-Salazar

Teachers College, Columbia University
New York and London

Published by Teachers College Press, 1234 Amsterdam Avenue, New York, NY 10027

Library of Congress Cataloging-in-Publication Data

Stanton-Salazar, Ricardo D.
    Manufacturing hope and despair : the school and kin support networks of U.S.-Mexican youth / Ricardo D. Stanton-Salazar.
        p. cm. — (Sociology of education series)
    Includes bibliographical references and index.
    ISBN 0-8077-4109-4 (cloth : alk. paper) — ISBN 0-8077-4108-6 (pbk. : alk. paper)
    1. Mexican American youth—Social networks—California—San Francisco Bay Region. 2. Mexican American youth—Social networks—California—San Diego.
3. Mexican American students—Social networks—California—San Francisco Bay Region. 4. Mexican American students—Social networks—California—San Diego.
I. Series.
HQ796 .S822 2001
305.235—dc21   2001027493

ISBN 0-8077-4108-6 (paper)
ISBN 0-8077-4109-4 (cloth)

Printed on acid-free paper

Manufactured in the United States of America

08 07 06 05 04 03 02 01   8 7 6 5 4 3 2 1

Para mi madre, *Rosario María Salazar De Melo*,
Para *Luis Silveira De Melo*,

In loving memory, *Juan Tomás Stanton-Jiménez*
(1899–1981)

Contents

Part III
The School as a Context for Social
and Institutional Support

Preface—Tale of My Expedition

Doubtless my interest in social networks, social support, and inequality began during my childhood in Southview, one of the four neighborhoods I studied for this book. Soon after returning to San Diego in 1990, I went to Southview to see what had changed, to visit old neighbors, and to reconnect with that *old hill* near my house where I'd spent so much of my childhood. From that hill, we kids would watch the neighborhood activity below and gaze at the various frontiers that existed far from our immediate world. This view from the hill, how magnificent it was—and still is.

Many memories and questions came to me as I strolled atop the old grassy knoll. Why had my life been so different? My contemporaries in the neighborhood and greater community were living lives more consonant with their native membership in San Diego's social bottom. In spite of living in the midst of geographic beauty and of wealth, we were *los de abajo*, the people who inhabited the middle and lower echelons of San Diego's working class. Walking around the old hill, I considered how easily my life could have followed the norm; but there were important mitigating factors.

Fortunately many of us, as children, had not been subjected to the worst the social bottom had to dish out. Vibrant kinship systems and various *urban sanctuaries* protected many of us from "the risks," paving the way to a somewhat secure working-class existence. Other key factors were put into play during my childhood that made me feel I was on a different trajectory. For one thing, I was never "turf bound," but many of my neighborhood buddies were. My network seemed open and dispersed; theirs seemed very localized and bounded. While I traveled about on bicycle, bus, ferry, and car, they guarded the neighborhood. As a prepubescent, up on the hill, I would pinpoint all the places I had visited and the places I would visit next; my friends, on the other hand, mostly Black and Chicano, talked mainly about the neighborhood activity below: the people, the other kids, the girls, the storefronts and Afrocentric murals, the occasional protest marches, the police, the fires, the frequent funeral processions, and the fancy cars. Although I was from a working-class family, my personal social network was spatially expansive, filled with diverse people and wondrous places. Criss-crossing sociocultural boundaries, neighborhood turf lines, and national borders was a regular affair. I had traveled to the very perimeter of the world as seen from *the hill*, and I wanted to go beyond. Yes, I was privileged: by my fair skin, by having an immigrant mother and family in Mexico, by having a Chicano mixed-race father who was steadily employed and had family ties to White folks in the suburbs, by being sentenced to Catholic school, by having a bicycle, by having blue eyes and looking somewhat White—and by being treated well by strangers who assumed I was.

But we were working-class in almost every important way. Being the older of two children, I had no older brother in college, or elsewhere for that matter. Although valuing education, my parents had little formal schooling. Money was always tight and we had debts. Virtually none of our extended family or family associates had gone to college; in fact, it was only after graduating from high school that I visited a university campus. Nearly all my friends living in the area were either poor or working-class, and a good number came from single-parent households. Although as a child I went to school with middle-class White kids from neighborhoods north of me, after school they went home to their neighborhoods and I walked home to mine. And while I occasionally visited their neighborhoods on my frequent bicycle excursions, I played mainly with the kids on my block, or with those kids whose families were similar to mine.

My personal *network*, that interconnected constellation of people, families, households, urban spaces, and geographic places, was something of an enigma. On the one hand, it permitted me to transcend the usually confining influences of class and race, but on the other, it kept from me those things and experiences that spelled authentic class privilege. From the hill, as a youngster, I could see how far and wide my personal network allowed me to go, but my daily experiences and social interactions informed me that this same network closed the door to many desired experiences and opportunities. Again and again, I witnessed activities that I could not actually experience.

The social-class constraints on my network and on my parents' network were revealed to me in other ways as well. Within earshot of my parents' daily discussions, quiet, observant, and attentive, I learned early about what working-class parents so anxiously and incessantly fussed about: How could they ensure I wouldn't fail third grade? Whom could they call for help, and would this person assist me, from the heart? Which of the two would call? And how would they repay? How could they possibly manage the debts next month? Whom could they ask for monetary help? Who was already indebted to them? Could they manage the shame that would come with asking?

Only years later did I come to understand what they were doing: trying to resolve life's problems and to accomplish their goals by surveying both the resources and the limitations of their own social support system, then assessing exactly how they would mobilize whoever was available. Years later, as an adolescent, I found myself making similar queries: Who could help me understand my chemistry assignments, and did I have the nerve, the self-confidence, to ask them? Who could help me find a summer job? Whom did I know who knew someone else who was attending college, particularly someone like me?

The "who" in the questions above points to the human resources that compose each individual's social support system. Each of us is situated within our own personal social web, and much of what determines whether our associates might possess the resources we need depends on our own social class and background. Although love, friendship, camaraderie, and exchanges of social support were always evident in my own family network, it was very rare for us to experience close exchange relations with people of middle-class means, such as those who had significant amounts of discretionary money, or who traveled to far and interesting places, or who had gone to college, or who knew people who did.

Manufacturing Hope and Despair has its roots in these early childhood and adolescent experiences in Southview. Although the scholarly literature and my academic training provided the analytical tools to articulate the role of social networks in adolescent development, it was my own childhood and adolescent experiences in Southview that drove me to ask the questions I ask in this book and that gave me the insights to see the obscure, often mundane, aspects of adolescent network-building as having profound theoretical and sociological significance.

Acknowledgments

This expedition has taken me back into my own early biography as an adolescent in San Diego, and forward into the lives of millions of youth across the country. Although it is far from over, the time has come to take a major turn, but not without thanking the many people and institutions that have made this expedition possible. First and foremost, I owe a great deal to the youth and their parents who willingly shared the most intimate details of their daily lives. My ability to sustain my attention to this project over the years was due in large part to their faith in my promise to tell their story. Their faith and honesty merited a sense of urgency—that their concerns and daily trials needed to be brought, once again, before the nation. With this book, I've kept my promise.

The administration and staff at Auxilio High School in San Diego also deserve my sincere gratitude; they allowed me to come into their midst, knowing I'd be a critical and inquisitive observer. During a full year and a half, they accepted my ubiquitous presence and facilitated my work at many critical junctures. My appreciation also goes to Alberto Ochoa, who reemerged in my career in 1991 to assist me in obtaining approval from the school district in San Diego and to encourage my efforts to study Latino youth.

The research project underlying *Manufacturing Hope and Despair* was labor-intensive, involving many research assistants who worked tirelessly with me, over long periods, to collect, organize, transcribe, code, and analyze the data. Their genuine enthusiasm for my project and their sincere desire to lend their talents and insights to the project will long be remembered and appreciated. Special thanks to Eva Galván, who took on considerable responsibility in helping me meet my sometimes overly ambitious fieldwork objectives in San Diego. Her solid interviewing skills exercised in countless meetings with the female subjects at Auxilio High School provided me a great deal of wonderful material.

The research underlying this book could not have been done without the financial support from both regional and national funders. The fieldwork in the San Francisco–San Jose Peninsula Area was made possible through financial support from the Stanford Center for the Study of Families, Children, and Youth. Support for the San Diego portion of the project came from multiple sources. Regionally, start-up support came from the California Policy Research Center and the U.C. Linguistic Minority Research Institute. My fieldwork in San Diego would not have been possible without my U.C. President's Postdoctoral Fellowship. The fellowship provided the time I needed and the collegial support that validated my early vision of this project. Nationally, financial support came from the Spencer Foundation, which provided me with my first major grant. At mid-stream, the W. T. Grant Foundation provided the support that permitted me to bring this project to completion.

Other institutions also came through at mid-stream to support and sustain my efforts. The Center for U.S.–Mexican Studies at U.C. San Diego provided me a fellowship year to finish the analysis of my data and to write up related work for publication. A major portion of this book was written while I was a visiting research fellow at UCLA during the 1997–98 academic year. This very productive year was made possible by the Ford Foundation Minority Postdoctoral Program, and by the Chicano Studies Research Center at UCLA, acting in conjunction with the university's Institute of American Cultures. Guillermo Hernández, Director of the Chicano Studies Research Center, played a major role in bringing me to UCLA and was helpful in getting me set up at the center.

Over the years, writing the lengthy grant applications, managing the subsequent flow of funds, and hiring my team of assistants could not have been possible without the support of Martha Neal-Brown, my department's fiscal officer. Martha was always there behind the scenes to ensure that the books were in order and that I met my project objectives.

A number of colleagues graciously made themselves available to read and critique portions of my developing manuscript. Their commentary, suggestions, and collegial support were always helpful and timely. Special thanks to Walter Allen, Patricia Gandara, Patricia Phelan, George Lipsitz, Bud Mehan, Michael Messner, JoAnn Moody, Rudolfo Torres, and Angela Valenzuela. Robert Tai, co-author of Chapter 10, played an important and instrumental role in the analysis and presentation of the book's statistical findings; his special combination of talents was always appreciated. My gratitude also goes out to all those colleagues over the years who, in their own way, provided validation and encouragement for what I was trying to accomplish. Academics are no different from other people engaged in creative endeavors—we need to hear from friends and trusted colleagues that our efforts are on the mark.

The last leg of writing a scholarly book is known for being arduous and painful: the near never-ending yet necessary editorial criticisms, revisions, and editing. At least part of this long process was enlivened by Jacquelyn Sorensen, my editor in San Diego. Jacquelyn combed every sentence of the manuscript, filling the pages of my chapters with a lot more than mini-lessons in grammar and usage. Her intellectually insightful, often brilliant, frequently enthusiastic commentaries made the latter part of the long editing process intellectually engaging and often pleasurable. Thanks also goes to those at Teachers College Press who shepherded the first book of my academic career, most notably my editors, Brian Ellerbeck and Aureliano Vázquez, Jr.; thanks as well to Wendy Schwartz at Teachers College Press who provided me with the first round of editorial comments on my manuscript.

Much of what *Manufacturing Hope and Despair* is about has to do with how the social support from significant others allows us to accomplish important objectives in daily life and, sometimes, to even move mountains. Bringing this book project from inception to completion was far more challenging than mountain moving, and could not have been done without the support from my own personal network of family and friends. Heartfelt gratitude goes to a cluster of very special people, beginning with my sister, Susie Hernández, who helped maintain the family web, and Olga Vásquez, whose friendship helped sustain me through graduate studies and the challenging nineties, and Lisa Catanzarite who was never far away. My UCLA writing partner, Otto Santa Ana, provided friendship and much-needed collegial support during a very important year in my academic career. A one-man show of applause to my Latino men's group in San Diego—*El Círculo de Hermanos*, as we call ourselves. Over the past 4 years, these special men have consistently fortified me by their example, their love and encouragement, and their indefatigable willingness to listen to me nonjudgmentally. A special thanks to my *Círculo hermanos* Eduardo Aguilar, Diego Davalos, and Paul Espinosa: Eduardo knew how to expertly weave the roles of friend, colleague, and teacher into something I experienced as fortifying, healing, and unreplicable; Diego entered the *Círculo* with love and changed everything. Paul (and his partner Marta Sánchez) provided that special extra support I needed during the 1999–2000 academic year. I must also mention Gail Pérez and Olivia Puentes-Reynolds, who, each in her own way, provided me much support with their friendship and faith in me.

While rightly acknowledging the support of my family and of so many friends, colleagues, and assistants, I must ultimately accept full responsibility for this project, particularly for errors incurred in the course of this study, including those of fact, approach, or interpretation. It is hoped, however, that even my errors will provide opportunities for all of us to amplify and extend the dialogue on the important issues raised in this book.

Although the book project was founded on a commitment to provide both careful fact and sound analysis, it was fundamentally driven by a profound desire to generate greater discussion concerning our nation's minority youth. If such a discussion can be aided by a heavy dose of scholarly criticism, than may it come forth like manna in the desert—plentiful and enriching to all.

Manufacturing Hope and Despair

1

Introduction

The two most searing stories of the past holiday season? One was
about the small Memphis boy who went home from school every
night to an apartment where his mother's body lay rotting. The
boy was so isolated, so afraid he'd end up in foster care that he
told no one of her death. In a similar story, a 7-year-old Massachu-
setts girl who told a teacher that her mother had died was report-
edly scolded, "You shouldn't say things like that." So the girl spent
that night alone with the corpse. I'm not blaming the school or the
teacher. But the uneasy truth is that children are often tragically
disconnected. The schools don't know their lives; the communities are clueless. Paying real attention to the younger generation is
labor-intensive. It consists of connections and discipline, expectations and second chances. It's harder to talk with troubled teens
than to profile them. But in raising kids, as a parent or country,
zero tolerance adds up to absolutely nothing.[1]
                    —Ellen Goodman, syndicated columnist in Boston

We know, from decades of research on children and adolescents, that healthy
human development and school success depend on regular opportunities
for constructing supportive relationships with various significant others
and agents across key institutional arenas (Bandura, 1969; Wynn, Richman,
Rubenstein, & Littell, 1987). Regardless of the community under study,
parents, siblings, extended family members, school personnel, peers, neighbors, and community agents all play a significant role in youth development. Yet, there are many children and adolescents from low-income families who routinely face school difficulties, an emotional crisis, or some
important developmental challenge alone, with little or no support. What
is perplexing is that such youth often are deeply embedded in a network
of family members, peers, and school agents who engage them socially,
who "care" about them, and who could very well serve as an important
source of social support.

1

What is particularly disturbing is that the process of social support is frequently short-circuited by children and adolescents themselves, by psychological orientations that either prevent them from seeking help or render them unreceptive to the supportive actions of significant others. Fear, anxiety, shame, anger, distrust, or loss of confidence in the support process are the usual culprits. Examples of these feelings abound throughout the present study: An adolescent tells of his fears that seeking support from his immigrant mother would add still another burden on someone he perceives as overwhelmed with economic problems and with her own cultural adjustments. Another adolescent is hesitant about going to her parents with her "boyfriend problems" because of generational differences in values and mores. In the arena of the school, an adolescent feels anxious about seeking academic assistance from a caring teacher because, in her own words, "things don't really sink into my head very easily, very quickly." This young woman not only fears taxing the teacher's patience, but also imagines the worst—that the teacher will detach in frustration, leaving her feeling like a hopeless case. Another adolescent admits he has never established the degree of trust and rapport with a teacher that would permit him to disclose his problems and to seek support.

All people, of course, at one time or another, or perhaps with some regularity, experience feelings that inhibit help seeking and network-building. Yet, when these human experiences and feelings are perceived in the context of the interlocking hierarchies of class, race, and gender, a set of fundamental sociological processes comes into focus. Although the difficulties inherent in the seeking of social support are genuinely human and experienced in similar ways by people in Western industrialized societies, for those consigned to the social bottom, such difficulties, if unresolved, carry the haunting prospect of stunted development, multiple marginality, and depressed life chances. And although the difficulties associated with network-building and help-seeking, as experienced by low-status youth, are often made manifest in conflictive relational dynamics and negative adolescent orientations, our task in this book is surely not to *blame the victim*; rather, it is to trace these observable processes to their structural roots, then back again.

Furthermore, the journey through this investigation is not always grim. Occupants of the social bottom or the lower classes also experience and benefit from instances of genuine support in ways that are distinctive and sociologically significant. Given the structurally vulnerable position and life circumstances of these individuals, occasions of authentic support often prevent them from experiencing the full and mortifying weight of social oppression—at least for a short time (e.g., Lomnitz, 1977; Stack, 1974; Williams & Kornblum, 1985). And thus we see the contradictory possibilities that underlie the social webs within which low-status youth are typically embedded.

WHAT IS *MANUFACTURING HOPE AND DESPAIR* ABOUT?

Manufacturing Hope and Despair presents a detailed study of the social support networks and help-seeking experiences of low-income Mexican-origin adolescents from immigrant families. In the course of this study, we come to know the life experiences, developmental challenges, and ecological risks that are common to this rapidly growing population. We also come to see the principal ways in which low-status adolescents cope with life's challenges and ecological dangers, and whether they are able to enjoy the support and protection of various significant figures in the home, community, and school. Too often, these adolescents do not enjoy such support and protection.

Latinos are the fastest-growing ethnic group in the United States today. By the mid-90s in California, Latino students in the K–12 school population already constituted the largest group (40%) of the new non-White majority. Yet, by most measures, particularly in educational achievement, Latinos lag behind other groups (López & Stanton-Salazar, in press). Behind the statistics lie the accounts of how social class, race, and gender restrict the mobility and life chances of Latino youth—and it is here that social networks and varied access to social support play a most definitive role.

Using social network data, excerpts from transcribed interviews, and statistical survey data, the book documents and elaborates on the numerous constraints and social forces that prevent many low-status youth from constructing the kinds of relationships and social networks that provide access to important forms of social support (e.g., academic assistance, career decision-making, emotional support, crisis intervention). Using representative data drawn from transcribed interviews, *Manufacturing Hope and Despair* draws the reader into private and highly sensitive conversations with a diverse sample of low-income Mexican-origin high schoolers, and exposes the often complex and distressing dynamics that make help-seeking and network-building so problematic, yet so potentially *resource*-ful. The book is both empirically rich and replete with elucidating analyses that offer new ways of looking at the life experiences of low-income urban Latino adolescents, particularly as they make the difficult transition into adulthood. Concepts such as *social capital, social networks,* and *help-seeking orientation* are key to the framework developed in the book, and are strategically used to explain not only how most working-class Mexican-origin

adolescents end up as working-class adults, but how some youth are buffered from the worst effects of class and racial oppression in society.

Manufacturing Hope and Despair takes us into the overlapping realms
of the neighborhood, the kinship network, and the school, and guides our
exploration of the relational dynamics peculiar to each context. We see, for
example, that obstacles to help seeking and social support in the immigrant
household are distinct from those obstacles arising in daily relations with
school personnel.[2]

Constraints on help-seeking and network development are mainly
divided into two distinct but highly related categories. The first is comprised of those constraints that become manifest in the social-psychological
orientations of adolescents (e.g., feelings of distrust, fear, and anxiety); the
second is those constraints most often identified as institutional structures
or organizational features. For example, high schools are frequently organized in ways that minimize opportunities for students and teachers to get
to know each other well. Student/counselor ratios in many urban/metro-
politan schools are often so high that counselors have little time to invest
in the school's most needy students. Attention is also paid in this study to
the whole range of social supports, although special attention is given to
those forms of institutional support that we know privileged youth normally enjoy and working-class youth do not—for example, expert guidance pertaining to college opportunities (Ianni, 1989; see also Appendix A).
In investigating the difficulties many low-status youth experience in
accessing institutional support, we pay considerable attention to the difficulties adolescents experience in forging trusting and supportive relations
with school personnel (Chapters 8, 9, & 10).

Although this study focuses on constraints to help-seeking and network-
building, considerable attention is also devoted to those social conditions
and adolescent orientations that *promote* the development of authentically
supportive relations. These findings, when they emerge, suggest to us how
some working-class ethnic minority youth become exceptional cases, weav-
ing social webs that promote persistence in school as well as empowering
forms of resiliency. In both cases, the role of social networks in shaping
young people's life-chances is elucidated.

The adolescents' own perceptions of relational dynamics, and of the
support process itself, lie at the center of this investigation. The objective
in this study was not to adjudicate the case of unsupportive relations between youth and their significant others, hearing in the process the testimony of all relevant parties. Rather, the objective was to explore how adolescent network experiences and help-seeking orientations are critical to
the development of adolescent support systems and how these orientations
and experiences are shaped by the various institutional, societal, and cul-

tural forces in which low-status youth are embedded. Thus, the focus on help-seeking and relational dynamics is necessarily grounded in the *emic* view of adolescents (i.e., from their perspective).

It is important to note, as well, that the theoretical literature on help seeking, coping, and network estrangement emphasizes the individual's appraisals of the human resources in his or her environment. Analytical attention to people's appraisals of their relationships, as part of the exploration of their support networks, has a very strong tradition in psychology (e.g., Belle, Dill, & Burr, 1991; Cochran, Larner, Riley, Gunnarsson, & Charles, 1990; Lazarus & Folkman, 1984) and in anthropology (Keefe & Padilla, 1987; Stack, 1974; Vélez-Ibáñez, 1980, 1983). Apart from a small number of ground-breaking or important studies conducted by sociologists (e.g., Lin, Dean, & Ensel, 1986; Lopata, 1979; Wellman, 1981), the dearth of analytical attention to such appraisals and orientations in contemporary or recent sociology cannot be fully explained by sociologists' heavy reliance on quantitative and survey methods. American psychology, of course, depends largely on quantitative methods. In any case, the qualitative methods employed in the present study did offer the opportunity to examine carefully the individual's own appraisals of the constraints on seeking support and on network development.

DEVELOPMENT OF THEORETICAL FRAMEWORK

The research presented in this book was motivated from the beginning by a desire to explore how several carefully selected tools of *social network analysis* might help us to better articulate the various and simultaneous ways class, gender, race, and ethnic forces affect the daily lives of low-status adolescents, particularly in the development of adolescent relationships and social support systems. Through the book's focus on the complexities of adolescent network-building and help-seeking experiences, I address how the structural effects of class, race, and gender can be articulated not only in terms of the objective ecological conditions within which low-status youth live (e.g., poverty, racial segregation, resource-strapped schools), but also in terms of the coping patterns that develop in response to these conditions.

Following a strong sociological tradition, I pay close attention to the linkage between structure and individual consciousness and, in particular, to the vexing problem of "internalized oppression," or in terms conveyed by the eminent French sociologist Pierre Bourdieu, how the dominated always contribute to their own domination (Bourdieu & Wacquant, 1992). And although the oppressed are often unwittingly complicit in their own oppression, we need to understand how this complicity is itself a product of the greater social structure.

Exclusionary or discriminatory structures in society are most easily understood in their concrete and objective forms, for example, housing segregation by class and race, or the middle class's historical refusal to fund our urban and suburban schools equally, or according to the needs of students (Berliner & Biddle, 1995; Lipsitz, 1977). More difficult to comprehend are the *subterranean* aspects of societal exclusion, that is, how low-income families, poor communities, peer groups, and urban schools are often forced to socially organize and cope in ways that lead many inhabitants to *play host to the system* and, and ultimately, to regulate their own oppression. Thus, we see many low-status youth grappling alone with sizable negative challenges to their healthy development, even though they are embedded in large webs of significant others and institutional agents.

Unlike the conventional approaches taken in most of the research on social and interpersonal networks, *Manufacturing Hope and Despair* selectively employs conceptual and methodological tools used in the analysis of social support and egocentric networks to articulate a new and, it is hoped, useful view of social inequality. This newly crafted approach shows how adolescent social webs routinely act as the conduits that deliver the harm underlying class and racial segregation in society. And yet, this approach allows us to see how these same webs can sometimes exhibit their wondrous potential for buffering youth from this systemic harm, and for propelling individual youth into the stratosphere of middle-class adult life—all the while, of course, maintaining the integrity of our class-, gender-, and race-stratified and exclusionary social system.

THE CONCEPT OF SOCIAL NETWORK AS
A SOCIAL SUPPORT SYSTEM

The concept of social network has been defined and described in many different ways, for example, as a "social web" that connects people to each other and that intertwines groups and communities into that integrated something we call society. Social networks have also been conceived as a "social support system," that web of relations that keeps us economically afloat as well as resilient and healthy, and that ultimately sustains our humanity. They have been conceived as "social freeways," permitting privileged people to move about the complex mainstream landscape quickly and efficiently. They've been theorized as "conduits" and "pipelines" through which resources, privileges, and opportunities flow to certain groups and individuals. To "expand the pipeline" usually entails changing people's networks, as well as bringing people into an institutional, resource-sharing network. Networks can be resourceful *and* exclusionary, like the *ol' boys* network we know exists in the corporate sector and in politics. Networks can also be resource-sharing and open, like those Mexican families that continually adopt fictive kin through religious rituals. Networks have also been referred to as "social prisons" that lock certain groups of people into urban spaces that generate despair and hopelessness. Networks can be any of these things, depending on the subject of conversation, or the object of scholarly study.

THE NATURE OF THE STUDY: SETTINGS, RESEARCH DESIGN, SAMPLES, DATA GATHERING, AND INSTRUMENTATION

The data featured in this book come from two distinctive research initiatives, each commenced by the author at a different research site and at a different time. The various data sets employed in this study and the types of data analyses conducted are summarized in Figure 1.1 and in Appendix B. The first study began with fieldwork I conducted in the San Francisco–San Jose Peninsula Area in the late 1980s. The second study was commenced in San Diego, California, in the spring of 1991. Below I provide an overview of both projects.

The San Francisco–San Jose Peninsula Area Study and The San Diego Study

Over the course of three months, a colleague and I surveyed 205 Latino high school students distributed across six high schools.[3] All six schools were already participating in a larger research study being conducted by the Stanford Center for the Study of Families, Children, and Youth.

Our semistructured research design generated a great deal of quantifiable data, much of it eventually subjected to statistical analysis. However, in the course of our survey of individual students, often occurring over two and sometimes three visits, a good deal of serendipitous and richly textured information came forth, much of it not systematically documented or transcribed due to our survey design and to strict time constraint. Most of this information was highly personal and *emic* in nature, and dealt with the subtle dynamics underlying students' relations with school personnel, family members, and peers. Some of this rich data did find its way into our logs after our interviews with a student; the qualitative data, however, was never systematically analyzed and written up. Soon after beginning

FIGURE 1.1. Data sets and Types of Data*

The San Francisco–San Jose Peninsula Area Study (1988–1989)

Egocentric Network Survey (N = 205 [N = 145]) — Quantitative Network Data (Descriptive and Statistical Analyses)

School-wide Questionnaire Survey (all six schools) — Quantitative Survey Data (Statistical Analysis)

The San Diego Study (1991–1992)

Replication of Original Network Survey (N = 75) — Quantitative Network Data (Descriptive Analysis)

Intensive Interviews with Students (N = 51) — Interview Data (Qualitative Data Analysis)

School-wide Questionnaire Survey (N = 1,187) (772 Latinos) — Quantitative Survey Data (Statistical Analysis)

Intensive Interviews with Parents of Students Participating in the Study (N = 18) — Interview Data (Qualitative Data Analysis)

Interviews with Adults Identified as Important Institutional Agents in School and Community — Interview Data (Qualitative Data Analysis)

Ethnographic Investigation (Participant Observation) of School and Community Social Structures — Ethnographic Data (Qualitative Data Analysis)

Demographic Profiles of Four Neighborhoods — Census Tract Data (Descriptive Analysis)

*Actual sample breakdown in Appendix B.

this project, it became clear to me that sometime in the near future I had to return to the field, most likely at a different site, and bring with me slightly modified research questions and a significantly different and mixed research design.

The opportunity came to me slightly less than a year after I finished and wrote up the original study in the Bay Area/Peninsula. Now in San Diego, California, my hometown, and with new funding, I sought out an urban-metropolitan high school that had a majority Latino student population. The school I located received adolescents from three of the largest Latino neighborhoods in the urban area; it featured a two-thirds Latino student body, mainly Mexican in origin. About 82% of the Latino student body came from working-class households, with about 55% from lower-working-class or low-income families.[4] Demographic inquiries into parental education showed that 75% of Latina mothers had not finished high school; 55% had completed 6 years of schooling or less.

Only one major hurdle stood in the way of commencing this new study: This was the school I had graduated from 17 years earlier. Although the old stone building was gone and most of the personnel I knew had died, retired, or moved on, and although the student body composition in the mid-70s was significantly different—the school had been much more ethnically diverse—this was still my old school, and old memories were stimulated. After several months of weighing the costs and benefits of entering such a research site, I decided to go ahead and begin my study at the school, which I eventually came to call, in symbolic fashion, *Auxilio* High School.[5]

The principal motivating factor underlying this second study was a desire to incorporate an ethnographic/intensive *interview* component into my research on Latino students' social and information networks. This I was able to do at Auxilio High, eventually replicating the original Bay Area/Peninsula network survey with a sample of 75 students, then following through with a series of intensive interviews with 51 students, drawn from the original sample of 75 (see Appendix B).

Soon after gaining entry to the school site, I received permission to give a self-administered questionnaire to the entire student body (about 1,500 students). The survey permitted me to query all the students at the school about their access to various institutional sources of information and social support. It also permitted me to acquire detailed demographic information from every student (e.g., national origin, family structure, residential mobility, length of residence in the United States, parental education, etc.), as well as information on additional issues of relevance to the study (e.g., educational plans, organizational participation, employment status, contact rates with school personnel, perceptions of social support, and perceptions of the opportunity structure).

Another vital component of the investigation entailed home visitations and interviews with the parents of students selected from the intensive-interview sample (N = 51). Although this sample includes students of all achievement levels, I was initially interested in investigating the support systems of "high-achieving" students from low-income families.[6] For this reason, and because the proportion of high-achievers from low-income families was low compared with the proportion of low-achievers, I tried to ensure that sufficient resources would be directed toward families with high-achievers. Interviews with parents entailed questions similar to those posed to students; however, the focus was on the parents' perception of the support process, including the obstacles they saw as inhibiting their children's access to various institutional sources of support and, finally, the parents' strategies for dealing with these obstacles.

During the academic year, I also reserved time to personally conduct ethnographic interviews with various adults identified by my adolescent informants as important and reliable sources of social support. I was particularly attentive to those identified as institutional agents working in various settings within the school (e.g., instruction, counseling, administration, extracurriculum) and in the community (e.g., federally sponsored programs, churches, voluntary civic and political associations, social clubs, and other small-scale institutions within and outside the residential colonies). These adults were asked to provide their perceptions regarding the social conditions and circumstances that had allowed them to be supportive, as well as the problems that exist in their own institutional domains that restrict their supportive capabilities.

I also tried as best as I could to immerse myself in the field, undertaking participant observation of neighborhood adolescents and staff working in various school and community settings. I was already familiar with the three residential communities in which my Mexican-origin adolescent informants lived. I grew up simultaneously negotiating my space in these three communities, and now, as a university academic, was living close by in an adjacent community. I had been gone for most of the 1980s, during a period when these three communities underwent considerable demographic changes, due principally to Mexican immigration. These important changes required that I reimmerse myself, and come to know these communities as they were being experienced by my informants.

AN OVERVIEW OF WHAT FOLLOWS

Chapter 2 begins the study by presenting an analytical framework for articulating the special roles played by social networks and help seeking in the lives of urban racial minority adolescents from low-income families. Many of the concepts and processes drawn from interdisciplinary studies on social networks are rearticulated here within a framework that uses the terms *social capital* and *social embeddedness* to make clear the connections between the problems of adolescent network development and the structural influences of race, class, and gender.

The findings of this study are presented across three sections, with each section concentrating on a major context in adolescent life. In Chapter 3, I describe the neighborhood and community settings in which the adolescents I studied resided. A demographic profile is presented, followed by an examination of how low-income urban neighborhoods and communities come to affect the social networks and life experiences of children and adolescents. Chapter 4 concentrates on the problems *barrio* youth and their families face in making use of the institutional and familial resources in the surrounding community. Supportive relations with older siblings and extended family members are highlighted. Chapters 5 through 7 concentrate on relations between adolescents and their immigrant parents. Chapters 8, 9, and 10 take us into Auxilio High School, and focus on relations between adolescents and school personnel—specifically, teachers and guidance counselors. Chapter 11 takes a retrospective look at the findings of this study, and provides summative analyses that can contribute to ongoing advances in network-analytic accounts of minority socialization and social inequality.

2

Social Capital and Social Embeddedness in the Socialization of Low-income Latino Adolescents in the United States

> It is clear that the real intellectual wealth of the individual depends entirely on the wealth of his real relationships.[1]
>
> —Karl Marx

In this chapter I lay out a social capital framework for looking at the network and help-seeking experiences of low-income minority youth, and for understanding how low-income families, schools, and communities are socially organized to reproduce social inequality. This framework also attends to those processes that allow individual exceptional cases to emerge— minority adolescents who are able to experience the necessary supports that not only buffer them from the worst effects of class, race, and gender oppression, but pave the way for a significant degree of social mobility. In laying out this framework, I present a number of cases that emerged as particularly revealing in this study, and that illustrate how so many adolescents coped with personal problems and stressors by withdrawing from various sources of support. Rather than framing this movement toward disengagement as a universal developmental stage in adolescence, I use these examples to show the ways that social class gender, race, and assimilationist forces often underlie the adolescent experiences of low-status minority youth.

FUNCTIONALIST BIASES UNDERLYING THE STUDY OF SIGNIFICANT OTHER SUPPORT AND SCHOOL SOCIAL INTEGRATION

The last dozen years have been marked by a good deal of scholarly interest and research focusing on social integration processes within the school and community (e.g., Coleman, 1988; Coleman & Hoffer, 1987; Tinto,

1993; Wehlage, Rutter, Smith, Lesko, & Fernández, 1989). Here we find evidence of fairly typical Anglo middle-class and functionalist undercurrents.[2] This social integration literature typically views student variations in academic learning, intellectual development, and persistence to degree completion as dependent on a student's level of personal engagement or *social integration* into the social and intellectual fabric of the school. According to these frameworks and their adherents, at the core of the problem of student underachievement and failure is the school's (or college's) difficulty in engaging, or socially integrating, particular sectors of its student body. Close relations or social bonds with parents, school personnel, and peers are given a good deal of importance. Governed by strong functionalist undercurrents, these frameworks interpret such relations in terms of key socialization processes that function to socially integrate the individual by conferring a new identity and facilitating adherence to the educational system's moral order and ideological foundations.

A number of researchers have called attention to the fact that the malintegration of minority students in urban schools is often invisible. While the most obviously disengaged students "disrupt classes, skip them, or fail to complete assignments," most disengaged students behave well in school and generally attend class (Newmann, 1992, p. 2). Yet researchers suggest that beneath the surface, this silent majority experiences a lack of psychological investment in learning, a lack of intellectual mastery of the curriculum, and a nagging sense of disconnection, if not alienation, from the core social fabric of the institution (Newmann, Wehlage, & Lamborn, 1992).

In one exemplary integration study, Gary Wehlage and associates (1989) draw our attention to a set of school integrative processes seen as fostering academic achievement in schools serving low-status students. In brief, these researchers isolated what they came to term "school membership," a process whereby students were able to develop social bonds to school personnel, thus connecting them to the school's core social fabric. In this scenario, the individual student is engaged in quasi-reciprocal relations and is "attached, committed, involved and has belief in the norms, activities and people of an institution" (p. 117). When such bonding between agent and student becomes a defining characteristic of the school community as a whole, students experience a certain "we-ness," a collective identity that is highly consonant with increased effort engagement and academic achievement. In sum: School personnel treat students in a caring manner, creating the conditions for "bonding"; in turn, students come to identify with, and conform to, the established order; now integrated, students experience a heightened degree of motivation and make the necessary efforts to meet academic demands.

Of course, interest in social interactions between peers and between school personnel and students has a long history in educational research— a history, I believe, that needs to be unpacked and examined carefully, then contrasted with alternative perspectives. For our purposes here, what is important is the relational transmission process that occurs through "integration," and how school success and social mobility are theoretically linked to this transmission process. According to the functionalist perspective driving most integration research, the engine that propels engagement, learning, and achievement is represented by key aspects or functions of social structure that inhere in relations between students and "significant others," particularly relations with parents, school personnel, and peers. For easy perusal, I have listed these aspects in Figure 2.1 below. The *social support* provided by school personnel, parents, and peers occurs through vital relational processes that function primarily to socialize (or resocialize [domesticate?]) youth into a particular psychological-motivational orientation and to move youth to behave in a certain prescribed and conforming manner. Conformity to the established order (e.g., the school system) brings rewards devised by the social system to facilitate everyone's integration, and ultimately to serve "the system's" greater interests—interests that are seen as rational, and that serve everyone who properly submits to the established moral order.[3]

FIGURE 2.1. Aspects [Functions] of Relationships That Foster Social Integration

---

1.   to instill trust, confidence, affective attachment, and loyalty;

2.   to engender specific and necessary psychological dispositions;

3.   to inculcate specific goals, standards of excellence, aspirations, values, norms, and mores;

4.   to confer a particular status and identity;

5.   to engender an appetite for certain extrinsic rewards;

6.   to obligate, to bring into debt, and to exact reciprocity;

7.   to apply pressures and sanctions for the purpose of enforcing normative standards.

Also implicit in this dominant perspective is the notion that responsibility for initiating and continually reinforcing this conformity lies with the student's family and community. The school is viewed as both enhancing the requisite psychological and cognitive traits and contributing to the proper academic cycle; in the case of "disadvantaged youth," the school is seen as valiantly providing students with a second chance to become part of this necessary socialization program.

Seldom addressed in these functionalist perspectives is the possibility that the school system's transmission process is not at all about instilling universal and rational values and traits, but rather about inculcating a psychological orientation that supports the culture and political interests of particular groups in society—groups that, in fact, effectively organize themselves into institutional networks on the basis of commonly shared class, racial, and gender attributes. Never addressed are the hidden ideological messages and the racist, classist, and sexist myths that might underlie the socialization forces mentioned above. Never addressed are the various adverse effects these ideological messages might have on the consciousness and coping patterns of different segments of the working-class minority youth population.[4]

Seldom addressed is the possibility that relations of detachment and conflict between low-status youth and their parents, and between these youth and school personnel, are founded on social antagonisms, contradictions, and divisions existing in the wider political economy. Such relational conflicts and antagonisms, when reluctantly addressed, are usually cast in the discourse of deviance and family dysfunction. In this light, the social-control mechanisms of the school and family are usually targeted. Following functionalist logic, either social controls need to be heightened— at whatever cost—or deviant students need to be loved into submission; in either case, the goal is to return all systems to a level of stability and cohesion.

The central issue here is that many scholarly works on minority youth, set as they are within dominant functionalist paradigms, insist on remaining ahistorical and disconnected from analyses that situate schools, families, and communities within our highly class-stratified, patriarchal, racialized, and segregated society. Such intellectual practices potentially carry dangerous consequences. The persistent decontextualization so characteristic of dominant perspectives often leads to explanatory accounts that are subject to misuse and distortion by those wishing to validate and promulgate their own class, racial, and gender biases.

This is not to say that conventional integration frameworks, when used conscientiously and without prejudice, wrongly target what are well-known dimensions of the educational experience (e.g., social relations with school agents, motivational dynamics, the fostering of pro-academic norms). Properly embedded within contextualized analyses that account for the various hierarchical forces that socially organize schools, school systems, communities, and the economy, this attention to norms and integrative processes can prove quite productive, significantly contributing to a deeper understanding of the persistent and pervasive problems experienced by so many urban minority youth.

Yet, when viewed through a critical network-analytic framework, what appears most troublesome in the socialization accounts of integration studies is not so much the hyperfocus on conformity (or nonconformity) to arbitrary norms and values, but the virtually complete absence of attention to the transmission and exchange of tangible institutional resources that are part and parcel of any privileged community, and are particularly characteristic of the social networks and social ties of the middle and upper classes. Seen in this light, integration frameworks do appear to be considerably invested in obscuring the divisive forces that organize our school system and society. Conformity to mainstream norms and values often requires regular access to class-based institutional resources and opportunities (e.g., a living wage, adequate housing, association with economically stable peers, etc.) (Rodman, 1964).

THE SOCIOLOGICAL SIGNIFICANCE OF SOCIAL NETWORKS: A DIFFERENT VIEW

In this section, I move toward a distinctive and network-analytic view of "social integration" and of "significant others" that I believe provides the basis for a far more penetrating perspective of the challenges faced by low-status minority youth today. A critical and network-analytic view of society sees individuals as deeply embedded in social webs that, in turn, are interwoven within other webs, with these webs further interwoven within ever larger webs or networks. At the nexus between class, race, and gender stratification, people's social relations and social exchanges become manifest at the individual level as *egocentric networks* (i.e., the *micro* level), at the community and institutional levels as *cliques* (i.e., the *meso* level), and at the societal level as *system networks* (i.e., the *macro* level) (Rogers & Kincaid, 1981; see also Brown, 1999). At the clique and system levels, networks are socially organized and tacitly governed by a distinctive structure and a set of cultural rules permitting communication, interdependence, solidarity, and, ultimately, resource exchange (Paxton, 1999). This same structure and set of rules, however, are also about exclusivity—that is, who is deemed an insider and an outsider in the network game (Barth, 1969; Phelan, Davidson, & Yu, 1998).

When applied to the study of social inequality, this critical network approach gradually reveals what Wellman (1983) so aptly calls the *social distribution of possibilities*, a term that refers to the unequal distribution of opportunities for entering into different social and institutional contexts and for forming relationships with agents who exert various degrees of control over institutional resources, such as bureaucratic influence (advocacy), career-related information, and opportunities for specialized training or mentorship.

Plainly stated, working-class people and middle-class people are embedded in quite different kinds of social networks. At the micro level, middle-class people have what we may call *cosmopolitan* networks, a set of relationships with a diverse constellation of people that translates into smooth access to the mainstream marketplace (meso level), where privileges, institutional resources, and opportunities for leisure, recreation, career mobility, and political empowerment are abundant (Fischer, 1982; Patterson, 1998; Wellman, 1983). The structural features of middle-class networks and cliques are analogous to social freeways that allow people to move about the complex mainstream landscape quickly and efficiently. It many ways, they function as pathways of privilege and power.

Working-class networks, in contrast, are often organized in response to structural exclusion, segregation, and scarcity, which trigger the need for conservation and coping mechanisms to deal with the trials of resource sharing and competition with other low-status groups (Eames & Goode, 1973; Warren, 1981). Working-class networks are relatively *smaller*, more *homogeneous, tightly knit* (everyone knows each other), and *turf-bound*, and have little *access* to institutions and diverse networks scattered throughout the mainstream. At both the micro and meso levels, working-class networks are *bounded*, as opposed to cosmopolitan; in the worst possible sense, working-class networks can become social prisons (Warren, 1981; Wilson, 1987). Working-class people select friends and associates from a "pool of eligibles" consisting of other working-class people with similarly bounded networks (Cochran, 1990b, chap. 15). The same goes for poor folk who are usually able to incorporate only other poor folk into their interpersonal networks (Eames & Goode, 1973; Lomnitz, 1977; Stack, 1974).

Social Embeddedness and Social-capital Formation

The very texture of an individual's daily existence (and ultimately, his or her life chances) is fundamentally shaped by structured and accumulated opportunities for entering multiple institutional contexts and forging relationships with people who control resources and who generally *participate in power*. An individual's social class, racial assignment, and gender play a decisive role in shaping these structured opportunities.

Concomitantly, opportunities, or the systematic blockage of these, prompt individual and group-based initiatives. For low-status people, such initiatives often involve exchanging social support with significant others in the extended family and community (e.g., Jarrett, 1995; Stack, 1974; Zavella, 1987). Smooth access to middle-class institutional agents, however, is another matter. In reality, access to institutional agents, significant others, resources, and pathways across multiple institutional contexts is a very messy business, often requiring the commanding, negotiating, and managing of many diverse (and sometimes conflictive) social relationships and personalities. And here again, an individual's class, race, ethnicity, and gender figure prominently.

The emphasis in this critical network-analytic perspective is, of course, quite distinct from frameworks lodged in classical social integration research. In contrast to the usual focus on norms and social control processes, attention is drawn here to a group of processes fittingly captured in the term *social embeddedness*, a concept taken from the work of Mark Granovetter (1985). According to Granovetter, individual purposeful action arises not out of rational choice or the mere assimilation of norms, but rather out of participation in multiple relationships and out of the social, micro-political, and instrumental dynamics that compose these relationships: the interplay of affect and conflict; the exchange of favors and support; and the negotiating, pressuring, and maneuvering that become nearly routine. This is to say that people make their way in the world by constantly negotiating both the constraints placed on them and the opportunities afforded them, by way of the social webs of which they are a part. Negotiations, compacts, social bonding, and assessments of differential power are all part of the process, although in different degrees depending on context and situation. The tension between constraints and opportunities, of course, has much to do with one's "embeddedness" in the multiple hierarchies of social class, race, and gender.[5]

It is precisely the engagement of individuals *embedded* in distinctive hierarchies that makes network relations so messy (and sociologically important and interesting). Consider, for example, the dynamics entailed when a lower-working-class woman of color negotiates with a middle-class White male principal over her child's access to special educational resources (see Lareau, 1987; Lareau & Horvat, 1999). Such structural dynamics and interactive processes are a significant part of what is meant by embeddedness. Here, notions of hierarchy, of differential power and exclusion, of social conflict, of human agency, and of privileged access to institutional resources all take center stage. As employed here, the concept of social embeddedness allows us to combine our focus on structural constraints with an appreciation of the psychological orientations and behavioral strategies people use to adapt to, negotiate with, and change certain aspects of their social environments (Baca Zinn & Eitzen, 1999).[6] The concept of social embeddedness is also meant to highlight how adolescents and their social webs (both at the ego level and at the meso or community level) are subject to the pull of various contradictory social, cultural, and ideological forces operating to shape the structure, composition, and resourcefulness of these webs. Indeed, the concept of social embeddedness shows us how adolescents themselves are active participants in this tug of war. For analytical purposes, I organize these external conflicting forces into two primary sets, which I will discuss next.

Sites of Stratification and Counterstratification

I see urban schools, families, and communities as three key institutional sites organized in ways that work in tandem with society's patterns of stratification and with a family's or a community's efforts at *counterstratification*.[7] This is to say that each site exhibits distinctive and contradictory potentials. On the one hand, such sites serve as fertile ground for the deleterious effects of class, race, and gender to operate on both the social webs *and* the subjectivities of lower-status children and adolescents (Bowles & Gintis, 1976; MacLeod, 1987). On the other hand, such sites are vital arenas where some low-status groups and individuals develop and exercise certain network resources and psychological orientations that allow them to cope in an effective manner. Such effective coping enables these individuals to access greater institutional resources (e.g., funded programs), neutralize the effects of deleterious societal forces (e.g., racist myths), maintain high self-regard and high levels of motivation, and engage school agents as key sources of social and institutional support (Frydenberg, 1997; Gurin & Epps, 1975; MacLeod, 1987; Ogbu, 1991; Valenzuela, 1999).

At the core of minority adolescent embeddedness we find a battleground where low-status youth are subjected to contradictory forces competing over the principal explicit and implicit functions of each institutional site (family, school, neighborhood, peer group, community organizations, workplace, church).[8] Thus, not only do we see a conflict between which set of values, ideologies, expectations, and emotions is most legitimate and "productive" in each particular site (i.e., Boykin's "triple quandary" [1986]); we also see a conflict over each site's positioning vis-à-vis the greater social structure.

With respect to education, Carnoy and Levin (1985) see schools, on the one hand, as reproducing "the unequal, hierarchical relations of the capitalist workplace," while on the other hand, representing "the primary force in the United States for expanding economic opportunity for subordinate groups and the extension of democratic rights" (p. 144).

Stratification forces in society shape the predominant pattern, while counterstratification forces create individual exceptions to the rule, and historically significant alterations to dominant hierarchical patterns. Women and minorities today, as two primary segments of our national community, continue to be subordinated, segregated, and underempowered, but not in the tyrannical and bleakly oppressive way they used to be. Similar to the multiple and contradictory dynamics underlying our public school system, working-class kinship and community networks operate to regulate social reproduction (Bowles & Gintis, 1976, pp. 142–147). However, such networks also hold the potential for resistance, for political empowerment, and for buffering the worst effects of class, gender, and racial oppression.

Just how do these contradictory societal dynamics operate on and through adolescent networks? The most powerful impact is through the forces of class and racial stratification, which operate by diminishing the *pool of effective sources* of social and institutional support through segregation and urban isolation (Cochran, 1990b; Wilson, 1987). As we shall see in Chapters 3 and 4, Mexican immigrant–based urban *barrios* are socially isolated, quite distant from the enclaves of privilege found in middle-class suburbia. The freeways that cut brusquely through inner-city neighborhoods were built as escape routes for suburbanites, not for inner-city folk (see Lipsitz, 1998).

The Master Subterranean Vein

Let me be explicit as to what I see as the foundation of social oppression as experienced by low-status children and adolescents in our society. All children and adolescents need to be embedded in multiple social webs organized for their empowerment and successful development (Bandura, 1969; Wynn et al., 1987). In the context of these (optimal) nurturing webs, young people learn to actively participate in social life, and in doing so, regularly seek help in a set of diversified social relationships with people capable of and oriented toward providing, or negotiating their access to, multiple forms of social support and institutional resources. This is to say that healthy development and social mobility in contemporary society rest squarely on forms of embeddedness that generate *social capital*—in other words, relationships and networks that transmit vital forms of resources and institutional support that enable young people to become effective participants within mainstream institutional spheres, particularly the school system (see Appendix A for how I have explicitly defined "institutional support"; see also Stanton-Salazar, 1997).

The reality of social stratification in U.S. society, however, is that young people experience distinctly different forms of embeddedness, depending on their respective enclosure in class, racial, and gender strata. In contrast to the developmental and institutional experiences of the dominant group, low-status children (and adults) are by and large embedded in social webs—at the ego, meso, and macro levels—that are socially constructed in ways that thwart or complicate this social-capital formation.

The data and analyses provided throughout this book draw our attention to the more subterranean currents of stratification in the lives of working-class minority children and youth. Within each of the major institutional arenas (e.g., neighborhood, family, school), macro forces (race, class, and patriarchy) engender network conditions and relational dynamics that systematically make it difficult for the existing *pool of eligible agents* to act as authentic and reliable sources of social and institutional support to low-status children and adolescents. Social ties and networks are stripped of their protective and productive capacities, cut off from their potential to act as conduits for the transmission of social, emotional, and institutional resources. This is the dimension of alienation that has been so sorely neglected in scholarly circles.

As formulated here, alienation is a condition of embeddedness in a social web that socially engages but does not nourish, a web that occupies and partially integrates but does not enable the young individual to actualize his or her full human potential. In a sense, these are the webs through which society manufactures the despair referred to in the title of this book—a despair many of us across institutional arenas are not willing or prepared to honestly address. I have termed this worst-case condition *alienated embeddedness*, and see it realized by a social construction process whereby network participants do the work of assembling the structures of class, race, and gender at the interpersonal and institutional levels. By "social construction," I do not suggest that any agents or groups consciously or deliberately "organize," "assemble," or "construct" young people's lives so that they experience limited access to key resources. Rather I refer to how social relations within many low-status communities exhibit certain enduring objective conditions and social patterns that continually short-circuit the social support process. Parents, kin, school personnel, neighborhood residents, police, and peers, constrained by external forces, are regularly forced to act, usually unwittingly, as the assemblers of social inequality. I shall return to further theoretical treatment of this issue, and of alienation, throughout the book and particularly in Chapter 11.

Counterstratification

In spite of embeddedness in social webs where structural currents are mainly organized to thwart the development of trust and of empowering networks, countervailing currents within the self, the family, the community, and the school are always present. When successful, these mitigating processes (set into motion by the individual, by the community, by institutional agents, or by all parties working either collectively or independently) gradually help selected youth construct egocentric networks characterized by trusting relations and authentic social and/or institutional support (i.e., social capital) (Maeroff, 1998; Stanton-Salazar & Spina, 2000). For low-status adolescents and significant others, empowering relations necessitate relational dynamics (negotiations, compacts, coping styles) that run counter to the logic of the surrounding institutional structures (e.g., a segregated, poor urban community; a stigmatized, resource-poor urban school environment). Usually, organized structures of resistance and collective engagement are required to generate relational dynamics that facilitate truly empowering forms of social support. But even here, such dynamics are often forced to attend more to defense than to authentic and lasting empowerment.

Although all children and youth require generous and positive forms of embeddedness in resourceful networks that facilitate and ensure their healthy development and long-term prosperity, for low-status children and youth and their agents, attempts to co-construct an empowering social web necessitate taking on additional, distinctive, and perhaps more primary burdens. These burdens entail a social dance oriented toward *buffering* the young individual from the full emotional and developmental consequences of family and neighborhood poverty, of racial segregation, and of acculturation stress (see Jarrett, 1995). While the participants in middle-class adolescent webs can focus on maximizing the privileges and benefits built into their structured embeddedness in networks at the *meso* and *system* levels, the participants we find in low-status adolescent webs must often focus their energies toward more defensive, buffering activities.[9]

Counterstratification efforts to protect, "empower," or provide support to low-status youth demonstrate varying degrees of success. Not only do such efforts attempt to counter the objective conditions of class, racial, and gender stratification (e.g., neighborhood segregation), they must do so within social and ideological structures tacitly organized to fracture and undermine such support (e.g., the uncritical push toward more standardized testing in schools without an influx of more resources; reactive "zero-tolerance" policies). These debilitating structures, in great part, do their work by shaping the dynamics of interpersonal relations (e.g., conflicts between youth and school personnel). In many cases, such dynamics lead adolescents to detach from mediation efforts organized by family, community, and school. When mitigating efforts fail, as they routinely do for many, the full weight of social oppression makes its indelible mark, leaving youth in perilous webs characterized by conflictive and distrustful relations, and by the general absence of genuine social, emotional, and institutional support.

The Adolescent as Active Participant

Minority adolescent embeddedness occurs on a social battleground where low-status youth are subjected to the contradictory forces of stratification and counterstratification; and yet, these adolescents are truly active participants in this battle. Social embeddedness is more than adolescents embedded in a battlefield that subjects them to constraints, socialization forces, organized mediations, and opportunities; their embeddedness is also marked by interactive processes that reflect their active role in network relations, including investments in certain coping styles, transformative epiphanies, negotiated settlements, compacts, forms of resistance, and cooperative activity.

The importance of understanding these interactive processes is highlighted by Mehan (1978, 1992), who reminds us that social structures are continually assembled and reassembled through social interactions and negotiations set within relations of differential power. This focus on the "constitutive activity" between social actors parallels Granovetter's (1985) emphasis on the relational dynamics underlying embeddedness. The concepts of embeddedness and constitutive activity can be dramatized by the idea that individuals and groups *wrestle* with social structure, and in doing so, continually recreate it—although not always in the same form. Sometimes we see this wrestling or constitutive activity working in the interests of reproduction; at other times, it provides the conditions for individual exceptions to reproduction; still at other times, it sets the stage for authentic social change. Determinism has no place here; structure and human agency together constitute the tumultuous and ever-moving bedrock of social embeddedness. Adding to Granovetter's and Mehan's insights into the embeddedness of social life, Lareau and Horvat (1999) aptly inform us that social reproduction is actually a quite "jagged" process, with multiple and multilayered forces at play.

The Formation of Minority Adolescent Network Orientations:
A Focus on Help Seeking

It is my contention in this book that examining the dynamics of help-seeking and social-capital formation among low-status minority adolescents affords us a view into the jagged and constitutive activities of social inequality in and across institutional sites. This is to say that the dynamics underlying help-seeking (and *not* seeking help) tap into fundamental aspects of inclusion and exclusion in adolescent life, and specifically, into whether young individuals are "integrated" within the flow of resources, privileges, and tangible support—not only within the arena of the school, but within the kinship network, the peer group, and the residential community. Through help-seeking, minority youth actively secure their survival on the battlefield; through their investment in unsponsored self-reliance, they become casualties of racial and class domination.

The issue of adolescent coping styles is fundamental to theoretical treatments that address not only the latent yet potent consequences of class, racial, and gender domination on child and adolescent development, but the active role youth play in assembling their current life conditions and life chances. Stratification and counterstratication do their work by organizing objective network conditions (e.g., network size) *and* by shaping network-related forms of consciousness (e.g., distrust of adults). By way of their embeddedness within a battlefield of contradictory ideological forces, adolescents living under class, racial, and gender oppression develop attitudes and beliefs that influence the ways they select and engage various relationships, and the manner in which they participate within and across various groups and institutional contexts. This developing network consciousness compels them to become active participants in their own socialization process—wrestling with multiple and conflicting manifestations of social structure and culture, tolerating contradiction, and actively negotiating both constraint and opportunity.

Network Orientation. An individual's network orientation constitutes an important dimension of human consciousness, and can be understood as a rather complex constellation of dispositions and skills related to network-building and adaptation to environmental demands, stressors, and opportunities. Let me first treat the broader dimension of network orientation, then address its more specific expression in people's help-seeking attitudes and behavior. As before, I will restrict my treatment here to low-status adolescents.

An adolescent's network orientation can be characterized in terms of attitudes and beliefs that inform or motivate the *personal initiatives* the adolescent takes in engaging various social relationships and in entering into various group affiliations.[10] For instance, an adolescent may say to himself or herself, "I'd like to be a part of some school organization, but I don't really do that kind of thing. People like me aren't really represented in them, and I don't want to feel like I'm intruding or I don't belong." Individual actions are always taken in light of social structural forces that not only expand or constrain an individual's options, but also facilitate or constrain self-empowering initiatives (Boissevain, 1974; Cochran, 1990b, p. 279).

For working-class minorities, network orientations assume a tolerance for operating from a hierarchically subordinate position. More broadly, these orientations manifest themselves in terms of coping strategies geared toward either defusing or sustaining (or resigning to) those latent yet imposing border dynamics and contradictions responsible for engendering social distance, conflict, and distrust of various agents and cliques (see Anzaldua, 1987; Blau, P. M., 1964; Erickson & Shultz, 1982; Lareau, 1989; Lyman & Douglass, 1973).[11,12]

Under certain oppressive conditions, the individual's network orientation may reflect a particular *distress pattern*,[13] shaped and repeatedly restimulated by micro-political dynamics, social conditions, and cultural practices within one or more institutional sites. Such dynamics may produce recurrent humiliation and/or frustration, combined with resentment and demoralization, that in time motivate the young individual to avoid, reject, or subvert various social relationships, institutional contexts, or social worlds. Such dynamics, too often, define relations with higher-status institutional agents (e.g., teachers and counselors; see Chapter 9); yet these conflictive and distancing dynamics also occur in adolescents' relations with members of their own kin network, peer group, and community. Resentment, rage, fear, and demoralization are clearly not the building blocks of adolescent social capital and healthy human development.

Adolescent network orientations are affected not only by relationships to people, but by relations to institutional contexts and social groups, for example the school, the neighborhood, the streets, recreational centers, churches, neighborhood gangs, the police, and the judicial system. An enduring feature of adolescent life at the bottom rungs of society is the presence of distress-inducing danger and of potential victimization within the neighborhood and community (Chapters 3 and 4). Exposure to urban social ills and to the distress patterns of community residents and institutional agents begins at an early age. Growing up "safe" in economically distressed urban environments requires a network orientation founded on a repertoire of knowledge, skills, and defensive practices for negotiating potentially dangerous spaces, groups, and classes of people. Regular access to local supportive resources, whether human or organizational (e.g., recreation centers), typically requires successful negotiation of these spaces and people.

Help-seeking Orientation. A particularly vital part of this network-relevant area of consciousness has to do with the individual's developing proclivity (or disinclination) to resolve personal, academic, and family problems through the mobilization of relationships and networks (i.e., coping by seeking help). Serious attention to this important aspect of consciousness, conventionally termed *network orientation* and originating in social anthropology (Barnes, 1972), is now seen in the work of community psychologists, epidemiologists, and sociologists who study mental health (Colletta, 1987; Lin et al., 1986; Pescosolido, 1992; Wallace & Vaux, 1993). Apart from a number of recent works that draw attention to a more expanded conception of network orientation (Cochran, Larner, Riley, Gunnarsson, & Charles, 1990; Erickson, 1996; Phelan et al., 1998; Stanton-Salazar, 1997), most explicit treatments of this phenomenon have focused on help-seeking beliefs and coping patterns. To lessen confusion, I use the term *help-seeking orientation* to address issues of help seeking and social support, and treat it as a key part of the individual's overall network orientation. *Manufacturing Hope and Despair* is largely about risk-filled attempts by Latino adolescents to seek support, and the emergence of orientations that reject help seeking as a viable coping strategy.

Throughout the course of writing this book, I engaged in many attempts to diagram a model that incorporates the major factors shaping network development among low-status minority adolescents and includes those factors that stimulate individual initiatives. Others have already accomplished the feat of drafting diagrams that include the many factors entailed in network development.[14] I strove for parsimony, and finally settled on Figure 2.2, which highlights the principal factors discussed in this chapter.

Social-psychological Constraints on Help-seeking: The Concept of *Confianza*

Of course, the crucial role of ethnicity, particularly of *Mexicano* immigrant culture, in network development must also be addressed, and is given due attention in Chapter 11 and in other work (Stanton-Salazar, 2000). For the moment, I provide here what I see as the bare essentials. Counterstratification forces in the ethnic community and kinship network, when effective, are usually founded on natural support systems that exhibit positive help-seeking orientations. Stratification forces ultimately win the battle when they erode these orientations and fracture these natural systems of support (see Martin & Martin, 1985).

To fully comprehend the role of trust (*confianza*) in the help-seeking orientations and network experiences of Mexican-origin youth, a brief introduction of this concept is in order. The term *confianza* is an important social construct within Mexican immigrant communities in the United States, and when used relationally, translates roughly into the trust expe-

FIGURE 2.2. Model Highlighting Principal Factors Affecting Network Development among Low-status Youth

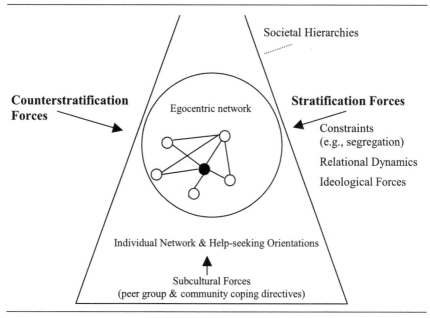

rienced within a particular interpersonal relationship. When individuals have *confianza* in each other, they are willing to make themselves vulnerable to the other, to share intimacies without fear of being hurt or taken for granted. *Confianza* also allows people to engage in important transactions without fear of being deliberately deceived and used. The saying *"No le tengo confianza"* is occasionally heard in Mexican immigrant communities, and communicates that one does not find a particular individual trustworthy and must be consciously vigilant in his or her presence. It can act as a siren warning others in the community to beware.

A closely related construct is *confianza en confianza*, roughly translating into "trusting mutual trust," which has been described by anthropologists and cultural psychologists as a fundamental organizing principle underlying the formation of Mexican/Latino interpersonal networks (Ramírez & Castañeda, 1974; Vélez-Ibáñez, 1980, 1983, 1997). *Confianza en confianza* is a construct learned early in life through relations with family members and community associates, and serves as a predominant mode of living and survival as much as it functions as a vehicle for self-reference, social esteem, and cultural meaning-making (Stanton-Salazar, 2000). It denotes a psychocultural expectation for ongoing exchange, mutual generosity, and reciprocity set in the context of trusting and intimate relations.

In Mexican immigrant communities, the solicitation of support as well as its provision is a valued cultural practice, governed by tacit cultural norms and associated values (Valle & Vega, 1980; Vélez-Ibáñez, 1980). At the individual level, help seeking depends on the internalization of the *confianza en confianza* norm, as well as on the positive appraisal of *confianza* in a potential source of support or aid.[15] However, the necessary conditions for the maintenance of *confianza* norms in ethnic communities are frequently undermined by a combination of structural, subcultural, and assimilationist forces operating within and across institutional contexts (e.g., vulgarized aspects of bourgeois individualism glorified in the media: the immediate satisfaction of personal whims and appetites and the accumulation of wealth without social responsibility). The potential for supportive relations between minority adolescents and parents, teachers, and peers always exists in the context of these disempowering forces. Before concluding this chapter, I provide several cases taken from the interview data that illustrate the texture of negative help-seeking orientations as expressed by many low-status adolescents. As we shall see below, and throughout this book, the lack of help-seeking initiative is usually founded on adolescent orientations that fail to reflect the *confianza en confianza* norm found in Mexican-origin communities in the United States.

ILLUSTRATIONS OF LATINO ADOLESCENTS' NEGATIVE HELP-SEEKING ORIENTATIONS

Many of the reasons provided to us by adolescents regarding their decision not to seek the support of a parent, a teacher, or a friend could be verified in many instances as accurate appraisals of the competencies and limitations of the agent or significant other. In other instances, their lack of trust or *confianza* and their hesitations could very well reflect emotional risks that were, indeed, too great. All relationships can, at times, be hurtful rather than supportive, and during certain periods some relationships become much more hurtful than supportive, so that withdrawal from the hurtful party becomes a wise defensive action. Yet, in many cases, we suspected that the reasons adolescents gave for not soliciting help, and the perceptions and concerns that were part of their appraisals, were being heavily informed by a help-seeking orientation that, in many cases, was quite negative (i.e., counter to the help-seeking process; a withdrawal from the belief that help-seeking is a viable coping strategy).[16]

In large part, these negative orientations were a product of the adolescent's accumulated relational experiences with family members, school personnel, and peers. For some youth, attempts at help seeking had been largely successful and rewarding, while for many others such a coping strategy had only led to cumulative disappointments and frustrations (sometimes within one particular context, and often across contexts). Many of these latter adolescents articulated varying degrees of resignation regarding the utility of relying on adults and peers for various forms of support. With regard to the kinship unit, the disabling forces of lower-class status, the burdens of immigration and resettlement, and the adolescents' own rapid acculturation rendered their immigrant parents ineffectual, their cultural knowledge questionable and alien, and their traditional value system unsupported by the dominant culture. Some families were able to shield themselves from such disabling forces, embedding the family unit in a larger supportive social network, often with the aid of a church or similar institution within the community (see Zhou & Bankston [1996] for one insightful case study). Most of the *Mexicano* families we studied, however, were without such supports.

Many of those adolescents most resigned to the limited influence and power of their immigrant parents in their lives became oriented toward other sources of support in their social network, for example, older siblings or school personnel. Others became quite peer-oriented, placing their faith in friends for needed support and validation. Others, while not social isolates, exhibited an orientation that reflected a new, though often ambivalent, commitment or resignation to what I shall term *unsponsored self-reliance*. Some of these latter adolescents adopted something close to what I describe in Chapter 11 as a *defiant individualist character*.[17]

That certain adolescents had adopted such an individualist character became quite evident in their subtle descriptions of how they coped with the many demands placed on them, the routine neighborhood dangers they faced, and the scarcity of needed resources to meet these demands successfully and without distress. Several illustrations are provided here.

Born in the United States, Lilia Escarza's father had long ago returned to Mexico to grow corn and tobacco. At the time of the study, Lilia lived on the east side of Harrison Heights with her four brothers, four stepsisters, and her mother, who was not currently working outside the home. Lilia was a 12th-grader who, despite working two jobs, showed considerable potential for becoming an academic high-achiever. With the proper support and intervention, Lilia could have easily accumulated a stellar academic record in high school. Yet a different story emerges here. Lilia described herself as a loner who had difficulty trusting others because of past experiences where her confidences had been betrayed. She seemed to have cut herself off from most of her friends, and had difficulty believing that the adults at school could really help her. In Lilia's words: "I live in my own world. I'm more comfortable. . . . People say that if you talk about your problems, you'll let 'em out, but it's not true; they're still there. I guess the problem is all in your mind."

Lilia's orientation toward help-seeking overlaps considerably with that of another young woman in our study named Angeles Machado, a bright, energetic, and motivated 12th-grader with aspirations of going to college. Angeles said she literally made herself sick trying to present herself "like a very strong person, [with a] very strong character." Angeles was, indeed, a very strong-willed, motivated, and ambitious young woman, yet her tacit awareness of her inadequate support system, combined with a coping strategy of withdrawal and self-reliance, produced internal contradictions that sent her spiraling into repeated anxiety attacks.

Juan Carlos Salgado, a serious and timid-seeming 11th-grader, nonetheless appeared highly motivated and engaged in school. An immigrant who had spent most of his life in the United States, he revealed mutually caring and respectful relationships with both his mother and his father. Yet Juan Carlos didn't feel comfortable seeking emotional support or counsel from either of them, stating, "I like keeping it all to myself." Juan Carlos acknowledged the many instances in which his immigrant parents had made efforts to assist and support him, but he had become all too wise as to the limits of what they could do for him—so Juan turned inward.

Sandra Jacobo, another 11th-grader who had lived in the United States most of her life, likewise conveyed a strong individualist orientation. Sandra came across to us as a highly resilient young woman, driven by high aspirations and showing a strong academic record. Sandra projected a very independent, mature, and friendly demeanor. She came from a large household composed of her mother and father, two sisters, two brothers, and two grandparents. Fortunately for Sandra, she was a participant in a widely heralded mentorship program at her school (Chapter 8), and thus enjoyed a support system built into her interpersonal network. Yet her responses to our network survey revealed only five likely sources of support, each source utilized very sparingly. Sandra preferred not to depend on people for support. In reference to her mother as a potential source of intimate counsel and social support, she said: "It's not that I don't trust her. It's just that I choose not to. I guess I'm just accustomed to it, doing things on my own, I'm a very individual person." Sandra's commitment to self-reliance extended as well to the issue of emotional support: "I keep a lot of things to myself, I mean. I'm weird. It's not that I've never had an emotional down time, but I've never actually had, you know, really trusted someone, really, really, you know, to go ahead and tell them, right?"

Role reversals in the home and the assumption of responsibilities as a cultural broker for immigrant parents can, under the proper ecological conditions, be quite developmentally empowering to *second-generation* adolescents (see Shannon, 1990). However, under other conditions, such occurrences in the home can have the effect of creating in older children an identity as caretaker, while simultaneously dampening expectations that they themselves are entitled and deserving—as young persons—to be taken care of; such dampening can undermine the rationale for seeking help and for developing supportive relations with caring adults and institutional agents.

Ana Helguerra's case is also illustrative. A high-achiever with 9 years in the United States, she made assessments of her parents' personalities, emotional capabilities, and class background that precluded her from perceiving them as viable sources of emotional support, intimate counsel, and academic support. Although Ana was able to extol the virtues she saw in each of her parents, we saw no evidence that Ana believed she could count on them to help her deal with the major stressors and demands she was currently facing in her life. From visiting Ana's home, and from talking at length with her mother, we saw evidence of a home life that certainly was economically stable and emotionally positive and cohesive. Yet Ana dealt with her challenges in school and community alone, and she had long come to accept this situation as the way it would always be. Ana's animated descriptions of her most significant relationships revealed her investment in the role of household caretaker and in an identity of someone self-reliant, mature, confident, and opinionated. An identity of an efficacious, forward-looking person who made strategic and regular use of her network of support was never salient in our exchanges with Ana or with any of the other adolescents who revealed similar orientations.

One problem with Ana's adoption of a strong individualist character is that it undercut the support available from a few of her teachers at her school who indeed saw in her the prospect of educational and career success. It also diminished Ana's ability to make the most of her participation in her school's mentorship program. The root of this conundrum lies not in the individual, but in public institutions, such as the school, that fail to recognize and attend to the difficult structural circumstances of low-status minority children—particularly children from working-class immigrant families. In the absence of enlightened intervention, children develop coping strategies that are defensive and individualistic in nature, and that, in time, function to exacerbate already difficult circumstances.

PREPARING FOR WHAT'S AHEAD

In assessing Pierre Bourdieu's contributions to our understanding of the ways inequality is continually reproduced, Lareau and Horvat (1999) credit him for always remaining attuned to "the strategies and actions that individuals follow in their daily lives." Nevertheless, they state, "he has not always been sufficiently aware of variations in the ways in which institutional actors legitimate or rebuff efforts by individuals to activate their resources" (p. 37). In a sense, Bourdieu has glossed over the "constitutive activity" and the wrestling that underlie the activation of resources, including the difficulties entailed in obtaining social support from significant others or in getting gatekeepers and institutional agents to "hand over the goods." This book promises to bring some of these constitutive activities to the forefront, demonstrating how adolescent webs work in numerous ways to assemble and perpetuate the savage inequalities of our times, as well as to provide for the emergence of exceptional individual cases.

The following chapters take us into the various institutional arenas and settings Latino adolescents participate in as they routinely confront different developmental challenges and as they prepare for adulthood as low-status members of society. In each of these major contexts, we examine the nature of social embeddedness experienced by different Latino adolescents, including the obstacles they experience as they attempt to access particular kinds of social, emotional, and institutional support from various agents and significant others. We also examine the consequences of these obstacles on their developing help-seeking orientation.

Part I

*Urban Neighborhood Ecology and
Adolescent Socialization*

3

Neighborhood Ecological Dangers
and the Socialization of Urban
Low-income Latino Youth

The repression of childhood pain influences not only the life of an
individual, but also the taboos of the whole society. . . . It is
precisely because a child's feelings are so strong that they cannot
be repressed without serious consequences.[1]

—Alice Miller

My desire and efforts to understand more fully the routine trials and developmental challenges faced by low-income urban Latino youth led me
to take a close and extended look at the urban neighborhood context. It is
in neighborhoods that we can usually locate the various overlapping social systems or embedded contexts that affect family processes and individual development (Bronfenbrenner, 1979). Neighborhoods also constitute the grand arena from which minority children traverse borders into
different, and often unfriendly, sociocultural worlds and institutional contexts (Boykin, 1986; Phelan et al., 1998), and from which they construct their
social networks of support (Cochran et al., 1990). Finally, minority-based
urban neighborhoods, in their geographical and segregated manifestations,
also function as invisible social prisons that underlie the reality of racial
segregation in American society.

These next two chapters introduce the neighborhoods and the larger
community in which most of the adolescents we studied resided. I describe
the neighborhoods' demography and ecology using census data, ethnographic data, city planning documents, and surveys of the adolescent's
kinship networks. The neighborhoods studied are referred to here by
pseudonyms, although we accurately locate them within the metropolitan
area of San Diego, California, known as Southeast. References are made to
local Chicano gangs and to important institutional sites in the neighborhoods (e.g., schools and parks), and here we also use pseudonyms or no

names at all. To further ensure cooperation from our informants, we promised full confidentiality, and to provide additional protection for them and their neighbors, the names we use to identify them in the text are also pseudonyms; other key identifying features are either obscured or minimized.

My interviews and ethnographic queries, over the course of several years, were motivated by the following underlying research questions: What is it like to grow up in Southeast? What are the challenges, posed by the ecology, that these adolescents must face and overcome in order to "make it" in mainstream or conventional terms? What it is like to raise children in Southeast? What are some of the ecological challenges immigrant parents and community leaders face in helping youngsters fulfill their human and social potential?

The adolescents and families in this study resided in four neighborhoods conjoined together at the western end of Southeast San Diego. For those living on the western boundary, the hub of the downtown financial district is no more than a mile away. Southeast San Diego is politically represented as a City Council District, and is known throughout the city as a place proud of its long history and close-knit community, but also as a place overwhelmed by city neglect, poverty, crime, and far too many disaffected youth.

DEMOGRAPHIC PROFILES OF SOUTHEAST SAN DIEGO

Southeast San Diego is a place of paradox. The community contains some of the city's most beautiful hillsides and vistas. In the neighborhood of Southview, from a small neighborhood park planted atop a small hill one gains a breathtaking panoramic view of the streets just below, and of the entire Southeast; in the backdrop lies the southern section of the San Diego Bay ("Southbay"), the city's famous ship-building and export industries, the naval base on Coronado, and, on the horizon, the blue magnificence of the Pacific Ocean. The view is dotted with late-19th-century Victorian homes, storefronts, and large commercial enterprises; the panorama is also marked by the steeples and domes of the many churches and occasional mosques serving the community. On a clear day, gazing directly southeast, one sees the plateaus, hillsides, and commercial buildings of Tijuana, Mexico, located just some 25 minutes away on the freeway. As one turns around, with one's gaze directed west, the tops of the downtown high-rises state their presence, with the northern harbor as their backdrop. During the 1920s, 1930s, and 1940s, Southeast, with its patchwork of neighborhoods and its many Victorian, Craftsman, and Spanish Colonial homes, contained a good portion of San Diego's white middle and upper-middle classes. Close by was the downtown area and the harbor, the yacht clubs, the many beaches, Balboa Park, and all the other splendors of the city's distinctive coastal geography and heritage. While the neighborhoods, historical sites, and natural geography remain, Southeast is known today more for its concentration of poverty, and as a place besieged by urban social ills. White flight beginning in the 1940s and lasting through the 1960s and dramatic trends in Mexican immigration during the 1980s, combined with many city, state, and federal policies and neglect, transformed Southeast, as we shall soon see.

The San Diego Mexican-origin Community

San Diego County has the third largest concentration of Latinos in California, following the Los Angeles and Orange County area and the San Francisco–Tri City Bay Area. According to the 1990 census, one in five residents in the county was of Latino origin (20.4%), totaling a bit more than a half a million people. About 86% of these Latino residents were of Mexican origin. San Diego County has historically served as the principal gateway for migration from Mexico and Latin America into the United States. In fact, the San Diego–Tijuana border is recognized as the busiest international border in the world. Mexican immigration to California is part of the long history of U.S.–Mexican geopolitical relations originally marked by the infamous war between the two countries (1846–1848). Today, Mexicans constitute the largest immigrant population in the country, and are also responsible for "the most sustained labor migration in the contemporary world" (Rumbaut, 1998, p. 6). The cities of San Diego and Tijuana, whose downtown centers are only 19 miles from each other, together represent a major component of the world's largest trading area: the Pacific Rim.[2]

San Diego's Latino population has historically been predominantly Mexican. More than 80% of Latino immigrants in the region come from Mexico. Most Latinos residing in the metropolitan and surrounding areas of the city are concentrated in communities and towns ranging from the downtown area to the border, along the inner perimeter of the South Bay. Other areas of significant representation (20–29.9%) are found in the coastal areas of north county, and in the unincorporated inland areas. As in other major California counties, San Diego County's economy is increasingly dependent on the Latino labor force. Latino labor participation in the county jumped from 12.8% in 1980 to 19.9% in 1990, and is quickly rising to 25%. While the 1980s saw Latinos heavily involved in the manufacturing sector, in the 1990s we saw Latinos much more likely to be involved in the construction, trade, and services industries. Upward occupational mobility for a substantial sector of the Latino population is circumscribed by depressed levels of formal schooling; this is particularly the case among immigrants. In 1980, 50.3% of the region's Latinos (25 years and older) had not completed high school or the equivalent.[3]

The growing presence of Latino youth in San Diego is most pronounced within the public school system, where demographic shifts have been remarkable. In 1977, White students constituted 71% of the county's student enrollment (ages 5–17); by 1989, this percentage had decreased to 54%. By 1996, 4 years after the initial fieldwork for this book was completed, Whites constituted less than 50% of the K–12 population. Latino students, representing by far the largest segment of the new majority, constituted about 27% of the county's student body (K–12). A rather large segment of the Latino student body in San Diego in 1990 was classified as Limited English Proficient (LEP) (42.6%), with a bit less than a third classified as bilingual, yet Fluent English Proficient (FEP). Another 28% are classified as English-dominant.[4,5]

The Neighborhoods

The neighborhoods of Harrison Heights, Augusta Heights, Southview, and Vista send most of their adolescents to Auxilio High School. About two-thirds of the Latino students at the high school, and a little more than a third of the African American students, reside in these four neighborhoods. Students walk to school, come in cars, or ride the bus or trolley. Other adolescents residing in these neighborhoods are bused to other public high schools in the city as part of a voluntary desegregation program. The two other high schools in Southeast serve the neighborhoods located in the eastern half of the community.

At the time of the study, Harrison Heights was a mixed Latino and Black neighborhood, and although it is divided into three census tracts, it has traditionally carried the same neighborhood identity. It is one of the oldest Mexican communities in San Diego, and remains the historic, religious, and symbolic center of the larger Mexican-origin community in the city. The 1930s saw the city rezone the area, opening up the neighborhood to many industrial and commercial uses. A slow deterioration of the area soon followed, including the new presence of toxic wastes and, by the 1960s, the proliferation of junk yards (e.g., automobile recyclers). The western end of the neighborhood was cut in half in the late 1950s with the construction of a new freeway facilitating travel between the downtown area and the communities of Southbay and Tijuana.

At the time of the 1990 census, nearly 74% of the neighborhood was composed of Latinos, who were overwhelmingly of Mexican origin. Between 1970 and 1980, the percentage of Black residents had decreased by 50% (from 39.7% to 20.7%), with concomitant movement into the central and eastern portions of Southeast. By 1990, their presence in Harrison Heights had further decreased to 13%. The other 13% of the population in 1990 were either White or Asian or Pacific Islander.

The neighborhood is nestled next to a massive industrial complex, representing both privately owned and military-run enterprises sewn along the rim of Southbay. At the time of the study (1991–1992), about 50,000 people were employed in these industries (shipbuilding, exports/imports, civilian employment in military enterprises), making the area the most labor-intensive in San Diego County. In spite of the proximity of this large industrial complex, a bit more than 48% of the neighborhood population lived on incomes of less than $15,000 a year, and only 4.8% of these families made over $50,000. Poverty was widespread, with a bit more than 44% of all residents, and nearly 55% of children (< 18), living below the official poverty line. Yet active employment was the norm, with nearly three-quarters of the men over age 16 in the labor force. About 77% of the occupied housing units were rented. As in the other neighborhoods we studied, here we find many families with working adults forming part of what David Ellwood (1988) calls the "working poor"—people employed in jobs with little security, poor wages, and no future. Many families whose yearly income falls just on the other side of the poverty line merely become part of the unofficial poor. As expected, a large proportion of those working fill nonskilled and semi-skilled jobs. Blue-collar workers account for about 70% of those employed in the neighborhood compared with 24% of similar-status workers citywide. Given the dominant presence of immigrant families in the neighborhood, it is not surprising that a significant portion of adults reported low levels of formal education. About 42% of adults 25 years and older had completed fewer than 9 years of schooling.

The neighborhoods of Augusta Heights and Southview not only share quite similar profiles, but in some important ways they join Harrison Heights as the same functional community. Most important, residents in these three areas share similar demographics and social life, a similar geographic space relative to the downtown area, and a similar sociopolitical relationship to the greater city. Mexican and Chicano youth, however, do make clear distinctions. Augusta Heights and Southview are normally cited as *turfs* separate and distinct from Harrison Heights.[6]

The neighborhood of Vista lies on the north side of a major freeway that serves as the northern border of Southeast. The area is divided into two census tracts, with the western tract featuring many two-story homes overlooking the downtown area below. For several decades, the freeway served as the "tracks," the space that separated White families from poor, non-White families. Through the 1960s, Vista had remained a predominantly White, mixed working- and middle-class neighborhood. As children grew up and moved out in the 1970s, new non-White families entered to diversify the neighborhood. With the spurt of Latino immigration in the 1980s and the limited stock of affordable housing units in Harrison Heights, Southview, and Augusta Heights, Vista saw its demography rapidly change. Vista has become a predominantly Latino-White neighborhood, although other groups are represented. In 1990, a bit more than 58% of the residents in both tracts were Latino, compared with nearly 28% who were white. Latinos are more prominent on the flat east side, while Whites are better represented on the hilly west side, an area that gradually descends into the periphery of the downtown financial district. Many of the old Victorian homes on the west side have been converted into law offices and private businesses. African Americans comprised about 7% of the residents, while Asians and Pacific Islanders constituted about 6%. Although Vista has yet to show the noxious signs of urban blight and neighborhood decay, poverty exists in the shadows. Nearly 30% of all residents and more than a third of all children (< 18) were living in poverty. About 87% of all occupied housing units in the east side were rented.

In the next section, I present an overall profile of these four neighborhoods mainly from the perspective of the adolescents and parents who lived there. I also examine how the ecology of urban Latino neighborhoods and communities affects the networks and the socialization of children and youth, and pay particular attention to their social-psychological orientation toward different community sites that are potential sources of social and institutional support, such as community recreation centers.

ECOLOGICAL DANGERS FROM THE PERSPECTIVE OF ADOLESCENTS, PARENTS, AND COMMUNITY MEMBERS

Growing up on the border zones of society begins in one's own neighborhood. As discussed in Chapter 2, although healthy development can be said to be founded on positive forms of embeddedness in social webs oriented toward the transmission of institutional support, for low-status children and youth, network processes often have more immediate functions, entailing efforts by youth and their families to shield themselves from the full weight of segregation and of concentrated neighborhood poverty. Defensive strategies and cognitive maps developed to ward off danger in the neighborhood, however, often run counter to the social skills and dispositions youth need to mobilize key agents and to build personal networks of support (Cochran et al., 1990; Garbarino, Dubrow, Kostelny, & Pardo, 1992). Given this "damned if you do, and damned if you don't" situation, other settings situated within the kinship unit, community agencies, and the school become particularly important as contexts for the development of network-building skills and of a positive help-seeking orientation. Yet too often, those class and racial forces in society responsible for turning urban neighborhoods into war zones also find their way into the organization of family life and schools, disabling those in the best position to be supportive.

We asked the adolescents in our study and their parents to talk about their respective neighborhoods; for example, we asked them to talk about the kinds of services and community resources they regularly enjoyed, or lacked, and the kinds of problems and hassles they encountered on a routine basis.[7] We learned that the absence of particular commercial services and conveniences, usually taken for granted in other communities, often functions to remind low-income residents that much of the mainstream private sector has little interest in investing in their neighborhoods.

One common issue raised by nearly all the mothers in the four neighborhoods was the absence of a major chain supermarket. The last major supermarket, nestled among the neighborhoods of Harrison Heights, Southview, and Augusta Heights, had been closed in the early 70s. The chain supermarket, lodged at the intersection of three different neighborhoods, had been a center of community and social interaction. It had served as a sign of inclusion and normality within the larger metropolitan community. Some years after the major chain vacated the building, the county converted the site into one of the two district welfare offices serving the greater Southeast community. This, of course, served to signal to community members a new trajectory oriented toward further marginalization.[8] From the time of the store's closing to the time of this study, the grocery needs of local residents were met by small corner markets and liquor stores run by Iraqi and Lebanese families. Dr. Cleo Malone, who ran a drug-abuse recovery center in the late 80s, resented not only the lack of a major supermarket, but also the absence of home-grown merchants:

> We have almost no merchants that are community residents. All except two are Iraqi Arabs that don't live in the community or support its churches. Nor do they employ [residents]. That's a hell of a drain on this community's economy.[9]

Many residents had long become resigned to traveling down the freeway to the nearby Southbay communities to stock up on their groceries. Those lacking transportation relied on the higher-priced local establishments.

Routine Exposure to Illicit and Dangerous Activities in Neighborhood

The greatest concern voiced by both adolescents and parents, however, had to do with safety, and with the foreboding signs of urban decay: drugs, crime, street youth, adult joblessness, and homelessness. This concern often emerged in well-articulated and passionate tales of personal encounters with dangerous neighborhood elements. Almost all adolescents and parents interviewed and living in these four neighborhoods expressed their distaste for the area they lived in. Community activists regularly conveyed residents' frustrations to the city council and to the press. The signs most distressing to residents are those rooted in the underground drug economy—in the daily activities related to the distribution, sale, and delivery of narcotics, activities typically played out in parking lots, street corners, and parks throughout the neighborhood. The primary actors on the street are usually late-adolescent boys and young adult men, although many recognize that younger boys and girls are often recruited to assist with delivery and surveillance. The older people who run the economy tend to remain out of sight. This illicit economy, of course, is situated in the larger backdrop of too many corner liquor stores, and the omnipresence of unemployed and underemployed men, high levels of alcohol consumption, and alienation.

The children of Southeast grow up exposed to an array of illicit drug activities, the urban rituals of public alcohol consumption, and the specter of gun-enacted youth violence. Parents and older kin strive to protect their children and siblings from such exposure, but must come to grips with the fact that their extensive work schedules severely limit their ability to control or monitor their children's contact with the environment.

Community residents commonly perceived that violence among youth was on the rise, and that it was intimately connected with the illegal drug trade and the greater availability of guns. Such perceptions appear well supported by research studies from around the country.[10,11,12] The theme of drugs and their devastating impact on community members reverberates throughout the city's newspapers. Michael Anderson, chairman of California's Martin Luther King, Jr., Holiday Commission and long involved in the area, conveyed in an article in the *San Diego Union-Tribune* the distress felt by so many residents: "The people of Southeast are afraid. They live behind bars. They're afraid to go out of their homes at night. Their children are being harassed and threatened. Their kids are being beaten up . . . [or] killed by the profit motive of drugs."[13] There is a fear among community leaders that the future of the community is in peril, and that there may not be sufficient young people who will survive, physically or psychologically, to lead the area.[14]

In our questionnaire survey of Auxilio High School, we asked students to report whether they had experienced any of a series of hassles or events related to urban living. Table 3.1 displays some of our results for Latino adolescents, with respective statistics for two of the three focal areas (Vista not included). A significant proportion of the two groups reported a good deal of crime and vandalism in their neighborhood (47.2% and 37.3%, respectively). A similarly high proportion of each group reported sighting a good deal of drug selling and drug use in their neighborhood (45.9% and 44.7%, respectively). Nearly a third of adolescents across both areas also reported their exposure to street and homeless people in the area around their homes. Finally, from nearly one-fifth to a bit more than a quarter of all adolescents from these two areas knew of a drive-by shooting in their

TABLE 3.1. Perceptions of Neighborhood Ecology*

	Harrison Heights Area (N = 231)	Augusta Heights/ Southview Area (N = 244)
A lot of crime and vandalism in my neighborhood	47.2%	37.3%
My house was broken into	7.4%	9.8%
A lot of drug-pushing and drug use in my neighborhood	45.9%	44.7%
There was a drive-by shooting in my neighborhood	26.0%	18.9%
A lot of street and homeless people in my neighborhood	31.2%	30.3%
Harassed (treated unfairly) by police	14.3%	15.2%

*Both samples (N = 231, N = 244) are comprised of Latino respondents with complete data on all six survey items. Since zip codes were used to generate samples, Vista could not be included in this analysis. Vista's zip code encompassed other neighborhoods as well.

neighborhood. These statistics were reflected in the vivid descriptions given by adolescents and their parents of their neighborhood and their security-conscious homelife.

Señora Ubilla, a 52-year-old mother of five and a long-time resident of Southview, described the false tranquility that permeated her neighborhood:

> *Where we're living it seems calm apparently; from time to time one can hear gunshots around there [in the area]. But as far as around here, Colonial Avenue, this whole street here, there's a lot of drugs and alcohol and things like that, all along Colonial Avenue. A few months ago, there were some people who sold drugs, living right in front here. Then the police came and took everybody. They were Latino.**

Sra. Ubilla still suffered from flashbacks to an event 17 years back when she was assaulted and robbed soon after getting off a bus near her home in Southview. *"They assaulted me and beat me pretty bad. I was beaten pretty bad. They stole my purse, but they didn't find anything. The pain in my back and my headaches still haven't gone away. They were black."* Before moving to her present home, Sra. Ubilla and her family lived in another section of Southview, and there, too, she described the nearly routine exposure to the drug scene, the associated violence, and the threat of victimization.

> *We used to live along an alley, near Kramer, for 5 years, and for about 3 years, while we were living there, right at the corner there was a house where they sold drugs, and there were often many problems; the people would fight each other over drug sales. Sometimes the house would be set on fire. And here they are, our neighbors, with all this happening.*

Like Sra. Ubilla, most of the other mothers we interviewed spoke about how they became quite adept at spotting the people in the street who were there to sell drugs. Sra. Cortes, a 44-year-old single mother of four, described the young men she regularly saw on major streets in Southview and Harrison Heights, *"Allá por la Veterans, y por la Colonial, los miro yo que andan por la calle, y luego salen con sus bolsitas* [Over there along Veterans and along Colonial Ave., I can see them along the street, and then they come out with their little bags]."

---

*Quoted text set in *italics* is used to signal that the original interview text was communicated in Spanish, transcribed verbatim in original Spanish text, then translated into English.

For a significant segment of the adolescents and mothers we interviewed in these four neighborhoods, the distressing presence of drugs,
traffickers, and victims appeared to spill over into yards and doorsteps.
One Saturday afternoon found me sitting in a living room conducting an
interview with Sr. and Sra. Montalvo, a couple in their late 30s and parents of four children. Their oldest son, Daniel, a participant in my study,
was seated nearby. The Montalvo's Harrison Heights home was situated
only a block from Colonial Avenue, a major neighborhood thoroughfare
known for its old storefronts, liquor stores, and corner markets, and its
montage of urban symbols of economic marginality and immigrant vitality.

In the middle of our animated conversation about drug addicts in the
neighborhood, Sra. Montalvo stood up and, taking my hand, led me to the
kitchen window overlooking the backyard. Beyond the back fence was an
empty lot where once stood a home and a yard. Strewn throughout the lot
lay a few worn shopping carts, piles of scrap lumber, old plumbing fix-
tures, empty steel barrels, and trash. According to her, 4 years earlier homeless people and drug addicts had "discovered" the lot; since then they
occasionally congregated in the lot at night, building fires in the barrels to
stay warm. "*¡Mire*," Sra. Montalvo said to me in an emphatic yet saddened
tone of voice, "*éste es lo que yo y mi familia tenemos que soportar!* [Look, this
is what my family and I must endure]!" Daniel walked into the kitchen and
explained: "There's an empty house next to the lot; they hang out in the
house and in the lot and do drugs. They used to have prostitution there,
but now the cops have been more active. Now that my mom has been calling them, it's lessened. You don't see that no more, but you still see the
drugs." Sra. Montalvo said that the drug addicts sometimes throw their
used hypodermic needles over the fence, and so she has to go out on a frequent basis, hunt for needles and other items, and dispose of what she finds.
For that reason, she didn't let her kids go into the backyard to play—much
too dangerous, she said. Returning to the living room, Daniel later commented: "When people come and visit us, they're like really scared. They're
intimidated by seeing the streets full of graffiti. They say like this is a really bad community."

Sixteen years old, Natividad Fernández lived virtually her entire life
in Harrison Heights. She told of the numerous community meetings with
police, the organized protest marches down Colonial Avenue, the Neighborhood Watch signs around the neighborhood, and yet she stated emphatically, "It doesn't seem to help. We just need to get those people off
the street." Natividad recounted the occasion when she found a "druggie,"
a young Latina woman, sitting on her porch. Natividad confronted her and
told her to get off the porch or she would call the police. "So I'm telling
you," she said, "these people are disgusting!" Lucita Alvarez, in nearby

Augusta Heights, had been in the United States for only 3 years. She felt that drugs will never go away, but what she wanted to see change is the selling of drugs around school sites and recreation centers. She worried about children growing up around the drug scene and what that might be doing to their moral development.

Many others we interviewed similarly complained of drug transactions too close to home, and of abandoned dwellings on their street subsequently converted into dope houses. Angeles Machado, a 17-year-old in the United States since infancy and a resident of Southview, told of a couple of boarded-up apartments around the corner from her house. Although her front gate remained locked, vagrants often jumped over her fence to get to the apartments, actions she and her parents found very annoying. She said they often took things from her yard on the way out. The few times she had called the police, they arrived too late to do anything. Angeles said she once spied a young woman her age sitting on the back porch of the abandoned apartments shooting heroin. Her description of her neighborhood, however, was mixed. For example, she complained about the poor conditions of the houses a few blocks down from her home, on Colonial Avenue. "They're like little shacks, and they're falling apart." A few moments later though, she finished her thought, "If it weren't for a couple of things, like the drugs and the shacks, Southview would definitely be one of those Ozzie and Harriet neighborhoods."

Harrison Heights, Augusta Heights, Southview, and the east side of Vista, like the other neighborhoods in Southeast, displayed the multiple and contradictory shades of decay and vitality, of alienation and resilience. Like the Montalvos, many families lived in rented houses and apartments that were in varying states of disrepair. Many single-frame houses, some 70 years old, confessed a sad and sagging fatigue, their sides covered with cracking paint, their porches having long lost their prideful gleam. Yet, in the same general area, many families lived in houses that remain in good condition, often with fenced yards featuring nicely tended lawns and gardens. In so many streets and pockets of the neighborhood, outsiders would readily perceive an ambiance reflective of stable working-class family life—a place where people strive to maintain a dignified and resilient presence. Regardless of the condition of the houses, to many of those raising children in the neighborhood, and to many of the children themselves, the signs of blight, multiple marginality, drugs, and danger had to be responsibly attended to. Fear and apprehension were widespread. The defensive posture of residents came with a heavy price, often obscuring if not contaminating the perception of other more positive signs in the neighborhood—especially those reflecting the coexisting normative presence of household stability and familial resilience.

In spite of the many positive signs in the neighborhood, the dangers were real, and the defensive postures of residents an unfortunate necessity. The majority of families we interviewed had some story to tell about gunshots in the vicinity or about a drive-by shooting they had actually witnessed. There in the living room, with his parents at his side, Daniel Montalvo talked about several recent incidents of shootings in the area.

> Like about six months ago there was a drive-by shooting on the corner of our street. And just a few days ago my dad and brother encountered another one. My little brother, he's 13, well, my dad took him to El Bazaar to sell fresh fruit and all of a sudden a whole bunch of guys just started gunning in the street. My dad and brother were still sitting in the car, so my dad just kept on driving and they ducked down and they tried to avoid anything. So, it's like occasionally, you don't see that everyday, but it'll probably get worse and worse with time.

Some of the adolescents we interviewed tried to cope with the violence by becoming desensitized to it or by suppressing their feelings of fear and dread. The strategy, however, didn't always work. Jaqueline Mora was another older adolescent whose family had been in Harrison Heights for a long time. Her grandmother operated a neighborhood market in the area, and Jacqueline had frequently helped out at the store. Her apparent fearlessness seemed to have been adopted from her grandmother and mother, who'd learned to interact confidently with all segments of the community. At first Jacqueline claimed that violence was not a problem in her neighborhood, although she regularly heard about such events in the media. "I do hear about shootings, like on the news, but I don't really pay attention, because, well, I don't know, I just don't." Later in the interview, however, she said:

> I see people like be in gangs and I hear about my friends that they have friends that got shot and stuff. And then my friend was telling me that he's seen his brother die and his friends dying, you know. I've never seen nothing like that. And I don't want to see it. I don't want to hurt like that. And I don't want to be around people who are always getting hurt by other people. My cousin has been killed, you know, and I don't like that. I just don't like to see people hurting each other.

Again and again in our interviews with adolescents, accounts of drugs and violence became the salient issues that colored our discussions about community life.[15] The fear of violence and victimization emerged as an intrinsic feature of adolescent life in Southeast. Miguel Angel Gonzales, in the United States since the age of 8, and 17 at the time of our interviews, was living out his adolescence in Harrison Heights. He felt his neighborhood, encompassing in his view all the homes in a surrounding three-block radius, was good by day, but not by night. At night, *los cholos* and *los negros* go out cruising and patrolling the streets;[16] he suspects that they are often drugged or intoxicated and that they could easily mistake him for a rival and shoot him. Even by day he worried, as when he joined his friends at the park close to his home: "*Sometimes I get scared that when I'm with my friends at the park, and since some of them are* cholos, *that they might shoot at us and that they might hit me. And this is why I'm afraid of being there with them.*"

Parents worried, too, that their child might find him- or herself at the wrong place at the wrong time, and in the line of gang fire. Horror stories circulated from household to household, street to street, their validity unchecked, but serving nonetheless to heighten parents' apprehensions. Sensationalized evening television accounts about shootings and murders were another typical way residents learned about dangers in their community.

Sra. Loza, a 49-year-old immigrant and mother of two teenaged daughters, recounted a news story she saw about an incident in the neighborhood in which a young Latino woman was found shot to death with her infant still on her lap. Apparently, the baby cried all night next to her dead mother before being discovered. Sra. Loza abruptly gasped for air, as if shocked by her own account of the incident. She said she wasn't sure whether the murder was gang-related or involved a jealous boyfriend. "*Le digo a mi hija Luz María, '¿Pero por qué lo harían?' Le digo, '¡Qué bárbaro! Ese niño sentado, en el estómago de su madre, ya muerta, y llorando toda la noche'* [I tell Luz María, my daughter, 'But why would they do that?' I tell her, 'How horrible! That child sitting on his mother's lap, now dead, and the child crying all night']."

Sra. Loza tells of another incident in which her *comadre's* daughter's crib was hit by a stray bullet, apparently from a drive-by shooting. The bullet narrowly missed the baby. As she told it:

> *My comadre had the baby's crib in the little room that faces the park. And the baby, well, she says that where the shot was directed, it was there that she always put her little head; but that day, imagine, by luck, she had her feet there instead. Well just imagine what would have happened if the baby would have been lying the usual way. She still has the crib there, with the mark from the gunshot.*

"Urban Learning": Learning to Read the Signs

The accounts of violence and victimization presented here are not new; they've appeared in books and articles on American urban neighborhoods over the last 30 years. Yet we are only now beginning truly to understand the developmental consequences of growing up in distressed environments filled with poverty-overwhelmed households, disaffected kids organized into cliques and gangs, guns and youth violence, roaming drug addicts and peddlers, and residents' fears about the daily risk of victimization.

In spite of the dangers, James Garbarino and associates (1992), who are at the forefront of such inquiries, state that "child developmentalists have estimated that up to 80 percent of all children exposed to powerful stressors do not sustain developmental damage" (p. 100). We need to be attentive, however, to what constitutes "developmental damage" and its distinction from, and overlap with, aspects of *anomie* and *alienation*. In any case, one reason for the positive statistic is that many children and adolescents, in spite of growing up in highly troubled ecologies, are situated in interpersonal networks that provide a necessary degree of protective insulation. These are networks that, among other things, permit young people to process emotionally their distressful feelings, and that emanate messages reassuring them of their value and of their safety (see Jarrett, 1995, for an elaborated treatment of this issue).

Another positive factor is that many children and adolescents are assisted by network associates in developing forms of consciousness and social competencies that help them cope with those ecological challenges and risks that are stressful as well as potentially damaging and dehumanizing. In total, such protective processes can go a long way toward fostering the development of basic and more global aspects of human consciousness (e.g., self-efficacy, self-confidence, and positive self-esteem), in spite of the dangers (Stanton-Salazar & Spina, 2000).

We see then that growing up "safe" in economically distressed and segregated urban environments necessitates a kind of socialization oriented toward helping young people effectively negotiate a trouble-filled urban social world. It includes what Lyn Lofland (1973) has called "urban learning," "the process of acquiring the requisite knowledge and skills for acting in a world of strangers" (p. 96). Such urban knowledge and skills include "a well-developed vocabulary for describing locations and whom one might expect to find in them" (p. 101). Personal safety, the avoidance or diffusion of antagonisms, and survival are the overarching objectives. Occasions and situations arise in which the child, adolescent, or parent is called on to code another's behavior as a means of identifying him or her as "safe," as unfriendly, or as dangerous.

To this end, urban learning involves the development of what Gerald Suttles (1972) refers to as "cognitive maps" of the city and the neighborhood. Cognitive maps are "part of the social control apparatus of urban areas" typified by a high degree of anonymity, sharp cleavages between social groups, the distress patterns of those overwhelmed by poverty, and the lack of "assurance that everyone will observe legal or customary norms" (p. 33). These cognitive maps help individuals to perceive the physical and social geographies of the urban environment as negotiable. They function to sort chaos into categories, knowledge forms, and rules that achieve a level of cognitive integration. They help the person decide whom to avoid and who can be considered neighborhood allies (Suttles, 1972). At the collective level, neighborhood allies band together to socially construct informal systems of surveillance, where key individuals (e.g., mothers, elders, gang members) "watch the block," identifying those who belong and noticing, if not confronting, those who do not (DeSena, 1990; Sampson, Raudenbush, & Earls, 1997; Sánchez-Jankowski, 1991). Thus arises what Suttles (1972) and others (e.g., Park, 1967) refer to as the "defended neighborhood," a place where informal mechanisms emerge for protecting the neighborhood from predatory or unwelcome elements.

Throughout our many interviews, the cognitive maps of our adolescent and parent informants across four adjacent neighborhoods revealed a very high degree of consistency. As outlined by Lofland (1973) and Suttles (1972), we find here a certain kind of mind set and vocabulary that disclose a defensive posture and hypersensitivity toward strangers and those in the neighborhood not deemed allies.

Elisa Montes was a U.S.-born 16-year-old who resided in a "nice" area on the west side (more upscale part) of Vista. She did, however, go into Harrison Heights and Southview to visit friends, and to help her older sister at her beauty salon on Colonial Avenue. She said this about the area: "To be honest, I really don't see anything really wrong with their neighborhood." By neighborhood, she means the community as a totality, its people, its social life. She was, however, acutely aware of the dangers. "It starts getting ugly around Colonial and Industry [a major street a block south of Colonial]." Here she mentioned, almost casually, the homeless, the drunks, the drug dealers, and the cops. Her familiarity with the dangers, however, was marked by her casual attitude: "You get so used to it, you don't really even look at it anymore; they just go there and sell drugs and stuff like that."

In some adolescents, like Elisa, a defensive posture seemed to operate just below the conscious level—effective in governing behavior, but with the fear or apprehension significantly muted or suppressed. In others, particularly those who'd been personally victimized, the defensive posture was a bit more conscious and palpable. Raul Ubilla, the son of Sra. Ubilla visited above, stated that "as soon as you step out of the house, you got to be looking out for danger." He went on to tell about recently being mugged in his own neighborhood:

> In the daytime I feel safe, but at night not as much. I just got robbed by two guys. I was walking from a friend's house on Stockton street to my house one night around 8 o'clock, and two guys came up with a bat and said, "Gimme your wallet"; and so I gave them my wallet and then they just walked away. I had like five bucks. I had my books though; I rather lose five dollars than throw down my books and run. They were both Mexicans, *cholos*; 22 years or so.

Gauging Quality of Neighborhood by Particular Criteria

The cognitive maps of adolescents and their parents were most sharply revealed in the criteria they used when entering into particular locations in the neighborhood and when determining how *defensive* they needed to be. They exhibited what Lofland (1973) calls "categoric knowing," a way of ordering details about the people who move within a particular domain. People are observed carefully for their clothes, their health condition, their gait in walking, as well as other signals and gestures with which their bodies communicate. Implications are drawn from the kinds of people identified; the response is either to "relax" or to "beware."

Figure 3.1 displays some of the most prominent criteria that emerged in our interviews. The congregation of *cholos* in parks, in parking lots, and on street corners—either gang members or merely kids dressed and groomed in a cultural *cholo* style reflecting a Chicano working-class oppositional identity—was one prominent sign. On the street, enacting a beware and alert posture took many forms; among adolescents, it could include a cool, fearless, yet respectful recognition of the group (e.g., walking by a group of *cholos* in the park). Among mothers, the feigned coolness and fearlessness might emerge, minus the respectful recognition. Physical signs of neighborhood decay and "respectability" were also used as clues regarding whether to assume a more conscious and active defensive posture, or to revert to a more automatic and relaxed one. Graffiti on walls, sidewalks, and fences was another prominent sign; others included houses and apartments in disrepair, drug paraphernalia or liquor bottles on the curb, metal bars on doors and windows, boarded-up houses, and cars parked in front yards. Positive signs were also recognized—for example, tended lawns and flower or vegetable gardens, houses and apartments in good condition, elders sitting on porches, small children playing on the sidewalk, and so forth.

FIGURE 3.1. Criteria Used to Determine Social Conditions and Safety of a
      Neighborhood

A.   Graffiti (including gang markings) on the walls and sides of buildings
     throughout the neighborhood.

B.   Existence of lighted alleys and streets at night.

C.   Whether one is able to leave possessions unsupervised in front of
     house.

D.   Metal bars on door and windows.

E.   Condition of single-family homes and apartment buildings; well-
     maintained or deteriorating.

F.   Drug paraphernalia found on street.

G.   Neighborhood talk about antagonistic relations with the police; whether
     police exhibit a "defensive posture" while patrolling community and
     interacting with members of the community.

H.   Frequent presence of police helicopters hovering about neighborhood.

I.   Talk about robberies and burglaries in the neighborhood.

J.   Talk about frequent gang violence in the area.

K.   Presence of elders on porches or tending gardens.

L.   Presence of young children on sidewalk.

M.   Presence of prostitutes ("hookers," *"prostitutas"*).

N.   Presence of "homeless people" in the streets.

O.   Drug use/dealing in public places, particularly when visible to young
     children.

P.   Public alcohol consumption on street corners.

Q.   Single-parent families.

R.   Presence/visibility of pregnant teens.

NEIGHBORHOOD CHARACTER: ANOMIC-TRANSITORY

Much of the demographic character of these neighborhoods is rooted
in the Mexican immigration boom of the 1970s and 1980s, a flow that continued into the 1990s. This dramatic increase was, of course, seen through-

out the state of California (Hayes-Bautista et al., 1988; López & Stanton-Salazar, in press). Up until the 1960s, second- and third-generation Chicanos constituted the majority in Mexican *barrios* across the state. In 1960, only 20% of the state's Latino population was foreign-born; three-quarters of all working-age Latino adults were U.S. natives, and two-thirds of Latino children were third-generation (López & Stanton-Salazar, in press). Renewed immigration over the past 30 years changed all that. By the mid-90s two-thirds of all working-age Latino adults were immigrants, and children were overwhelmingly the children of immigrants—many of whom were (and are) economically distressed. The dramatic increase in poorly educated Mexican immigrants, their concentration in dead-end, low-paying manual and service-oriented jobs, and their segregation into very dense urban *barrios* with other transient "working-poor" households have created neighborhoods that lack the stabilizing influence of "old families" and of well-known merchants who raised their families in the same *barrio*.

Many of the older Latino residents in Augusta Heights, in Southview, and particularly in Harrison Heights speak of an earlier time when *gente* in the neighborhood knew each other well, and would interact frequently at church, weddings, baptisms and *quinceañeras*, in corner markets, and in community centers. [17] Corner-store merchants were often Mexican-American. Kids, both Black and Chicano, regularly played in the streets, usually supervised discreetly by adults and elders who knew the children's parents. Vice existed, of course, but in the shadows, away from children and neighborhood authority figures. Chicano gangs existed as well, but their existence was not intricately intertwined with the proliferation of firearms and gun-enacted violence. The Mexican sections of Harrison Heights in the 60s were predominantly Mexican-American *barrios,* with many of the households headed by adults who were U.S.-born or immigrants with many years in the country. Children were predominantly U.S.-born. Recent immigrants in the neighborhood served to continually revitalize Mexican cultural traditions as well as the neighborhood's tradition of bilingualism and biculturalism. Although poverty was apparent, so was home ownership, as were households that had attained long-term (working-class) economic stability.

By the early 1990s, these neighborhoods, particularly sections that show a high proportion of low-income Mexican households, revealed a number of mixed characteristics that can be specified using Donald Warren's (1981) distinctive descriptions of "transitory" and "anomic" neighborhoods. Using Warren's description of transitory neighborhoods, we see the disjunction between an earlier time when the neighborhood (particularly Harrison Heights) was stable and highly socially integrated, and currently, when rental arrangements predominate, and with families continually on the move, usually seeking better housing, more affordable rents, and less drug activity on the street. At the time of this study, the neighborhoods were divided into social cliques, representing immigrant newcomers on the one hand and the remaining old-timers on the other, between the majority of highly mobile renters and the significant but dwindling minority of established homeowners.[18]

DEVELOPMENTAL CONSEQUENCES AND RISKS: ENVIRONMENT, CONSCIOUSNESS, AND MENTAL HEALTH

Adolescents throughout our society are called to devote their energies and inner resources to making key developmental and scholastic transitions. The portrait painted here of life in these four neighborhoods should remind us that many urban youth also carry the extra burden of having to develop urban skills and orientations to ensure their daily safety and survival. The street is yet another stress-provoking social world urban youth must contend with in their already arduous transition into adulthood, a world with noxious borders fundamentally poised toward their dehumanization, if not their destruction. For many who lack embeddedness in a network of caring and resourceful adults and peers, these two sets of challenges are simply incompatible and overtaxing. Continued exposure to urban social ills, beginning at an early age, does not magically inoculate children against negative outcomes; instead, as Pynoos and Nader (1988) argue, "it tends to increase their susceptibility to developmental harm and post-traumatic stress." Overexposure to social ills, particularly to street violence, combined with the lack of coordinated support from family, friends, neighbors, and institutional agents, can lead to a premature closure on identity formation or a premature entrance into adulthood—an adulthood without the resiliency, maturity, skills, and self-confidence necessary for successful living (Gorman-Smith & Tolan, 1998; Pynoos & Eth, 1985). Overexposed and overtaxed urban adolescents usually have overtaxed parents, who themselves become susceptible to the dark perils of fatalism and hopelessness.

Prolonged and unprotected exposure to violence and social ills observable on the street can also bring a desensitization to danger, and thus a heightened risk of its worst effects (e.g., getting shot or beaten) (Garbarino et al., 1992). We found many adolescents talking about violent incidents they had personally witnessed as if they were describing a particular day's bad weather. Many others oscillated between disgust and anger, on the one hand, and dispassionate observation, on the other, as if unsure what to do with these lived experiences and their associated feelings. Similar psychological profiles emerge in studies of children and youth growing up in war-torn areas of the world (Garbarino, Kostelny, & Dubrow, 1991). Chronic negative conditions and the lack of a protective social web can ultimately lead to coping strategies that may promise immediate protection, but may also seriously diminish the individual's life chances, exacerbate conditions of multiple marginality, and raise the risks of incarceration and, ultimately, of early death. Initiation into gang life, of course, is one prominent high-risk strategy taken by some urban youth (Moore, 1994; Vigil, 1988).

Of course, these concerns are quite distinctive from the "normal" challenges socially built into the developmental pathway toward adulthood that we antiseptically call adolescence. After puberty, we expect adolescents to do their part in maintaining good physical health and in acquiring the essential skills that will permit them to fulfill adult social roles and responsibilities. We expect that they will strive to construct a self-system that will lay the foundation for healthy self-esteem, a sense of self-efficacy, and a growing social identification with adult-centered communities. And we expect them to make such efforts in cooperation with institutional domains, such as the school, that devote their efforts to teaching literacy and technical skills deemed important in economic and in civic life.

For Latino children and adolescents in urban America, this "normative" socialization agenda cannot be separated from the challenges associated with developing a bilingual-bicultural *border* orientation, a means of successfully negotiating participation in multiple and often conflicting cultural worlds—particularly as represented in the cultural divide between school and home (Darder, 1991; Phelan et al., 1998). Success in meeting these distinctive developmental challenges, set within the worlds of the street, the school, and the home, depends on how well various socialization settings are constructed to provide committed, capable, and supportive individuals who become integral components of adolescents' social support network. Such construction, however, is made difficult at many levels. To begin with, proximity and access to adult kin and neighborhood youth services simply may not exist. Furthermore, when neighborhood services do exist for youth and families, the ecological dangers discussed in this chapter often function as invisible walls that prevent their full utilization.

In the following chapter, we consider some of the social as well as institutional resources *barrio* families do often have at their disposal, such as extended kinship networks and recreation centers; we also consider some of the complexities entailed in their full utilization. Beyond the consideration of worst-case scenarios, we pay special attention to how human and institutional resources, when fully accessible, provide an important basis for embedding low-status youth in viable social support and "buffering" systems and for securing their long-term resiliency.

4

Protective Familial Webs, Strategies of Defense, and Institutional Resources in the Neighborhood

We know that the negative effects of poverty and environmental stressors are neither direct nor inevitable. Many families and young people actively strategize to shield themselves from the harmful distress patterns of others, and they do so by engaging in any number of defense-oriented behaviors (e.g., surveillance, avoidance) and by seeking out various protective resources within the kinship unit and community.

Some neighborhoods are fortunate enough to have organizations and social programs oriented toward helping community residents remain resilient in a trouble-plagued environment (e.g., churches, mosques, recreation centers, schools and educational centers, rehabilitation programs). Also, some family units are large and cohesive enough to provide an adequate "buffering system" for their members (Anthony & Cohler, 1987, p. 12). In this chapter, we consider recreation centers, extended kin in the community, and supportive ties to aunts, uncles, and older siblings as important constituents of the support and buffering systems of low-status Latino adolescents.

I suggest here that when the supportive capacity of buffering systems is fully mobilized, the potentially harmful effects of environmental stressors, including the experience of adolescent distress and alienation, are kept at bay and the resiliency of those protected is heightened. However, we should consider as well that when adverse neighborhood conditions also impact the utilization of community resources, and when kinship networks are unable to enact their supportive potential, adolescents may reach their highest levels of vulnerability.

PARKS AND RECREATION CENTERS

I saw recreation centers in the focal neighborhoods constituting an important part of the buffering system of many adolescents. Such centers provided supervised recreation, a milieu for engaging in constructive activities with friends and peers, and a place that afforded informal counseling with caring and committed adults. And yet, the *perceived* threatening elements in the neighborhood that caused our informants to be perpetually vigilant also functioned to make these recreational sites unappealing to many parents and adolescents; again, safety was the issue.

Two major recreation centers run by the city operated in the area studied; one was located in Veterans Park, on the east end of Harrison Heights, and the other in Vista Park, located in Vista.[1] No recreational center existed in the Augusta Heights/Southview area at the time of the study, although the city did provide a recreational attendant at Southview Elementary School, a staff person charged with dispensing board games and ball equipment and with providing some supervision. Five neighborhood parks were distributed throughout the area. In Harrison Heights, Veterans Park is situated on the east end, and Cuahtemoc Park is situated on the west end. In the combined area of Augusta Heights and Southview, Southview Park stands solitary, up on a hill overlooking Southeast San Diego. Just east of Southview Park, in the neighborhood of Kearny, lies another small neighborhood park. Vista Park is located on the northern perimeter of Vista.

In terms of centers and organizations serving the youth community, Harrison Heights was rich. Local churches and mosques provided social clubs for church-going adolescents; the public schools in the neighborhood provided a number of after-school sports activities; and Veterans Park Recreation Center boasted a committed staff and offered arts and crafts, board games, 16 different sports teams, and special events (e.g., seasonal carnivals). On the periphery of Veterans Park are Harrison Heights Elementary School and Veterans Academy (the corresponding junior high school). After school, many students walked to the various recreational centers in the park, which included the Boys and Girls Club and the Girl's Club of America, which similarly offered recreational opportunities for eligible girls in the neighborhood. The Little League had been serving the community for decades. On the west end of Harrison Heights, La Raza Center, a social service agency funded by government bodies as well as by the private sector, focused on working with gang members in the greater area and on serving the needs of Chicano prison inmates, parolees, and their families. Yet the real story of recreation centers and youth services in the community is mixed and complicated.

At the time of the study, Humberto Smith was an area parks and recreation manager for the city of San Diego; he managed three recreation centers, supervised all the recreational personnel distributed throughout the area, and oversaw all the parks in the western half of Southeast. Mr. Smith, a Chicano who came to his position with a lot of lived knowledge

about the community he served, lamented the biased coverage the media
provided about the community.

> There are a lot of organized activities in this community, even the
> church groups provide activities for the youth; it's just that, unfor-
> tunately, you never get to see that in the news; all you see is the
> negative element, the problems. This community has a lot of
> tradition. The Little League has been here since 1940; there are a lot
> of church groups that have been here for years and years. The
> recreational center here [Veterans] has been in operation since 1961.

Mr. Smith spoke about how the various organizations, agencies, and schools
serving the neighborhood had recently organized into a "superblock," an
interagency organization devoted to better coordinating their collective
services and programs. Other neighborhoods, however, were not as fortunate. For many of the residents of Southview and Augusta Heights, the
recreational sites available in Harrison Heights and Vista were just too far
away to be routinely or easily accessible.

Although Harrison Heights appears rich in recreational resources, the
quiet specter of danger seemed to loom over each site. A fire had recently
destroyed the recreational facilities at Veterans Park; evidently, arson was
the cause. The recreational center now occupied the Seniors Center, located
across the park. A new facility was in the final planning stages, this time with
an architectural design including many more security features. Vandalism
and theft at the recreational center had been a regular problem during the
preceding year. Mr. Smith and Ms. Selena Gaitán, the Veterans Recreation
Center director, talked openly about the challenges, rewards, and dangers
involved in working at the various recreational sites in Southeast.

Job candidates undergo a good deal of screening; they must bring a rare
combination of enthusiasm, commitment to the community, job experience,
street knowledge, fearlessness, leadership ability, and perseverance, and a
solid reputation. Once hired, they undergo considerable training and tutored
supervision by their more experienced comrades. As Mr. Smith states:

> A *BA* in Recreation doesn't necessary make you qualified here. A
> lot of our staff don't have a lot of [formal] education, per se; but
> they have real life experience. Oftentimes that counts more than
> classroom experience. Why? Because they've gone through it; they
> understand what these kids are going through.

Local gangs utilize the areas' parks as meeting places; for those involved in the drug economy, the parks serve as drug distribution sites. For

these local gangs, parks are also places that reflect neighborhood identity and "protected" gang territory. Given these realities, it is understandable that such public places are where intergang rivalries and drug-related conflicts often play themselves out—although mainly in the late afternoons and evenings. Both Mr. Smith and Ms. Gaitán had accumulated considerable knowledge about the two Chicano gangs operating in Harrison Heights, and about the respective Chicano gangs of Augusta Heights, Southview, and Vista. They had also established diplomatic rapport with particular members within each of these groups.

Recreation staff members must supervise the young people who come into the center for recreation, while perpetually surveying the terrain, often negotiating with gang members and other people who come to the park with different agendas. Job candidates were routinely asked how they might respond to gunshots and "drive-by's" in the area. Ms. Gaitán spoke about how the director of another center in Southeast was recently caught in the line of fire attempting to corral young patrons during a drive-by shooting. Luckily, his injuries were not fatal. Mr. Smith talked about the kinds of risks staff members routinely confront on the job:

> Each and every person here, staff members, has had conflict with someone out there, either with a patron, with gang members, with anyone. Selena's car has been vandalized on two or three occasions. My car has been vandalized. I've had incidents with gang members, but it's how you deal with them. It's not easy. Staff members here know they could get a job somewhere else, but they understand that it is more gratifying to work here.

Staff members are encouraged to go beyond supervision, to serve as informal mentors to those who are receptive and in need. They are also encouraged to reach out to the most troubled children as a preventive measure against future problems that could disrupt the activities at the center. Mr. Smith talked about how he personally directed his staff to embrace this role:

> Sometimes I tell my staff that sometimes you have to see who you can deal with, if you can deal with the parents of the child, if you can deal with the child directly, that would be the best thing. If you can deal with some of the counselors at school, fine; you try to use all of your resources, but I'll be honest with you, sometimes we try all angles, but we ourselves don't have the resources. It would be great if we could provide counseling services here; but that's not our primary objective. And yet we do understand, if we are to, at

least, assist in trying to make a difference in our communities, we have to take time and say to each other, "Hey, bring him in, talk to him, tell him what the consequences of his actions are."

As long as recreational centers and parks are perceived as unsafe by many in the community, many adolescents and families simply decide to stay away. Thus, the apparent abundance of parks and recreational sites in Harrison Heights must be seen in context. Such sites remain, unfortunately, unutilized or underutilized community resources. Many of the adolescents we spoke to, especially the girls, but many of the boys as well, commented that their parents placed restrictions on their going to local parks, for fear of the gangs or the *cholos* hanging out there. Ms. Gaitán, center director, spoke of having to arrange transportation for the girls' softball teams in order to appease apprehensive mothers. Each interviewed adolescent and parent had a story to tell of someone shot at the park, or of a shooting between rival gang members, or of drug transactions taking place in the open.

Sra. Villanueva, whose family had been in the United States for only 3 years, felt that there were not a lot of recreational activities available to her children. Veteran's Park seemed a bit too far, and Cuahtemoc Park, which was close, didn't seem safe. In her own words:

> *No, there's nothing here except for one to take them to the park, over here to Cuahtemoc Park, but you know how "choteado" that park is* [ridiculed because of its run-down state], *that people get killed there, that there are a lot of drug addicts hanging around.*

Another parent, Sra. Pullido, an established resident of Harrison Heights, said she used to take her children to Cuahtemoc Park when they were smaller. She commented how she was always on the lookout to see who else was in the park. She refused, she said, to share the park with *cholos*, and would collect her children and leave when she saw them.

Most of the youth identified as *cholos* in public spaces are not gang-affiliated nor do they participate in the neighborhood drug economy. The adoption of certain working-class stylistic conventions in dress associated with urban Chicano identities, combined with normal clique formations among young adolescents, serves, however, to mislabel them as "trouble" in the eyes of many community residents. The combined dictates of economic necessity, youth identity formation, and fashion lead many to dress in the *cholo* style—without participation in the darker aspects of street life. And yet, the real threats of danger in the streets necessitate defensive strategies on the part of residents, usually leaving little room for finer discriminations of youth who are not personally known.

IMPORTANCE OF EXTENDED KIN IN THE NETWORKS OF LATINO
ADOLESCENTS: PROFILE OF FAMILY NETWORK DATA

In spite of the negative ecological forces that impinge on youth from segregated urban neighborhoods, many adolescents do find themselves embedded in a buffering system strengthened by the presence of primary and extended family members in the local community. Yet we are still left with the question of just how many is "many," a question that can be reworded in the following ways: "How likely is it that [urban] low-income, Latino parents with adolescents have local kin they can call on to help monitor and care for their children?" and "How likely is it that adolescents will make use of local extended kin as sources of social support?"

In an extensive review of qualitative studies, Robin Jarrett (1995) identifies and describes an array of strategies utilized by African American families to buffer their adolescent children from the risks of growing up in poverty. Families that were socially embedded in "extended, often socio-economically heterogeneous, kinship networks" were able to construct a strong buffering system that included key mediated links to institutions and networks that facilitated social-mobility opportunities (p. 120). Such networks included grandmothers, older siblings, godparents, and other biological and fictive kin, and were often interwoven with adult neighbors who provided additional care, concern, and resources. Supportive ties to "better-off" kin provided an especially important advantage.

To answer the question regarding the representation of extended kin in the social support networks of Mexican-origin adolescents, we go to our original network survey, administered during the 1987–1988 academic year. The survey was administered to 205 Mexican-origin students from six high schools in the San Francisco Bay–San Jose Peninsula area.[2] Adolescents were asked to name people they usually went to for 12 different kinds of social support. Descriptive statistics were produced for adolescents who were immigrant or second-generation (N = 145). Statistical comparisons were conducted by acculturation level, as indicated by nativity and language proficiencies and use (Highly Bilingual and English-Dominant adolescents, n = 93; Spanish-Dominant immigrants, n = 52).

Our adolescent sample was close to evenly divided between those who elected extended kin as likely sources of support and those who didn't, with just over half the overall sample electing at least one extended kin member (this measure includes only aunts and uncles, cousins, godparents, and grandparents; it does not count siblings living outside of home or in-laws). The more acculturated subgroup (Highly Bilingual and English Dominant adolescents) appeared to be a bit more likely to incorporate extended kin as sources of social and emotional support (58.1% vs. 50% for social support, 23.7% vs. 11.5% for emotional support). I suspect that this may be due to the greater proximity of extended kin among those adolescents with longer residency in the Bay-Peninsula Area. Our measures, however, were not designed to tell us whether nonelection was a matter of preference or lack of available kin. For those who did elect extended or secondary kin, the average of kin was between two and three people. Out of all the people elected as sources of social support, between a fifth and a quarter (1 in 4 people) were extended kin.

What exactly do we know about the structural characteristics of Mexican kinship networks in the United States? Susan Keefe and Amado Padilla (1987) collected kinship network data in three working-class Mexican-origin communities in California and found a high degree of local extended family organization (i.e., structural familism) despite the impact of acculturation and urbanization.[3,4] They also found important intergenerational differences that run counter to classical assimilation models (e.g., Gordon, 1964). Immigrant families, particularly those in the midst of the resettlement process, tended not to have the advantage of a large and localized kin network. Although there was heavy reliance on selected secondary kin, especially in the beginning, many immigrant families built their community networks largely by incorporating nonkin (e.g., neighbors, church associates, work mates). Fifty-two percent of all social contacts were nonkin. Only with time, and with greater economic and residential stability, did localized kinship-based exchange networks begin to take root and grow. Among the second-generation or family households with U.S.-born parents, rather than a decrease or weakening in structural familism, we see an increase. Much of the increase in the size of the kinship network had to do with increases in contact and exchange with secondary kin who settled in the same geographic area. We also see that primary and secondary kin were equally important for the exchange of goods and services. Nonkin friendship ties did not necessarily become less important, but rather were incorporated into the family support system, sometimes formally, through the practice of *compadrazgo* (godparentship).

We return to the question of whether Latino parents in low-income communities have the option of socially embedding their children in localized kin networks. Research by Keefe and Padilla (1987) suggests that due to a combination of cultural and economic factors, many second-generation families and those immigrant households with longer residency are able to mobilize local kin much more than recent immigrant-parent households are able to. Given these findings and given that the youth in our study are from immigrant-parent households (as were virtually all the Latino youth enrolled at Auxilio High School), we would not expect to find a high degree of structural familism in the neighborhoods we studied.

Our San Diego survey of adolescents' social networks included a count of the number of primary and secondary kin in the area. Two survey methodologies were used. Our first survey was administered to our initial interview sample (N = 75), and included a count of the number of primary and secondary kin in the neighborhood as well as in San Diego county. Our second survey of kin networks relied on an inventory incorporated into the self-administered questionnaire survey of all students at Auxilio High School. In administering the first survey (N = 75), we explained to our adolescent informants that "neighborhood" was defined for the moment as the general local area, and was not necessarily to be restricted to the actual neighborhood they lived in (e.g., Harrison Heights). The survey asked about siblings, aunts and uncles, cousins, grandparents, great-grandparents, and godparents (in-laws—for example, sisters-in-law—were not included in this measure). Table 4.1 displays our findings. The statistics reported here are based solely on data from adolescents who lived in the two zip-code areas that encompassed our four focal neighborhoods (N = 55). For this data set, the sample is divided by immigration status. Students who had been in the United States 7 years or less were differentiated from everyone else. We refer to this survey below as Kin Survey I.

Our high school questionnaire inventory included siblings, aunts and uncles, cousins, grandparents, and great-grandparents, and asked whether any of these relations lived in the "neighborhood or community (but *not* in your house)." Students were able to indicate the number of each kin type, including "none." As with the first survey, we again constructed a variable measuring adult kin in the area (cousins were left out) and a separate measure for number of cousins. Here the sample was divided by immigration status and language proficiency, with one group identified as Spanish-dominant immigrants (n = 288), and the other group containing everyone else (N = 171). We refer to this survey as Kin Survey II. Table 4.2 displays these survey findings. As with Kin Survey I, the demographic statistics presented here are restricted to the two zip-code areas that encompassed our focal neighborhoods.

We see in the results derived from Kin Survey I that from 52% to 55.8% of the adolescents surveyed reported having at least one adult relative in the neighborhood or local area. The percentage derived from Kin Survey II is similar (55.8%). Overall, group differences appear reflective of the findings from Keefe and Padilla (1987). These percentages are also similar to the Bay Area data, showing about half of the adolescents citing extended kin as likely sources of social support. However, from Kin Survey II, we see that nearly three-quarters of Spanish-dominant (recent) immigrants at Auxilio High (72.9%) did not have an aunt living close by, with access to aunts increasing with length of residence. Yet, even for the English-

TABLE 4.1. Primary and Extended Kin, Neighborhood and County (SD Network Data)*

	SAN DIEGO KIN SURVEY I	
	U.S. Resident 7 years or less (N = 21)	U.S. born/ U.S. resident 8 years or more (N = 34)
At least one adult kin in community/local area	52%	55.8%
Mean number of kin in community/ local area**	5.36 (N = 11)	3 (N = 19)
At least one adult kin in San Diego County	61.9%	73.5%
Mean number of kin in San Diego County*	5.23 (N = 13)	6.28 (N = 25)
At least one cousin in community/local area	42.8%	20.5%
Mean number of cousins in community/local area*	8.22 (N = 9)	2.43 (N = 7)

*Using original sample (N = 75); data only taken from those who lived in two zip-code areas that encompassed our four focal neighborhoods (N = 55).

**Means calculated only for those with at least one kin member in specific area.

proficient group, a bit more than half (53.8%) reported not having an aunt nearby. As we shall discuss later in this chapter, aunts (or *tías*) play a particularly important buffering function in the lives of many Latino adolescents.

All in all, our findings suggest that quite a large proportion of households in our study do not enjoy easy geographic access to local kin support. Recent immigrant households, as suggested by the Keefe and Padilla (1989) study, particularly feel the scarcity of kin. A significant segment of our recent-immigrant sample remains without any kin in the neighborhood (48% in Kin Survey I; 48.3% in Kin Survey II) and in the city (38% in Kin Survey I). The picture improves somewhat when we look at adult kin liv-

TABLE 4.2. Kin in the Community/Local Area (Auxilio High Survey Data)

| | SAN DIEGO KIN SURVEY II | |
	Spanish-dominant Immigrants	English-proficient Adolescents
At least one kin member in the community/local area (non-parent)	51.7% (N = 288)	62.6% (N = 171)
At least one aunt in the community/local area	27.1% (N = 288)	46.2% (N = 171)
At least one cousin in the community/local area	29.2% (N = 288)	42.7% (N = 171)

ing somewhere in San Diego. Here we see in the findings from Kin Survey I that, as expected, adolescents and their households with longer residency in the United States report a greater likelihood of having adult kin in San Diego. Length of residence in the United States leads to an increase in localized kin.

Perhaps some of the recent immigrant families are able to compensate for their isolation through visitations with family in Tijuana just across the border (about 19 miles away). In our survey of the student body at Auxilio High School, we asked students to report whether they had kin residing in Tijuana. Almost 50% (49.3%) of all recent-immigrant students surveyed (n = 424) reported having family residing in this Mexican border city. An even greater percentage of the more acculturated subsample (n = 329) reported family residing in Tijuana (64.7%). The regular visiting of relatives in Tijuana may very well ameliorate feelings of isolation, but such relatives cannot help with the routine monitoring of adolescent children as they traverse the streets of Southeast. Furthermore, for those parents who remain undocumented, the possibility of regular visitations is ruled out completely.

Returning to our findings from Kin Survey I, we see recent-immigrant households that do have adult kin in the neighborhood appear to have, on average, slightly more adult kin in the neighborhood than do their more acculturated counterparts (5.36 vs. 3.0—respondents with at least one adult relative in the neighborhood—Kin Survey I). Households with longer U.S. residency, however, appear to have a slight edge regarding kin distributed throughout the city (6.28 vs. 5.23). Nonetheless, we see that some recent-

immigrant families do have some kin, and in these particular neighborhoods, it may be that these recent-immigrant families may be temporarily
quite dependent on a few secondary kin, compared with those more established residents who enjoy larger and more diversified kinship networks, just as we saw in the findings of the Keefe and Padilla (1987) study.

OLDER SIBLINGS AND EXTENDED FAMILY MEMBERS
AS SOCIAL RESOURCES

Past discussions of the role of social capital and schooling have tended
to focus exclusively on parents. The singular focus on parents is similarly
found in the research on social capital and mobility chances among low-
status youth (Furstenberg & Hughes, 1995). In immigrant families, key
influences in terms of institutional support, moral guidance, and discipline
often include the routine practices of the oldest children. The eldest children,
now adults, are sometimes the only viable sources of emotional, social, and/
or institutional support in the household and community. Whether or not
they are sought after as sources of social and institutional support, the oldest
children usually wield a good deal of power and influence over family
decisions and over the social development of younger siblings. The personal networks of older siblings also play an important "buffering" role in
mitigating the effects of environmental stressors on adolescents.

Statistical Results on Older Siblings and Extended Family
Members as Sources of Social Support

Our investigation of older siblings and extended kin included examining the relationship data collected from the social support network survey of Auxilio High School students (N = 75). The sample is divided by
gender and immigration status (recent immigrants and everyone else).
Let's look first at the number of *multiplex* relationships with older siblings. Multiplexity is defined here in terms of whether the sibling was a
recognized source for two or more forms of social support (12 possible
forms of support; does not include "hanging out together" and sharing a
favorite pastime); the age cutoff for identifying older siblings was 21 years
of age or older. Table 4.3 displays the results of our tabulations.

Immediately notable is that boys appear to be a bit more likely to have
identified an older sibling as a multiplex source of support, although also
notable is that the majority of each category of boys did not identify such
a relationship. Immigrant boys show the highest percentage of those iden-

TABLE 4.3. Ties to Older Siblings and Extended Kin as Sources of Support (SD
Network Data, $N = 75$)

	Girls	Boys	N
Percentage of subgroup indicating at least one supportive relationship with *older sibling* as a *Multiplex Tie*			
Recent Immigrant ($N = 10$)	20% ($n = 10$)	42.9% ($n = 14$)	24
Acculturated	23.1% ($n = 26$)	30.4% ($n = 25$)	51
Percentage of subgroup indicating at least one supportive relationship with an *extended kin member* (excluding cousins under 21 years of age)			
Recent Immigrant	50% ($n = 10$)	78.6% ($n = 14$)	24
Acculturated	62% ($n = 26$)	65.2% ($n = 25$)	51
Percentage of subgroup indicating at least one supportive relationship with an *extended kin member* as a *Multiplex Tie* (excluding cousins under 21 years of age)			
Recent Immigrant	20% ($n = 10$)	42.9% ($n = 14$)	24
Acculturated	22.2% ($n = 26$)	30.4% ($n = 25$)	51

tifying supportive relations with older siblings (42.9%). Overall, for those who did identify such a sibling, the range was between one and two siblings. Of course, a major problem with the data is that we did not control for whether adolescents had an older sibling in the first place; thus, many of our adolescents may not have had such a person, as when, for instance, they themselves were the oldest children in the household.

Adolescents were much more likely to name an extended family member as a source of social support, as we see in Table 4.3. For these calculations, all extended family members (including brothers-in-law and sisters-in-law) were counted when they were a source of at least one form of social support (again excluding "hanging out together" and sharing a favorite pastime). Cousins who were under 21 years of age were not counted. The greater likelihood of selecting an extended family member (vs. an older sibling) is probably due to this relationship category's having a much greater range of people (e.g., aunts and uncles, in-laws, godparents, grandparents). Again, immigrant boys exhibited the highest percentage of those identifying extended family members (78.6%), and immigrant girls, the lowest (50%). Still, for three of the groups, the majority of adolescents did identify at least one extended kin member, with the range roughly between two and three people. We should keep in mind that gender groups may differ in their assessments of who is a likely, reliable, and trustworthy source of support. Immigrant girls, for example, relative to immigrant boys, may have a higher threshold and more stringent criteria for identifying supportive individuals. Immigrant young women may also be more likely to see themselves as *caregivers*, rather than as persons who seek and depend on the support of others.

CASE ILLUSTRATIONS DRAWN FROM INTENSIVE INTERVIEWS WITH ADOLESCENTS

Our interview findings clearly demonstrated to us the importance of older siblings and extended family members in the lives of adolescents with immigrant parents. This is not to suggest that among those who in fact had an older sibling, or a nearby aunt, all enjoyed a congenial and supportive relationship. A good deal of evidence emerged pointing to conflictive relations or to relations that lacked *confianza* and emotional closeness. What I wish to highlight in this chapter is that genuinely supportive relations with an older sibling or an extended family member provided another important avenue for adolescents to accumulate familial social resources and to receive the type of support that fostered their resiliency.

Older Siblings

Antonio Barrera, a high-achieving senior who had resided in the United States since age 7, lived in a small apartment with his mother and two younger siblings. Although his parents were recently divorced, his father visited the family frequently. At the time of our home interviews, the family was being supported by government welfare. In a family of eight children, Rosalina, 36 years old, was the oldest of the Barrera children; she worked as an elementary school teacher and lived with her husband and child in a north county community, about 20 miles north of where Antonio lived. Also mentioned in our interviews with Antonio was his brother Mario, 21 years old and, at the time, serving in the Marine Corps.

Antonio spoke extensively of the role his sister Rosalina had played in his life and of how she kept a watchful eye over the family: "Well, she's the oldest of us all. She likes to know what's happening to everybody, even the nephews and nieces, down to the little kids. So she gets involved with everybody's life; she can't avoid it." Antonio was one of the few adolescents in the sample with an older sibling in the professions. This vital link is better understood in terms of Rosalina's own personal network, in which Antonio frequently participated. There was Rosalina's husband, Patricio, who was an engineer, and Patricio's mother, Velia, who had worked many years as a volunteer nurse. There were Rosalina's colleagues at the elementary school where she taught. Antonio often spent a month in the summer with his sister and her family, an extended visit that usually included a camping trip. Occasionally during the academic year, Rosalina would take her fourth-grade class on a field trip and ask Antonio to assist with supervision. Antonio joined his sister with the school principal's approval. Many of Rosalina's students were the children of agricultural workers; others were children of parents no different from Antonio's parents.

Rosalina was a source of many forms of support for Antonio, including intimate counsel, advice on school matters and post–high school plans, and help with school assignments. Patricio, the engineer, regularly provided help with Antonio's math homework. Velia, Patricio's mother, often provided unsolicited advice regarding matters of sex and girls; she also helped him financially with his school-organized trip to the Soviet Union (in 1991).

Just before our interviews began, Antonio had been seriously considering whether to enter the Army or to go directly into a university, which his grades would have made quite possible. His sister Rosalina preferred that he go directly to college and even offered to assist him financially. In Antonio's own words:

> She pretty much left the decision up to me, but kind of edging me away from it [the military] in a way, saying, "If you need money, I can take out a loan. I'll do this for you, you know. You don't have to join the Army." Yeah, she was willing to support me, whatever I decided. . . . That's what I like about my family. They're like, they have their own opinion, but at the same time, if it's against their opinion, they'll [still] back you up.

How Antonio ultimately decided to join the Army will be taken up later in another published work. Suffice it to say that Antonio, in spite of his household's low-income status, enjoyed a key connection to the middle-class world, via his sister's college education, her marriage to an engineer, and her work as a professional educator. A world minus Rosalina (and her network) would certainly have spelled a different set of choices and life chances for Antonio. It is interesting that current indicators of family socioeconomic status, used in educational studies, rarely include the educational attainments of older siblings (and other intimate caretakers).

Most accounts of highly supportive relations with older siblings, however, were not about forms of institutional support, but rather about the regular enjoyment of intimate counsel and moral and emotional support. Such support was qualitatively different from the support of parents, fundamentally because these adolescents could assume that the older brother or sister could "relate to" or understand their perceptions, perspectives, and dilemmas. These older siblings had already gone through what the younger ones were currently experiencing, and had garnered lessons from their own adolescent struggles. As Antonio Barrera says of his Marine Corps brother, Mario:

> I feel more comfortable around him than anyone 'cause he, I don't know, 'cause he's been through most of what I'm going through now, and I can ask him how he dealt with it, what he did. Many times like I don't take his advice that much 'cause he, he's pretty much a pessimist and stuff. He looks at everything kind of from the low side.

What Antonio took away from his discussions with Mario was not so much his brother's solutions to the problems and challenges they both have had to confront, but rather validation that these problems are common to similar and significant others, as well as opportunities to see and to discuss alternative solutions to problems commonly shared. We see then that the psychological charge underlying the emotional and moral support often accessible from older siblings has its basis in common experiences as children of immigrants growing up in a similar ecology and exposed to similar societal circumstances (e.g., low socioeconomic status, segregation, racism).

Raul Ubilla, the unassuming and soft-spoken 12th-grader born in the United States, spoke of the pressure he felt from his parents to conform to their strict religious practices. Raul had three older brothers and two older sisters, along with his two younger brothers who lived with him at home. In the network survey, he cited all three of his older brothers, yet it was his sister Olivia who was his greatest source of social support. Olivia, age 28, was married with three children and lived in San Bernadino. Raul described his relationship with her by saying, "We're like twin brothers, except that she's 28." He felt that his sister had always had a special affection for him, and admitted there were hardly any issues he couldn't discuss with her. He stated that Olivia usually made the effort to examine things from his perspective, such as his half-hearted involvement in his parents' church. Olivia was a recognized source of intimate counsel and emotional support; Raul knew he could count on her for other forms of support as well, although institutional support was not one of them. When he had a terrible argument with his girlfriend, he turned first to Olivia. By his own account, his relationship with Olivia was reciprocal, with Olivia often calling Raul to talk about her own troubles; as he revealed, "She gets into arguments with her husband a lot, and she calls me to talk about it." Raul was also close to Olivia's husband, Lalo, and admitted that although he felt close to his three older brothers, he would prefer going to Lalo before seeking out his brothers. Similar to Antonio's relationship with his sister Rosalina and her spouse, Raul felt he could turn to his sister's home for occasional refuge and solace.

Evidence also emerged showing that older siblings were critically important during an adolescent's emotional crises or during key developmental transitions. Elisa Montes, an articulate, highly motivated, and attractive 11th-grader, and a member of her school's AVID program (see Chapter 8), told the story of her depression following her sister's engagement and marriage. Her sister Reyna had been her closest sibling, a confidante and a highly multiplex source of support, including homework assistance. Elisa was very attached to her sister; in Reyna she had confided all her secrets. Then Reyna became engaged and gradually began to direct her emotional energies toward her fiancé and her upcoming marriage; with this, the world began to come apart for Elisa. At the time of our interviews, Reyna had already married and moved to Tijuana, Mexico; Elisa became quite emotional when asked to talk about what had transpired. She felt resentment toward her sister for disengaging so fast, and toward her sister's new husband, who took her away. *"¡Nunca me cayó!"* [I never really liked him] she said, still in pain. Elisa talked about how her sister's departure affected her as well as her friends:

> I mean she was also really good friends with my friends, too, and they got really close to her, 'cause a lot of them don't have like an older sister, so they would look at my sister as an older sister, and whenever they needed advice, they would go to her and stuff; and all of a sudden she wasn't there anymore, not just for me, but for them either. It was hard on them, but it was greater for me, 'cause, you know, she was always there, at home, I lived with her, I talked with her; it hurt.

Notice Elisa's continuing ambivalent feelings over her sister's departure: "I don't know now, now I'm used to it, I don't feel that way anymore and sometimes I might act like, 'No!, I don't care!' you know, it's OK, [pause] but deep inside, I do care."

Yet the real story here is that this change in Elisa's core support network set in motion dynamics that opened up new relationship possibilities. Although core network losses often precipitate an emotional crisis and may generate temporary feelings of loss and isolation, such changes may also stimulate the emergence of new relationships and the emotional activation of once-dormant ones. Such was the case with Elisa; although her boyfriend, Ray, could not adequately provide the emotional support she needed, he did arrange for Elisa to speak to his mother about her minor depression—and in this arrangement was born a new relationship. Most importantly, the change in the relationship with Reyna provided the context for the kindling of Elisa's relationship with Micaela, her second oldest sister. Needing help at her beauty salon, Micaela asked Elisa to help out on the weekends, and there a new sense of sisterhood was cemented. Elisa was surprised to find she could establish such intimate rapport with this sister, given the difference in their ages (Micaela was 31). In Elisa's words: "It was really shocking; I never really thought I, I mean I knew that I could talk to her, you know, but I never really thought I could [pause] confide in her, like I had with Reyna." Micaela became a source of many forms of support, including, and most especially, intimate counsel and emotional support. She was also there when Elisa decided to break off her relationship with her boyfriend, Ray. In turn, Elisa was very pleased to be able to act as a confidante to her older sister, and listened intently to Micaela when she shared with her the problems and challenges experienced by a mature, married, and entrepreneurial Latina woman.

Throughout our interviews, we saw that close relations with older siblings exhibited a number of important and overlapping functions. Already mentioned is the sense of validation felt when adolescents learn that their older siblings had experienced similar trials as Latino adolescents from an immigrant household and a problem-plagued neighborhood. They also received a preview of the trials that awaited them as young adults, as well as opportunities to learn from their siblings' successes and mistakes. In this sense, older siblings acted as role models, providing ample opportunities for vicarious learning (Bandura, 1969). The stronger the identification with the older sibling, the more likely the adolescent seemed to take these lessons to heart.

Finally, close, multiplex relations with resilient and supportive older siblings provided opportunities for these adolescents to practice the principles of mature and responsible adult relationship (Youniss & Smollar, 1985). This we saw clearly in the relationship between Elisa and her sister Micaela, and in the relationship between Antonio and his sister Rosalina. Through these relationships, these adolescents were bound by the norms of *mutual trust* and *symmetrical reciprocity* (Youniss & Smollar, 1985). Adolescents also learned that seismic shifts and changes in their personal networks, while bringing a sense of loss, also opened opportunities for new relationships and new sources of social support, as witnessed in Elisa's case. Although the accounts provided above were revealed with an air of normative commonality—a stereotypical cultural feature of Mexican life in the United States (Keefe, Padilla, & Carlos, 1979)—on close scrutiny, our data show that such highly supportive relations between adolescents and older siblings, although frequent, were *not* the norm.[5] They do, however, provide a glimpse of the circumstances that bolster resiliency among many urban Latino adolescents, and that often allow these individuals to *overcome the odds.*

Extended Family Members

Older siblings, of course, are not the only kin who intervened in the lives of these adolescents. As we saw in the statistical findings derived from our network survey data, adolescents also established supportive links to extended family members, although our data suggest that it was harder to develop the multiplexity and intimacy we saw in relations with older siblings. As with the data on older siblings, few extended kin emerged as viable sources of middle-class forms of institutional support. This was primarily due to the similarly low socioeconomic status of extended kin members. Under the best of circumstances, supportive relations included intimate counsel, emotional support, and small amounts of monetary aid (e.g., lunch money); also common were offers to take the adolescent in (temporarily) when distressful conflicts erupted in the adolescent's home.

Aunts (*tías*) represented key figures in these adolescents' networks, although uncles (*tíos*) were occasionally cited as sources of support as well. Aunts and uncles often took the role of co-parents and surrogates, providing much the same kinds of support parents give their own children. In a few cases in our sample, adolescents had been raised by aunts and uncles. It is also not uncommon within Mexican enclave communities for adolescents to leave their parents in Mexico and to join an aunt and uncle in the United States (Hondagneu-Sotelo, 1994).

The sentimentality of adolescent relations with their aunts is exemplified in the account provided by Soledad Arroyo. Soledad had gone back and forth between Mexico and the United States since infancy. Most recently, she spent 4 years in schools in Mexico before returning to the United States 3 years prior to our first interview. Soledad talked extensively about her spellbound and adulterous father and the great distress his behavior brought on her family. In the midst of this domestic turmoil emerged Soledad's relationship with her maternal *Tía* Josefina, a woman of 43 who served as a source of many forms of support, including intimate counsel and emotional support. Soledad talked about how her aunt tended to her and her siblings when her mother became ill: "*When my mom would be sick, she would buy us whatever she could afford. She would give me money for my lunch, for the bus, and to buy clothing.*" Soledad acknowledged her aunt's patient and tender disposition and her ability to inspire trust: "*Well, I trust her, my aunt is very patient. She has a lot of patience for everything.*" Soledad spoke of her aunt with obvious fondness, pride, and appreciation in her voice. From time to time Soledad visited her aunt and, seeing that she needed help with ironing and housecleaning, offered to help.

Daniel Montalvo, in the United States since infancy, spoke with similar affection about his relationship with his *Tía* Leti, his father's older sister. Daniel stated that she paid a lot of attention to his progress in school, regularly offering advice and guidance about school matters as well as about his educational future. In the network survey, Daniel also cited her as a source of emotional support. She was generous with Daniel, and offered material support when she saw that he needed it, like the time she obtained a camera for Daniel to use for one of his photography class projects. He likened her to a "second mother"; and although she was his father's sister, she usually sided with Daniel's mother on family and educational matters, thus reinforcing his mother's strong authority and influence in the household. As he saw it, his mother and *Tía* Leti stood as a formidable team, although it is obvious that his aunt's generosity and genuinely loving disposition toward Daniel softened his position toward the significant influence and authority she wielded in the family and in his life.

In these families, as with other similarly fortunate adolescents we interviewed, aunts and uncles played a significant role in forming an extended family web that generated additional care, concern, and resources. Similar adult structures have been found in the research on resilient African American youth (see Jarrett, 1995, for review). Furthermore, the homes of older siblings and extended family members offered many of our adolescent subjects a home away from home, a temporary sanctuary where love and support were bestowed and enjoyed, and a place to receive special counsel from respected older siblings and family elders on emotionally perplexing issues. These are precisely the mediating network processes many scholars believe contribute to resiliency (see Garbarino et al., 1992), processes that served to differentiate a subset of our adolescent subjects from the others whose personal networks placed them at considerable risk.

Unfortunately, a high degree of structural familism and propinquity among our adolescents did not always translate into supportive and emotionally congenial relations with extended kin. Propinquity could also provoke gossip and conflictive relations. Many of the adolescents we interviewed were beginning to find help seeking and emotional closeness to significant others a rather troublesome coping strategy. Repeated experiences with betrayed confidences, disappointing help-seeking experiences, and a growing lack of *confianza* underlying relations with friends, school personnel, and kin members made the development of a negative or a defensive network orientation a high probability. Such orientations often short-circuited the potential for ongoing supportive relations with kin who were, in fact, quite capable and positively predisposed to help-giving and to the rules of *confianza en confianza* (trusting mutual trust).

In other cases, the problem was not a history of betrayed confidences or spoiled relations, but rather that closer relations with adult (immigrant) kin had to be considered in light of the life-style and social activities enjoyed by the adolescent, particularly when such activities were outside the social norms and moral dictates of the adult kin community. Seeking intimate counsel and emotional support from adult kin usually required disclosing the intricacies of their personal lives (e.g., issues of teen romance or sexuality, tagging and graffiti). Congenial and sentimental relations with an aunt or uncle, or godparent, did not necessarily translate into intimate disclosures! Adult kin could be generous in their provision of material and social support, and yet remain inaccessible as a source of intimate counsel. Such intimate relations of trust and disclosure required arriving somehow at a very clear compact of trust, nonjudgmental rapport, and confidentiality.

María Toledo, 9 years in the United States and daughter of a devout Jehovah's Witness, spoke of her relationship with her *Tía* Nelly with both affection and reservation. "Out of all of my aunts, she's my favorite one," she said. Yet "favorite" didn't necessarily translate into intimacy and trust. Although *Tía* Nelly was cited as a source of six different types of support, and thus qualified as a highly multiplex relationship, she was not cited as a source of intimate counsel or emotional support. To complicate matters, this aunt had recently moved to a distant city; as María stated: "We don't talk that much because she moved to San Francisco and she's busy right now. [pause] When we do talk, we do get along. She's nice. It's really not that close, but we get along real well." Moments later, María finally wrestled with the issue of trust and confidentiality: "Sometimes I feel that I can trust her, but sometimes I don't. I guess sometimes I'm afraid that she'll tell my mother stuff I tell her. That's what I'm always scared of." Asked whether her aunt ever betrayed her confidence, she stated, "No, not that I remember." Yet the fear remained.

The fact that her relationship with her mother was not one of mutual trust raised the stakes. As we shall see in Chapter 7, María was fearful of her mother's reactions whenever personal issues surfaced in their daily interactions. María articulated her apprehension, stating: "Every time that I try to talk to her, it scares me because she might scream at me or do something or tell me [pause] that's why I feel sometimes that I can't trust her." Without a clear declaration or compact of trust with her aunt, María pondered the risk of her mother's learning of her social life, of her peers, and of her moral ruminations, so far painstakingly kept outside her mother's purview. Ultimately, María considered the risk too great.

María wanted to maintain her relationship with her boyfriend and her other friends; she wanted to feel "normal," to engage in the social activities enjoyed by her peers. To do so she had to maintain a quasi-secret life, which included keeping aspects of her life hidden from the purview of adult kin—however emotionally giving and congenial they appeared to be.

CLOSING ANALYSIS AND REFLECTIONS

In this chapter we examined recreational centers and extended kinship networks as two institutional domains within the community that potentially play a decisive role not only in insulating youth from negative environmental forces (e.g., criminal activities), but in assisting youth to meet the developmental challenges associated with these urban segregated environments (e.g., avoiding undue risk and danger; building supportive ties to resilient peers and caring adults across contexts). Our findings provided a mixed picture. Although some youth in the neighborhoods studied were embedded in networks that included generous interaction with extended kin and regular access to recreational centers, many did not enjoy such embeddedness. First, some neighborhoods (Augusta Heights and Southview) simply did not have organized recreational centers. Second, in Harrison Heights where recreational sites were plentiful, the specter of danger compelled many parents to prohibit their children from visiting such places. With regard to regular contact with extended kin, we saw that many immigrant households in our study did not have easy access to a proximal kinship network (especially to an aunt or an uncle). To complicate matters, geographic proximity and regular interactions between adolescents and kin did not automatically translate into social support. Relations of mutual trust, a help-seeking orientation that placed a value on kin support, and a kin member's emotional availability and commitment to confidentiality were also necessary for relations of support to emerge. Without neighborhood kin who were geographically accessible, as well as trustworthy and dependable, and faced with invisible walls preventing access to recreational sites, many youth in these four neighborhoods spent a good deal of time unsupervised by adults and without the benefit of safe and organized recreational activity.[6]

As we shall see throughout this book, the negative effects of class and urban segregation are not always apparent. For many low-status youth, access to supportive and buffering resources is blocked by mediating forces and circumstances that are often quite invisible to the average observer. Structural forces are usually understood in terms of their direct effects, such as the concentration of poverty in urban spaces. Yet structural and institutional forces also work indirectly by preventing or undermining positive mediations, or by turning individual circumstances into an express ticket to heightened vulnerability (e.g., a temporary lack of adult kin in area; living in a one-parent household; a defensive or self-protective help-seeking orientation). For many youth, the lack of successful mediations by family, school, or community translates into embeddedness in a social web that fails to buffer and protect, thus subjecting these adolescents to the full weight of class and racial stratification. Successful and empowering mediations are visible, however, in places like Harrison Heights, Southview, and the other focal neighborhoods; and although positive mediating forces can be rooted in empowering ethnic practices (cultural agency), they can also be rooted in proper institutionalized interventions. These mediations (i.e., counterstratification forces), when they result in embedding youth in a supportive and protective web, can turn the many trials of urban segregation into challenges successfully met and overcome.

The chapters that follow permit us to closely examine adolescents' relations with parents and relations with school personnel. These two relational contexts have long been seen as vital sources of support for low-status adolescents, particularly as they confront different developmental challenges and ecological dangers, and as they prepare for adulthood. Let us see what these particular Latino adolescents encounter as they engage with parents and with school personnel, and as they attempt to access different kinds of social, emotional, and institutional support.

Part II

*Immigrant Parents
as Sources of Social
and Institutional Support*

5

Immigrant Parents' Educational Values and Aspirations for Their Children—Constraints on Converting Values into Practice

> I think that most Mexican immigrant parents, they push you along,
> they tell you for the one millionth time that you've gotta work
> hard so that you can do something they never did; or, you know,
> just climb the social ladder like they never did and never will.
> —Angeles Machado, in the United States since infancy

So states a young 12th-grade female living in the United States since infancy, her sentiments quite reflective of the views of so many of the other adolescents interviewed. The statement embodies an underlying credo, transmitted by immigrant parents over many years as a way of motivating their children to stay on the academic path—in spite of the difficulties. It communicates the idea that success in school is a matter of familial obligation, and that, ultimately, doing well in school will both justify and honor the sacrifices and tribulations of immigrant parents.

The erroneous assumption that Latino children perform poorly in school because, in great part, Latino parents are ambivalent or uncaring about education is still widespread. In early 1990, then-Secretary of Education Lauro Cavazos, an appointee of President Bush, while announcing that Latino parents have historically placed a high value on education, nevertheless finished his statement by lamenting that "somewhere along the line we lost that" (cited in Valencia, 1991, p. 323). Although he was forced to resign later in the year due to widespread complaints about his lack of strong leadership, Cavazos's conservative views and rhetoric did serve to reinforce the dominant discourse pertaining to the problems encountered by minorities in the educational system.

Absent in this dominant discourse is a clear understanding of what it means to be working-class, non-White, and immigrant; absent is any concrete knowledge of the many problems Mexican-origin and other Latino parents encounter as they try to influence the educational trajectories of their children. Also absent is what it means to be an adolescent child of immigrant parents who themselves have only 3 or 4 years of formal schooling. What is given prominence in this dominant American discourse is the notion that the success or failure of individual Latino children can be ultimately traced to the decisions, investments, and values of their parents.

HOW MEXICAN PARENTS EXPRESS THEIR HOPES FOR THEIR ADOLESCENT CHILDREN'S FUTURE SUCCESS IN SCHOOL

Throughout our interviews, Mexican immigrant parents communicated an unequivocal value for the continued education and schooling of their children. Their hope for their children's success in school was characteristically framed in the context of their own limited educational opportunity as children. The high premium placed on education, however, did not usually translate into either a deep comprehension of what their adolescent children were going through in school or any efficacious sense of their role in helping their children plan a post–high school educational strategy.

Parents varied in whether they clearly articulated an understanding of the importance of a college education. A subgroup of parents did appear to be quite explicit about wanting their children to go to college. A mother whose son stayed with his father in Mexico, then later rejoined her in order to continue his schooling, declares:

> Yes, of course, he should go to the university . . . if he studies to be a teacher, then he should still continue studying something else. I always tell him, never stop learning about things, you should never stop learning, understanding, or knowing.

Señora Cortes adds that it is important for all her children to get good grades, stating that she is *"muy vanidosa; yo quisiera que mis hijos tomaran el primer lugar* [I'm a very vain woman; I always wish that my children finish in first place]."

> —Sra. Cortes (44 years old; mother of four; separated; son Joaquin stayed with father in Mexico while she came to the United States with three younger sons)

Other mothers asserted similar feelings, although in these cases in reference to their U.S.-born or 1.5 immigrant children. Note, however, the tinge of uncertainty in their statements.

Well, yes, now there are teachers that encourage them and tell them that in order to accomplish great things, you have to go to the university, you have to continue to study.

> —Sra. Jacobo (37 years old; mother of six; sixth-grade education, 13 years in the United States; not currently working)

I want him to finish his education. I would like him to go as far as he can. He should go to the university or college, depending on how much our economic situation would allow, since, well, the university costs more. And there, can't they give him a scholarship? It seems that Raul already filled out an application for the university. He was telling me that; I asked him what he wanted to study and he told me psychology. Yes, we have spoken with him.

> —Sra. Ubilla (52 years old; mother of five; graduated from preparatory school in Mexico; 14 years in the United States; not currently working—disabled)

Well, she should finish and then continue on to college. I believe those are her plans. God comes first, then we'll see, because one can never really know.

> —Sra. Loza (49 years old; lives with husband and two daughters; 16 years in the United States; not currently working)

Although many of the other parents may very well have harbored a hope that their children continue their studies at the university level, their educational aspirations for them were expressed in different terms. What these lower-working-class parents shared in common, and what is revealed in their statements, is a pattern of nonexplicit intervention in their adolescent children's schooling. While expressing much support for their children's educational endeavors, they did not explicitly articulate any precise aspirations or goals, preferring to allow their children to define their own educational plans. These parents appear to follow the lead of their adolescent children's interests, talents, and motivation. Their hopes are clear, but such hopes reveal a noninterventionist parenting style.

Sra. Urquilla wanted her daughter Marisol to pursue a career; she and her husband were willing to support her as long as she was willing to put forth the effort. She stated it this way:

Well, we'd like for her to finish her education; whatever she'd like to study, depending on how much we can help. As long as she's willing to study, we'll continue to help her in any way possible.
        —Sra. Urquilla (about 40 years old; mother of three; fifth-
              grade education; 3–4 years in the United States; has
              never worked outside the home)

Sra. Urquilla stated that Marisol and her son are doing well because they are motivated. They are extremely happy with their children's progress, but they are not pushing them; the children are doing well because they want to. As she put it, "*Right now they are doing well because of their own efforts, because of their own desire. We don't put pressure on them.*"

Another mother, Sra. Barrera, admitted that she never really had any conscious, outspoken goals for her children in terms of an occupation or career. In her own words:

I've never given them any goals, well, because, they should, they have formed their own goals, . . . I only hope that they really study. I've never told them, "You'll do this or you'll do that." They've decided what they're going to do. I only ask that that they study and that they do what they like as long as it's in their best interest.
        —Sra. Barrera (53 years old; mother of four; recently
              divorced; no formal schooling, but literate; 10 years in
              the United States; not employed)

Nonetheless, Sra. Barrera was clear that whatever her children's decision, it should involve "studying" and academic preparation. The aspirations held by many of the mothers were couched in similar terms; they wanted their children to study, to take advantage of existing educational opportunities. They wanted their children not to experience the indignities and poverty they themselves had endured. They wanted their children to take personal responsibility for their future, to make sound and mature decisions, to be purposeful; in their own words, "*Ser responsable y honrado*" (to be responsible and honorable).

Sra. Hernández, in the United States for 6 years, spoke in regard to her son Leonel: "*Well, that he decide to study. And that he makes a real effort in his studies. Because if not, if he doesn't make an effort to plan for his future, what will happen to him?*"

Sra. Iglesias spoke of her wishes for her daughter in the context of the family's motivation for coming to the United States: "*We want them to have*

the very best schooling; we want them to prepare themselves well for the future
... this is why we came here."

> —Sra. Iglesias (39 years old; mother of three; second-grade
> education; 6 years in the United States; works at a
> veterans' used-goods store)

Note the strong association between academic preparation and becoming an honorable, morally upright, self-sufficient person. Sra. Villanueva, in the United States for 4 years, expressed her hopes for her daughter in this way:

> *I want the best for her, that she study and that she, well, be able to do*
> *something with her life. I want her to prepare herself; so she won't be*
> *tied down to her husband, because my husband sees a lot of people, a lot*
> *of girls at the high school, they get ruined with a man, with any man*
> *and then they're good for nothing; because you know what times are*
> *like.*
>
> > —Sra. Villanueva (47 years old; mother of four; third-
> > grade education; 4 years in the United States—but lived
> > in United States from 1976 to 1981; not currently working)

Again, Sra. Barrera, speaking in reference to all her children:

> *The only thing that has concerned me is that they be good, that they don't*
> *have any vices, and that they be responsible; with that, I think, things will*
> *turn out well for them; but hoping that they'll be a doctor, or an engineer;*
> *honestly speaking, it might happen, but economically, I don't think so.*
> *Well, it's enough that they study hard, that they be responsible persons*
> *and that they like their job. Like I tell my children, "You aspire what you*
> *want, you study what you can, I will help you with whatever I can, and*
> *that's it." Well, of course, all mothers hope that their child will experience*
> *success, but I say, if they are able to become lawyers, or doctors, it's*
> *because they've been responsible and that they like what they're doing.*[1]

Although the immigrant parents we interviewed left no doubt that they *valued* education for their adolescent children, seldom did this translate into being actively engaged in their schooling. Restrained by constraints imposed by their own limited education, their status as newcomers to the United States, and their lower-working-class background, parents searched for more culturally appropriate ways of actualizing their educational values. As evidenced by Sra. Barrera's statement, and as we see later, Mexican immigrant parents try to foster the academic achievement of their children through actively shaping their children's moral development. The belief is that a morally strong and responsible child will experience success in school, according to his or her abilities.

The widespread practice of calling into question the educational values of Latino and other minority parents doesn't usually include an examination of the social forces and life experiences that severely circumscribe these parents' ability to act according to idealized middle-class parenting standards. Mexican parents are themselves cognizant of their own limitations, and do express them, often in lamenting fashion.

Many of the parents spoke of how their own limited schooling prevented them from being more academically helpful to their adolescent children. The statements of Sra. Loza and Sra. Pulido presented below are typical. Sra. Loza considered it extremely important for her daughter to continue studying. She pointed out to us that she did not have access to formal education in Mexico and that she now hoped her daughter would take full advantage of the opportunity to study in the United States. In her own words:

> "Because,—I say, since I,—I didn't really have any schooling. We just didn't have the opportunity, you know. My parents, well, they were very poor."
> —Sra. Loza (49 years old; lives with husband and two daughters; 16 years in the United States; not currently working)

Likewise, Sra. Pulido was aware of her limitations when it came to providing her children with academic instruction in her home. She seemed, however, to take it all in stride, repeating what she has told her children:

> I tell them, "That's your job. It's your obligation. How am I going to sit there by your side, and say, 'Look, do it like this,' or 'Do it like that,' it's very likely I don't know the material. 'I really can't help you. How can I, if I don't have the knowledge or I never studied that particular material, how can I be expected to help you?'"

When we queried adolescents about the difficulties they may have encountered in obtaining academic and other forms of institutional support from parents, distressful responses were more likely to be voiced by the more acculturated adolescents. Although recent-immigrant adolescents recognized their parents' limitations as sources of support, the fact that they shared a common identity and experience as immigrants may have served to mute the issue.

The experience of María Jesús Iglesias was fairly typical; a 12th-grader with 4 years in the United States, María Jesus spoke about not being able to go to her mother for help with her schoolwork, given that her mother didn't receive formal schooling. She did, however, frequently seek her mother's opinion regarding school matters. María's strategy was to employ her mother as a sounding board for school-related issues outside the realm of academic subject matter.

In contrast, the responses by the more acculturated adolescents revealed varying degrees of distress and resignation. This does not necessarily indicate that they didn't understand or empathize with the sociocultural limitations placed on their parents. Rather, it seemed to reflect more their accumulated, often distressful, schooling experiences over the years, confronting and coping with school problems without the benefit of knowledgeable and efficacious parents. This response also seemed related to the fact that they no longer identified their experience as *immigrant,* and understood that neither did school personnel. This suggests that school personnel now evaluated their performance in school on the same terms they evaluated that of U.S.-born groups.

Lázaro Bonilla, a 12th-grader and in the United States since infancy, commented that his mother had seldom been able to help him with the problems he faces in the outside world, including his schoolwork.

> Like my mom she doesn't help me with my homework. She's never helped me with my homework because she doesn't know. Because like my mom doesn't know how to read or write. My mom just knows how to write her name, that's all. That's all she knows. Like I read everything to her. So, I never had help from my mom. I'll tell her, "*Má,* I don't know how to do this, and she just tells me, '*No sé*' [I can't help you]."

The more acculturated adolescents spoke of a split between the world of school and the world at home, and there are varying ways in which these youth cope with this multiple world experience. Sandra Jacobo, a high-achieving 11th-grader residing in the United States since the age of 3, had learned to accept it, embracing a sense of independence that left little room for sharing her academic world with her parents:

> They try to get involved, but I tell them, I consider it to be part of my personal life. My studies, my education. Since I was young, they really haven't had much involvement with my school work. So in a sense I have grown accustomed to it and I don't get them involved. They are apart from school work. They are apart from my, [long

pause] my life in general. I think they are just two separate things. I don't share with them.

Rosario Zárate, a mid- to low-achieving 12th-grader residing in the United States since infancy, stated that her mother did talk to her on occasion about school and college, but felt that she could not really expect her mom to help her academically. She stated, "They [my parents] really can't help me with my work because they don't understand it. All they can do right now is just talk to me." Rosario felt, however, that if her mother had a higher level of education, she would very likely seek her mother's help.

Rosario hadn't kept her mother informed of her progress in school, feeling that her mother didn't have the knowledge base to truly comprehend the academic difficulties she was experiencing. At the same time, Rosario more than hinted at her frustration with her parents' passive engagement in her academic life, feeling that her situation might not be so precarious if her parents would go to the school and inform themselves. Such ambivalence was widely shared among the more acculturated students in the study.

Most parents were not well informed about their adolescents' academic or social situation in school, apart from occasional queries and discussions with their children about report cards, which came periodically in the mail.[2] The evidence also suggests that adolescents who were doing well in school kept their parents much better informed than did the low-achievers. Only one recent immigrant and three long-term immigrant parents talked extensively about their self-initiated and periodic visits to the high school to speak with teachers and counselors. Most of the other parents could not provide any significant descriptive information on their adolescent child's teachers and counselors. When these parents talked about visits to the campus, it was usually about visits to see their children perform in a talent presentation (i.e., *rondalla*), or a sporting event.

A few of these parents gave unsolicited excuses for their lack of involvement. Sra. Zamora, mother of Robert, blamed her lack of direct involvement in her son's school affairs on her chronic arthritis. Sra. Ubilla, mother of Raul, spoke about various illnesses she had suffered during the past year, combined with difficulty in walking. It is important to note, however, that Sra. Ubilla, a devout "Christian," attended church services almost daily, usually taking her children with her, a practice her son Raul was finding increasing problematic, in part because it interfered with his homework and leisure time.

Among these particular immigrant parents, the seeming lack of involvement in their adolescents' high school education conceals a larger story. Most of the parents interviewed had younger children in elementary and junior high school, and revealed a much more active involvement and interest in their school affairs. Faced with limitations on their time and energies, these parents concentrated on the needs of their younger children. Similarly, these parents also spoke of their greater involvement during the early years of their adolescent children's schooling, with progressively less involvement as they matured into adolescence.

PARENT INVOLVEMENT IN THE ACADEMIC AFFAIRS OF THEIR ADOLESCENT CHILDREN: PRESENTATION OF QUANTITATIVE SURVEY RESULTS

As another way of inquiring into the degree of parent involvement in students' school and academic affairs, we included some relevant items in the questionnaire survey, administered to the entire high school student body near the end of the academic year. Table 5.1 displays our findings. Analyses were conducted to differentiate between Spanish-dominant immigrants and students who were English-proficient—both immigrant and U.S.-born. The first question we consider here asked: "How many times this year has your parent(s) or guardians(s) come to school to talk with a teacher or a counselor?"

Among the 398 Spanish-dominant students who reported, nearly 60% of their recent immigrant parents made either no visit (37.4%) or only one visit (22.1%) to the school to speak with staff. Put differently, 62.6% of recent-immigrant parents did make at least one visit to speak to staff. Only

TABLE 5.1. Visits to Auxilio High School by Immigrant Parents (as reported by student)

	Not once this year	Once	Twice	3 to 5 Times	More than 6 Times
Spanish-dominant immigrant students (N = 398)	37.4% (n = 149)	22.1% (n = 88)	17.6% (n = 70)	17.8% (n = 71)	5.0% (n = 20)
English-proficient students (N = 311)	48.4% (n = 150)	20.9% (n = 65)	18.3% (n = 57)	10.0% (n = 31)	2.6% (n = 8)

*Survey administered in May (toward the end of the academic calendar); students asked to report on parental visitations during the academic year.

a bit more than a fifth of the parents visited on three or more occasions. In contrast, among the 311 English-proficient and U.S.-born students who responded, 69% of their parents either made no visit (48.2%) or only one visit (20.9%) to the school. Alternatively, 51.8% of these parents made at least one visit, nearly 11% lower than the percentage of recent-immigrant parents. Only 12.5%, or a bit more than one-tenth, visited on three or more occasions, about half of the percentage of recent-immigrant parents.

Of course, these data are complicated by the fact that we don't know what percentage of visits were parent-initiated; some parents could have been called to school because of some school policy violation on the part of the adolescent. Nonetheless, it is important to call attention to what amounts to a counterintuitive finding: that recent-immigrant parents made more visits to the school than did long-term immigrant parents (differences were statistically significant, p < .05). Acculturation and longer U.S. residence don't appear to bode well for parent involvement in high school. In any case, a large segment of both recent- and long-term immigrant parents does not appear to be significantly engaged in the school affairs of their children.[3] The social science literature on parent involvement suggests several key explanatory factors: the lack of middle-class cultural capital on the part of working-class parents, combined with the level of naive trust among immigrant parents; also the tacit, paternalistic, and distancing messages communicated by school personnel toward working-class parents in general.[4]

The second survey item we consider here is divided into two questions, the first of which asked:

My *mother* (stepmother, female guardian) keeps close track of how well I am doing in school.

Students responded by indicating either *True, False,* or *Does not apply.* Table 5.2 displays our findings. Again, recent-immigrant parents appear to have an edge. Among recent immigrants, 72.5% reported that their mother closely monitored their academic progress; in contrast, among the more acculturated English-proficient students, 63.9% reported close monitoring by their mother. The differences were statistically significant (p < .001). The subsequent item inquired about the incidence of monitoring by the father. A similar trend emerges, with recent-immigrant fathers revealing a higher likelihood of parental monitoring (again, statistically signficant; p < .001). As expected, a greater percentage of mothers were engaged in monitoring behavior than fathers. Although these are crude measures, they do suggest that a solid majority of Mexican-origin parents do attempt in some way to monitor their adolescent children's progress in school, in spite of their low socioeconomic background and constraints. At the same time, we see

TABLE 5.2. Parental Monitoring of Adolescent Child's Progress in School (as reported by student)*

	MOTHER MONITORS			FATHER MONITORS		
	True	*False*	*Does not apply*	*True*	*False*	*Does not apply*
Spanish-dominant immigrant students (*N* = 396)	72.5% (*n* = 287)	19.2% (*n* = 76)	8.3% (*n* = 33)	54.8% (*n* = 217)	28.8% (*n* = 111)	17.2% (*n* = 68)
English-proficient students (*N* = 313)	63.9% (*n* = 200)	30.0% (*n* = 94)	6.1% (*n* = 19)	41.9% (*n* = 131)	37.7% (*n* = 118)	20.4% (*n* = 64)

*Item worded: "My *mother* [father/guardian] keeps close track of how well I am doing in school." Student asked to indicate *True, False,* or *Does not apply.*

that a significant proportion of adolescents in this study, particularly the more acculturated, perceived that their parents either did not or *could not* closely monitor their academic situation.

PARENTAL INVOLVEMENT: WHAT THE LITERATURE TELLS US

Overall, the findings above largely substantiate earlier studies on parental involvement in school among low SES Mexican-origin families. In a study published in 1986, Harriet Romo studied and contrasted the schooling perspectives of undocumented recent immigrant parents, transitional families (i.e., legal residents), and parents who were second- or third-generation Chicanos. The high value placed by parents on the education of their children across these three categories was confirmed. However, the barriers that prevented parents from being more actively involved in their children's education, although similar in some respects, were also distinctive across categories.

Recent immigrants expressed the strongest feelings of isolation and, due to their lack of English proficiency and poor literacy skills, were inhibited from actively engaging school personnel. Nonetheless, this group registered the strongest support for school teachers and staff. Transitional families, while apparently accommodating well to the school's routines, "lacked the knowledge of how the system worked, how to get information, and how to make things happen for their children in the schools" (Romo, 1986, p. 188). Although they were often present at school meetings, confronting school authority and vocalizing their concerns continued to be troublesome for them. Chicano parents, in contrast to the other groups, expressed the most antagonism to and alienation from the schools. As noted by Romo, the fact that their children acquired full fluency in English, even at the expense of Spanish, hadn't really translated into their children's school success. Although significantly involved in parent groups and in school affairs, parents were still marginal to the centers of power and influence at the school and at the district headquarters.[5]

In another, more recent study conducted in Austin, Texas, Harriet Romo and Toni Falbo (1996) examine the various strategies undertaken by Latino parents, schools, and youth to ensure high school completion. These researchers also revisit the problems many low-SES immigrant Latino parents confront in shepherding their children through the schooling process. Romo and Falbo summarize some of the burdens many of these parents carry:

> Uneducated parents had less opportunity to monitor their children. And because poorly paid, low-level jobs are often done in the evenings and night, the parents had less opportunity to supervise their children's departure from school or their arrival home. Moreover, they were unable to control the time when their children went to bed or got up in the morning . . . many of the parents, especially the least-educated ones, were [also] unable to be an advocate for their children when their children needed help in overcoming administrative obstacles within the school. . . . These parents did not know *when* their advocacy was needed, they did not know *how* to be an advocate, and they were discouraged from doing so by their children. Many parents told us that their children begged them not to go to the schools because the students were ashamed of them. (pp. 196–197; emphasis added)

Clearly, these problems cannot be fully comprehended on the basis of simplistic cultural and linguistic disjunctions between the family and the school. The problems delineated above are characteristic of many other families and ethnic communities occupying the social bottom in the United States, including Whites. The alienation and skepticism of well-established Chicano families in Romo's (1986) earlier study also parallel what we know about the alienation and distrust felt by other low-SES parent communities throughout the country (e.g., Fine, 1991; Lareau, 1989; Ogbu, 1991).

In some important respects, Latino parents with children in high school, as an aggregate, do not differ significantly from parents across the class and ethnic spectrum. Sophia Catsambis and Janet Garland (1997), in a national study of multi-ethnic 8th- through 12th-graders, provide a mixed picture of parental involvement in adolescent schooling.[6] We see that Latino parents communicate with the school about their adolescents' progress at about the same level as do parents from other ethnic groups, with rates for all groups remaining stable between 8th and 12th grades (an average of 52.3% of parents [with 12th graders] maintain this form of parent-school communication). By 12th grade, Latino parents also approximate White and Asian parents in the level of aspirations for college completion by their children (Latinos 37%, Whites 41%, Asians 38%, African Americans 23%).

Latino parents also share more or less in the proportional *decrease* in communication with the school about their children's academic program (Latinos go from 68% to 41% between the two grade levels—8th grade and 12th grade). The decrease in this form of parent involvement is, however, compounded for some groups; Latino youth are much more likely to make academic decisions alone (61%) relative to Whites (only one-third of students), although this is probably more a function of social-class differences than of ethnicity or racial status. In some important ways, high schools do see more parental involvement (across all groups) than is the case in junior high schools; particularly with respect to parent volunteering, we see an average increase of about 16.5%. Nevertheless, most parents, regardless of ethnic group, do not volunteer (volunteering Whites 43% vs. Latinos 32%). Although we know that family socioeconomic status plays a big role in the nature of parent-school relations, Catsambis and Garland (1997) found that the strongest predictor of parent involvement in the 10th grade is "prior parental involvement." Keeping in mind Romo's (1986) and Romo and Falbo's (1996) research, it would be reasonable to suggest that the institutional experiences immigrant parents accumulate while interfacing with elementary schools not only register immediate effects on their children's academic development, but also set the stage for later parental involvement in high school. Positive involvement in the early grades heightens the chances for continued involvement in the junior and high school years, in spite of the general trend toward gradual disengagement among all parents.

WAYS MEXICAN PARENTS TRY TO ENCOURAGE ADOLESCENT CHILDREN TO DO WELL IN SCHOOL

Given that we know that many low-income (and low-education) Mexican parents do not visibly and directly engage themselves with high school personnel or provide assistance with their older children's schoolwork, it is easy to see how outsiders may impute to these parents a lack of interest in or an ambivalence about their children's performance in school. We have already seen how lower-working-class Mexican parents often frame their hopes for their children's educational future in more generalized terms, with the emphasis on motivating their children to make the most of the opportunities afforded them.

Parental exhortations framed in the context of the family's oral history emerge as one important way parents attempt to instill and reinforce educational values and to motivate their children to persist in their schooling. Consistent with the findings of Margaret Gibson and John Ogbu (1991), the Mexican parents we interviewed articulated their children's opportunities for schooling via references to the limited opportunities and hardships they themselves endured as children in Mexico. As illustrated in the quotation that prefaced this chapter, adolescents carry the burden of their parents' hardships. Immigrant parents can be relentless in their exhortations, ensuring that their children will not forget that although they as immigrant parents cannot help them directly with academic affairs, children, the generation of hope, cannot disengage from school without rendering in vain their parents' many sacrifices.

Sra. Loza, whose daughter Liliana has received all her education in the United States, spoke of her own lack of educational opportunity and Liliana's struggle to persist academically.

> *My parents, well, they were very poor. Over in México, that doesn't exist [for everyone]. The opportunities that exist here [pause] well, if a person doesn't study here, it's really because they don't want to. Right? Then again, well, how should I say it? It's hard. I know it's very hard. English is not that easy because I see sometimes how Liliana struggles to do some of her homework. But she does it.*

Sra. Machado was almost livid in her account of her own blocked opportunity and of her desire for her children to avoid the kind of working conditions she has been subjected to:

> *I'm someone who cleans toilets, who cleans houses, who takes the jobs which are the most strenuous, the most difficult, and which pay the least; all because I didn't study. It wasn't that I didn't want to, but because they [my family] wouldn't let me. When I came here with a baby girl in my arms, I wanted to get ahead, hoping that God would let me, hoping that my children would be something more than what I was; not for my own benefit, but for their benefit, so that they wouldn't have to kill themselves like me. Look, I was a young woman, 25–30 years old, and already my*

back, already the doctors told me that it was impossible that I, being so young, should have my back in such bad condition. "What kind of job have you had?" they would ask. I don't want that to happen to them; that's why I want them to study.

Other parents voiced a similar theme, exhorting their children to do well in school to avoid the miserable jobs and economic woes they've had to contend with. Sra. Villanueva was regretful that she had not learned English, and attributed her lack of proficiency in the language to her limited formal schooling. She clearly understood that her limited schooling combined with her limited English prevented her from obtaining a better job: *"I want her [Dolores] to prepare herself. I tell my children that if I would've attained a better education, I would probably have a good job."*

Exhortations to children were frequently framed within accounts of the family's journey to the United States. Sra. Urquilla, here with her family almost 3 years, spoke of their motivations for leaving the coastal city of Rosarito in northern Baja California. Reflective of the motivations of so many other parents, their hopes were to better themselves, and to provide their children a better education than they could receive in Mexico. Sra. Urquilla persuaded her husband to come first, while Maribel finished junior high school; then the rest of the family would join him in San Diego.

Another more recent immigrant parent, Señor Gonzales, stated with great satisfaction that his older children had been able to pursue university studies in the United States, but tearfully recounted how his family's initial undocumented status threatened to undermine his hopes for his children's education in the United States.

We're living very well. They've gone to school. They're trying to make a better life for themselves. When we first arrived, we didn't have any documents. When my daughters wanted to go to the university, they asked for the "green card," and we didn't have it. So, I felt like crying. Because my daughter had left behind her [college] program in México, and here, she couldn't continue. But thanks to God, we immigrated due to the [government's] amnesty program; that was a miracle, right? I see it as good luck. So, now my children are studying again, and we now have a better life.

Evidence that such parental exhortations play a vital part in the socialization of children of immigrants was also replete in our conversations with adolescents. Although both recent immigrants and more established adolescents conveyed such influences, explicit examples were more plentiful in the accounts of the more acculturated. It is possible that recent-immigrant parents don't have to tell their immigrant children what the latter already know—a tacit understanding of each other's hopes and longings as immigrants is shared. Given that long-term immigrant parents with many years of U.S. residence have lived remarkably different lives compared with those of their U.S.-reared children, these parents may feel that retellings and exhortations are more necessary. Furthermore, in these cross-generation families, immigrant parents have had more time for past life experiences in Mexico to age into parable-like accounts, and more time to retell them over a course of a child's upbringing.

Supportive and close relations between adolescents and parents often serve as a good medium for such retellings and *consejos* (attempts to impart parental wisdom). Depending on the family context, these *consejos* can serve either to strengthen relations or to strain them. As we shall see in the next chapter, not all adolescents we interviewed enjoyed close relations with their parents. In any case, parental exhortations are intended to instill a sense of familial obligation, payable in terms of staying out of trouble and doing well in school. Victoria Melendez, a second-generation high achiever, had no problem expressing how important it is for her parents that she do well in school.

> I admire my parents a lot. I love my mother because even though my mom never went to school, and she didn't have her academic education, she's a very smart person. *El apoyo de mi madre está siempre conmigo; y ella es la que me empuja. Ella quiere que haga lo que yo quiera hacer; no quiere que yo pase por actos difíciles, como ella, por falta de una educación académica* [I always have my mom's support; and she's the one who pushes me. She wants me to do whatever I aspire to do; she doesn't want me to go through difficult times like she did, because she didn't get a good formal education].

Elena Guerrero and Daniel Montalvo, both in the United States since infancy, provided similar accounts. Although Elena's parents attained a higher level of schooling in Mexico than most of the other parents, Elena felt that her mother's slow acculturation limited how much her formal education could directly benefit her daughter. Elena stressed that her father only finished ninth grade, and that although her mother had some college education in Mexico, neither could really help her because neither had facility in English. Her parents, keenly aware of the limits restricting their ability to assist their daughter academically, used their life circumstances as a way to further motivate (if not pressure) Elena. "So they like make me feel if I don't, like, to go school and get an education and have an opportunity they didn't have, then I'm not gonna be worth as much." Daniel

Montalvo's account emphasized the theme of avoiding miserable working conditions:

> [My mother] tries to keep that dream alive in my head, so it continues, so it doesn't die off like other stuff, like when you like a record, and the next day you say "Ah, I don't like it anymore." My parents just emphasize the importance of an education, and they give examples, like the kind of job they have, and where I'm going to end up if I don't finish. Maybe that has helped me, but I don't think so, because if I didn't like school, I wouldn't be in school right now, it doesn't get me scared or anything.

Antonio Barrera, also a high-achiever and also here since age 7, was likewise very cognizant of his parents' difficult life. He was one of the few students we studied whose father had finished high school in the United States. Antonio's father believed he could have reasonably finished college, but didn't. Mr. Barrera differed from the other fathers in the sample in that he immigrated early in his life, and thus, grew up having experiences similar to many Mexican American youth in the late 60s and 70s; during this era, we did see a significant wave of Chicanos entering and finishing college (for example, with the GI Bill, Affirmative Action programs, and first generation of "academic outreach" programs). Although there were success stories during this era, there were also many cases of attrition. Antonio felt that his father's frequent and mournful retellings of his failure to stay in school had been quite instructive. In response to a query about his father's capacity to help him develop a post–high school strategy, Antonio commented that although his father completed 2 years of community college, he made a lot of regrettable decisions. "He's always telling me, 'I should've stayed in school,' 'I should've done this; I should've been more assertive.'" Antonio felt that his father had learned from his mistakes the hard way and very much wanted for his son to avoid them. Robert Zamora and Chris Rocha, both born in the United States and both exhibiting a high degree of acculturation and loss of Spanish proficiency, nevertheless provide similar remarks. Robert was very much aware that his parents see their life of hard work and sacrifice as purposeful, that the payoff would come in the educational opportunities their children would enjoy. Robert didn't want to let them down. Chris shared a similar account in this way:

> My parents usually just talk to me; they say if you don't want to do good in school you're gonna have a hard job, and they say, "You don't want a hard job do you?" And I go "No"; so then I say I will try harder in school. My dad gives me examples of his life. Like he

had to go pick in the fields when he was like 15 or something like that. I don't want to be like my dad. I want to have a good job.

The economic and emotional hardships Mexican parents have endured and the many sacrifices they've made on behalf of their children can be seen as part of an immigrant family's treasury—a form of accumulated folk capital. From time to time, the treasury is opened and the capital is laid out for family members to assess and appreciate. The children of immigrants come to know it well, particularly when parents are good storytellers. Through many retellings, and the bestowing of *consejos* [advice] and exhortations, parents try to instill and reinforce in their children a core set of values and a sense of familial attachment and obligation. When these retellings, values, and exhortations are mirrored in the greater kinship network or throughout an enclave or community network, they become normatively stronger. In any case, the children of immigrants learn that their efforts and accomplishments, and their failures, are a family matter. Immigrant parents attempt to compensate for their inability to act as institutional agents by exploiting the family treasury of parental sacrifices. For many adolescents, the sense of attachment and obligation to parents is firmly internalized, and school striving is an attempt to honor those sacrifices—to pay back. For others, however, the road to school success is too difficult and the burden of paying parents back overwhelming.

MEXICAN PARENTS' MODEL OF SOCIAL MOBILITY AND ANGLO-PROTESTANT CONCEPTIONS OF ACHIEVEMENT

At a time when conservative civic leaders are heard lamenting the decline of traditional values in the United States, Latino and Asian immigrants are serving to resow and revitalize these "lost values" throughout America. It is ironic that such lamentations are closely connected to xenophobic reactions to these brown and yellow "aliens," precisely the folks who are largely responsible for reconstituting old-world "family values" within our national borders.

Through our conversations and interviews with immigrant parents, we saw plentiful evidence that they subscribed to an educational ethos and a view of social mobility that significantly overlap with key aspects of traditional Anglo-Protestant individualism. This is particularly the case in those aspects or ideals that have historically shaped mainstream notions of status attainment based on model meritocratic processes. Prominent in the achievement views of these parents was the primacy of parenting and family processes, manifested in part by *orgullo* or pride in the family's unity and cohesiveness, and coupled with a belief that such an environment provides a strong foundation for success in school and in life. We also found parents distressed when they saw their family's cohesion and stability threatened by such things as unremitting poverty or the rapid and unbalanced acculturation of their children to American values and *vicios* (vices).

Another way these immigrant parents emphasized the primacy of parenting processes was by exhibiting a strong predisposition to address the problem of Latino underachievement by chastising other Latino parents for their lack of responsibility and effort (for not being *padres responsables* [responsible parents]). Criticisms of other Latino parents far outweighed criticisms of the schools.

We also see a high premium placed on the development of moral character; by guarding and nurturing the moral character of one's children, one ensures their success in school and society. Part of this development of character results from an emphasis on the value of hard work and sacrifice, and on the necessity of embracing these twin engines of human accomplishment—termed *empeño*. On the flip side of this emphasis on hard work is a strong condemnation of idleness, and of those who are perceived as wasting opportunities to improve themselves—actions that can bring on one the infamous label *sinvergüenza* (literally, one who is shameless).

Belief in Authoritative Parenting Behavior

Sra. Jacobo, mother of Sandra, exemplified the parenting behavior subscribed to by many of the other parents we interviewed. She kept a very close watch on her children's social network, but without smothering them—at least from her point of view. She wanted to know who her children's associates were and what their families were like.

> *Perhaps I'm a bit strict since I don't let them go whereever they want by themselves; it's not that they don't have any freedom, rather that they have to abide by certain moral restraints. "Mom, can I go with a friend?" First, well, I ask them, "Let's see, invite your friend over so I can meet him. Where does he live? Well, let's go see where he lives." And you know, who knows what's going on inside his house; I say, "If you want to invite him over here. What are you going to do over there? Whatever you were going to do over there, you can do here." I see a lot of kids going around in bolitas [cliques], and if that isn't enough, they're learning things from the older ones. You already see young kids running around in cliques, already going around with their rayadero [i.e., their markers and spray cans].*

Sra. Jacobo, a full-time homemaker, discussed the importance of having her husband's support with regard to the discipline of their children, and said she carried the primary responsibility for their monitoring. Following a well-known pattern in Mexican immigrant families, Sr. Jacobo deferred to his wife's judgment, believing that it was she who knew the intricate details of how their children were getting along. *"Well, we also talk and I tell him, "Did you know this or that, and did you know"* [pause]*; well, it's true, I am like a newspaper* [laughs].

Sra. Ubilla's statements also exemplify the value placed on family cohesion and stability. Speaking about a neighbor's difficulties with her son, she commented:

> *Well, many times the problem is within the household. Many times it's something psychological. I think that in the case of this young boy, that's it. I think that there are problems in his house, whether it's because of a sibling, or the father, or the mother. Here in this house, my husband doesn't have any vices; he doesn't drink, doesn't smoke, we don't create scandals.*

And so we see that social conservatives who lament the decline of family values and the undermining of parental authority have only to turn for validation to the inner city, to those very same people charged with threatening the hegemony of American old-time values.

Concerns Regarding Loss of Parental Authority and Acculturation of Children to a Different Value System

Parents varied in the degree to which they were able to control and monitor their children's relations with peers and other outside influences. When monitoring was not possible, whether to trust adolescents to regulate themselves became the issue. The majority of parents we interviewed communicated a firm trust in their adolescents' moral regulation. Sometimes, however, this trust was not warranted, and was more a reflection of immigrant parents' anxious hope that, since they had now lost the ability to monitor their adolescents' engagement with peers, the values they had instilled in their children over the years would somehow protect them.

The concern of one obviously anxious mother is instructive. Undocumented, and in the United States only 5 years, Sra. Hernández was separated from her husband and not employed outside the home; her oldest son worked to support her and his four siblings. Sra. Hernández had suspicions that her 15-year-old daughter had become involved with a gang.

She had tried repeatedly to counsel her daughter to be more careful in choosing her friends. She had told her that she was not mature enough, nor wise enough, to understand that her friends could get her involved in activities that might very well do her harm.

> INTERVIEWER: *Do you think that there are some problems that Mexican youth face here in this community?*
> SRA. H: *Well I believe so.*
> INTERVIEWER: *What kind of problems have you seen?*
> SRA. H: *Well, I've heard from other people. But in the case of my daughter, she doesn't want to lose her friends. That's what the problem is, the wrong crowd. I tell my daughter, I tell her, "Look, I appreciate how important your friends are to you. Yes, have your friends, but be aware of who you're with, because you are still a young girl." I tell her, "You haven't fully matured," you know, "like the other girls." "And they can get you into a bad situation," I tell her, "without you even knowing." But she doesn't listen.*

Sra. Hernández betrayed a sense of desperation and lack of control over her adolescent children's exposure to a sociocultural environment she feared would harm her children. Given her limited education, her undocumented status, her unfamiliarity with this new societal context, and the lack of a father figure in the home, it is not difficult to understand why this immigrant mother found it nearly impossible to translate traditional Mexican family values into an effective support system for her children.

Concurrent with the belief that good parenting, positive moral development, and success in life are strongly connected, the majority of parents expressed another prominent anxiety and concern, that is, whether their children were putting sufficient effort into school and whether their children's gradual internalization of mainstream values and attitudes would occur at the expense of traditional Mexican values. The fear of rapid acculturation among immigrant parents reflects a deep concern regarding their children's moral development, which in turn, they believed, would affect their chances of success in school.

Although parents strongly desired their children to attain full educational and economic success in this country, they believed such success could be had while maintaining Spanish and a strong cultural identity. Sra. Machado believed that some parents wrongly encouraged their children to culturally assimilate, and commented on how distressing it was when she saw Mexican children, "*morenitos, . . . que no les gusta hablar español. Tienen el nopal aquí en la frente, pero nunca quieren aceptar que son mexicanos* [young, dark-complected Mexican children . . . that don't like to speak

Spanish. They have the *nopal* (cactus) right here on their foreheads, but they don't want to accept that they are Mexicans]."

Sra. Pulido articulated the same concern in a slightly different way. *"Yo he crecido aquí; pero a mí me enseñaron a respetar mi cultura* [I grew up here, but I was taught to respect my culture]." She commented further that to respect one's culture, one must live it in the fullest sense.

> *Knowing that we have to make chile with a molcajete, that it must be eaten, and things like that. That we have to make the tortillas by hand. How to dress, how to act, how to be, all of that. All that is around us, right?, part of one's culture; and that's one of the things that we were taught.*

Sra. Urquilla believed that children reared in a family with strong Mexican values would be able to resist morally damaging influences in the greater social environment. She felt that because she had been able to raise her oldest children in Mexico, she and her husband have been able to exert a lot more control over those children. The underlying belief was that the values of parental respect and obedience widely shared in a Mexican context, and successfully internalized in her older children, would continue to guide them in a distinctly different cultural environment.

Although we find key points of overlap between the value systems of Mexican immigrants and certain ideological tenets of Anglo individualism, it is important to stress that immigrant parents are subscribing to the former. Little or no evidence emerged to suggest that parents were motivated to assimilate a new value system—that is, at the expense of their own. The evidence, in fact, suggests the opposite. Even in the case of parental responsibility and involvement in the schooling affairs of their children, a quintessential ideal in Anglo middle-class conceptions of meritocratic status attainment, we can see that this too is firmly implanted in the value systems of Mexican parents.

This is not to deny that immigrants are influenced by the ideal norms of middle-class society. Research on immigrants tells us that they are as saturated as anyone else by the media's depiction of middle-class life as the ideal norm. The point here, however, is that immigrants arrive with those values traditionally associated with school achievement already in place. Exposure to the ideal norms of middle-class society pertaining to education merely reinforces the core values they already hold.

In a similar fashion, the propensity of the Anglo middle-class to see itself in terms of ideal norms, rather than its true social practices, is mirrored in the immigrant community.[7] So is the practice of condemming in others the lapses in value-prescribed behavior, which one is unwilling to admit to sharing. The disjunction and tension between deeply held values and mores, on the one hand, and observed behavior of those in the community, on the other, was plainly evident among our immigrant parents.

Belief in the Importance of Parent Involvement in Children's Schooling and Social Development

Parents not only were emphatic in their belief that parental involvement in children's schooling was key, they also criticized immigrant parents they perceived as uninvolved or nonparticipatory. Sra. Machado, feeling that the foundation for a good formal education should be set by parents, criticized those Mexican parents who believe that once they are here, there is little need to become involved in the school; their rationale appearing to be that, because the material standards seem so superior to those of Mexican public schools, they can assume their children will be all right. Sra. Machado complained that many immigrant parents, rather than coming to the United States with the spirit of improving their family's prospects, instead disempowered their children and themselves by their passive, nonparticipatory behavior. These immigrant parents, she stressed, needed to get more involved so that *"el Angosajón no toma la idea de que todos los Mexicanos somos 'indios ignorantes'* [Anglos don't get the idea that all of us Mexicans are ignorant Indians]." Sra. Machado, noting the racist undertone of her comment, almost immediately qualified her statement about *indios* by saying that *"el verdadero indio, el indio puro es bien educado, en su forma de ser—muy elementaria—pero bien educado* [the true Indian, the pure Indian (in Mexico), is well educated, in the way he conducts himself (i.e., well socialized)—very elementary—but well socialized nonetheless (i.e., dignified, exhibiting proper etiquette and poise)]."

Sra. Barrera lodged a similar criticism, but also called on those parents who are literate and who have attained a higher level of education, and who have the time, to get involved in the schools, to help teachers, and to contribute to the schooling of Mexican-origin children. Speaking in the first person, she confessed:

> What happens is that sometimes we parents don't support our children, we aren't monitoring them carefully. Because all the schools are good, but I think that in order for our children to be well educated, well, we have to support the teachers. Like the people who know how to read, and have the time, that they should go to the school, that they should help, like I say, to watch over the children, to talk to them. That's what's missing, that the parents, those with the time, like the mothers who sometimes have the time and have had schooling, if they could. If each mother could dedicate a

quarter of an hour, there at the school; because, you know, the teachers can't do it by themselves.

In a more critical tone, Sra. Barrera complained:

There are parents that don't even call the school, they never call to check up on their kids; the teacher always has to call . . . on the other hand, if the parents would call the schools, we would be observing; like I say, if each person could give just a little bit of time.

Sra. Jacobo voiced similar criticisms of Mexican parents. When asked why she felt these parents did not participate more, she listed the reasons, then qualified them with a critical note:

It's because of a lack of confidence, we don't feel comfortable going to the school; many because of the language; many because they work; they come home tired and they don't have the time; oh! these are just excuses [pause], just to avoid having to visit the school.

Sra. Cortes spoke not only of the language barrier that prevents many parents from becoming more involved in the schools, but also of their *vergüenza,* their embarrassment over not having proficiency in English and not having much formal education. Sra. Cortes, however, also blamed many parents for making excuses and for being irresponsible or lazy, stating that in every school there are people who will gladly translate and assist Mexican parents.

It is important to note that for different reasons, Sra. Jacobo, Sra. Machado, and Sra. Barrera, and most of the other parents who criticized Mexican parents, were not among those actively involved in the school affairs of their adolescent children. Some parents may have felt that their criticisms were justified, given their own involvement in the school affairs of their younger children. For others, their criticisms may be an example of what psychologists term *projection,* the tendency to ascribe to other people the feelings, thoughts, and weaknesses present in oneself. In this case, such projections may be a way of relieving feelings of *vergüenza,* or guilt regarding the disjunction between one's deeply held values and one's experience of not realizing them in day-to-day life.

Certainly though, parents were not unaware of many of the reasons they and other immigrant parents remained uninvolved. For example, parents cited undocumented status (and fears of apprehension and deportation), illiteracy or limited education, lack of English proficiency and its accompanying shame, chronic illnesses, the stresses of low-wage work, and the embarrassment sometimes exhibited by older children when parents showed up at school. Yet such knowledge did not truly function to exonerate them—or relieve their shame. They understood that their nonactivist or passive engagement in their adolescents' school and social world (outside the home) could jeopardize their children's chances of success in U.S. society; they understood that school authorities and *anglosajones* (Whites) often held them in contempt for their lack of visible involvement. In the end, they feared that, however formidable the obstacles they faced, they were not being true to their deeply held traditional Mexican values pertaining to education.

CLOSING ANALYSIS AND REFLECTIONS

Parents' lack of involvement continues to be targeted as the underlying reason for Latino underachievement in school. The charge, however, is usually couched in terms of parents' fundamental educational values and expectations, rather than in terms of the constraints experienced by people in captivity at the bottom of society's class and racial hierarchies. Our interviews with Mexican immigrants clearly show that they held both strong educational values and great hopes for their children. The evidence also shows that most parents do attempt to monitor their adolescent children's progress in school—for example, by reading progress reports and talking with their children. Cognizant of their own limitations due to their often scant educational preparation and their marginal position relative to the cultural mainstream, parents found more culturally appropriate ways of remaining true to their values. Through the bestowing of *consejos* and through exhortations, parents tried to morally obligate and thus motivate their children to forge ahead in their schooling.

Such a value-centered strategy of supporting their adolescents, however, while creating a strong family-based moral structure with clearly dictated proper behavior, did not directly translate into a support system that could yield needed institutional resources and support, nor did it shield these adolescents from multiple threats in the greater social environment. Little evidence emerged showing that the families we studied were embedded in tightly knit kinship networks, and only a few families were integrated into church communities or other similar organizational domains. Thus, the potential was lost for social-control processes that would validate and reinforce a family's moral structure and monitor adolescents' social conduct in the school and community.

Adolescents were experiencing a stage in their lives when parents increasingly shifted their attention to younger siblings, and, in many cases, required their adolescents to share in adult responsibilities (childcare, housework, brokering for parents). Adolescents were also expected to manage their own school and academic affairs, and to do so responsibly. As I intend to show, the adolescents we studied valiantly attempted to do just that, to manage their own school and academic affairs and their lives—though not necessarily alone, in the literal sense. Although they were lodged in networks composed of significant others, more often than not, such networks did not provide the institutional supports that would help them fulfill the expectations and hopes of their immigrant parents.

6

Parent-adolescent Relations of Conflict: Class/Race/Gender Comparative Perspectives

The schooling and developmental experiences of low-income minority youth are seldom examined within a comparative analysis of the systematic privileges, opportunities, and community-based resources afforded middle-class suburban adolescents. Success in the educational system has been traditionally framed, in great part, in terms of parental efforts to instill the proper values and to develop achievement motivation and autonomy in their children. Parent-child and parent-adolescent interaction processes are typically viewed as paramount for all groups (across social classes and ethnic groups). These processes are clearly evident in mainstream theories of adolescent development; here we see the emphasis on family interaction patterns that allow for natural developmental processes to run their course, permitting adolescents to develop full individuation, mutuality with parents, more varied forms of social reasoning, greater social skills, and higher self-esteem. The problem, I suggest here, is the habitual and largely unquestioned decontextualization of adolescent developmental processes in the research literature. This widespread practice is problematic precisely because middle-class patterns of child and adolescent development, whether tacit or explicit, are portrayed as *universal*, rather than as *cultural phenomena* of a particular subgroup entrenched within a set of institutional structures and ideologies oriented toward preserving their privileged access to resources and power. At the same time, the different developmental experiences of groups other than middle-class Whites become characterized, though usually in subtle terms, as "cultural" phenomena and as non-normal.[1] Before I develop this criticism, let us look more closely at how many psychologists within the mainstream of their discipline have theorized the family context of adolescent development.

THE POSITIVE FUNCTIONS OF FAMILY CONFLICT
IN ADOLESCENT DEVELOPMENT

Psychologists have moved away from the view of adolescence as an inevitable period of "storm and stress," where adolescents gradually sever their ties to parents and gravitate toward full autonomy and individuation. In its stead, the parent-child relationship is now viewed as an enduring bond that undergoes renegotiation and change during the adolescent years (Grotevant & Cooper, 1986; Hunter & Youniss, 1982; Richardson, Galambos, Schulenberg, & Petersen, 1984). Relational patterns move from unilateral authority toward mutuality, i.e., negotiated authority, shared responsibility, and cooperation (Youniss, 1983a; cited in Grotevant & Cooper, 1986). While parents continue to monitor, counsel, profess their values, and set standards, adolescents strive to arrange more cooperative and equitable relations with their parents, lessening the discrepancy between the hierarchy of parent-child relations and the mutuality of peer relations (Smetana, 1989; Youniss, 1980).

In spite of the move away from a rigid storm-and-stress paradigm, many psychologists concede that this transition from childhood to adulthood is inherently stressful, particularly during and shortly after puberty, when adolescents experience profound biological, psychological, and social changes. Adolescents are believed to lack the cognitive and social skills to cope effectively with these changes, and consequently experience disorientation, moodiness, and what has been termed "transitional stress" (Montemayor, 1983). Such stress is thought to have inevitable influences on routine relations between parents and their teens—adolescent distress usually becomes family distress. Although psychologists concede that relational tensions and stress may be an enduring feature during this renegotiation process, they also emphasize that turmoil is not (Lipsitz, 1977). Moreover, the stresses that emanate from these changes are cast by mainstream psychologists in a positive and constructive light; that is, these tensions are viewed as contributing to adolescent development.

Although some psychologists have drawn attention to the fact that the degree of transitional stress and family conflict varies greatly across families, and that the important question lies in why this period is very stressful for some families and not for others (Montemayor, 1983), mainstream psychologists have yet to seriously examine the incidence, the antecedents, and the consequences of parent-adolescent conflict across social classes (i.e., middle-class vs. working-class families).

Pioneering research that has taken a more ecological approach has looked at those factors that may mediate the degree of transitional stress, and here we find some important leads. One key mediating factor suggested by this research is *anticipatory socialization* (Montemayor, 1983, referencing Burr, Leigh, Day, & Constantine, 1979). Significant adults mobilize to prepare young adolescents for the physiological and status changes they are about to undergo, and for the requirements, responsibilities, and benefits associated with the role of adult. The process is said to include the tailored transmission of values and behavioral norms as well as opportunities for both observing appropriate role models and for rehearsing adult behaviors and social practices (Burr et al., 1979).

Thus, adolescents who find themselves with such support, and who gradually learn how to behave appropriately in their new set of roles, experience an easier transition. Much of the mainstream empirical literature on adolescents suggests that most adolescents receive such critical support from parents. The jagged edges of parent-adolescent conflict are thus softened when viewed within the context of this important socialization support. Family conflicts, in normal cases, are not seen as threatening the cohesion of the parent-child bond (Montemayor & Hanson, 1985). However, we again need to bear in mind the types of families that are normally examined in these empirical studies.

In spite of an awareness of the variations in family conflict and distress, assessments of parent-adolescent conflicts are usually articulated in terms of their contributions to personality development and the development of social competencies (Cooper, Grotevant, & Condon, 1983). Such conflicts provide key opportunities for learning to express and negotiate individual positions and for developing more varied forms of social reasoning (Smetana, 1988). Thus, conflictive relations provide an important vehicle for the development of what psychologists call *individuation*, a concept that has evolved into several distinctive dimensions. In its classical representation, it refers to a level of ego development marked by disengagement from infantile object relations with parents and a clear sense of self (Blos, 1979). A new dimension is now thought to exist, described in terms of the quality of relationships in the family, and defined by four separate properties: *separateness*, the ability to differentiate one's own thoughts and feelings from those of others; *self-assertion*, the motivation to communicate one's personal views clearly to others; *mutuality*, a respect for, and sensitivity to, the different views of others; and *permeability*, a receptivity to the views of others.

Thus, parent-adolescent conflicts are seen as carrying the potential for stimulating the cognitive growth of adolescents (Connell, Stroobant, Sinclair, Connell, & Rogers, 1975; cited in Frydenberg, 1997) and for promoting individuation, with the latter functioning to enhance self-esteem (Demo, Small, & Savin-William, 1987). In the final analysis, conflictive relations between parents and young adolescents function to emancipate the latter from an infantile attachment, and set the stage for reattachment to occur on a more mature, equitable level later in adolescence. Psychologists concur that this transitional process must ultimately occur within a context of supportive and nurturing family relations; conflicts and tensions are beneficial to the degree that they are negotiated in a way that preserves the cohesion of the parent-adolescent bond (Hill, 1980; Montemayor & Hanson, 1985).

This is, however, not always the case. Psychologists have, in fact, shown that a high degree of parent-adolescent conflict, rather than promoting psychological growth, can lead to a variety of adolescent problems (Montemayor, 1983). Frequent, intense, and unresolved conflicts, in time, can lead to physical abuse (Garbarino & Sherman, 1980), running away from home (Blood & D'Angelo, 1974), drug abuse (Costa, Jessor, & Turbin, 1999; Dryfoos, 1990), early sexual activity and pregnancy (Dryfoos, 1990; Koenig & Zelnik, 1982), and involvement in gangs (Vigil, 1988). Psychiatric disorders are an additional risk (Rutter, Graham, Chadwick, & Yule, 1976), as is suicide (Dryfoos, 1990).

Yet the dark side of parent-adolescent tensions tends to be deemphasized in the psychological literature, with the spotlight held on the developmental benefits that can accrue from family conflicts. Why is this so? There are several possibilities worth pursuing. Empirical studies on middle-class and upper-middle-class suburban adolescents—which represent the majority of empirical study samples—show that, most of the time, parent-adolescent conflicts are negotiated in a constructive fashion.[2] Also, the potentially toxic consequences of family conflicts tend to be framed in a discourse of dysfunction, maladjustment, and pathology; they are viewed as non-normative, and thus relegated to the domain of psychiatric disorders and family dysfunction. Another possible explanation is that there exists a widespread tacit acceptance that these non-normative cases are linked to family processes thought to be prevalent among working-class, low-income, and racial-minority groups in society. Given mainstream psychology's lack of disciplinary tools for comparative analyses, researchers are unable to adequately decipher the complexities of family life in non-normative groups. Given this situation, many mainstream researchers either turn to the study of psychiatric disorders or altogether avoid addressing group variations and cross-cultural issues.[3] In many cases, issues of social class, culture, and other sociological factors are simply accorded minimal acknowledgment and relevance. The conventional and exclusive use of White middle-class suburban samples in such studies makes this avoidance fairly easy.

The systematic indifference toward sociological considerations in contemporary analyses of family interaction processes only reinforces the mythology of "natural" or "normal" developmental processes, and of the middle-class family as existing independent of macro-social structures. However, many non-middle-class (lower-status) adolescents and their families live in ecological or social-structural conditions that not only prevent the potential benefits of family conflict from emerging but, perhaps more important, imbue conflict with the power to undermine a family's ability to sustain the only support system the adolescent may have.

Sociologically *uninformed* models of child and adolescent development also distort and hide from view the many trials routinely faced today by suburban middle-class households with adolescents. Deindustrialization and corporate restructuring have also adversely affected many middle-class families throughout the country, placing enormous pressures on many parents to move, become retrained, and resituate themselves in a different niche in a rapidly changing economy (Baca Zinn & Eitzen, 1999). With the increasing prominence of women in the workforce, two-career or dual-worker households are now the rule. Corporate and labor policymakers and government bodies have been generally resistant to taking some responsibility for the new burdens families face. And with this new reality, we see households experiencing higher levels of work-family conflict and strain. Family scholars are telling us that such pressures and conflicts do not necessarily emanate from the reality of both parents working, but from time-devouring and family-unfriendly work schedules and careers (Hughes, Galinsky, & Morris, 1992; Voydanoff, 1987). This situation applies to families across the class spectrum, including middle-class suburban families. While the scholarly focus on working-class families is usually on resource deficits, increasing focus on stressors within middle-class families centers around what Sylvia Ann Hewlett (1991, p. 62) refers to as the "time-deficit," the dramatic decrease in time that middle-class adolescents spend with their career-burdened parents. Increases in family-work conflicts are also closely associated with what Arlie Hochschild (1989, p. 11) refers to as the "stalled revolution" in gender roles—particularly the meager contributions of men to domestic chores and child rearing, and the concomitant weightier burden on women to manage both family and work. The burden of adolescence set within these family-work conflicts often translates into middle-class youth unable to activate the parental social capital inhering in their own egocentric networks, a problem founded, of course, not on the absence of parental knowledge and network resources but rather on the considerable occupational and career demands now carried by middle-class parents.

Higher levels of parental separation and divorce (compared with those in the 1960s) have also wracked middle-class suburban life. A 1988 study by the National Center for Health Statistics found that children in single-parent families (including those whose parents never married) are more likely to drop out of high school, become pregnant as teenagers, abuse drugs, and get into trouble with the law than are those living with both parents.[4] In 1993, Nicholas Zill and his associates reported that children of divorced parents are, regardless of their economic circumstances, twice as likely as others to have poor relationships with their parents, drop out of high school, and receive psychological help.

We see then that problems stemming from family conflicts cannot be easily attributed to dysfunctional families on the periphery of American life, or to non-normative working-class families of color. Family conflict and adolescent distress, during our postindustrial age, may now be endemic to American family life across the social spectrum. The pivotal issue may then be the differential resources and long-term consequences of family distress between the social classes; while middle-class youth may ultimately recover from family distress associated with family-work conflicts or from divorce, most working-class and poor adolescents may find such experiences operating as an express ticket to alienation and chronic distress patterns during early adulthood.

What theoretical questions, then, might represent important advances in the development of *sociologically grounded* models of adolescent development—models that would be applicable to all adolescents and families, yet sensitive to the social-class circumstances within which particular groups of families are embedded? With specific regard to the issue of parent-adolescent relations, we can ask: Under what macro-structural currents,[5] ecological conditions, and cultural forces do we find a heightened level of conflict and long-term dysfunction? Under what conditions do we find parent-adolescent conflict promoting positive developmental gains? Are these conditions the same for working-class and middle-class families? For families living under the forces of racial and class oppression (e.g., residential and occupational segregation and discrimination), as well as for immigrant families attempting settlement and stability, what ecological conditions and cultural strategies allow family stress and parent-adolescent conflicts to be negotiated in a way that promotes positive developmental gains (meta-cognitive development, psychological resiliency, individuation, etc.)?[6]

Sociologically grounded models of child and adolescent development, by definition, contextualize parent-adolescent relations, situating family interaction practices within the local community ecology and within society's racial, class, and gender hierarchies. This eliminates the view of middle-class family life as normative or *generic*, as well as the practice of rendering working-class families (and ethnic/racial minority families) invisible and irrelevant. In contrast, family relations, set with sociologically grounded analyses, are examined in terms of the degree of access to institutional resources and support. Family relations are also examined in terms of widely shared coping strategies that, for both working-class and middle-class families, are rooted in collective perceptions regarding the group's relation to the major sources of power, privilege, and opportunity in society.

MIDDLE-CLASS VERSUS WORKING-CLASS ECOLOGIES
AND ADOLESCENT DEVELOPMENT

Research by Francis Ianni (1989) fortunately provides a much-needed window into the ecological conditions that support middle-class adolescent development. As with other studies, Ianni found in middle-class communities such as Sheffield problems of communication and disputes over discipline and other matters. Tensions and conflicts between parents and adolescents were clearly evident. Yet, as young people moved into their later teens, their demands for greater independence and their complaints over sanctions were usually met by parent-adolescent negotiations that rearticulated and justified the controls in terms of preparations for a socially and economically promising future. This relates to the issue of *anticipatory socialization* as a key factor in mediating transitional stress.

Through the normal course of family conflicts and disputes and the more routine parent-adolescent interactions, parents demonstrably respected and even encouraged their adolescents' individuation and movement toward mutuality; yet these developments were carefully and subtly circumscribed by parallel efforts on the part of parents to ensure conformity to behavioral norms they believed to be the bedrock of school success and social mobility.

What is most significant here is that these family processes were set within a larger system of institutional supports within the community. Ianni's (1989) careful description of the middle-class suburban community of Sheffield provides a key illustration of how some middle-class ecologies "work" for families and young people. Adolescent development in communities such as Sheffield occurs within certain structural conditions that Coleman (1988) has referred to as "intergenerational closure," a situation where family norms are upheld and reinforced by the various institutions within the community. This is in contrast to the disparate and conflictive social worlds many minority youth experience (Boykin, 1986; Phelan et al., 1998).

Ianni (1989) tells us that in Sheffield, "parents can and do plot a steady course for their children through the long and arduous educational preparation in order for them to achieve an occupational and life style similar to their own" (p. 59). There is a certain inevitability about the future that permeates adult-adolescent relations. Uncertainties have to do with each adolescent's degree of competitiveness and ranking among peers, not with inclusion in the society's opportunity structures. Ianni emphasizes that the confluence of values and expectations in Sheffield produces a place where "the community *is* the family, and adolescents experience it that way" (emphasis in original). He goes on to say:

> Like the other suburban areas we studied, Sheffield is child-centered, and all of its resources are directed to advancing the lives of its children as extensions of the family. There is little or no discrepancy between the private world of the family and the public preoccupations of the community. (p. 59)

Suffice it to say that an accurate understanding of parent-adolescent conflict, and of adolescent development in general, in communities such as Sheffield would be impossible without a clear articulation of the community's empowering ecology. Included here is the community's ability to sustain both intergenerational closure and the political organization that directs its collective economic and institutional resources toward ensuring that Sheffield adolescents will eventually enjoy middle-class status and all its associated privileges and benefits. It is important to emphasize that the "community ecology" within which many middle-class families are embedded goes far beyond the interwoven networks of other families of similar status; equally, and at times more, important is the matrix of nonfamily institutions: the school board, city council, churches and clergy associations, the chamber of commerce, employers and business organizations, corporate representatives and agents, residential associations, state and federal lobby groups, elected officials, and the local media.

The shared class interests and the racially based solidarities exhibited by the agents of these institutions converge to make for a strong ecological context, and function to imbue parental exhortations, values, and norms with a considerable degree of power and force. In the case of family dysfunction, or career-burdened parents, the institutional matrix of the community is there to serve as a strong safety net. That this collective power is exercised within an ideology that exalts independence, self-reliance, and meritocracy is a testament to how complex adolescent socialization processes truly are. It is also a testament to the ecology's profound and inescapable grip on the developing consciousness of middle-class adolescents.

Thus, middle-class and upper-middle-class youth, such as those from Ianni's (1989) Sheffield, learn to publicly dramatize the ideals of self-reliance and independence, all the while embedded in the social, material, political, and intellectual resources available within their community's ecology. In contrast to the social webs of low-status youth, the social webs of privileged youth are socially constructed for the tacit transmission of mobility-related resources, which flow through routine relations with kin, friends, associates, and institutional agents and through involvement in organizational life (e.g., church). In moving through the stages of middle-class adolescent development, adolescents gradually learn to articulate and *make sense* of their behavior within a discourse of independence and utilitarian individualism, thus interpreting *and* experiencing the power inhering within their ecological niche and system networks as their own individual ability, talent, and potential to determine their own destiny.

Ianni's (1989) description of Southside paints a very different ecological picture, showing a multiethnic inner-city (geographic) community situated within a major eastern metropolis, and "bounded by massive public housing projects and squalid aging tenements" (p. 24). In contrast with Sheffield, in Southside the concepts of *family* and *community* take on very different meanings. While the community of Sheffield *is* the family, in Southside, essentially, *the family functions as the community*. The ecological conditions of Southside overlap with those of many low-income urban residential areas throughout the country, including places such as Harrison Heights and Southview. In Chapter 3, we saw, among other patterns:

1. social interaction reserved for people living in the house and for proximal relatives;
2. little exchange with neighbors (i.e., little network exchanges of social and material support);
3. most of the families in our study (four focal neighborhoods) living in what were essentially defended households, physically but not socially close to their neighbors; household members were often afraid or suspicious of others who were not somehow related or in some way connected to the family;
4. little "intergenerational closure" (school, extended family, household, church) (see Coleman, 1988);
5. nonfamily institutional spheres not dominant in routine family life—recreation centers and other places that cater to "at-risk" youth were perceived as potentially dangerous places, to be avoided.

THE PROBLEM OF RELYING ON THE "FAMILY AS COMMUNITY"

Let us consider the risks entailed when low-income and working-class immigrant families become "the community," particularly for adolescents. It is not hard to see that adolescents' relations with parents and adult family members take on exceptional importance, since many of these families are not embedded in a strong ecological support system. While in communities such as Sheffield, parent-adolescent relations act both as a receptor for and a channel to the enormous resources exchanged within the surrounding institutional context, in places such as Harrison Heights, Augusta Heights, Southview, and the east side of Vista, adolescent-family relations are configured very differently. In many cases, familial relations are left to collectively function as an insecure life-raft in a turbulent sea, struggling to transport adolescents safely into early adulthood with the least trauma possible. Under such conditions, ambivalent, detached, and/or conflictive relations with parents do not make for a safer and more secure journey.

The Heightened Importance of Emotional Support and "Intimate Counsel" in the Lives of Youth Living Within a Toxic Community Ecology

Following the "turbulent sea" metaphor above, family processes oriented toward survival and resilience become key. Consider the limited ability of many immigrant parents to act as effective agents of institutional support, due primarily to their low levels of formal schooling, their low occupational status, their less-than-fluent command of English, and their restricted experiences in the host country.

Consider, as well, that most working-class immigrant families cannot afford private professional help (e.g., psychotherapy). Given these circumstances, parental provisions of emotional support and thoughtful counsel on personal problems—supports much less dependent on formal schooling—take on increased if not extraordinary function and importance. In the face of a hostile and unsupportive ecological context, the emotional and social support systems of the family network often provide the only basis for sustaining and enforcing behavioral norms and parental values, and for accommodating those cultural features of the dominant society that are requisite for individual mobility. A highly bicultural accommodation strategy usually entails continued valuation of many traditional cultural practices, as well as a rejection of those cultural features within the mainstream that may be psychologically debilitating or demoralizing (e.g., racist myths, norms of conspicuous consumption, eccentric individualist values, youth subcultures espousing an apolitical *antagonistic acculturation* style).[7] As I discuss below, however, such a bilingual, bicultural accommodation style is not consonant with high levels of parent-adolescent conflict.

Predictors of Family Conflict in Low-SES Latino Immigrant Families

Heightened parent-adolescent conflict, particularly in low-SES immigrant families, may undermine a household's capacity to act as a viable system of support for rapidly acculturating adolescents. Let's consider a number of household factors that point to those families most at risk of generating excessive and debilitating levels of conflict.

Rubén Rumbaut (1996), drawing from the data collected from the Children of Immigrants Longitudinal Study (CILS),[8] analyzed a number of key variables for their value in predicting adolescent-parent conflict in immigrant families.[9] Gender emerges as a significant determinant of immigrant parent-adolescent conflict; teenage daughters are significantly more likely than sons to report conflicts with their immigrant parents. This statistical finding is confirmed many times over in our interview data, as we shall soon see in Chapter 7. Rumbaut suggests that this finding is a "reflection of the clash between restrictive parental standards for behavior and dating and the girls' increasing sense of and desire for individuality and independence from parental control in the transition to adulthood" (p. 163). Included in these "restrictive standards" is the practice of placing a lot more responsibility on daughters for the management and upkeep of the home and for interfacing with institutional agents and bureaucracies.[10]

I see another, perhaps even more fundamental reason why girls experience more family conflict—or at least why they tend to *report* higher levels of conflict. Basically, relative to boys, the young women in my study were more psychically in touch with, and invested in, their relations with parents and adult family members. Although greater psychological involvement and social interaction create a context that can foster more opportunities for both tacit and explicit social support (a plus), they also create more opportunities for conflict (a potential negative as well as a potential plus). Feminist scholars have argued that boys are socialized to be somewhat inept and guarded when it comes to close relationships and interpersonal communication at the level of feelings; in contrast, girls develop a refined discourse for talking about relationships. The boys in my study tended to evaluate family social support (i.e., emotional support and intimate counsel) in terms of "crisis intervention," whereas the girls tended to evaluate the supportive potential of parent-adolescent relations in terms of routine interactions that were validating and reassuring. Of course, these same criteria among girls also carry the potential for appraisals of parent-adolescent interactions to be cast as nonvalidating and nonreassuring—and thus may account for the higher reports of conflict. As we shall see later, such criteria may also be responsible for girls' lower levels of *perceived parental support*, relative to boys (analyses reported below).

As expected, Rumbaut (1996) found that mother's level of education was another important factor associated with reports of parent-adolescent conflict. Poor and precarious economic conditions generate anxieties and irritability in all family members, and relational closeness between adolescent and parent may serve only to stimulate each person's distress patterns. Poorly educated immigrant parents may be more isolated, experience more acculturation stress, and be less sensitive and less adept at helping their children deal with the challenges of adolescence and coercive assimilation.

This distressful situation appears to be particularly salient among the most recent immigrants; as suggested in the CILS data, immigrant families begin the settlement process with a good deal of parent-adolescent conflict. One can imagine recently arrived immigrant parents pulling the reins tight as they are introduced to the lax moral standards they perceive in the mainstream of American society—and particularly when they see their children attracted to the liberties taken for granted by acculturated and disaffected youth in the community. Acculturation pressures, in fact, do not bode well for immigrants, particularly when the result is native language loss on the part of adolescents. Loss of facility in Spanish, registering in the CILS study its positive association with conflict, is a likely proxy for communication problems between parents and adolescent; and less communication usually spells the loss of parental control and authority—a process of *decapitalization* in the family system (Buriel, 1984; Valenzuela, 1999).

Rumbaut (1996) also found feelings of embarrassment significantly associated with parent-adolescent conflict. Coercive assimilation functions in the United States, in great part, by framing low-income immigrant parents—in the eyes of their children—as submissive and powerless cogs in the American labor system, out of touch with newly emerging cultural trends and standards, and highly invested in a third-world pariah culture. Of course, not all children and adolescents succumb to this racist framing, but Rumbaut's findings show that when they do—most probably unconsciously—parent-adolescent conflicts increase proportionally.

Perceived Support as a Generator of Help-seeking Behavior

In Chapter 2 we discussed the mediating and buffering functions that underlie perceptions of support and satisfaction; these perceptions also appear to be important generators of active help-seeking behavior. In Chapter 10, we present statistical analyses showing that *perceived support* (i.e., appraisals of support from teachers and counselors) is an important predictor of actual help-seeking behavior within the context of the school (i.e., seeking assistance from teachers and counselors). Phrased differently, we see here that students who register low levels of satisfaction with support or who feel that school personnel are not at all supportive are the least motivated to engage in active help-seeking behavior.

Our own finding regarding perceived support in the school context, combined with the results from published studies, suggests to us that adolescents who register low or negative appraisals of support from parents, *and* who exhibit a negative help-seeking orientation, experience a kind of double jeopardy: Not only are these adolescents psychologically disinclined to seek assistance from parents in times of crisis or considerable need, but they may also be in a state where they are not able to benefit psychologically from genuine attempts by parents to be supportive (Barrera & Baca, 1990).[11]

Results from Statistical Analyses of Adolescents' Perceptions of Parental Support

Exactly what characteristics of immigrant Latino families and of adolescents are associated with negative perceptions of familial support? My desire to pursue this question among students at Auxilio High led me to incorporate relevant survey inventories (questionnaire items) pertaining to both school personnel and family members. Both inventories were adapted from an assessment scale developed and tested by Procidano and Heller (1983). The inventory pertaining to familial support is composed of 16 items.[12] Through factor analysis, two measures of perceived support of family were constructed. Items for the first factor included "I get good ideas about how to do things or make things from my *family*" and "I rely on my *family* for emotional support." This first factor was labeled *Perceived Supportiveness of Family Unit*. Items for the second factor included "Most other people are closer to their *family* than I am" and "When I confide in the members of my *family* who are closest to me, I get the idea that it makes them uncomfortable." The second factor was labeled *Familial Cohesion*.[13]

Table 6.1 presents the results of two multiple regression analyses, each predicting a separate measure of *perceived familial support*. My presentation here is limited to the Latino respondents with complete data on all measures (N = 604). We examined a carefully selected set of potential objective and subjective predictors, including age, gender, self-reported grades, and English proficiency. For family socioeconomic status, we used the average of both parents' levels of formal education. Following the lead of Barrera and Baca (1990), we included two separate but related measures of help-seeking orientation (*Confidence in the Support Process* and *Interpersonal Openness*; see Chapter 10 for details on the construction of these two measures).

Gender emerges as a significant determinant of perceived familial support, paralleling Rumbaut's (1996) findings on family conflict. Adolescent Latinas are significantly more likely than their male counterparts to

TABLE 6.1. Predictors of Perceived Familial Support

Independent Variables		Perceived Supportiveness of Family	Family Cohesion
Parental Education	B	.117**	.130**
	s.e.	.146	.062
	beta	.395	.192
Gender	B	.094*	.067
	s.e.	.367	.156
	beta	.846	.261
Age	B	.022	-.051
	s.e.	.180	.077
	beta	.010	-.098
English Proficiency	B	-.134**	.011
(of student)	s.e.	.164	.070
	beta	-.503	.017
Grades	B	.118**	.123**
	s.e.	.182	.078
	beta	.531	.239
Confidence in the	B	.138***	-.061
Support Process	s.e.	.060	.025
	beta	.202	-.039
Interpersonal	B	.031	.220***
Openness	s.e.	.066	.028
	beta	.050	.155
$R^2 =$		.0628	.0992

Unstandardized coefficients in italics.
$^+p < .10$ $^*p < .05$ $^{**}p < .01$ $^{***}p < .001$

report perceptions of *low* support (i.e., *Perceived Supportiveness of Family Unit*). However, differences in *Familial Cohesion*, by gender, did not reach statistical significance ($p < .096$). Similarly, English proficiency registered a significant negative effect on *Perceived Supportiveness*, but not on *Cohesion*. Yet these results do suggest that Spanish-dominant recent immigrants are more inclined toward positive appraisals of familial support than are their more acculturated counterparts. Of course, this association does not necessarily parallel Rumbaut's (1996) findings, which show that being a recent arrival (fewer than 10 years in the United States) was associated with higher levels of adolescent-parent conflict. Our own auxiliary analyses of other perceived support indicators suggest to us some possibilities worth considering.

In our analyses of perceived support of school personnel, we found perceived support to have different effects across ethnolinguistic groups (i.e., Spanish-dominant immigrants vs. everyone else; see Chapter 10). Perceived support predicted help-seeking behavior among students, except for Spanish-dominant Latino students; in other words, high perceived support did not translate into help-seeking for Spanish-dominants as a group. It is possible that *perceived familial support* among many Spanish-dominant adolescent immigrants may be highly intercorrelated with *attitudinal familism*, on which adolescent immigrants tend to score higher relative to their more established and acculturated counterparts. Valenzuela and Dornbusch (1996) described attitudinal or ideological familism as a collective orientation where "the needs of individuals are subordinate to the needs of the family" (p. 53). Thus, reports of perceived support among recent immigrants may not be closely aligned with actual conflictive relations in the family; that is, perceived support may remain high for some recently immigrated adolescents, regardless of conflictive relations with some family members. More research is needed to bear this out.[14]

Family socioeconomic status (SES) would be expected to play an important role here—especially with regard to recent immigrants; yet our original SES measure did not register an independent effect on either of our two measures (using Blau and Duncan's [1967] indicator of SES).[15] When we substituted the average of both parents' education levels for the original measure, however, positive effects registered in both models. Adolescents reporting parents with low levels of formal education were more likely to report negative perceptions of familial support, relative to their peers whose parents had more schooling. This finding does parallel Rumbaut's (1996) results, which show that "frictions are more likely to occur in families where the mother is less educated and where the economic situation of the family has perceptively worsened" (p. 164).

Grades (self-reported) register positive effects on both our measures of perceived support. Academic high-achievers, net of the other factors, are significantly more likely to report positive familial support than are low-achievers. We already know that high-achievers in general have dispositions that reflect more self-efficaciousness and higher self-esteem than their low-achieving counterparts have.

At this point, we see that lowered appraisals of familial support are mainly associated with being female, acculturation (i.e., English proficiency), low level of education of parents, and poor academic performance. Of course, these risk factors can occur together, and when they do, as in the case of low-achieving, highly acculturated girls, parent-adolescent relations may be subjected to considerable tensions, particularly when immigrant parents have minimal formal schooling.

Perceptions of familial support also appear here to be affected by adolescents' help-seeking orientations. *Confidence in the Support Process* registered a positive and significant independent effect on *Perceived Supportiveness*, but no effect emerged for *Familial Cohesion*. In contrast, our measure of *Interpersonal Openness* registered a positive and significant effect on *Familial Cohesion*, with no effect on *Perceived Supportiveness* (i.e., high *Confidence* and high degrees of perceived support go together; *Openness* and reports of *Familial Cohesion* go together). Overall, these two results do provide supplemental support for the findings reported by Barrera and Baca (1990) that help-seeking orientations are closely associated with perceptions of support as well as with psychological distress and well-being. Considering the findings of these researchers, it remains quite tenable that adolescents' help-seeking orientations mediate (i.e., facilitate or obstruct) the restorative and empowering potential inhering in family exchanges of support. Yet these findings remain undertheorized in the literature. It is also quite possible that negative help-seeking orientations among working-class Latino youth may not necessarily stem from unsupportive and uncaring family members. Rather, what we may be seeing is a level of skepticism and resignation that frames genuine familial support as insufficient and poorly tailored, given the acculturation pressures, developmental challenges, and ecological dangers that these adolescents normally face. Thus, reflective of the overall findings reported here, we might easily imagine these youth telling us the following: "My family cares for me, but they can't really help me."

THE IMPORTANCE OF HELP-SEEKING INITIATIVES AMONG LATINO ADOLESCENTS FROM LOW-SES IMMIGRANT-BASED FAMILIES

Emotional support and *intimate counsel* represent two key subsets of those supportive interactions that impact physical and psychological health, and more broadly, adolescent development—whether directly, or indirectly through positive appraisals of enacted support or through appraisals of the potential support inhering in relations with significant others. In their enacted form, each of these two types of support represents a process where recipient and provider jointly acknowledge the inevitability of human vulnerability and pain, while engaging in a cultural practice where one yields to the ministering of another in a compact of trust and caring relations. It is the regular act of receiving emotional support and intimate counsel that functions to create a sense of psychological embeddedness in a protective web; it allows the individual to assert himself or herself in a challenging—and sometimes turbulent—world, to experience the feelings of sponsored independence and efficaciousness, possible only when the self is sufficiently and positively embedded.

Although they are intimately related, one key difference between perceptions of the supportive potential of significant others and enacted support is that the latter is often initiated by the act of soliciting help. What exactly is significant about the act of solicitation or help-seeking among adolescents? By their mid-teens, adolescents are experiencing a significant private life. Parents often do not readily know the events that are transpiring in the greater social world of their adolescent children, nor are they in a position to know how their children are coping with the more stressful events (e.g., hostile provocations by peers, gangs, or bullies at school; souring relations with a boyfriend; antagonistic relations with school personnel). Given parents' conflicting roles—as authority figures and sanctioners as well as caregivers—efforts by adolescents to maintain a veil over their private lives are not uncommon. The generational and cultural differences between immigrant parents and their acculturated children often exacerbate the divide. Penetrating this veil usually entails a supportive familial context, a particular parental orientation, and a good deal of social skill. Whatever the degree of distance between parents and their children, solicitations and sharing on the part of the adolescent often provide the only possibility for parental support and intervention to occur. Furthermore, without the benefit of adolescent solicitations and explicit episodes of enacted support, adolescent perceptions regarding the supportive potential inhering in parent-adolescent relations may turn less than positive. Framed in this way, obstacles to adolescent help seeking take on paramount importance.

This view of the fundamental importance of adolescent help seeking is informed by the research on adult and adolescent coping styles (see review by Frydenberg, 1997; Stanton-Salazar, 2000; Stanton-Salazar & Spina, 2000). In the process of coping, the individual makes several key appraisals of the situation, one of which is made to determine the options and resources that may be available (Lazarus & Folkman, 1984; see also Frydenberg, 1997, p. 35). With regard to the possibility of soliciting help, another key appraisal entails an assessment of the potential costs, risks, and benefits entailed in the solicitation (Gross & McMullen, 1983). The adolescent, for example, may ask himself, "What will happen to me if I tell my mother that my friend in trouble is a *pandillero*, a gang member?" Another adolescent may ask herself, "What will my mother say if I tell her that I think I'm pregnant?" Still another adolescent may ask himself, "What will my counselor say if I ask to be placed in college-preparatory classes? Will he laugh at me or discourage me?" The potential costs are real, particularly to adolescents who have a history of losing face, of regular humiliation, or of dealing with the punitive capacities of authority figures.

RESULTS FROM STATISTICAL ANALYSES ON PARENTS AS ELECTED AND UTILIZED SOURCES OF EMOTIONAL, PERSONAL, AND INFORMATIONAL SUPPORT

Although parents are certainly not the only important sources of emotional support for developing adolescents, in a hostile and problem-plagued community environment they may represent one of the few reliable sources. Statistical data collected by the author on the social support networks of Mexican-origin adolescents in the San Francisco–San Jose Peninsula region and in San Diego provide us with a way to examine how prominent parents are as elected sources of social support. Qualitative data collected in interviews with adolescents in San Diego offer a more focused look at relations of support between Mexican-origin adolescents and their parents.

Parents as Sources of Emotional Support

In the course of our social network survey, adolescents were asked to identify who they turned to for fourteen types of support, including emotional support, personal support, and information. Table 6.2 displays the findings stemming from our queries pertaining to the three principal forms of support studied. Our indicator of *emotional support* is based on one item in our network survey. Our indicator of *personal support* was composed using four of our survey items: material or monetary support, personal services, help with schoolwork, and intimate counsel (i.e., advice on personal matters). Personal support from parents (PARPER = 1) was indicated by the adolescent's electing parents for at least one of the four forms of support, including intimate counsel (i.e., advice on personal nonacademic matters). *Informational support* was composed using seven of our survey items, with support relating to the acquisition of information pertaining to: (1) post–high school options, (2) part-time employment opportunities, (3) legal aid, (4) treatment for substance abuse, and (5) psychological services. Adolescents were provided with hypothetical situations and asked

TABLE 6.2. [Immigrant] Parents as Elected Sources of Support (Bay Area/Peninsula Data, N = 145, Statistics shown for First- and Second-generation Adolescents Only)

Parent(s) as an Elected Source of	Both Parents Elected (N = 145)*	Mother Elected**	Father Elected**	At least One Parent Elected**	No Parent Elected**	N
Emotional Support	13.8% (n = 20)	39.1% (n = 52)	18.1% (n = 21)	40.6% (n = 54)	59.4% (n = 79)	133
Highly Bilingual		38.1% (n = 16 of 42)	23.7% (n = 9 of 38)	42.9% (n = 18)	57.1% (n = 24)	42
Spanish-dominant		42.3% (n = 22 of 52)	19% (n = 8 of 42)	42.3% (n = 22)	57.7% (n = 30)	52
English-dominant		35.9% (n = 14 of 39)	11.1% (n = 4 of 36)	39.9% (n = 14)	64.1% (n = 25)	39
Personal Support	48.3% (n = 70)			83.5% (n = 111)	16.5% (n = 22)	133
Highly Bilingual				76.6% (n = 33)	21.4% (n = 9)	42
Spanish-dominant				88.5% (n = 46)	11.5% (n = 6)	52
English-dominant				82.1% (n = 32)	17.9% (n = 7)	39
Informational Support	45.5% (n = 66)			82.0% (n = 109)	18.0% (n = 24)	133
Highly Bilingual				78.6% (n = 33)	21.4% (n = 9)	42
Spanish-dominant				82.7% (n = 43)	17.3% (n = 9)	52
English-dominant				84.6% (n = 33)	15.4% (n = 6)	39

*Based on N = 145 sample, which includes adolescents who didn't have both parents available to them.
**Percentages based only on those adolescents who reported living with or having parent(s) technically available to them.

whom they would seek out for the pertinent information or for help with acquiring the necessary information. Apart from these five types of information, adolescents were also asked to identify sources of particular forms of counsel regarding: (1) academic decisions and (2) post–high school plans. Receipt of informational support from parents (PARINFO = 1) was indicated by the adolescent's electing parents for at least one of the seven forms of such support.

Adolescents, on the average, reported between two and three people as potential sources of emotional support, and between one and two sources of actual support during the prior four months. Among adolescents who lived with their mothers (n = 133), 39.1% indicated their mothers as a source of emotional support. Among adolescents who lived with their fathers (n = 116), a much lower proportion—18.1%—indicated their fathers as a source of emotional support (statistics based on restricted sample; see Table 6.2). With regard to emotional support, affective ambivalence appears widespread; about 61% of adolescents did not elect their mothers as a potential source of emotional support, while 82% chose not to elect their fathers as a source.

Overall, parents are usually not a common or first-order source for adolescents seeking emotional support, although the data show that parents do stand a one in five chance of being asked during times of need. On the other hand, these adolescents do make intensive use of the nuclear family unit for this purpose, with family members experiencing close to a 45% chance of being sought for emotional support; in different terms, a family member was likely to be at least one of the two or three persons acknowledged as a preferred and ready source of emotional support. Peers make up the other half (i.e., 48%, translating into one or two people).

For purposes of investigating whether differences existed by level of acculturation, adolescents were divided into the following three groups, according to language proficiencies and usage: (1) Spanish-dominant, non-English-proficient; (2) bilinguals (high proficiency in both Spanish and English); and (3) English-dominant or monolingual English. Statistics again were calculated only for those who had potential access to the respective parent. Table 6.2 also displays these results.

Analyses by language group did not reveal statistically significant group differences, or a different pattern of reliance on parents. For each group, the majority did not cite mother as a preferred source of emotional support, and at least four-fifths of each group did not elect father for this support.

Analyses by gender did suggest that adolescent boys were a bit more likely to elect their mothers and fathers as sources of emotional support than were girls, although only the difference in the election of fathers was statistically significant (p < .03).[16] In any case, the majority of both gender groups did not elect parents as sources of emotional support.

Parents as Sources of Personal and Informational Support

Adolescents seemed much more comfortable electing parents as potential or viable sources of personal and informational support, with the large majority electing at least one parent as a source. Given the high number of opportunities to elect parents at least once, it is understandable that the percentage would be high. Data are not readily available on the number of times parents were selected as sources of specific types of personal and informational support (i.e., multiplex relations). Although parents may be elected as potential sources, this does not always translate into actual help-seeking. Parents may be trusted as sources of support, but adolescents may not actually turn to them as viable providers of the support they need, particularly when it comes to informational support. However, in terms of indicators of personal support, our calculations showed that election of potential sources of personal support did indeed overlap extensively with actual help-seeking. Among those who elected one or both of their parents as *potential* sources of personal support, about 85% actually had sought such support during the last 4 months. How do the above findings fit with what we already know about adolescent-parent relations? This we consider next.

Differences in Relations with Mother and with Father: What Other Researchers Have Found

What, in fact, do we know about the content of the interactions between adolescents and their parents, and about the differences between interactions with mothers and those with fathers? Research by James Youniss and Jacqueline Smollar (1985) provides us some notable insights and answers. Their findings certainly make clear how much more multistranded and complex mother-adolescent relations are relative to father-adolescent ties. From relations with their mothers, adolescents appear to be learning how to engage in ongoing exchange relations complicated by differentials in power and authority, and in which conflictual relations are tempered by intimacy, self-disclosure, and mutual caring. However, as with much of the psychological literature on parent-adolescent conflict reviewed earlier, Youniss and Smollar similarly neglect to interpret their data in terms of the ecological context in which these relations are embedded. Also neglected are the greater institutional forces that ultimately shape what we see in their data (i.e., class forces and privileges, patriarchy, and ethnicity— Anglo utilitarian individualism).

To their credit, Youniss and Smollar (1985) let us clearly see that middle-class status, in and of itself, does not have any positive, automatic, and transformative effect on father-adolescent relations. Emotional distance and a defensive posture are still the rule among adolescents in middle-class White families. What still needs to be established is how societal patriarchy intersects with Anglo-individualist culture to produce what we see in the Youniss and Smollar data. And more pertinent to the study presented in this book, we also must ask how Mexican colonialism, Anglo racism, and lower-social-class status have impacted father-adolescent relations within immigrant families in the United States. This book may not answer this important and complex question, but it may motivate us to do the necessary research.

EXEMPLARY CASES OF CLOSE, EMOTIONALLY GRATIFYING RELATIONS BETWEEN ADOLESCENTS AND IMMIGRANT PARENTS: FROM THE ADOLESCENTS' PERSPECTIVE

Although many of the adolescents we interviewed in San Diego conveyed highly affective, mutually supportive, and trusting relations with their mothers, from half to two-thirds within each subgroup conveyed the existence of ambivalent or conflictive relations. Given the prevalence of such strained parent-child relations in our discussions with adolescents, those acknowledging close and supportive relations with their mothers stood out. Relations of *confianza* (nonstressful, emotionally gratifying, and trust-inspiring relations) did occur among both recent immigrants and their more acculturated cohorts, and it would be instructive to visit some of these cases before we go on to the more conflictive accounts (Chapter 7).

Marisol Urquillo, a high-achieving immigrant with only 2 years in the United States, lived with her mother and father and two older brothers. In spite of her undocumented legal status, at the time of our interviews Marisol, a 12th-grader, was busy filling out applications to different universities. At school, she was involved in both the school *rondalla*, an acoustic guitar ensemble, and the band; outside of school, she was an active member of her church youth group. Marisol revealed a rather large support network, with 22 people cited, including two sources of emotional support—her mother and her friend Angeles (age 18). Three more sources of emotional support were added in the fall—her new best friend, Isabel, another friend, Sonia, and her father, Regino.

Marisol appeared to have a positive and prosocial network orientation, successfully interweaving a support network comprised of family members, friends, teachers, and counselors. She seemed to be quite invested in these relationships, and was eager to reciprocate. Her older brother Victor attended a local community college and served as a close companion; she recognized the high degree of rapport they shared and that she confided in him a lot. However, much of this support appeared tacit, since Victor was not explicitly cited as a source of emotional support and intimate counsel. When actively seeking out preferred sources, she turned to others. Marisol admired her brother's considerable artistic skill, and spoke at length of his ability to draw.

Marisol strongly identified with her mother and didn't understand why other youth do not listen to their parents. Asked whether she was satisfied with her parents' counsel regarding whether to begin seeing a boy who would have been her first official boyfriend, she commented:

> *I'm very satisfied because although I also count on my friends, I saw that many didn't, no one would listen to their parents, and I say, why? Yeah, you tell your friends things, you get things off your chest, but you feel better when you tell your parents; they know what you're like, what you think, what you want.*

Although Marisol recognized the importance of friends as confidants, she was emphatic in her view that parents are a superior, more emotionally gratifying source of emotional support and intimate counsel. We asked Marisol about the degree of trust and confidence she had in her mother, *"Do you trust your mom a lot?"* Marisol responded, *"She's like my twin.* [pause] *She's my best friend."* Our queries also revealed a good deal of reciprocity. Marisol's mother is cited as a source of eight different forms of social support. Marisol, in turn, helped her mother translate mail documents and pay bills; she also acted as a translator and cultural broker in various public settings. In this regard, Marisol shared much in common with many others in our study who assisted their parents in these ways.

Victoria Meléndez, who is U.S.-born and also a high-achiever, likewise spoke proudly of her relationship with her mother. In Chapter 5, Victoria expressed her admiration for her mother, stating that her mother's past sacrifices and encouragement motivated her to strive academically. Again, in her own words, *"El apoyo de mi madre esta siempre conmigo para todo* [My mother's love and support is with me in everything I do]." Although her mother was not cited as an elected source of bureaucratic information and institutional support, Victoria and her mother did have a multiplex relationship, with her mother providing various forms of support, including intimate counsel on personal issues. In spite of her mother's low level of formal education, Victoria said she could count on her mom for anything, including speaking to the principal when she disagreed with scheduling decisions made by the counseling staff.

The fact that Victoria did not explicitly elect her mother as a source of emotional support may have had to do with Victoria's sense of self-reliance and help-seeking orientation toward highly emotional or personal issues. No one, in fact, appears in her survey responses as a trusted source of emotional support. Victoria was the oldest of five children, in a household of nine. She carried a lot of responsibilities in the household, and was expected to look after her three younger sisters and her younger brother. The family unit appeared quite emotionally cohesive, due in large part, Victoria asserted, to the stabilizing influence of her stepfather of 8 years. In school, Victoria had learned to defend her right to a good education, challenging administrative decisions she felt were not in her best academic interests. Although not able to articulate in detail how racism operates within the school system, she did acknowledge it existed and operated in her life. However, she asserted that she didn't feel too constrained by it. This, again, may have had to do with her heightened sense of self-confidence and efficaciousness.

Her stepfather had been a strong influence on Victoria. Switching back and forth between Spanish and English, she stated, "My stepfather is great, too. He's the father I haven't had. We get along just great." Victoria had no contact with her biological father. Victoria's stepfather owned a business that provided legal and accounting services to the local Latino community (e.g., immigration, taxes, and divorces). Victoria stated that she had been working for him for 3½ years. She really enjoyed working there and had framed her future career plans in relation to her positive experience working with her stepfather; furthermore, through this work experience she had come to truly appreciate the importance and usefulness of being highly bilingual. "I think I have a great advantage because I'm bilingual and I feel good when I can help somebody."

As uplifting as these accounts are, through our many hours of interviews and conversations with our sample of adolescents we found that the majority did not acknowledge their mothers or fathers as a vital, emotionally gratifying, and multiplex source of social and emotional support. Thus, our ethnographic interview findings served to substantiate our statistical results.

When we looked for notable differences across our four principal subgroups (recent-immigrant boys and girls, and the more acculturated boys and girls—comprised of 1.5- and second-generation adolescents),[17] we found both male and female immigrant adolescents to be slightly more likely to have close relations with their mothers, relative to their more acculturated counterparts. This finding appears to confirm previous work showing the rise of intergenerational dissonance in working-class and poor immigrant families with more acculturated adolescents (Portes, 1996; Rumbaut, 1996; Zhou, 1997).

About half of the more acculturated girls showed evidence of close relations with their mothers, and half showed evidence of ambivalent or conflictive relations. The more acculturated adolescent boys showed a slightly greater likelihood of close relations with their mothers, yet these parent-adolescent relations were seldom as emotionally intense as was seen with the girls—a finding that mirrors what we see in the Youniss and Smollar (1985) studies.

Our ethnographic interview data on *relations with father* produced similar trends. Although our data on recent immigrant boys was affected by the high incidence of absent fathers (e.g., parents separated, or father still in Mexico), our interviews with recent immigrant young women did allow for some cautious comparisons. We found female immigrant adolescents to be significantly more likely to have close relations with their father than their more acculturated female counterparts were. Less than half of our more acculturated female adolescent informants who had a father present (four out of nine) spoke of having close and trusting relations. The confluence of this finding with those of Youniss and Smollar (1985) suggests the overarching and inhibiting effect of patriarchy across social classes and ethnic groups.

Interestingly, about 90% of our more acculturated adolescent males spoke of close attachments to their fathers (9 out of 10). This finding, however, needs to be juxtaposed with our statistical results showing that 82% of our male Bay Area sample did not elect their fathers as a chosen source of emotional support. This suggests that while Mexican-origin male adolescents may identify strongly with their fathers, such affective identification does not easily translate into explicitly supportive interactions. Given the role reversals prevalent in immigrant households, much of the explicit supportive behavior may be from adolescent to father.

CLOSING ANALYSIS AND REFLECTIONS

As noted before, there are instances when the process of emotional and other forms of support can be acted out in tacit fashion within routine interactions. Given what we know about the pressures and burdens working-class immigrant families regularly endure, it is reasonable to suggest that both explicit and tacit forms of support may be threatened by aggravated and accumulated tensions between immigrant parents and adolescents. At the same time, the existence of close affective relations does not always translate into the identification of parents as a likely and preferred source of support; for various reasons, many adolescents maintain certain, though subtle, reservations, even under the best of emotional circumstances.

However, close affective relations—particularly when founded on the principle of trust—might still be crucial within immigrant families: (1) by preventing the kind of relational dynamics that can undermine the family's function as the adolescent's sole system of social support and moral development, and (2) by creating the necessary conditions for occasional parent-adolescent conflicts and disputes to serve the purpose of stimulating the cognitive growth of the adolescent. In this latter scenario, we can begin to see the developmental possibilities outlined by psychologists, where adolescents engage in ongoing relations of exchange and support with parents and adult family members, and learn in the process how to deal effectively with supportive relations complicated by differentials in power and authority. This is precisely the type of relations children and adolescents encounter in school. Under appropriate familial conditions, conflictual relations and disputes, tempered by intimacy, self-disclosure, and mutual caring, provide opportunities not only for cognitive growth but also for the development of important social competencies that pay dividends in mainstream institutional life (i.e., social capital).

In the final analysis, our interviews revealed that the majority of adolescents were not seeking out and soliciting support from their mothers and fathers, even in cases where adolescents spoke of their relations with them in affectionate and appreciative terms. In the next chapter, we explore some of the reasons why these adolescents would not or could not seek emotional support, intimate counsel, and other forms of support from their parents.

7

Constraints on Supportive Relations
with Immigrant Parents

In this chapter we explore the reasons adolescents gave for not soliciting the support of their parents, and particularly, their mothers. The factors inhibiting adolescents from actively seeking support from parents fell into two principal and conceptually distinct categories. The first category, labeled *Institutional Circumstances and Conditions*, is comprised of difficult circumstances, life-events, and family arrangements that interfered with supportive parent-adolescent relations. The second category, labeled *Social-psychological Constraints*, comprises a number of intrapersonal and individual factors that inhibited the adolescent from seeking support from parents and other relevant family members. Within the realm of the family, Social-psychological Constraints appear as the most salient in the data, with issues of trustworthiness and appraisals of parents' ability to be supportive being foremost in the accounts of adolescents. In this chapter, we concentrate on Social-psychological Constraints.

SOCIAL-PSYCHOLOGICAL CONSTRAINTS ON HELP-SEEKING

Many adolescents we talked to, particularly the young women, spoke of conflictive relations with their mothers, so much so that actively soliciting emotional support, intimate counsel, and other forms of support from them was virtually impossible. The reasons varied, but a lack of *confianza* and intimacy in mother-adolescent relations was the driving force in their appraisals.

La Falta de Confianza: Conflictive Relations and Help-Seeking

María Toledo's mother was a Jehovah's Witness and very protective, closely monitoring María's friendships and social activities. Living close to Colonial Avenue in Harrison Heights with its array of street people and commercial bustle made Sra. Toledo even more protective. She didn't permit her daughter to have a boyfriend, although María maintained a secret relationship with a boy named Alex. María was afraid of her mother's reactions whenever personal issues surfaced in their interactions: "Every time that I try to talk to her, it scares me because she might scream at me or do something or tell me [pause] that's why I feel sometimes that I can't trust her." María stated that she would have liked to go to her mother for emotional support or intimate counsel, but felt that she could not. She indicated that she had made a number of attempts to approach her mother to discuss personal problems or issues: "I've tried, but every time we fight. She thinks it's me and, uh, we just end up arguing again, and I'd rather just forget it. And I have told her before that I can't trust her and I don't think she has a problem with it."

This, however, is not the story of a wicked mother; rather it is one that conveys the complexity of immigrant mother–adolescent daughter relations in the *Mexicano* community throughout the United States. María, at other moments in our interviews, tells of a mother who is generous to her friends, "maybe not with money, but with support, and she'll probably talk to the person about what to do." María related how her mother had helped a number of her girlfriends by talking to them about their personal problems.

Sra. Toledo, a single parent, appeared to nurture her immediate and extended family, providing material and monetary aid, advice on school decisions and career planning, and spiritual guidance to María and her three sisters. The daughters did not always get along with their mother, who in turn complained that she didn't feel appreciated for the efforts she had made for her family.

Mariana Zedillo was a U.S.-born high school senior who grew up not in a *barrio*, but in an adjacent mixed-SES and multiethnic neighborhood. As a child, she lived with her mother and three older sisters; her father was estranged from her mother and seemed to have many problems, such that she really never knew him as a father. Her family's economic situation had been "low income" for most of Mariana's life. Her mother had worked as a seamstress, providing the principal support for the family. At the time of the study, Mariana lived with her mother, stepfather, and two sisters.

Mariana came from a home that imposed a great deal of structure on her personal life. This probably enabled her to stay away from high-risk behaviors and activities (e.g., binge drinking, illicit drugs, coerced sexual intercourse, delinquency, etc.), but Mariana's sentiments reveal that such a high degree of parental monitoring may have acted as a double-edged sword. Mariana felt that she had little support from her family, emotional or otherwise, although one comes to learn that her immigrant mother is very concerned about keeping Mariana out of trouble by restricting her

freedom. There seemed to be quite a bit of intergenerational conflict between her and her mother. Mariana felt that her mother could not relate to
her life and how difficult adolescence was for her, both in and outside of
school. Her stepfather and mother admitted to not having the necessary
knowledge to help her arrange to go to a community college the following
year. Sra. Zedillo seemed resigned that college was out of reach for her
daughter because the economic barriers were perceived as too high.

Mariana frequently found herself the object of her mother's scolding.
Evidently, Sra. Zedillo also regularly told her older daughters of Mariana's
trespasses, and they in turn made reprimanding faces and remarks at her.
Mariana complained of often feeling depressed, but with no satisfactory
outlet for her feelings.

> It's like I keep it all to myself, I never talk to no one. It's like it all
> stays inside and sometimes I like get into tears. And then, I guess I
> get depressed and I feel like talking to someone, but I don't talk to
> no one about it. And so all that does is just like build up inside me
> and sometimes I just get like depressed. Sometimes I feel like I'm
> getting sick or something, you know.

Mariana recounted a recent occasion when she cried all night, then fell
asleep, only to wake up the next morning with a headache. "So I figured it
was because of that. But then I didn't want to tell my mom because then
she's gonna say, 'Well why didn't you say anything about it?'" Mariana
felt that her mom wouldn't provide her the emotional support and validation she desired:

> I can't say she won't care, but it's like she'll think of it different. It's
> like, I don't know, I just would rather keep it to myself, I guess,
> since they don't understand it. They don't say what I would want to
> hear. You know, they never told me like what I would want to hear.
> So I just keep to myself.

Feelings of unfairness also infused themselves in her relationship with
her mother, and tarnished Mariana's appraisal of her mother as an attractive and approachable source of support. When queried about what Mexican immigrant parents do that may discourage kids from doing well in
school, she stated emphatically:

> God, I guess when they don't really see or understand how hard it
> is to do all the work to get good grades. Parents don't recognize all
> the effort and hard work you put into it. They react based on what

little they see, and not on what the kid has really accomplished. It
pisses me off!

Mariana didn't necessarily object to her mother's monitoring behavior, but to its excessiveness. When asked about other parents, she said,
"Some of them are strict, and some just let their kids do what they want. It
all depends on the way you're brought up or what nationality they are.
But I know a lot of girls that their parents are strict. Some don't care and
wish their parents would care."

In the end, several factors merged to create a nearly impenetrable
wall between Mariana and her immigrant mother. Mariana felt that in
her mother's valiant efforts to raise three daughters alone, keeping them
out of "trouble" had come at the price of close and trusting relations. Appraisals of her mother's lack of validating behavior and authoritarian rules
prevented Mariana from conceiving her mother as a reliable and approachable source of support.

Our conventional notions of family life, defined by a nuclear kinship
structure with two parents at the center, have been archaic for some time
(Baca Zinn & Eitzen, 1999). Family structures today are much more varied, with changes spurred by national and global transformations in the
economy and the emergence of more fluid gender roles. Within immigrant
communities in the United States, the exigencies and stresses of migration,
resettlement, and poverty make for a wide range of household structures
(Hondagneu-Sotelo, 1994).

Lucita Alvarez, a 12th-grade high-achiever with only 2 years in the
United States, lived with two grandparents, two aunts, one uncle, and four
younger cousins on the east side of Harrison Heights. Her parents and most
of her extended family remained in Tijuana, Baja California. Lucita was
articulate, highly opinionated, and forthright about the tensions that existed in her new home, particularly the friction that existed between her
and her aunts. She was determined to continue her studies, not to marry
early, and to prepare for a good career. She spoke enthusiastically about
her involvement in her Catholic church group and about her participation
in the school *rondalla* (acoustic guitar ensemble). Her parents made occasional visits to see her, and had traveled to Auxilio High to attend school
meetings and open house.

Lucita acknowledged loving her mother very much, but felt distressed
that she didn't experience with her mother the same *confianza* and emotional closeness she had with her father, whom she considered a role model.
She wished she were closer to her mother, both geographically and emotionally. Yet she also appreciated the distance, although not without some
guilt. Lucita admitted to having a strong character, and to being oftentimes

obstinate and unyielding to her mother's attempts to impose strict limits on her social activities. These attempts at monitoring, she stated, had led to a lot of disagreements and fights. These same tensions had now emerged in her relations with her aunts.

Soliciting counsel from her grandparents and aunts regarding events in her personal life appeared out of the question, mainly due to Lucita's appraisal that their views regarding moral standards and adolescent social practices were in conflict with her own. She knew that her grandparents cared deeply for her, but the intergenerational divide in values and attitudes was simply too great to bridge.

Parent-adolescent tensions in immigrant families seldom remain constant, but rather go through periods where they heighten, then wane. There are some good days, then some bad days. Even when tensions are high, family life continues, and mutually supportive interactions between parents and adolescent—though often subtle—are common. These tensions do not undermine the norm of *confianza en confianza* [trusting mutual trust] in family life, but they do complicate it considerably. Although I consistently emphasize in this book the importance of direct and conscious solicitations of support—as an important adolescent coping strategy—it is essential that we remain attuned to the fact that routine interactions between immigrant parents and adolescents indeed contain many tacit instances of mutual support. Although adolescents may not explicitly solicit support from parents when tensions exist, they may still tacitly communicate the need for support, while also remaining receptive to the subtle but important supportive behaviors of parents. Although the lack of *confianza* at the dyadic level can certainly interfere with explicit or active soliciting of support, the existence of *confianza en confianza* within the family domain does allow for tacit supportive interactions to continue.

Confianza en confianza in family interpersonal relations is a resilient cultural entity, although it may temporarily weaken, prompting individuals to withdraw for self-protection. In families where the norm of *confianza en confianza* has a strong foundation, the occasional conflict and the subsequent defensive posturing of family members are often followed by conciliatory family rituals and the mutual reconstruction of interpersonal *confianza*. Thus, the prospect for the restoration of *confianza* at the dyadic level is usually only an encounter or an episode away.

Occasionally, however, certain family episodes (or a series of episodes) carry the potential for lasting and deleterious effects not only on the degree of *confianza* the adolescent feels toward the parent, but also on the very foundations of *confianza en confianza* within the family unit (Rumbaut, 1996).[1] The case of Dolores Villanueva is representative. Dolores had been in the United States for 3 years, having come from the state of Guerrero with her family and a complicated personal biography. She projected a very pleasant persona and charm, and was quite responsive to queries about her family and social network. Yet her cheerful presentation of self hid the grief and alienation from family that are, again, the main headlines of this story. It also masked what Dolores admitted to being, a young woman with a very strong temperament and one who was frequently rebellious.

Her mother died when she was only 15 days old, and Dolores was soon adopted by her uncle Ebodio and her aunt Velia—whom she has come to know as her only parents. Dolores blamed her biological father for her mother's death, as he evidently subjected her mother to a life of misery, and ultimately disregarded the wound inflicted when she stepped on a rusty nail while pregnant with Dolores.

Along with her parents (i.e., uncle and aunt), Dolores lived in Harrison Heights with two older brothers and one younger brother (her biological cousins), and a sister-in-law. Dolores portrayed her home as a very conflictive environment, attributing most of the trouble to her father, Ebodio, but also revealing her refusal to submit to what she considered his overbearing and authoritarian manner of parenting. Dolores admitted to frequent tensions and arguments with her father, some escalating to the point where her father hit her and she resisted.

She recounted an incident during the past year where her father had called the police when she failed one evening to come home on time. By her own admission, she had developed the habit of coming home later than the hour her father normally prescribed. According to Dolores, on this particular occasion she had arrived home on time (about 6:00) after doing her homework at a friend's house, then left again to ride her bicycle in the neighborhood. Her father, believing she had not come home at all, waited for her to return, only to block her way into the house. Wanting to avoid a prolonged and distressing confrontation, Dolores turned around and left again on her bike, going to the home of Doña Rosa, a close neighbor and friend. Sr. Villanueva, incensed, then called the police and reported her as a runaway.

> DOLORES: *I rode to Doña Rosa's house and I told her what had happened; well soon after, my mother telephoned Doña Rosa and told her to send me home. I left to go home and saw that the police were already there waiting for me since my dad had reported me as a . . .*
> INTERVIEWER: Runaway?
> DOLORES: *Yeah. And then we spoke with the police. My dad was telling them that I had arrived too late, and that I had yelled at him, and that I took off again on the bicycle. I then turned to my dad and said, "You wouldn't let me in, right?" No way is he going to make me look stupid.*

Dolores related another argument where she finally declared to her father that he would never hit her again. One evening she remained outside conversing with a neighbor and his girlfriend. After Sr. Villanueva called several times for Dolores to come in, he lost his patience and went out and grabbed her, leading her forcefully into the house.

> *He drags me inside, and he says, "When I tell you to come in, you come in," and he grabbed me like this, and he slammed the door and he hit me with a belt, and I got real red right here, and I told him, "You know what, this is the last time you're going to hit me; you'll see how much I'm going to change with you, you just watch!"*

Yet another fight between her and her father soon followed, this time provoked by her attempt to intervene in an argument between him and Dolores's mother. When Sr. Villanueva attempted to strike her, Dolores blocked his hands, then mocked his angry outburst.

> *"Ay," I tell him, "those feeble little hits!" It's just that he has a funny way of hitting. It also made me laugh, and he got really mad and then he got his belt. "Come on!," I tell him, "only don't say that you fight like a man with your fists." It's just that when you're mad you don't know what you're saying, and if I remember right, I told him, "Uuuu!," I told him, "you don't know how to fight like a man!" [pause] Yeah, I also have a temper, a strong personality.*

Dolores sees this willingness to fight as a definite family trait. "*Sí, tenemos un caracter, somos, mi familia, digamos, muy orgullosa* [Yes, we have a strong character; we are, my family, let's say, very prideful]." In her family, she says, no one apologizes for anything.

Dolores felt that her family should be there to provide her emotional support when she needs it, especially her mother, but that they were not. Although she viewed her father as the primary source of most household conflicts, her mother rarely intervened, and many times sided with her father. She said her mother gets nervous when Dolores complains about having difficulty finishing her homework, perhaps feeling powerless to help her daughter. On other occasions when Dolores tried confidently to show her mother how to handle a particular technical or accounting issue, her threatened sense of pride became quite evident: "She'll answer, '*And who knows more, me or you? You all think you know more because you go to school!*' Well, you can't talk to her."

In contrast, Dolores spoke eloquently of Doña Rosa, the mother of her schoolmate and friend Gilberto. Doña Rosa appeared to take the role of surrogate mother for Dolores, always making herself available when Dolores needed someone to talk to. Dolores describes her in quite affectionate terms: ". . . *almost like a kind of, well, like part mother, part friend; especially right now, given that my mom and I don't get along too well. Doña Rosa, although she's quite old, she's got it all together, she always tries to communicate with people."*

Abusive behavior in family life, of course, doesn't manifest itself only in parent-child relations. Depending on the household composition, it can also manifest itself in sibling rivalries, or in the figure of an aunt or uncle who is accorded some authority and power in the household. The incidence of an abusive older sibling arose a number of times in our interviews, and the resentment it generated was directed not only toward the sibling, but also toward the parent the adolescent believes should have been more vigilant and protective.

Robert Zamora, a U.S.-born 11th-grader, lived with both of his parents and his older brother in a neighborhood adjacent to Vista. Life in the Zamora home was economically secure, and both parents appeared to emphasize the importance of doing well in school. Robert confided in his older sister, Ana, who had recently married and moved to a northern county just outside of San Diego. Their relationship was multiplex and emotionally close. His relations with his slightly older brother, Javier, however, were quite conflictive. For many years, Robert explained, he had gotten into many arguments and fights with Javier, who had a mean temperament; in Robert's words, Javier was "always mad," "a punk!" He described several past altercations where Javier "messed up my back, my legs, tried to kill me." The tension existing in his relationship with his brother was coupled with a quiet resentment toward his mother. Robert felt she had never really understood the long-standing problems he had with his brother, nor had she ever actively intervened on his behalf. These feelings had existed for some time, and had served to distance him from his mother, causing routine frictions in their relationship and undermining what appeared to be legitimate attempts by her to monitor his activities and progress in school.

Fractures in trust between immigrant parent and adolescent are a two-way street; just as the adolescent may come to lose *confianza* in a parent due to what are perceived as parental failings, so too can strained relations and loss of mutual trust result from the adolescent's misdeeds. The case of Héctor Ordaz, in the United States since the age of 3, is illustrative. He was a low-achiever who had recently been placed in the Block program, an alternative curriculum program within the school for students deemed to have long-standing difficulties conforming to the academic and behavioral norms of regular classrooms. Héctor lived with his mother, father, two stepsisters, and two stepbrothers in a community about three or four miles south of Harrison Heights.

Héctor admitted to being a "tagger" and participating in a "crew" that roamed different neighborhoods and freeway sites with their "utensils" (i.e., markers and spray cans), looking for key places to leave their graffiti artwork. Although never arrested, Héctor told of many occasions when he'd been "in trouble," particularly at school for things like ditching, fights on school grounds, talking back to the teacher, and other classroom disruptions. He was once caught shoplifting in a store, but was not detained. "I got caught once, but they let me go out. We didn't take anything. They let me go. I was scared because that was the first time I got caught."

Héctor conveyed loving feelings for his mother, and although he talked to her every day, he regretted that they did not have "personal conversations," and their relations were often strained. Héctor felt that his past troublesome behavior had fractured his mother's sense of trust in him; he also understood that he was currently engaging in activities that complicated and worsened the situation. Under such conditions, Héctor felt it almost impossible to approach his mother for the moral, emotional, and social support he wished he could receive from her. Héctor admitted that it boiled down to "problems, problems that I had, still have. Well, I know what I'm doing right now [tagging], I don't know what she'd do if she found out. She probably would get mad, real mad. I want her to help me."

Héctor seemed caught in a bind. He wanted his mother's love and support, and longed for her to trust him, but was unwilling at this time to take full responsibility for his behavior or to cease his tagging activities. He also feared the loss of privileges and freedoms he'd grown accustomed to; so Héctor focused his energies on managing the damage to his reputation, rather than on changing his behavior.

> I don't want people to find out what I, other people, 'cause my
> mom's like the type of person that believes everybody, like, they'll
> just tell her a lie about me, she'll believe it. 'Cause this lady told her
> that I was drinking and all this stuff, getting high and everything
> else. My mom started getting mad at me and I go, "I don't even do
> that. You can even take me to the doctor and everything and check
> me out," and she said "No"; she kept quiet.

Héctor described how his mother normally reacted to the problems that he created, and how he typically responded: "She lectures me. It kind of helps. I just listen 'cause if you keep on talking, she'll never stop. Just keep quiet and she'll stop." Many adolescents, like Héctor, became considerably adept at managing their strained and complex relations with their immigrant parents, although these competencies were rarely refined enough to resolve the contradictions and impasses that arose.

Throughout our interviews we saw variations in the development of competencies pertaining to the micropolitics of network relations, including conflictive kinship relations; adolescents with low competency usually suffer the most from familial tensions. Considering this situation, recent trends toward instituting programs that teach conflict resolution is certainly a welcome development in public education.

Generational Dissonance: Incongruence in Values and Cultural Perspectives

Conflictive or antagonistic relations were only one of a constellation of factors that inhibited adolescents from perceiving their parents as viable and approachable sources of emotional and social support. Adolescents also provided evidence showing how they appraised the various risks involved in self-disclosure or in seeking help from a parent. Would a parent listen carefully and validate the adolescent's feelings? Would he or she get angry easily? Would a solicitation for help turn into an argument, or worse yet, a punitive action? These appraisals were just as likely to occur in nonconflictive parent-adolescent relationships as they were in the conflictive relationships we encountered. Almost all the evidence for such appraisals emerged from our interviews with 1.5- and second-generation girls (see note 17 for Chapter 6). The cases of María Toledo and Mariana Zedillo, featured above, are illustrative of such appraisals, involving heightened adolescent sensitivity regarding a parent's reaction to self-disclosure and requests for support. Intergenerational cultural differences between immigrant parents and their acculturated children appear again as a major source of the problem.

In one way or another, differences in values and cultural perspectives and in the degree of adherence to traditional ways complicated the relations between immigrant parents and their Americanized or rapidly acculturating children. This issue emerged in nearly every interview, including instances where attachments were positive and emotionally intense. Studies of relations between middle-class parents and their adolescents have shown a remarkable degree of congruence in political, moral, and religious views (Berndt, 1979; Kandel & Lesser, 1969; Sebald, 1986; Youniss & Smollar, 1985).

The situation, however, is far more complicated within low-income or working-class immigrant families (Zhou, 1997). A family's migration and resettlement experience, and the consequent changes in family relations, may last until the death of both parents; certainly, the frictions are at their height during the adolescent years when youth, whether immigrant themselves or not, are developing their identities as young adults, and are still under the care and authority of their parents.

Although both parents and children are undergoing acculturation, each is coping with the experience while lodged in different cultural vessels—like two different ships being thrashed in a storm. For some families, at least, members experience more or less the same storm, as well as having embarked from the same place and having been similarly molded by cultural experiences in the motherland. In the case of immigrant parents and U.S.-born youth, however, parents and adolescents are not only lodged in different vessels but have embarked from different places, and now experience life in very different storms. The latter case produces the greatest "generational dissonance," a term coined by Portes and Rumbaut (1996, Chapter 7) to refer to circumstances when parents and adolescents experience drastically different acculturation experiences. Although parents and children usually meet their distinctive challenges within the same overall ecological context and share in whatever support systems are available to them, their separate vessels and different points of departure lead to very different experiences.

For U.S.-born and many 1.5–generation children, the storm consists of a partial and uneasy embeddedness in distinctive and conflicting socialization contexts that compete for their allegiance (Stanton-Salazar, 1997, 2000). While recent adolescent immigrants (e.g., Marisol U., Chapters 5 and 6) experience early development and the pressures of acculturation within a consciousness (a vessel) largely constructed and fortified in the land of their parents, U.S.-born and 1.5–generation youth experience acculturation in a vessel largely or completely constructed in the United States, in a society still defined by de facto racial segregation and multiple forms of institutionalized racism (Rumbaut, 1996; Stanton-Salazar, 1997). Also, while recent adolescent immigrants experience the storm near the threshold of full adulthood, their U.S.-born cousins have been in the storm since infancy. While recent adolescent immigrants and their parents make sense of the storm in terms of a hope-inspired journey from the motherland, their cultural counterparts experience it through the lens of *multiple-marginality*, and reflected in the well-known phrase *ni de aqui, ni de alla*.[2] Immigrant parents and foreign-born relatives, lodged in a different vessel, cannot truly fathom the storm in which their U.S.-born children and kin are cast.

Angeles Machado was a bright and articulate 12th-grader who lived with her stepmother, aging father, and younger sister in Harrison Heights. She was a moderate- to high-achiever, and had hopes of going away to college in the following year. She had been elected president of a small company as part of the Junior Achievement program organized by her economics teacher.

Angeles, originally adopted as an infant, was 9 when her adoptive mother passed away. Her father remarried, but Angeles almost never got along well with her stepmother. Angeles spoke of a clash in values with both her stepmother and her father. Although Angeles described her immigrant stepmother as "uneducated" and "old world," she credited her for reading a good deal. Angeles admitted to finding herself engaged in interesting conversations and social criticism with her stepmother, but complained: "She's not open-minded. She's not willing to accept other people's ideas. She's very, very biased. When you're open-minded, it's just, you're a completely different person than if you're closed-minded." At another point in the interview, Angeles remarked: "Yeah, we talk, but we bump heads at the same time [laughs]. Always. Always, always, always."

When queried about whether she saw her stepmother as a source of support, or whether she felt uncomfortable with the idea of soliciting help or advice, she said: "I'm comfortable, because I know what's coming as soon as I ask for something. Sometimes she knows what she's doing and saying. Well, like I said, I don't take her advice too seriously."

Her relations with her father were also characterized by a certain degree of dissonance and distance. Angeles explained it in terms of the significant age gap between her and her father, who was 73, but also in terms of an intergenerational clash in values. "It's very regrettable, but like I said, I understand the age gap and that his sense of values and morality are a lot different from mine. I understand. So we don't talk too much." Angeles found that attempts to engage her father in issues, either personal or important to her, became too distressful for the both of them. She stated, "No I have to be very [pause], I have to beat around the bush a lot; he can't deal with it at all." This didn't mean that Angeles felt that her father was unsupportive or uncaring. In spite of their differences, she felt he would be there for her in a crisis or in a time of need: "He's always there, you know. If something comes up, he's always there, and I think that as far as right now, I wish we could be a little closer but [stops]. Neither he nor I are [sic] expressive. I never go to him for my personal life."

Angeles had become very interested in Latin American politics, and talked excitedly about the author Carlos Fuentes, whom she'd read in government class. "I love how he writes. He's very good. I like what he says about what our society should be like." Her interest in politics, she admitted, had its roots in her father's personal stories about his own political adventures in Mexico. "When he was young he went to Mexico City and got involved in politics. He climbed the social ladder, and that's sort of my dream. I mean I love politics and I think that's the sort of the thing I'd like to do."

On the surface, Angeles conveyed a strong, independent, and forward-looking attitude. When asked to address the role of parents in providing emotional support and intimate counsel to their adolescent children, Angeles revealed a curious mix of ambivalence and resignation.

> That's what I'm saying, I don't think anyone has the responsibility. Well [laughing], I would say my parents should be there for me. I say it'd be nice, but I can't say they *should*. [long pause] I feel fine because I know that not every family is like perfect, not everybody's Ozzie and Harriet and that sort of thing; I just feel that I've got what I've got and I've just got to learn to accept it, so.

Angeles admitted that she put up a good front, of someone strong and independent, but the price appeared quite high. She confessed to having had "several" stress attacks resulting from home and school pressures.

> I make myself sick. I've only collapsed once. I get really nervous, nervous, I have a stupid giggle, a stupid giggle, I lose it [pause] I lose it. It's happened like once at home; once here at school. Well, I usually have medication for it, or they usually let me sleep it off or something. I sleep a lot, I sleep a long time. Tonight I'll go to sleep at 6:30 and wake up tomorrow morning.

When we probed her about why she thought she had these attacks, Angeles revealed a glimpse of remarkable insight: "I feel like I portray myself to everybody like a very strong person, very strong character, and I'd like to think of myself like that, you know; but deep down, you know, I've gotta break it down sometimes. I can't keep going on like that forever." Such insight, however, did not appear to be coupled with a desire for social support. When asked whether she has sought help in dealing with these pressures more effectively, she answered: "Like I said, I usually sleep it off or work it off. I've started working on it myself."

Religious devotion and extensive integration in church activities on the part of immigrant parents can affect family life in several ways. On the one hand, such parental religiosity can serve to embed family life in a strong support system, providing various social control functions (Coleman, 1988) as well as a buffer against the vagaries and stresses of immigrant adaptation (Portes & Bach, 1985; Zhou, 1997). The case of Marisol Urquilla, visited in Chapter 6, illustrates this. Marisol's parents decided to look for a new church community precisely because they wanted their children integrated in church-sponsored youth activities. Marisol and her siblings welcomed the move. On the other hand, high parental religiosity, when coupled with adolescent disinterest, can serve to accelerate and deepen intergenerational differences in acculturation, providing an arena for conflict that may severely fracture relations of *confianza* and household *familism*.

Raul Ubilla presented himself as an unassuming and soft-spoken 12th-grader. Born in the United States, he was a mid-achiever who lived in

Southview with his mother, father, and two younger brothers. Although he cited 20 people in the network survey, half of whom were peers, he described himself as a loner. Raul's mother appeared as a source of multiple forms of support (e.g., advice regarding school matters and post–high school plans, various types of informational support); yet Raul stated that he tried not to get too personal with his mom, then murmured "I don't know why." Later Raul admitted that his parents, particularly his mother, placed a great deal of pressure on him to conform to their religious commitments. They self-identified as "Christian," and belonged to the Church of God, a nondenominational church serving a predominantly local Latino congregation. As with many other Mexican-origin youth in the United States, Raul's socialization within a Mexican immigrant household was defined by the degree to which cultural values and mores of his immigrant parents were molded by religious beliefs and practices, whether Catholic or Protestant.[3]

Three or four times during the school/work week, from 6:30 to 9:00 in the evening, Sr. and Sra. Ubilla took their family to worship services. During the past 3 years, Raul had tried to present convincing reasons for not being able to attend these evening services (e.g., homework) and, in general, had attempted to distance himself from the church community— but not without creating a strain in his relationship with his parents, especially with his mother.

Raul's feelings regarding his parents' religiosity were complex. He admitted that the church had protected him from the dangers and risks visible throughout Southview and adjacent neighborhoods. Yet his desire for autonomy from the church community had steadily grown. Besides his parents' discomfort over this gradual detachment, Raul perceived that the adults and other teens in the congregation silently scorned him for not being interested or invested in church activities. Although Raul remained an occasional participant in church services, he refused to mingle with the other teens, stating, "They're into their own little group. I hate them anyway." The problem appears twofold; on the one side is a tightly knit church community oriented to the needs, dispositions, and tastes of its immigrant congregation; on the other side are acculturated youth, like Raul, who fail to see this church body speaking to the identity issues, assimilation pressures, and deep spiritual needs associated with their bicultural and working-class existence.

Raul had regular but different degrees of contact with five older siblings, including two older sisters and two older brothers who have moved out, and one older brother in prison. He was particularly close to Sonia, who registered in our network survey as a strong and multiple source of support and counsel for Raul. Sibling religiosity also played its role here.

Sonia was no longer active in the church. Sara, another sister, lived in the neighborhood and shared her parents' religiosity and, from Raul's perspective, the congregation's scorn for him. He mused about the possibility of moving in with his brother Tony, who lived in the northern part of the county, as a way of staying close to his girlfriend, who had plans to attend a small community college in the area. However, his move wouldn't be ideal, considering that his brother Tony was "also into that religion." Nevertheless, he felt his brother would give him considerably more liberty and wouldn't force him to go to church.

There was little evidence of overt conflict between Raul and his parents. For the most part, Raul abided by the limits his parents placed on his social and recreational life. He was not the rebellious sort, and communicated a quiet respect for his parents' efforts to raise and protect their children in a neighborhood ecology that had long been problem-plagued. But the ambivalence was there, marked by his feeling that his parents were out of touch with the kind of young man he had become, unperceptive of the difficulties he experienced in attempting to reconcile his difficult participation in culturally disparate worlds.

Appraisals of Provider Capabilities

As we have seen, active help seeking as a coping strategy entails a complex set of social-psychological processes. First and foremost, such a strategy is shaped by a number of cognitive appraisals, which in turn are heavily influenced by the individual's developing network and help-seeking orientations.[4] One key appraisal is an assessment of whether a potential source of support is capable and competent, and whether the person would be a skillful provider. In varied ways throughout our interviews, adolescents articulated their appraisals of whether a parent was—in the present tense—*psychologically* or *emotionally capable* of acting as an effective source of support. A number of examples can illustrate how important these appraisals are in inhibiting certain adolescents from seeking help from their parents.

Leonel Hernández arrived in the United States 3 years prior to our first interview; together with his mother, two sisters, and two older brothers, he settled into their new home in Southview. His father remained in Mexico, having separated from Leonel's mother some years prior to their move north. Sra. Hernández's family was supported by her older children. Throughout our interview, Sra. Hernández conveyed an anxiety over her and her children's undocumented status. In response to whether he had recently needed emotional and social support from family members, Leonel admitted: *"Yes, yes I've had, but I don't feel comfortable talking with other people.*

With my mom yes, yes; I mean, I have spoken to her about such things." Leonel soon told of a number of incidents that had caused him much distress: *"Yeah, like I had that problem when the kids at the park wanted to hit me."* With regard to his experiences at school:

> *Well, when it comes to school, whenever I go to school, I don't feel like I belong there. Because many people look at me as if I were less, less than them, like the [white] American and Black kids. They look at me, at us Mexicans, they look at us as if we were less than them. I feel bad and at the same time angry.*

There was ambivalence in Leonel's appraisal of his mother as a viable source of emotional support and counsel—although of a different kind. He described his relationship with his mother with respect and affection. *"Well, she's an understanding person; she understands the problems that I have in school, with my studies. She's always motivated me to keep studying and she's helped me a lot, with my studies. She's given me a lot of advice (i.e., consejos)."*[5]

Yet Leonel admitted to being very careful in what he told his mother, stating, for example, that he never told her about the park incident, *"para que no se preocupara ella de eso* [so she wouldn't worry and become anxious about this situation]."* In the network survey, Leonel did not cite his mother as a source of emotional support or as a source of counsel regarding personal problems (e.g., harassment by peers), preferring to go to his older sister María and his older brother Beto. María registered, in fact, as a strong multiplex relation for Leonel in our survey. In reference to his perception of racial prejudice at school: *"I talk to my sister, the oldest one. She tells me to talk to the counselors, but I tell her that I don't feel comfortable talking to them."*

Another recent immigrant, Marisol Urquilla, told of similar decisions to not seek help from her parents. Marisol spoke of the great affection and respect she had for her father, but considered the many burdens he already carried; she experienced great discomfort when circumstances were such that she had little choice but to approach him for assistance. Marisol tried, as much as possible, to take her burdens to others in her family.

> *Yeah, sometimes I feel bad because, for example, there are times like the other day when I needed him to help me with some scholarship stuff and it was almost 11 at night and he hadn't come home from work yet. I knew that he was going to come home tired, but well, I had to do it, so then he got upset and I also got upset; we almost fought, but we didn't. I don't like asking him for many things because I know he has a lot of problems that he worries about and everything, but he always helps me.*

As with Leonel and his mother, we again see that the perceived need to protect a heavily burdened immigrant parent sometimes complicates the decision of whether to seek parental support.[6]

The case of Héctor Ordaz, whom we visited earlier, presents another clear-cut example of an adolescent's assessment of both a parent's capability to be genuinely supportive and the potential effectiveness of the support. Where Héctor's relations with his mother were ambivalent—highly affective, but strained—his relations with his father stood out as distant and uneventful. Héctor cared deeply for his father, and worried about how his weekend drinking could be raising his blood sugar and damaging his health. Héctor stated, "He gets drunk sometimes. [pause] He shouldn't be drinking." Asked about how his father reacted to his family's concerns, he said, "No, that doesn't make him upset. He stopped once like for a year; but he's back. On weekends, Saturdays and Sundays." There were no words of disdain or anger in Héctor's voice as he described his father and their relationship; in fact, one hears an occasional word of affection, and even of praise. Yet, when asked whether he would go to his father for intimate counsel, Héctor said no. "He [his father] wouldn't understand because he's been through badder things."

Héctor viewed his father's drinking problem as evidence that his father, at this time, was not a reliable source of support. Furthermore, Héctor knew of his father's past failings, and saw them as providing no moral basis from which his father could counsel him. However, it wasn't so much his father's troubled past that disqualified him as a source of counsel, but rather his father's inability to learn from his mistakes. This is precisely why Héctor admired his older brother so much, and why he regularly sought him out for intimate counsel. Héctor spoke at length about how his brother was once involved in gangs and how he put all that to the side, to work and help his family.

Throughout our interviews many adolescents spoke of people they knew—parents, siblings, peers, community people, and counselors—who were able to turn their lives around, to move from a dark and trouble-filled time in their lives to one that was far more positive and empowering to self and others. Adolescents found such individuals very worthy of their admiration and trust, and sought them out frequently for various types of support, and especially for intimate counsel.

Finally, we present the case of Ana Helguerra, a high-achiever, a senior, and a participant in her school's AVID program.[7] She had been in the United States for 9 years and spoke English like a native speaker. Ana exhibited a certain self-assuredness, was quite opinionated about the people in her life, and appeared surprisingly pragmatic in her orientation toward them. Ana lived with her mother, father, and younger sister in an inconspicuous apartment building in a section of town known for its older homes and middle-class white urbanites. Ana's younger sister Virginia, an unwed mother, had a 5-year-old baby at home.

Ana's relationship with her father exemplifies a common experience within immigrant families, a situation in which the father separates and travels to the United States alone, then brings in his family at a later date (see Hondagneu-Sotelo, 1994). As the story unfolds, Sr. Helguerra left his family to work in the United States when Ana was only 9 months old. She would turn 7 years of age before she and her family reunited permanently with her father in San Diego. Ana stated that during those early years, her father visited the family in Mexico during the summers, but she remembered him only as a friendly stranger who would arrive once a year with gifts. By Ana's account, the first years of reunification were hard for their parents—and particularly stressful for her mother—mainly because Sr. Helguerra had become quite accustomed to the freedom he enjoyed during the years of separation. Only now, in the past 3 or 4 years, had Ana and her father been able to forge a close relationship—although one with very clear and defined parameters.

Ana clearly had a lot of affection for her father; she liked his sense of humor, admired his artistic abilities, and acknowledged that they do, in fact, share much in common:

> We have the same tastes, we like the same stores, we like the same people; we love the same entertainment, we love the movies, we love to gossip, we like nice things, and we *really* like money, we never disagree over that. We like the same kinds of friends. He really loves me, because I was the first child, and he used to change my diapers, so he really got close to me; then he left us, so there was sort of a gap right there that he missed, about 7 years.

Ana seemed quite cognizant that her father's absence interfered with the development of what she perceived would have been an otherwise positive and strong father-daughter relationship. When asked about the depth of their relationship, she said:

> It's a very superficial thing. We can't get too personal or too close to each other, because deep inside, we're really like different. He says I'm very opinionated and critical. So we try to keep it, not distant, but not too close. That's how we get along, just talking about other things, besides the family. He's like a friend that's [pause] always there to have fun, but that's it {pause} not to get serious.

Regarding her father as a source of advice and intimate counsel, she said:

> No, I wouldn't go to him for advice because, first of all, he cannot
> give advice, he always says the wrong thing. He uses the wrong
> tone of voice at the wrong time. So you cannot go up to him,
> because he'll make you mad; he will, you'll think he's taking it
> lightly, or he's just making fun of you. So, he's just a fun guy, you
> can go to him for money, for help in drawing, because he's a real
> good artist.

We wondered whether she had ever talked to her father about her deep-
seated feelings regarding their relationship; Ana stated that she wouldn't
risk it. She saw her father trying his best to be attentive to her—for example,
by showing fatherly pride and giving encouragement when she did well
in school. She saw these as positive and compensating influences. Ultimately she felt that to broach these deeper emotional issues "would really
damage our relationship, [pause] too much closeness, that's really not our
style."

Ana's case shows how the psychodynamics of immigrant parent-
adolescent relationships are often deeply entrenched in the structural circumstances of Mexican poverty, parental migration, and subsequent family reunification. Our investigation uncovered a number of adolescents
whose emotional attachment to their fathers—and mothers—had been developmentally undercut by the parent's migration north during a critical
period in their childhood.[8] This separation turned out to one of the principal issues emerging within the category of *Institutional Circumstances and
Conditions* (see Figure 7.1). Also significant here is Ana's clear appraisal of
her father's social competencies, and of his ability to provide effective counsel. Furthermore, Ana intimated that long before our interviews, she had
already arrived at a careful analysis of the strengths and weaknesses of her
relationship with her father, of what the relationship could successfully
sustain and provide, and of what it simply could not.

Ana's assessments of her mother's personality and emotional capabilities likewise precluded her from perceiving and approaching her mother
as a viable source of emotional support and intimate counsel. The evidence
that emerges depicts a classic case of parent-adolescent *role reversal*, as
sometimes mentioned in other studies on immigrant families.[9] Although
Ana spoke of her mother as very giving, the language of reciprocity and
interdependency did not emerge here. Rather, the principal dynamic in
their relationship is described in terms of Ana as *confidante and informal
provider* of emotional support and intimate counsel and her mother as *recipient and dependent*. Ana described her mother as "passive" and lacking

Figure 7.1. Relational Appraisals and Emotions That Determine Whether Adolescent Seeks Support from Parent(s)

I. INSTITUTIONAL CIRCUMSTANCES AND CONDITIONS

A. *Lack of Social Interactional Opportunities* (lack of easy access due to geographical separation or to difficult circumstances—e.g., family-work schedules)

B. *Permanent Separation—Loss of Ties* (death, abandonment)

II. SOCIAL–PSYCHOLOGICAL CONSTRAINTS

A. *Assessments of Parent Capabilities* (parent not perceived as an effective, appropriate, or reliable source of support)

B. *Lack of Confianza/Trust* (set within ambivalent or conflictive relations with parent[s])

C. *Generalized Lack of Confianza/Trust* (set within good relations with parent[s])

D. *Intergenerational Incongruence in Values and Cultural Perspectives* (leading to a lack of trust and rapport)

E. *Assessments of Parent Capabilities* (fear of or anxiety about further burdening parent)

F. *Anxieties Regarding Parent's Reaction* (that parent won't understand, or won't validate feelings, or may apply negative sanctions)

G. *Capability of Adolescent* (an adolescent's *help-seeking orientation*: generalized feelings about help-seeking as an unviable *coping strategy* and about the inability of others to provide effective support [low trust]; low degree of confidence in the social support process) in self-confidence. However, such assessments were juxtaposed with a definite understanding and appreciation of the many trials and deprivations her immigrant mother had had to endure over many years. Yet Ana found it difficult to relate to her mother's deep self-sacrificing disposition and saintly devotion to her children, calling her at one point "a female Jesus Christ." At another point in the conversation, she tried to capture this dominant trait: "She's like the super most weakest person in the whole world; she'll do anything, you can do anything, you can go anywhere, as long as you ask her, and she'll do anything for you. [Pause.] She'll [even] take a beating for you." Asked whether she and her mother have disagreements from time to time, she said:

> We haven't had the chance to have disagreements. It seems that, all the problems that she's had, I've sort of had to help her with them, listen to her, and comfort her for whatever she was going through. So whatever she has to go through, I have to understand it. I really can't disagree with the decision she takes, because that's the same decision I would take if I were a nicer person.

Ana wished that her mother weren't so "nice," that she could be more assertive and self-confident—that she could be, perhaps, a little more like Ana.

REVIEW OF SOCIAL-PSYCHOLOGICAL ISSUES THAT PREVENTED ADOLESCENTS FROM SEEKING SUPPORT FROM THEIR PARENTS

Through an analysis of our interview data pertaining to parent-adolescent relations, we discovered seven major relational and social-psychological issues that repeatedly inhibited adolescents from actively seeking emotional support and intimate counsel from their parents. These issues are listed in Figure 7.1, in order of salience. For four of the first six issues, we could not find any substantive differences between relations with mother and with father. The two exceptions will be discussed in a moment. It is critical that we note and emphasize that these six issues are not mutually exclusive; there were many instances where we found significant overlap among two or three. Nonetheless, from the perspective of the responding adolescent, the strain in the relationship was articulated mainly in terms of one particular issue or concern.

The most prominent relational issue that emerged pertained to the adolescent's appraisal of the parent's capability or competency in providing emotional support, intimate counsel, and other forms of nonmaterial support conventionally provided by parents (II.A. in Figure 7.1). Adolescents made appraisals as to whether relying on a particular parent would be an effective or productive strategy, whether the parent would be reliable, and whether the support provided would be effective. Adolescents made the assessments regardless of whether their relations with parents were strained or not.

This appraisal issue was addressed in Chapter 6, regarding whether parents were seen as effective providers of *academic support*. Because of the low level of formal education and Mexican immigrant status, the parents were assessed as ineffective or inappropriate providers. However, for most adolescents this issue did not significantly and adversely affect the emotional intensity of the parent-adolescent relationship; in other words, adolescents did not hold their parents personally accountable. More often than not, they recognized their parents' accomplishments, in spite of the blocked educational opportunities and deprivations their parents had had to endure.

Héctor's assessment of his father's weekend alcoholism and its adverse impact on his father's continued emotional growth prevented Héctor from feeling that his father was an appropriate and effective source of emotional support and intimate counsel. This, combined with Héctor's awareness that his father couldn't help him with his academic problems, cast Sr. Ordaz as an ironic father figure who still enjoyed the love, respect, and praise of a trouble-prone son, but, ultimately, could not be conceived as a worthy or reliable source of support by the same son who desperately needed parental intervention.

Ana Helguerra's characterization of her mother as a martyr, and as weak and nonassertive, prevented her from visualizing her mother as a source of effective support. Role reversals within immigrant families appear to contribute to such negative appraisals, particularly when parents find themselves more dependent on their adolescent children than the adolescent children are on them. The lack of fluid reciprocal relations, and the adolescent's reconceptualizing of a parent as helpless, dependent, or overburdened, provides fertile ground for the emergence and reinforcement of these types of assessments.

Negative appraisals of parental competencies sometimes appeared secondary to other more salient issues affecting the relationship, as when adolescents were involved in emotionally guarded relations with their parents. Although the lack of *confianza* and the emotional guardedness may have been most salient in the mind of the adolescent, both issues appeared tightly coupled. Such coupling tended to occur when appraisals were framed in terms of anxieties about further burdening an overburdened or distressed parent. Appraisals of this sort emerged as the fifth most salient concern in our data, and provided the first of two instances where we saw differences between relations with mother and with father. All except one of these "burden" appraisals were associated with difficulties in seeking support from the mother.

Leonel Hernández worried that telling his undocumented mother about being physically harassed at the park or about the prejudice and depreciation he felt at school would seriously upset her. Perceiving her already generalized anxiety stemming from her status as a poor and undocumented immigrant, and fearing she would feel powerless to do something about these situations, Leonel opted to keep silent about his hurtful experiences—in a sense, managing what she learned about his own adjustment experiences as a recent and undocumented immigrant in order to not adversely impact her already attenuated mental health. The possibility that such relational management may serve to infanticize immigrant parents, as well as prevent them from asserting themselves as caring parents, fails to appear in these adolescent appraisals. However, it could very well be that Leonel's calculations were accurate as well as keenly sensitive—ultimately, what we are left with is simply another conundrum in adolescent-immigrant parent relations.

The coupling of concerns referred to earlier was evident in the case of Dolores Villanueva, who lost confidence in her mother when she refused to intervene between her and her authoritarian father. Dolores, however, also understood that relations between her parents were conflictive and quite stressful for her mother, too. Besides experiencing *una falta de confianza* [lack of confidence] in her noninterventionist mother, Dolores felt a strong ambivalence heightened by her empathetic awareness that her mother was also in a stressful relationship with her volatile father, and that seeking her support would most assuredly overburden her.

CLOSING ANALYSIS AND REFLECTIONS

What do people really mean when they say "low-income immigrant Latino families" or "urban minority adolescents" in their writings and conversations? There exist countless untold stories and hidden structural realities that lie encrusted in these terms, and that are never adequately unearthed when used in academic texts. The accounts in this chapter are intended to provide a glimpse into some of the micro-structural realities that lie beneath our clumsy attempts to code and classify these families and youth as inhabiting a distinctive reality within society's social bottom.

We should be cautious, however, lest our understanding of such deep structure lead us to think of these adolescents and families as somehow apart from society; rather, we should view these glimpses as a mirror of the contradictions and ramifications of how our society is socially organized as a whole. Simultaneously, much of what we see in this chapter may very well have parallels to what we see in many middle-class families. The difference may only be in degree and severity, in the coping resources available to families, and in the long-term consequences of such alienated embeddedness—specifically, that the adolescents in this chapter pay the price for their estrangement from parents in ways that privileged youth do not.

Although the adolescent-parent estrangement we see here may be evident in some form across the class spectrum, the familial embeddedness of these low-income, urban Latino youth does point to certain stratification processes that are unique to those occupying the social bottom. In low-income immigrant communities throughout the country, macro-forces engender economic conditions, neighborhood ecologies, and relational dynamics that systematically make it difficult if not impossible for immigrant parents to act as authentic and reliable sources of social and institutional support to their children. These stratifying forces do their work, in great part, through the *social decapitalization* of immigrant parent networks—by sustaining conditions that isolate immigrant parents and that deny them the ability to increase their own social and cultural capital, and thus the opportunity to mitigate the effects of neighborhood ecology, their acculturation status, and their low levels of formal education. Daily interactions between adolescents and their immigrant parents are usually plentiful and often loving, although such interactions, by structural design, are unable to transfer key forms of middle-class cultural capital. Nor can these interactions—no matter the degree of love and parental sacrifice involved—normally organize around the task of ensuring that children and adolescents will master the environment. As occupants of the social bottom, many of these youth are forced to negotiate the multiple borders and overlapping hierarchies that structure their lives without the aid of adult kin and other resourceful agents.

More importantly for us here, this decapitalization process also operates to systematically alienate low-status children and adolescents from the very people we hold accountable for developing these youths' creative, moral, and productive potential as soon-to-be adult members of society. Instances where parents do have the power to act as effective protective agents and sources of emotional and social support are systematically sabotaged by forces rooted in our society's dominant cultural system: the press toward unilinear acculturation (e.g., California's Proposition 227; the "English Only" Movement), which exacerbates cultural conflict in the home; the social isolation of immigrant parents, which leads to their overdependence on their adolescent children; our general ambivalence toward immigrants in society; the middle-class fetish around self-reliance; and young people's feelings of embarrassment emerging as a result of the stigma parents carry as low-income Latino immigrants charged with doing society's dirty work. As we shall discuss in Chapter 11, the social decapitalization of adolescent-agent relations among low-status youth is accomplished in distinctive ways across institutional arenas and social contexts (i.e., conditions that prevent the accumulation of social capital; see also Valenzuela, 1999). In these past three chapters, we've seen how this decapitalization is accomplished by the gradual estrangement of Latino youth from their immigrant parents, in spite of the love and commitment both parties may feel toward each other. In Chapter 9 we shall explore how this decapitalization is also accomplished in the arena of the school.

Part III

The School as a Context for Social and Institutional Support

8

Empowering Relations of Support Between Students and School Personnel

I think he's the greatest teacher in the whole world! . . . He's like a friend, he's like my second dad. I can ask him things that I couldn't ask my dad, and he knows things that my parents don't know.

—Rosario Zárate, in the United States since infancy

Seldom in the public arena do we seriously explore the possibility that teachers and guidance counselors do far more than teach and organize class schedules. In fact, they are often key participants in the social networks of low-status children and adolescents, and play a determining role in either reproducing or *interfering with the reproduction of* class, racial, and gendered inequality. To see this happen we must descend, somewhat like geologists, into the subterranean world of the school.

That the most important practices occurring within our public schools and classrooms happen at the tacit, hidden, or subterranean level, and that it is these practices that have the most lasting effects on children, are both premises lodged deeply in the sociology of education. Such notions are not easily or frequently communicated in the public discourse on education and low-income minority youth. It is these hidden social practices that motivate so many sociologists of education; yet they are also practices that need the light of public discourse, as well as the careful attention of teachers and other school agents who are continuing their professional training.

Conventional thinking defines the various roles assumed by school personnel (e.g., teachers and counselors) in terms of a narrow range of formal and professional duties; yet a good deal of research in schools strongly suggests that the multiple roles assumed by school agents, as well as the relations between agents and students, are far more complex and fascinating. The social position of teacher, for example, can be characterized by multiple roles and functions that are inherently inconsistent, ambiguous, and contradictory. Survival and long-term effectiveness require school personnel to learn to integrate those roles and duties that are amenable to integration, and to cope effectively with the tensions and ambiguities that prove irreconcilable. Such coping normally entails ongoing negotiation as well as moments of resistance.

The most salient tensions exist between a school agent's explicit professional responsibilities, his or her tacit roles and functions, and the moral imperatives inherent in the teacher/educator role. A teacher's explicit professional responsibilities are fairly straightforward: to develop students' literacy, provide academic support, enforce discipline, and develop talent. Yet the position of teacher is also weighted by a number of unofficial and latent roles and functions. Lodged within the core social networks of children and youth, and deeply implicated in their students' developmental histories, teachers and other school agents operate far beyond their function as pedagogues. School agents frequently find themselves acting as co-parents, informal mentors, child advocates, and informal psychologists. Yet the established social order of the school system also obligates school agents to act as purveyors of unequally distributed rewards and punishments, as gatekeepers and controllers of scarce resources, as self-interested and self-advocating members of unions, and as representatives, and often unwilling "agents," of a classist, sexist, and racialized societal order.

THESIS STATEMENTS

The moral dilemmas and imperatives inherent in the roles and daily lives of school personnel are quite real. How do teachers and counselors manage the tension between their role as agents of social reproduction and their role as co-parents and informal mentors? In schools where personnel interact with working-class and minority youth, this tension becomes exponentially more salient, particularly because the advocate-mentor role is one of considerable transformative power. Given the low structural position of these adolescents in the principal hierarchies in society, and the contradictory roles of school personnel as both agent-advocate and gatekeeper, relations between adult and student, when they become genuinely supportive, carry the potential to transform a student's life chances in very positive and lasting ways.

Even the concepts of social capital and institutional support become uncomfortably constrictive when we contemplate this transformative potential. Given the family and community circumstances of many of the youth we studied, school personnel many times went beyond the mere provision of institutional resources, classically defined; some, indeed, acted as co-parents and fictive kin. At moments, a few acted as co-conspirators against the established order. The existence of caring and nurturing relationships between students and school personnel became plainly evident. Instances of teachers and counselors providing emotional support and exhibiting loving parental behaviors emerged throughout our interviews and observations. The importance of these relationships and their impact on students were quite evident, as we shall soon see. Our data, therefore, leave no question that such relationships do emerge in schools serving working-class minority students. Whether such relationships constituted the norm at such schools is another matter, and one explored in this section of the book.

In network-analytic terms, the inclusion of one institutional agent in the social network of a youth from a working-class or low-income family carries far more potential transformative power than such an inclusion would carry in the social network of a typical middle-class youth. Of particular theoretical importance, then, is how supportive ties to school personnel potentially embody differential value and power, depending on the social background of the student.

Given the social order of the school and the contradictory roles, functions, and demands foisted on school personnel, to what extent are the latent and transformative powers of teachers and counselors given full expression? This particular section of the book, comprising three chapters, is devoted precisely to this important question. This chapter, drawing from our intensive interviews with students at Auxilio High, features remarkable instances of trusting and supportive relations with particular school agents, and explores how such relations were able to emerge. Also drawing from our interview data, Chapter 9 examines from the students' point of view how organizational features of the school may inadvertently make help-seeking behavior and the formation of supportive ties with school agents very difficult and stressful. Finally, Chapter 10 reports a series of quantitative and statistical analyses designed to capture the prevalence of supportive ties between students and school personnel. These analyses also explore some of the more probable antecedents associated with prosocial help-seeking orientations among adolescents and with actual help-seeking behavior within the school. Before we proceed, a brief description of Auxilio High's history and demographic characteristics is provided below.

DESCRIPTIVE PROFILE OF AUXILIO HIGH SCHOOL

Auxilio High School's relationship to the city of San Diego is set within the complex juxtaposition of established wealth and prosperity and segregated urban poverty; such juxtapositions are regularly found throughout the United States. Yet, when compared with other large cities in the country—New York City, Los Angeles, Chicago, Houston, Philadelphia, Detroit, San Francisco, Miami—"San Diego is comparatively a more affluent, better educated, still primarily native non-Hispanic white population, with a 4-to-1 ratio of professionals to laborers in its labor force" (Rumbaut, 1997, p. 4).[1] Most Auxilio High students, those from working-class or immigrant backgrounds, know they live in the midst of prosperity; they also know that their own communities are not sharing in the wealth generated by this city's economic boom.

Auxilio High School's history bears the legacy of mid-century White flight and of the demographic transformations of the 1980s. Founded at the turn of the century, Auxilio High School began as a predominantly middle-class Euro-American school, then recreated itself as an ethnically mixed and socioeconomically diverse school in the 1960s and 1970s, then finally transformed into a predominantly "Mexican school" in the 1980s and 1990s. Mexican-origin youth from Harrison Heights and the other adjacent neighborhoods have been part of Auxilio High's history since the early part of the century, but now they find themselves in the majority and without the ethnic and socioeconomic diversity and balance that characterized an earlier era. In the mid-1970s, Auxilio High underwent another major transformation when its turn-of-the century architecture was traded for an uninspired and cost-contained replacement. Security features throughout the school are abundant; windows are scarce. The school looks more like a modernized 17th-century coastal fortress than an institution of learning and cultural enrichment. Such are the realities of our contemporary ambivalence toward "other people's children" (see Grubb & Laserson, 1988). Issues of cost containment, security, and public miserliness toward urban segregated schools have historically tended to go together.

San Diego's school district is the nation's eighth largest; in 1990, the district enrolled 133,000 students, K through 12. And despite voluntary desegregation efforts, as in many other large districts, racial and socioeconomic segregation remain contested issues in San Diego (see Orfield, 1994). Although Latino/a students in the district's senior high schools represented about 24% (in 1991), their enrollment at Auxilio High hovered between 62 and 67% during the time of the study. And while Euro-Americans in senior high schools throughout the district constituted about 37% of the overall school population (in 1991), 4 of the 16 senior high schools exhibited slightly White majorities (50.2%, 51.2%, 54.7%, 62.5%). In contrast, the presence of White students at Auxilio High, mainly by way of the *International Baccalaureate* magnet program, stabilized at around 18%.[2] African American students during the period of the study constituted about 11% of the student body. Other groups represented at Auxilio High included Filipinos, Pacific Islanders, Indo-Chinese and Chinese, and American Indians. The Latino/a student population at the high school fluctuated the most. Due to the school's proximity to the border and to several Latino metropolitan neighborhoods, as well as the city's function as a corridor to the economies of Orange and Los Angeles counties, recent-immigrant students raised or lowered the school's enrollment by between 20 and 25% during the course of the year.[3]

Most students retained their fall semester teachers in the winter/spring semester. During the course of the academic year, most students had an average of eight teachers. As in many other urban high schools in the country, teacher composition did not begin to reflect the demographic composition of the student body. Although Auxilio High's principal was of Mexican origin, only about 15% of the full-time teaching faculty were Latino/a, a bit more than half of whom were either in Foreign Language, English as a Second Language (ESL), or Special Education. The overwhelming majority of the staff at Auxilio High was Anglo- or Euro-American.

Guidance counseling in many urban high schools is woefully inadequate, with student/counselor ratios that preclude any close monitoring of mid-achieving and low-achieving students. At Auxilio High, with only four full-time counselors and a student body fluctuating between 1,500 and 2,000, ratios ran from 375 to 500 students per guidance counselor. With two Latino counselors who were fluent in Spanish, and about a third of the student body Spanish-dominant, the ratio between Spanish-speaking counselors and students hovered around 200 to 1, not including bilingual students who preferred the bilingual counselors. We need to keep in mind that students were normally assigned to counselors alphabetically, and that many Spanish-dominant and bilingual students preferred seeking assistance from the counseling staff in their native language, if only as a measure of establishing relations of rapport and *confianza*. This means there was a significant *informal* trend toward Spanish-speaking counselors' carrying a heavier load. Periodic distress calls by Auxilio High's counseling staff for more personnel were typically met with blank or exasperated stares by district personnel.

Although by the 1980s, Auxilio High had gained a reputation as a "Mexican school" or "minority school," serious efforts were made to attract metropolitan and suburban Euro-American students as a part of the district's voluntary desegregation efforts. The great majority of Euro-American students enrolled at Auxilio High come for the school's International Baccalaureate magnet program, known as IB. "IB is a two-year preuniversity curriculum designed to prepare students for the intellectual demands of university study in nearly every country in the world. It was originally designed to meet the learning needs of expatriate students who wished to return to their own national systems for university study" (Greene, 1986, p. 16).

The IB program is widely recognized as the most challenging pre-university curriculum in the world. Although this high-powered curriculum has brought some of the city's most gifted teachers to Auxilio High, the real story here is that the program exists as a school within a school. At the time of the spring survey (May 1992), approximately 66% of surveyed Latino juniors and seniors had not enrolled in at least one IB course that school year, and only about 8% had taken six or more such courses. Of those surveyed Latino students who enrolled in one or two IB courses, the most frequent selection was Spanish literature. African Americans did not fare much better; about 65% of surveyed Black juniors and seniors had not taken one IB course that year. In contrast, 40% of surveyed Euro-American juniors and seniors reported not taking at least one IB course that year.[4]

EXPLORING SUPPORTIVE RELATIONS WITH TEACHERS AND COUNSELORS

We shall now explore how access to multiple forms of social and institutional support from school personnel is contingent on the establishment of relations of trust and positive sentiment. Close relations of trust and support between school agents and our adolescent subjects were most easily identified by their multiplex characteristics, that is, regular supportive interactions that involved tacit or explicit forms of emotional support and intimate counsel as well as institutional support.

Not all laudatory appraisals by adolescents pointed to a multiplex relationship that acted as a likely source of emotional support and intimate counsel; many times students made repeated use of a particular teacher or counselor solely as a source of informational or academic support. What clearly emerged in our interviews is that enactments of academic and institutional support by agents, when they did occur, signaled developing relations characterized by patience, a substantive degree of caring, and a responsiveness to the adolescent's special needs. This is to say that enactments of academic and institutional support did not occur in a social vacuum, or in some rationalized dispensing fashion; rather, they occurred in the context of authentic relations of trust and rapport.

Furthermore, our interview data also suggest that in many cases, when emotional support, moral support, and intimate counsel were provided, it was not the consequence of explicit adolescent help seeking, but rather the by-product of an ongoing caring relationship between a student and a school agent. Again, whether we speak of provisions of intimate counsel, emotional support—tacit or otherwise—or institutional support, the vehicle that carried such support was a caring and trusting relationship between adolescent and agent.

Through these caring relations, teachers and counselors emerged as very important participants in students' core support networks—networks often made precarious by perceptions on the part of the adolescent that alternative sources within the family were not currently available. In other words, adolescents often turned to trusted school agents when needed support from parents, family, and peers was deemed inaccessible. At other times, when support from these latter sources was available and effective, trusted school agents acted to supplement that support. Throughout our interviews, adolescents gave testimony that caring and nurturing relationships with school personnel provided the necessary conditions for them to persist in school or to survive an emotional crisis, such as the sudden death of a friend or parent or even the breakup with a boy- or girlfriend.

Methodological Overview

In determining how to present the interview findings for this chapter, I thought it would be useful to focus on the major types of positive appraisals articulated by adolescents when identifying different sources of adult support at school. Four main categories of appraisals emerged in the data, although by no means were these appraisals mutually exclusive. Their categorization only represents the relative emphasis placed on each by the adolescent.

The most common articulation had to do with fundamental qualities attributed both to the personality of the agent and to typical interactions with the adult. Issues of *confianza*, mutual respect, and informal mentorship formed the basis of these appraisals. Evidence of substantial emotional attachment usually also surfaced in these testimonies. The second category, clearly related to the first, had to do with qualities and competencies attributable to the agent's professional demeanor and persona. Appraisals of this sort conveyed that such qualities functioned to distinguish the agent from others at the school, making the agent quite attractive as a reliable and comfortable source of support. The third category pertained to appraisals that tended to focus on a specific problem or crisis, and on how an agent was found to be an effective and trustworthy source of support. Finally, the fourth category pertained to appraisals regarding past support. Here adolescents gave testimony to the history of their relationship with a particular agent and to the regular instances where they received valuable support. The ethnicity of teachers or counselors did not emerge as a major factor in these accounts; both White and Latino teachers and counselors were cited as positive sources of support. However, ethnicity (including social identity, social-class identifications, and language abilities of the adult) did emerge in students' accounts of dissatisfaction with particular school personnel, and this will be discussed in Chapter 9.

RELATIONS OF *CONFIANZA* AND INFORMAL MENTORSHIP

The quotation that began this chapter comes from Rosario Zárate, a mid- to low-achieving 12th-grader we visited in Chapter 5. Her richly multiplex relationship with Coach Shane, her biology teacher, exemplifies how school agents take on parent-like aspects. The relationship described by Rosario matured over the course of 3 academic years, going back to Rosario's first semester at Auxilio High. Rosario confidently stated that she could ask Shane for anything, and said she consistently relied on him for academic and informational support, intimate counsel, and emotional support, as well as for a variety of miscellaneous favors. Her dependence on Shane is all the more evident when we see that she reported only one other staff person as a source of support, Coach McGuire.

Yet we can fully comprehend Shane's importance in her life only when we also understand how stressful Rosario's last year at Auxilio High was turning out to be. Rosario's accumulated sense of low academic self-esteem was easily apparent. At moments, a sense of despair over her academic difficulties in school overcame her. When she was prompted to talk about the possibilities of college, tears began to well in Rosario's eyes. "When you talk about college I feel stupid talking about it because I've always had bad grades. It's like I feel dumb even thinking about college. It's just [long pause] I don't want to talk about it." Rosario, as with many other students we interviewed, felt caught in a perilous current—a set of circumstances she felt she could not change. She was resigned or determined to ride it out, to survive, to get by, with the hope that she could find the right current later, perhaps during the following year, or once she enrolled at a community college—given that she finished high school. For Rosario, persisting through high school completion was the immediate goal. Meanwhile, she saw Shane as her lifeline, one of the few adults at the school she could trust to be fully responsive to her many special needs.

The fondness and emotional attachment many students felt toward key teachers served as important sources of academic motivation and resiliency. Throughout our interviews, the notion that schooling occurs in the contexts of real human relationships became abundantly evident. María Toledo, a mid- to low-achieving 11th-grader we visited earlier, described her drama teacher, Ms. Keaton, as a teacher, a mentor, and a friend, someone she could comfortably go to for various types of support. Although María defined their relationship as one of teacher and student, she felt that this designation didn't readily communicate the mutual friendship and "fun" embodied in their routine interactions. "Sometimes it's not like that [typical teacher-student relations]; sometimes it's like friends, that we talk; [pauses] I trust her. I feel comfortable."

In more than a few instances, close relations between teacher and student emerged after some disagreement or minor conflict, or after the teacher took some disciplinary action against the student. María spoke of an occasion when Ms. Keaton, her drama teacher, reprimanded her for being disruptive and unhelpful during a rehearsal. María subsequently ditched a number of classes, feeling embarrassed by the episode. "When I came back, she was happy I was back, because she says that, well, I'm her favorite student. We're not mad at each other any more." Having ditched, María was waiting for rejection and reprisal, but instead received not only a welcome, but a gesture that made her feel very special. From this point on, María became Ms. Keaton's fervent supporter and ally.

In many other cases, close attachments to school agents seemed to emerge out of a series of episodes that created a basis for lasting trust. These relationships can truly be appreciated only when viewed within the larger context in which routine interactions with school personnel are more typically characterized by emotional guardedness and impersonality. Relations of *confianza* with school personnel were never a given at Auxilio High. It seemed, instead, that students entered new relations with school personnel with heavy armor and then waited to see whether it was safe to divest. Some students, unfortunately, became too accustomed to their armor even to consider occasionally lightening their load.

Different groups of students appeared to have different motives for self-protection. Recent immigrants, while motivated to appraise their new school in positive terms, felt that their limited language proficiency and their marginal status as newcomers restricted them to the core of ESL teachers officially charged with their care. Many of the other students, long-term immigrants and the native-born, carried with them the lessons of unsponsored independence and impersonality that had defined their schooling experience since their entrée into junior high school. In any case, caring relations with school personnel emerged as revelations, founded on interactions and episodes that shed light on an agent's nurturing and supportive capabilities. Elena Guerrero, the mid-achieving senior visited in Chapter 5, admitted to being normally shy in public, so when a friend encouraged her to try out for the cheerleading squad, she initially refused. Her friend insisted, and Elena eventually tried out and won a place on the squad. A number of highly supportive relationships with school agents subsequently followed her initiation as a school cheerleader, particularly her relationship with Ms. Rogers, a teacher who formally sponsored the squad. In reference to her experience as a cheerleader, Elena recognized, "It has been one of the most wonderful experiences in my life." Evidently, her entrée into this new social world was most timely. She credited Ms. Rogers for encouraging her to stay in school during a period when she considered dropping out. "There was a time when I just didn't want to go to school, and I'd talk to her about it and she'd say, 'If you just stick it out now, it will be worth it.' And I know that she's there for everybody, not just cheerleaders." Yet Elena admitted that she was quite leery of Ms. Rogers in the beginning. "At first I didn't trust her because, I guess, people have to prove themselves to me first." It appears that Ms. Rogers did just that, by agreeing to sponsor the cheerleaders and inviting them to sleep over at her house. "She had us sleep over, so I guess that's how we got close." In time, their relationship became quite multiplex. To stay on the cheerleading squad, Elena needed to maintain a 2.5 grade-point average, and Ms. Rogers made it a point to monitor her academic progress and to advocate for her when the occasion arose. As a cheerleader, Elena found that other school agents also became key sources of support.

Mr. Nielsen, the head counselor at Auxilio High, came to figure prominently in her core network of support, as both an informal mentor and a role model. Elena described Nielsen as a highly competent counselor who is fair and who could be relied on for sound advice and guidance. In her own terms, "I can count on him for anything. He will always be there if I have a dispute with a teacher. He won't take sides until he hears the whole thing. I know that he will not, just because she or he is a teacher, he will not automatically take their side. So he's a really good counselor." Mr. Nielsen also served as a sounding board when her parents' restrictions on her social life became unbearable. "He helped me to realize that everything comes to those who wait." Elena also commented that earlier in the year she found herself repeatedly postponing a minor medical operation, and Nielsen persuaded her to set up an appointment and go through with it. She admitted that his encouragement and support gave her the courage to go through what was, for her, a stress-provoking medical procedure. Asked whether she ever hesitated before seeking support from Nielsen, she stated that she always feels comfortable approaching him, "because I know he won't criticize me."

Overall, a picture emerges of a school agent as a confidant and informal mentor, providing the type of support she could never imagine receiving from her father—given the circumstances at home. Through her regular interactions with this caring counselor, Elena was able to sort out her feelings, develop sensible approaches to her problems, improve her academic standing, and maintain her personal sense of balance. Under these conditions, help seeking and help giving appear to lose their clinical connotations, becoming embedded within an ongoing relationship that is mutually gratifying to agent and adolescent.

Mr. Nielsen frequently emerged in the accounts of other students we interviewed. The complex dynamics through which trust and rapport are forged are particularly illustrative in Salvador Baca's account of his early interactions with Nielsen. Salvador came across as a particularly astute, forthright, and streetwise senior with keen insights into adolescent emotions, interpersonal relations, and the many affiliational pressures within the school and in the neighborhoods. I soon learned of his knack for fluidly moving in and out of different groups and social cliques at school while maintaining a certain autonomy. Salvador was noticeably school-weary and somewhat uncertain as to how he had survived in school given his poor academic record. He carried with him a number of emotional burdens as well as memories of past traumatic experiences that awaited future resolution. Yet I was left with little doubt that Salvador was a determined and aspiring young man.

His own orientation toward help seeking reveals the same fundamental ambivalence evident in the accounts of so many of the others we interviewed. For Salvador, the connection between help seeking and "makin' it" as an adult is quite clear.

> I've always been attracted to find somebody who talks about how to make it, you know. If I see the opportunity to learn from the person, I'll go for it, you know what I mean? Whether I'm gonna look stupid by asking stupid questions or whatever; or whether I'm gonna you know, break out with real emotional problems, or whatever. But as long as I can get it into my head that I can make it. You know, no matter how hard it's been, no matter how hard it's gonna be, I can still make it. I've met a lot of people, from the university, other people, Mexicans, homeboys *también* [as well], you know, that have made it. People like that, you know, have influenced me. They get the point across.

Yet Salvador was also aware of his own ambivalence toward approaching certain people, in this case Mr. Nielsen. Here, issues of gender becomes quite explicit.

> I wouldn't go to Mr. Nielsen, I used to hate him, you know. He's helped me out a lot, I give him a lot of credit. I wouldn't go to him; I

don't know, I wouldn't go to another guy for help. If I had a problem, I'd always go to a girl, whether it was school, personal, or whatever; and that would affect me in school, because if I had a really bad problem, I couldn't concentrate on my schoolwork. When I needed a guy's point of view of a problem, I could never go to another guy because, being *macho*, you know, another guy can't see you cry.

Salvador's eventual connection to Nielsen seems partly attributable to his propensity for hanging out in varied social spaces within the school, including the counseling office. It turns out that Salvador often accompanied his classmate and close friend, Miranda, as she regularly visited her mother, a clerical worker in the counseling office. On many occasions after school, Salvador chatted with Miranda's mother and the various counselors and paraprofessionals who congregated to gossip and muse about the latest school events. This provided Salvador within an opportunity to build rapport with Mr. Nielsen and with other school agents and to find out what in their lives had special relevance for him. In reference to Mr. Nielsen, Salvador commented:

He's the one that mostly influenced me; 'cause, I mean, for a while, my grades and everything were fucked up. *Y él me decía que no, que* I'm not gonna make it [And he'd tell me that no, that I'm not going to make it]. I mean, everyone would tell me, you know, like, "I don't think you'll be able to go to college 'cause your grades, you know, unless you work on your grade point average," and all this shit, you know. But, he told me in different ways that I could do it. You know, I kind of liked the way he did it, you know. I'll be going to a community college, getting my two years, you know, the A.A., whatever you call it. And that transfer program, they automatically accept you to the U.C. system.[5]

How Mr. Nielsen came to assume a place of extraordinary significance in Salvador's life is most informative. Asked to explain how and why Nielsen came to be so influential, Salvador asserted:

'Cause he's the one that, although he's not Mexican, you know, he's White, but still, *you know*. He was in jail. Um, he went to the war. He was a little bit of a fuck up, you know, but look where he's at now. Making a lot of money, bought a new house, bought a new car.
        RSS: So he's been through some rough times?

> Yeah; the same way as every typical Mexican that you know from the *barrio* that would be like, you know, causing trouble; he was the same way. You feel that a person that had it easy doesn't know where you're really coming from. They don't really know how you're struggling.

Asked to clarify his own notions of what it means to make it, Salvador stated:

> . . . getting out of the *barrio*, living in a place that's stable, a good environment. Working somewhere where you don't have to put up with the bullshit of, "Are they going to fire you tomorrow, are you going to get laid off." That your son got beat up on the way home from school because your boy is the wrong color, you know, shit like that. That's makin' it.

For Salvador, Mr. Nielsen represented not only a laudable standard of success, but a reasonable and accessible one. Although Nielsen is White, evidence of class *co-membership* overshadowed the potentially distancing influence of race. Salvador was able to reframe Nielsen as someone who faced a similar working-class existence, who survived the temptations of the streets *and* the ravages of war, and who, in the end, triumphed. Yet his identification with Nielsen went beyond Nielsen's personal account of his youth, finding repeated reinforcement in an authority figure whose speech, dress, and personal demeanor tacitly signaled enduring working-class loyalties while simultaneously demonstrating he had reaped the benefits of middle-class life.

Many other accounts by students focused on the nurturing qualities and extraordinary supportive efforts of various teachers and counselors. Evident in these accounts is the affection and respect students felt for these adult figures. Lilia Escarza, who described herself as a loner and as someone who experienced difficulty trusting others, nonetheless found a reliable source of support through Coach Shane. "He's not just a teacher; he's a friend. . . . I feel great about it, because, you know, I feel I can go to him at any time."

Antonio Barrera, a high-achieving senior who had lived in the United States since age 7, described his relationship with his physics teacher, Mr. Hines, as a playful one, with a lot of teasing and joking between the two. Mr. Hines was also known for playing casual basketball with his students. Yet one could sense the respect Antonio felt for this teacher. Mr. Hines tutored Antonio in physics, as he apparently did for many other students, during lunch period and after school.

He has his lunch in class, except on Wednesday when he has a staff meeting. There are always kids in there. [Pauses.] He's fun to be around with; I think he understands a lot about where people are coming from. [Regarding playful joking.] I don't think he takes it too seriously. You expect the same from him as what you give to him.

Through his tutoring and recreational experiences with Mr. Hines, Antonio had come to see this teacher as an approachable and reliable source of other forms of support. Mr. Hines appeared as a teacher with a fluid and expansive conception of his role as teacher. Through humor and play, combined with a visible devotion to his area of expertise, Hines was able to establish a relatively high comfort level with his students. Here, knowledge of physics was imparted in the context of caring and even playful relations between teacher and student. Students, however, gained much more than knowledge of physics; they also gained an additional and reliable adult link in their school-based social network.

Alejandro Ponce, brother of Aida, who also attended Auxilio High, was an 11th-grader and a participant in the school ROTC. Both siblings are native-born. As with Aida, his grades were a combination of As and Bs. Like Lilia Escarza, Alejandro described himself as someone who kept his personal problems to himself. His participation in ROTC enabled him to develop a binding relationship with Mr. Horner, an older man who, by Alejandro's account, acted like a caring uncle or *padrino* (godfather). I came to learn that Mr. Horner was usually quite informed about what was happening in the personal life of this supposedly private young man. I also saw that the special attention Alejandro enjoyed was accorded to other students who similarly found in ROTC a tightly-knit community overseen by a caring mentor.

> *Mr. Horner? He's good people, he helps people a lot, like when we, the whole group, go to some place, like to Magic Mountain, and you see that someone is poor and doesn't have any money and they say, "No, I can't go with you guys," he, Mr. Horner, gives him money and everything. One time he bought me tennis shoes, I didn't have any tennis shoes, [laughs] and I wore those damn tennis shoes for awhile, until I got a job and I was able to buy myself a pair.*

Many of the close relationships we documented developed through interactions outside of normal academic or administrative routines, through participation in school organizations or clubs, athletic teams, formal extracurricular activities, remedial classes, after-school detention, or special elective courses. For some students, like Salvador, such relationships emerged through casual interactions within those few social spaces conducive to bringing staff and students together informally; the large and spacious counseling office at Auxilio High was one of the few places on campus that afforded such opportunities.[6]

ORGANIZATIONAL PARTICIPATION

Given that organizational participation represents a major avenue for establishing close supportive ties to school agents, how many Latinos at Auxilio High were placing themselves in this avenue? We examined non-athletic organizational participation for both Latinos and non-Latinos at Auxilio High. Table 8.1 displays our findings on organizational participation. We see that organizational involvement for Latinos was quite low, with only 25.5% of Latinos reporting some participation. Among Latinos, girls did tend to be slightly more involved than boys. Thus, for most students, the development of informal and close relationships was dependent on near-random, accidental occurrences. Salvador happened to find him-

TABLE 8.1. Organizational Participation (Percentage of each group who participated in a nonathletic school-based organization, Auxilio High School, N = 1082)

Variables	ETHNO-LINGUISTIC GROUPS[*]				
	Latino (English-proficient)	Latino (Spanish-dominant)	African American	Asian	Euro-Am. (White)
Males and Females	28.2% (n = 309)	23.4% (n = 389)	38.6% (n = 114)	43.6% (n = 55)	48.8% (n = 215)
Males Only	20.7% (n = 145)	20.2% (n = 223)	30.4% (n = 56)	39.3% (n = 28)	45.4% (n = 97)
Females Only	34.8% (n = 164)	27.7% (n = 166)	46.6% (n = 58)	48.2% (n = 27)	51.7% (n = 118)

[*]Native Americans (N = 5) were not included in this table because of the small number of students in this category.

self with an opportunity to get to know Mr. Nielsen on a very personal level, yet it could just as easily not have happened. Most low-status students in the same precarious position as Salvador do not have a Mr. Nielsen embedded in their social web of support. Elena just happened to have a friend who insisted that she try out for the cheerleading squad. Then one night Elena happened to find herself in the home of a caring teacher; yet her story easily could have evolved very differently. Antonio took physics from a teacher with a knack for building relationships with students through verbal play, the basketball court, and lunchtime tutorial sessions. These were adolescent webs made perilous by the exceptionality of good fortune and by the consistency of negative class forces that impinged on their daily lives.

When not speaking of the fundamental aspects of a teacher's or counselor's personality or life story, adolescents frequently addressed an agent's professional demeanor and persona. Such accounts reveal students' capacity for assessing teachers and counselors based on rationalistic and professional criteria. Students generally held school personnel to very high standards and, as we shall see in Chapter 9, they became quite irate when personally affected by an agent's perceived incompetence or lack of professionalism. On the other hand, students were often generous in their praise when they were able to benefit directly from interactions with a school agent deemed exceptional.

Susana Beltrán, a high-achieving immigrant student with only 2½ years in the United States, spoke glowingly of Ms. Rollins, who helped her transition out of ESL English in a very short time. Susana considered Rollins to be the very best ESL teacher at the school, emphasizing Rollins's patience, her caring demeanor, and great sense of humor. Although no longer in Rollins's class, Susana admitted to returning regularly to Ms. Rollins for assistance with assignments from other classes. Susana also spoke of Ms. Castañeda, her assigned counselor during the previous year. She admitted to continued visits to Castañeda, in spite of a newly assigned counselor, because of the degree of trust and rapport established during the previous year. She especially appreciated the fact that Castañeda consulted with each student and asked for his or her individual opinions as she worked to arrange a student's schedule.

Marisol Urquilla, another high-achieving immigrant, similarly found Ms. Castañeda's way with students praiseworthy. Asked to describe her relationship with Castañeda, Marisol commented: "*Well, she's like my counselor, it's like she tries to be friends with the students; and that's what makes you trust her.*" Marisol freely talked to Castañeda about the difficulties she encountered planning for college, given her problematic status as an undocumented immigrant. Various court decisions affecting the enrollment of undocumented persons and foreign nationals, and the disparate policies across California's state university and community college systems, made college planning quite an awesome feat for most undocumented students at Auxilio High.[7] That a good number of such students were doing well academically and were highly motivated made the situation more contentious among students and counselors.

It is important to note here that successfully confronting these obstacles was again dependent on the help-seeking initiative of the student and on relations of *confianza* between student and counselor. Auxilio High maintained no formal or systematic policy or counseling service to address the special post–high school needs of undocumented students. Marisol was one student who did receive extensive help with various scholarship possibilities that would compensate for her ineligibility for federal financial aid. Her close relationship with Castañeda provided the necessary assurances to allow Marisol to comfortably discuss her precarious legal situation, as well as her aspirations for social mobility in her new country.

Antonio Barrera's description of his English teacher, Ms. Roberts, differed in important ways from his characterization of Mr. Hines, yet both descriptions shared a common theme. First, the teachers' personalities were vastly different. Antonio stated that initially, Roberts came across to students as a strict, no-nonsense teacher. In Antonio's own words: "Everybody used to think that you had to be polite, to look kind of straight, but now that I've gotten to know her, she's real, you know, a loose kind of person [personable]. She doesn't mind if you say something wrong. She'll correct you, but not in a negative way. She's OK." In reference to her capacity as a source of academic support: "She's real open about if you need help. She's always there. She makes time out on Tuesdays and Thursdays for whoever needs help." While Antonio's description of Mr. Hines reveals students' attraction to a teacher who combines a colorful character with a visible commitment to students' academic learning, his description of Ms. Roberts reveals that teachers also gain students' trust and respect by genuinely acting as dedicated and caring professionals. Students encountered little funny business in Ms. Roberts's classroom, but behind Ms. Roberts's austere demeanor, students recognized a real person, a dedicated and personable teacher, and a reliable source of academic support.

Our adolescent subjects were also noticeably moved when they saw a teacher or counselor assume the *extra-officio* duties of co-parent, advocate, or informal therapist. Given the many stressors these students confronted in their daily lives, opportunities for school personnel to act in these capacities were potentially abundant. Yet, more often than not, a teacher or a counselor became aware of a student's plight only when a relationship of trust and rapport was already in place. Below, we consider a number of exemplary cases in which students' appraisals focused on a specific problem or crisis.

Lourdes Acuña, a senior and a mid- to high-achiever with 3 years in the United States, grieved over the loss of both of her parents who had recently died within 4 months of each other. Lourdes's mother died of a heart attack at 60, and her father of pneumonia at 94. These deaths occurred between our first meeting with Lourdes and our follow-up interview in the spring. Besides the profound sense of loss Lourdes was feeling, she was also coping with the fact that her friends had not really been there for her. Lourdes explains how her combined experiences of loss and disappointment changed her life:

> *Now my life has changed. Everything changed for me, as if it's made me more independent, tougher. But when one doesn't have their parents* [pauses] *it's different. They understand everything* [pauses] *you never cared about anything else or anyone else. Yeah the others were there, O.K., but they weren't always there. But now that I don't have my parents, when I need a friend or one of my brothers, I notice when they're not there for me. It was different before, because all the attention and all the love I got from my parents filled all the empty space of my life. And now when a friend lets me down or something, I notice it and that's when these feelings surfaced* [pauses] *like now I don't think that my friends that I had before are as important. I needed them more after the death of my parents,* [pauses] *"my friends," and I say that in quotation marks, to Tonia, to Daniel, to Humberto, to the other Daniel, and to Veronica. I expected them to understand more, to be more supportive. Like when they invite you to go out to take your mind off things, things like that, a telephone call, whatever, and no, they didn't do that.*

Lourdes explained that in her time of grief, it was Mr. Puente, the detention officer and Spanish-speaking community aide at Auxilio High, who stepped in and helped fill the void. With his help, she said, she was able to continue school, while coping with her sudden and painful loss. Lourdes saw Mr. Puente as a friend and a constant, reliable source of emotional and social support. She credited him for his sensitivity and for knowing how to calm her down. In her own words: *"Whenever I talk to him, I feel more secure, more at ease."*

The death of Lourdes's parents set into motion a series of important network-specific social dynamics: the realization of her new emotional dependency on her older siblings; the awareness that her "friends" were unreliable, if not vacuous, sources of support; and the knowledge that she somehow needed to cope effectively with her new aloneness. Because she was an immigrant adolescent living in a low-income community, Lourdes's tragedy and tenuous support network could easily have rendered her invisible. Yet, through Mr. Puente's efforts, the school provided a web of relations that offered the regularity and support that Lourdes needed to continue her life in a constructive, resilient, and healing manner.

Soledad Arroyo, another high-achieving immigrant student, again conveys the role that school personnel play in helping minority adolescents manage the social and psychological burdens they carry with them to school. In January, Soledad contemplated dropping out of school to care for her sick mother. Both her mother and Ms. McKinney, her ESL teacher, advised, if not insisted, that she stay in school. Soledad's threat appears to have served more as a distress signal than as a real intention to drop out. Through this episode, Soledad was able to share with Ms. McKinney, an older Latina woman, many aspects of her home life that proved emotionally taxing. Ms. McKinney, in turn, responded with generous and genuine support. On a different occasion, Soledad shared with Ms. McKinney her desire to find part-time employment in order to help her mother financially. Again, Ms. McKinney advised her to reconsider. As Soledad explained it: "I told the teacher, Ms. McKinney, I told her that I wanted to work, because, well, to help my mom, but she told me to first concentrate on my studies, that if I worked, I wouldn't get much sleep and my grades would go down. So, I didn't look for a job."

As with many recent-immigrant students at Auxilio High, Soledad's ties to school personnel were restricted to Spanish-speaking ESL teachers. But even such ready access to Spanish-speaking personnel did not automatically translate into social capital for immigrant students. During our initial network survey, Soledad failed to indicate any ties to teachers or counselors. Only with our follow-up interview did she mention Ms. McKinney, a teacher Soledad was only beginning to see as a trustworthy and comfortable source of social and institutional support. And with this one source, Soledad had already received the guidance and support she needed to avoid making choices that would have seriously compromised her academic status and future life chances.

Social capital is said to embody a form of power that can make people do things they would not otherwise do unless under pressure or enforced obligation. Throughout our interviews and observations, students regularly conveyed how they were often at the mercy of a counselor's authority and discretion, particularly in terms of scheduling. For many students, individual appeals or exhortations for schedule changes or for counselor intervention did not bring the desired results. Other students learned to mobilize their social capital, and in doing so, learned an important lesson in how high-status and highly *capitalized* adults often get their way in the worlds of business, bureaucracy, and civic life.

Aida Ponce, sister of Alejandro, was a senior and a member of the school ROTC as well as a member of the girls' varsity volleyball team. She talked insightfully about the multiple functions of coaches, and of the symbiotic relationship between the coaches and student athletes:

> The coaches need you to play for them; but while they need you to play for them, they need to make sure that you have the grades and everything, so they're being like a counselor also. To help you, they sometimes go to the counselors and talk to them. They deal with them, so that you can get wherever you need to go.

Aida offered an example of just how her volleyball coach intervened once on her behalf:

> I went to Coach Davis because I was failing a chemistry class and my counselor didn't want to let me out of it, and I was afraid the class would hurt my GPA. It was like a 2.7; it wasn't a great GPA, and I didn't want to make it worse. And so Coach Davis went and talked to the counselor and said that it was hurting my playing, that they needed me playing; she made up all this stuff, and then they got me out of the class.

Whether another approach to Aida's problem might have been more beneficial for her certainly merits consideration. Nonetheless, we begin to see that students' ability to exercise control over their lives, as well as their ability to influence the decision making of school personnel, is significantly associated with their accumulated school-based social capital—in this case, a connection with a coach willing to intervene assertively on a team member's behalf.

The most reliable accounts of students' close and multiplex relations with school personnel came when students spoke of a relationship with a particular agent extending over several years. Here we found adolescents citing a number of different instances when an agent provided valuable support, under varied circumstances. Coaches, again, appear to take a special place in students' school-based networks of support.

Mateo Hinojosa was a U.S.-born 11th-grader who earned Cs in most of his classes. He was a varsity football player and, in the spring, a member of the track and field team. Mateo found in football a vehicle for personal accomplishment and social esteem, and hoped to continue into college football, thus continuing his education while playing the sport he loved. Through his athletic pursuits, Mateo had been able to build relationships with a number of coaches who, in turn, have acted as informal mentors and as sources of multiple forms of support.

Mateo spoke warmly of Coach Thompson, his football and track and field coach. Over several years, Thompson had provided Mateo with academic support and advice and guidance on school matters, as well as intimate counsel and emotional support. In our original network survey, Thompson appeared as a source of eight types of support. Mateo indicated that on a number of occasions, Thompson has spoken to teachers on his behalf. Mateo went on to explain that Thompson always seemed to be there when he needed him, even providing an occasional ride home from school or money for snacks or for the bus. Mateo tried to emphasize that most of Thompson's supportive behavior was *instrumental* in nature. This emphasis makes sense in the context of Youniss and Smollar's (1985) analysis of interactions between father and son, with 48% of interactions classified as instrumentalist ("teach me things," "give me advice about my future," "give knowledge to me").[8] When asked to share how he felt when asking for help from Coach Thompson, Mateo, with a deep and resonating voice, explained it this way: "*Na, just straight out, hey I need help with this, how do you do this? Just like that, straight out, nothing out of the ordinary, everything's fine.*" Mateo stated that he didn't like to talk about personal stuff with others, unless they were very close family, or were like close family. He did eventually admit to sharing intimate details of his life with Thompson on several occasions, but he preferred to talk about his more instrumental exchanges with his coach. Again, on further probing, we learned that Thompson provided a good deal of intimate counsel, but that most of this support occurred not as a result of Mateo's help-seeking initiatives, but rather as by-products of routine interactions between coach and athlete.

Mateo also talked extensively about his relationship with Coach Shane. Similar to his multiplex relationship with Thompson, Mateo indicated Shane as a likely source of 11 forms of support. Mateo initially met Shane in the seventh grade, then didn't see him again until his first year at Auxilio High. He described his relationship with Shane in this manner: "He's a teacher of U.S. history . . . and everybody respects him as a teacher and a counselor. When I was in his class, he made me work, man. He's like the only teacher that ever made me work. He makes you think about the future and stuff like that." Mateo also commented on Shane's honest and forthright way with students: "He talks to you, you know like . . . heart to heart. He tells you what's up. But he's also got an attitude. But, I mean, it helps you real good later on. You know, he's cool." Beside Coaches Thompson and Shane, Mateo also was close to Coach McGuire, a reported likely source of 10 forms of support. Mateo has similar things to say about McGuire, who also acted as an informal mentor and who is a strong authority figure. He too was characterized as a "friend" and a reliable source of support.

As with the other coaches, McGuire's connection with Mateo is situated within a larger collective of coaches and student athletes who embrace similar goals and values.[9] Like a tight-knit family, the team is headed by coaches who exhibit many parent-like functions; also similar to family structure, a coach's authority over an individual athlete is tied to his or her authority over the team. Authority and discipline occur in the context of goal-striving, rationalized in terms of rewards and privileges experienced both individually and collectively, and overlain with strong affect and loyalty commitments.

When *multistranded* relations between student and teacher are contrasted with similar relations between coaches and the student athlete, the latter appear to be far more explicit and publicly visible. Multistranded relationships are those involving multiple roles or functions, compared with multiplex relations, which I have described as entailing multiple forms of support. The two are clearly related, but conceptually they are independent. Although teachers often take on the latent and multiple functions of co-parent, social worker, and informal mentor, the manifestation of these functions in routine interactions between coaches and athletes appear not only more explicit and visible, but also more positively sanctioned by the school system. Teachers get the message that they should concentrate on their teaching; in contrast, coaches are usually expected to expend the requisite time and energy to ensure that other areas of a student-athlete's life are in order: academics, personal health, family life, and the minimization of high-risk behaviors.

For many student athletes, the coach emerges as both the master builder of their social network and the wellspring of many forms of social and institutional support. Throughout our interviews, student athletes consistently spoke of being taken to local and distant places for both competitive events and recreation, of learning to work hard and stay on the "straight and narrow," and finally, of having an advocate at school ready and willing to intervene administratively on their behalf.

However, an important caveat is in order. Amid the ranks of high school coaches across the country, particularly in the highly competitive male sports domains of football and basketball, are coaches reputed to be overzealous and self-serving mini-chieftains of the sports world (Messner, 1992, pp. 102–105). These coaches appear willing to subordinate their athletes' academic and moral well-being to championships, school prestige, team rivalries, or a lucrative sports scholarship for a star athlete. Many male high school athletic teams also carry the mark of subcultural formation (Eckert, 1989). Under certain conditions, we find athletes creating distinctive modes of expression, norms, and meaning systems that function to create a sense of solidarity and group identity, separate and apart, although never independent, from the greater student body.

The issue here is that such athletic youth subcultures often appropriate the most noxious elements and contradictions of their patriarchal-capitalist parent culture. Athletes thus revel in their exaggerated cultural style, establishing their dominance both on the field and in the quad through a male supremacist discourse that ultimately denies them the means to interrogate critically their own exploitative socialization by economic interests and self-serving adults—including their own coaches. In the final analysis, coaches embody several contradictory potentials: On the one hand, coaches often do maximize their special position within the school, functioning in a multiplicity of ways to empower student athletes' academic, moral, and social development; yet on the other hand, as mini-chieftains of a male-dominated and ruthlessly competitive sports world, they sometimes succumb to inculcating modes of thought and expression rooted in what many feminist writers see as the darkest substratum of our mainstream culture.[10]

As we have already seen, nonathletes also made special references to coaches, most often when they served as classroom teachers. Coaches in the classroom were attributed a special status, and were viewed as having qualities that altered the usual dynamics between student and teacher, thus making them attractive and approachable sources of support. Students knew coaches as school agents who were already intimately involved in the personal and social lives of student-athletes. They saw coaches as people who were much more in touch with, and responsive to, a young person's many (nonacademic) needs. Given that coaches were readily seen as having to manage multiple formal functions within the school, students correctly perceived a coach's position as teacher as more open, fluid, and multistranded. Coaches, of course, do not have a monopoly on multistranded renditions of their role as school-based institutional agents, although it does appear that they have a slight built-in advantage. As I have already shown, many teachers are quite motivated to reconfigure their positions as school agents, and students do respond accordingly.

Classroom subject matter and classroom organization also play a significant role in shaping relations between teacher and student. Some attention has already been paid in the research literature to important contextual influences on help seeking. In another work (Stanton-Salazar, 2000), I mention some of these organizational arrangements within the classroom:

... the nature and organization of tasks, including rules, procedures and norms for carrying out these tasks, the allocation of roles, opportunities for publicly demonstrating diverse competencies, and finally, evaluation procedures. These structures, whether within the workplace or the school site, not only dictate the conditions and norms under which resources are shared and how the transfer of support is interpreted (Ames, 1983; Nelson Le-Gall, 1985), but also how individual performance and competency is socially interpreted. (Simpson & Rosenholtz, 1986, pp. 215–216)

These classroom structures, of course, also dictate the kind and quality of relations between teacher and student. Yet high school teachers vary in terms of the degree of restriction they face in reorganizing curriculum and social relations within the classroom. Some teachers are afforded many opportunities, given the nature, organization, and objectives of their classroom curriculum.

Juan Santiago, a mid-achieving 11th-grader who has spent most of his life in the United States, talked at length about his close relationship with Mr. Carlton, his auto-mechanics teacher. Student-teacher interactions within the shop appear qualitatively different from those in other classrooms where more college-oriented subject matter is taught. Students in Carlton's shop come highly motivated to engage the subject matter; the tasks assigned are often conducted with peer support; and there exist many opportunities for help seeking as well as for good-natured conversation with the teacher. The fundamentals of trust and rapport are often built while working over the motor of a student's car. Juan spoke to Mr. Carlton every day, and felt that he could go to him for help with any issue, including academic problems brought from other classrooms. *"I tell him, 'Oh!! I'm having a problem with my homework in this class,' or 'I failed this test,' things like that."* Juan viewed Carlton as someone who could help him with anything and with whom he could converse with on an informal basis. *"He can help you with math, anything. I mean, and* [voice trails off]. *It's a good situation, I go almost every day. Every day he says hi to me. Sometimes we talk about stuff, you know, about school."*

We see here that more goes on in Carlton's shop than the learning of auto-mechanics. We also see that close ties with a teacher in one classroom, even in auto shop, can translate into academic assistance with work assigned in other classes. And again, interesting network dynamics were at work here. Juan's mathematics teacher, Ms. Carlton, was married to Mr. Carlton and both were cited as multiplex relations of support. Moreover, the affect and trust involved in Juan's relation with Ms. Carlton was buttressed and strengthened by his relationship with Mr. Carlton, and vice versa. Juan viewed his relationship with Ms. Carlton as *"poquito más de una profesora* [something more than just a teacher]." As a teacher, however, she received high marks from Juan: "She's like a clown sometimes. She makes it [math] interesting and fun. *Es fácil aprender; bien fácil* [It's easy to learn, real easy]." As with Mr. Carlton, Juan relied on this math teacher for much more than help with his algebra; over time, Ms. Carlton had assisted Juan with course scheduling and college planning. Juan carried with him a history of supportive and caring relations with both Carltons.

The fact that both sources were intimately connected increased the individual influence and power of each teacher. In this case, Juan's relation with Ms. Carlton cannot be divorced from his relation with Mr. Carlton; one informed the other, and Juan knew it. Such is the basis of most of the influence and normative pressure embodied in tightly knit network relations (Boissevain, 1974; Coleman, 1988). The same influence is exerted by coaches over student-athletes—alienate one coach and you risk forfeiting the support of the entire coaching staff. Influence, power, and institutional support, the holy trinity of sociology, comprise the basic stuff of all network relations. Some students are afforded opportunities to learn this lesson to their advantage; many, however, are not.

THE AVID PROGRAM AT AUXILIO HIGH

In this penultimate section, I wish to showcase one classroom and one teacher that richly embodied the potential of urban high schools to enrich and *capital*-ize the social webs of working-class minority adolescents. In no other place did classroom organization so profoundly affect teacher-student relations than in Ms. Michaels's room, and nowhere did we find so highly integrated the roles of coach and academician than in the person of Ms. Michaels. I must state from the beginning, however, that Ms. Michaels's room was never designed to be a conventional classroom, nor was she hired to act in a conventional manner. Ms. Michaels, an enthusiastic and talented teacher in her early 40s, was hired to implement and staff an innovative school program at Auxilio High known by its acronym "AVID," which stands for "Advancement Via Individual Determination."

AVID was developed to assist a particular class of high school students: underachieving ethnic minority pupils from low-income families who have indicated, through standardized tests taken in eighth grade, that they have the academic potential to go on to college. As in other urban-metropolitan schools in the district, the two ethnic groups most represented in AVID were African American and Latino.[11]

Under the direction of their AVID teacher, students come together each day to participate in a mentoring class where they receive special help in managing their advanced-placement or college preparatory classes. Additionally, the program invites college counselors to the AVID classroom to answer questions, assist students with college and scholarship applications, and help students become better acquainted with numerous colleges and universities.

Students enter the AVID program as early as their freshman year, where they are enrolled in an advanced history class, an advanced English class, or an advanced math class. If a student shows good results, he or she is placed in more advanced classes aiming to fulfill the "a–f" sequence of courses required for admission into California State University, the University of California, or similar institutions. Overall, the program's goal is to help students get accepted into college.

AVID, however, is not merely an innovative high school program that prepares low-status students for college who otherwise might never go. AVID also represents a cultural space where social life is organized on very different principles than those normally found throughout the school (Stanton-Salazar, Vásquez, & Mehan, 2000). AVID students come together in a collaborative learning environment that reframes "academic success" as a group experience rather than as an individual one. The AVID teacher embodies the functions of mentor, academician, coach, and cheerleader. Students are encouraged to bring not only their academic problems into the classroom, but their personal issues as well, particularly those that may be interfering with their ability to study and excel in school.

Ana Helguerra, the self-assured and opinionated senior we visited in Chapter 7, described Ms. Michaels as a mother figure who made it her business to look out for everyone in AVID. In her own words, "She is very protective. I think she does more than Mr. Nielsen for me; she's actually the one that made things happen for me. She's the one that sort of gets there first." A few minutes later Ana adds:

> It really cheers you up when you see somebody so dedicated and so interested in your affairs. I mean, it's like when you see her and you say, "I can't do your test, 'cause I have to do something else," she'll wait. I feel that she is like the most wonderful teacher I've ever had. I don't think she's ever been upset with me; she's never yelled at me.

Daniel Montalvo, the 11th-grader in the United States since infancy, described how Ms. Michaels strove to build an unequivocal sense of trust between herself and her students:

> She tries to get closer to us by telling us about her family. She is always willing to help you, not only in schoolwork, but in family problems, support, anything. She's like a parent. I trust her a lot.

Javier Soto, a U.S.-born 11th-grader and star baseball player, described Ms. Michaels as "kick back." "She understands you, she knows how to talk to you." In this case, Javier reserved his baseball coach, Mr. Sánchez, for questions pertaining to his post–high school plans. This choice makes sense given Javier's hopes for a baseball scholarship. However, Ms. Michaels emerged as his sole multiplex relationship at school, and was referred to as a source of academic support *and* intimate counsel. Asked whether he would seek such support from anyone else, Javier flatly remarked, "I don't want to ask nobody else." When Javier's girlfriend unexpectedly became pregnant, Ms. Michaels, with his mother's acknowledgment, spent considerable time counseling him on how to manage his new responsibility. The friendly relationship between his mother and Ms. Michaels reinforced the latter's *familial* status in Javier's core network of support. As he began to consider the various colleges that might offer him a sports scholarship, Javier placed considerable trust in Ms. Michaels's judgment. After returning from an AVID tour of different colleges in California, Javier was left quite impressed with the U.C. Santa Barbara campus. "Ms. Michaels said it would be a good school for me 'cause she knows how I am; anyway, she said I should go there, I could play baseball for them."

The students in Ms. Michaels's AVID class exhibited an extraordinarily high degree of trust and confidence in their AVID mentor, so much so that student-teacher relations took on a binding and familial quality. I came to see that there was a clear social compact in this extraordinary classroom. On the one hand, I saw students believing that Ms. Michaels genuinely "cared" and was "invested" in the learners themselves, not merely in the intervention. On the other hand, I noticed a teacher secure in the knowledge that her students would not only be invested in the intervention, but highly receptive to her influence. We see here a mutual and binding trust, each party conveying an implicit commitment to honor the trust of the other.

As with the teacher-coaches who emerged in our student interviews, Ms. Michaels similarly assumed an agent role fundamentally oriented toward both multiplex and multistranded relations with her students. However, unlike the roles of most teacher-coaches at Auxilio High, Ms. Michaels's role was formally associated with academic excellence and college preparation. And unlike most classrooms at Auxilio High, the AVID classroom was carefully developed and managed to provide students with tailored and multiple forms of emotional, social, and institutional support. Inevitably, then, the AVID environment functioned to situate the AVID teacher as a principal adult figure in the adolescents' core social network, with this figure often assuming the status, authority, and affective elements of co-parent.

CLOSING ANALYSIS AND REFLECTIONS

A number of important themes emerged in this chapter—first and foremost, that teachers and counselors often do play a fundamental role as caretakers in the lives of working-class minority adolescents. Key here is the idea that these adolescents were receiving emotional support and intimate counsel from middle-class institutional agents who also possessed the capacity to transmit highly significant forms of institutional support. Through our many interviews, we see that the emergence of *caring relations* between agent and adolescent (i.e., the tacit provision of emotional support and intimate counsel) established the conditions that permitted not only the potential flow of institutional support, but also a high degree of receptivity to such support. This is not to suggest that high quality institutional support automatically flowed from relations of trust and rapport, only that trusting and caring relations created the necessary conditions for its effective transfer.

This study did not evaluate the actual provision of social and institutional support, or its quality. Except with the AVID students we interviewed, there is reason to suspect, given the socioeconomic background and academic histories of most Latino students at Auxilio High, that many of the caring relations we documented did not always become conduits for high quality institutional support, particularly support oriented toward academic excellence and college admission. This is not meant to trivialize the caring relations that existed between adolescents and school agents. Our understandable obsession with academic achievement sometimes blinds us to the positive latent functions school agents often fulfill in the lives of urban minority youth.

Can we safely assume that low-status adolescents, when they make decisions pertaining to their personal lives based on input from authentically caring school agents, make the kinds of decisions that ultimately help them avoid the many risks associated with living in oppressed communities of color? The support Soledad received from Ms. McKinney may not have been overtly geared toward college entrance, but indications are that it did prevent Soledad from worsening her academic circumstances and life chances. This interpretation is not meant to let urban schoolteachers and counselors off the hook; it is clear to many that as a collective, urban school educators are thrust into acting as unwitting agents of social reproduction. However, many educators as individual agents are woven into the social support networks of individual low-status students, and once woven, they do provide forms of support that contribute to the adolescents' social-psychological embeddedness in school, academic persistence, and developmental resiliency. Through caring relations of support, enacted through routine school activities, many low-status adolescents are buffered from the worst alienating effects of class, racial, and gender oppression.

It is also important to emphasize again that the student-agent relations of support we documented constituted real relationships; this is to say that there existed elements of occasional ambivalence and episodic disagreements between agent and student. More often than not, such occurrences set in motion overtures and negotiations that served, in time, to strengthen the tie. Yet, given the differential degrees of power and maturity between parties, initial overtures usually depended on the initiative of school agents. As we saw in the case of María Toledo, it was Ms. Keaton who gave the welcoming gesture to María after she had skipped a number of classes.

James Garbarino and associates (1992), in concluding their international study of children growing up in environments plagued by chronic community violence, make a strong case for a rearticulation of public schools as an important caregiving environment for affected children and adolescents. They make their case in light of their acute awareness of the pessimism that pervades current debates over whether schools can ameliorate the damage done to children by their families' and communities' economic and social marginality ("disadvantage"). In their own words:

> Not only are schools one of the most continuous institutions in children's lives (Wallerstein & Kelly, 1980, chap. 15) but "after the family, schools represent the most important developmental unit in modern social systems" (Comer, 1980, p. 268). Furthermore, as public institution, schools are more accessible than the family—or indeed, the "infrastructure"—as an appropriate unit of intervention. Accordingly, we believe that school settings represent a significant context—a secondary care giving and learning environment—that can be influenced and shaped to play a vital role as a protective factor in children's lives. (p. 121)

Garbarino and associates observed that, despite the overwhelming pressures low-status children and youth often encounter in school, 75 to 80% of this population "can use school activities as a support for healthy adjustment and achievement *when schools are sensitive to them and their burdens*" (p. 121; italics in original).

As this chapter sought to convey, the school's supportive potential is realized by students' school-based support network. Although each adolescent is embedded in an overall social web that extends into different institutional domains, certain ties gain salience and positive influence when the fundamentals of trust and social support are set into motion. Social ties to school agents become activated once the adolescent arrives at a new school; and for crucial periods of time in a young person's life, it is ties to school agents that often act as major conduits for intimate counsel, emotional support, and, of course, institutional support. Furthermore, for most working-class adolescents, ties to parents and family do not normally permeate the boundaries of the school, or for that matter, adolescents' schooling experiences. Family networks and school-based networks are usually linked only —and most tenuously so—through the individual adolescent. The burden of socially integrating these two subnetworks often falls on the working-class adolescent.

Many students in our study of Auxilio High were able to cite at least one supportive relation with a teacher and counselor; yet highly multiplex and multistranded relations tended to be enjoyed by that subsector of students who were able to become involved in school organizations, extracurricular activities, or special academic programs. A few students were able to develop close relations with school agents by their persistent presence in those social spaces where personnel would informally congregate. Agent-student interactions in these organizational or extracurricular settings and social spaces allowed for more regular and informal relations centered around activities enjoyable or satisfying to both students and staff. With authority and power relations becoming relaxed, if not transparent, emotional attachments could develop. Yet overall organizational participation was low for Latinos at Auxilio High. Similarly, Auxilio High had few social spaces on campus that generously allowed for informal engagement between students and school personnel.

The development of multiplex and multistranded relations with school personnel is a complex issue. Multiple forms of measurement and observation are necessary to truly know just how extraordinary or common these relationships are. In Chapter 10, we continue with our exploration of multiplex relationships, using various quantitative survey measures common in the field of network analysis. In spite of network survey indicators showing that a large proportion of our interview sample reported ties to school personnel as likely sources of multiple forms of support, our interview findings raise the possibility that our quantitative indicators may be reflecting "wishful thinking," rather than actual social capital. Although, in this chapter, we have been able to witness and appreciate the significant impact that school agents can have on the lives of low-status adolescents, over the course of the year our interviews left us with the bitter suspicion that the majority of students at Auxilio High were never truly successful in interweaving school agents into their social web of support. We shall explore the various causes for this difficulty over the next two chapters.

9

Constraints on Supportive Relations
with School Personnel

Schools are institutional settings designed to place considerable academic and social demands on young people, and doing so, at least officially, for the purpose of advancing their intellectual and social development. These settings are also designed to supply, at least technically, the intellectual and human resources and support that would permit young people to meet these intellectual and social demands successfully. Working-class and low-income minority students, however, must also contend with emotional burdens and psychocultural challenges originating from pressures found in the home, the minority community, and the society (Boykin, 1986; Clark, 1983; Stanton-Salazar, 1997). Yet, as we saw in the last chapter, school agents can, and do on occasion, provide the emotional and social supports that help students cope effectively with the many burdens they carry. Whether most low-status students actually gain access to existing resources and support to successfully meet the academic, social, and psychological challenges they face is another question, and one that most well-informed people would find easy to answer in matter-of-fact fashion. To address the complexity of this problem, however, requires us to examine the dynamics that arise and that interfere with the formation of caring, supportive, and *resource*-ful relationships between school personnel and minority youth. The formation of such relationships, or social capital, is understood here as contingent on two principal factors: (1) the social structure of the school and (2) students' help-seeking orientation. In more sociological terms, the construction of social capital within the school is considered dependent on the complex interactions of structure and agency.

This chapter explores students' help-seeking orientations as well as aspects of the school's social structure, and considers the influence of each on actual help-seeking and on the formation of supportive and caring relations with school personnel. Although we have seen that close and supportive relations do exist between low-status students and school personnel, many readers might rightfully harbor suspicions that the majority of

low-status students normally find the task of approaching school personnel for support a risky and anxiety-provoking endeavor. Is it possible that
the subterranean *structures* of urban schools are designed tacitly to engineer the malintegration and alienation of the majority of their students? If
this were so, I believe it would be evident in commonly shared sentiments
of distrust and emotional defense that would become manifest in discussions with students around issues of help seeking and social support. The
following pages reveal the feelings, attitudes, and orientations of many
Latino students regarding the supportive potential of school personnel.
Their accounts also shed light on the organizational features of the school
that may inadvertently make help-seeking behavior and the formation of
supportive relations quite difficult.

SOCIAL-PSYCHOLOGICAL CONSTRAINTS ON HELP-SEEKING AND ON THE FORMATION OF SUPPORTIVE RELATIONS

Sandra Jacobo, a moderately high-achieving 11th-grader in the United
States since early childhood, conveyed an independent and assertive personality. Although she was an AVID student, she was not readily trusting
of school personnel and was accustomed to keeping things to herself. In her
statements, Sandra revealed perceptions of teachers at Auxilio High common to many students—that they are professionals usually motivated to
provide academic assistance when approached, yet generally inaccessible
as multiplex and multistranded sources of support. She conveyed no dissatisfaction or ire, mainly due to her minimalist expectations. As she put it:

> I think they're [teachers] very willing to help. If you ask for the
> help, I think they'll give you the help that you need. Not personal
> advice, but as far as the class is concerned or any other material; if I
> have any questions, I'll go ahead and ask them and they'll help me,
> they'll give me an answer, the best answer they can.

However, when asked to describe, from her perspective, the extent to which
students at Auxilio High can develop close and supportive relations with
teachers, Sandra responded:

> To a minimum. You can't really establish a relationship or become
> real friendly or anything like that. Well, I never really looked for it,
> I mean, looked for support from them, anything like that. I don't
> feel that I'm really close to my teachers to ask them, you know, all
> kinds of things or anything.

Sandra's less-than-positive help-seeking orientation extended to counselors as well, but in this case, her views appeared framed perhaps in more rationalistic and substantive terms; these views are at least reasonable and persuasive given the inordinately high caseload that guidance counselors normally carry at Auxilio High. Asked to comment on counselors as viable sources of academic guidance, Sandra stated: "I don't really go to them if I can help it. We know they're there and everything, but I wouldn't even think about going. Because of my friends' experiences, things I've just seen or observed on campus, I just don't like them." Asked whether she trusted the judgment of Mr. Nielsen, she admitted:

> Not really, because I don't really think he knows me enough to counsel me, or if I need to change to a certain class, I already don't feel that he knows what I am capable of. The counselors don't really know you as an individual, to actually know what you want and what kind of person you are. They don't really know you enough to know if you're capable of handling a certain class. I pretty much, you know, do my own schedule. I pretty much make the decisions myself, what I feel is best for me; they [these decisions] don't really concern anybody but me, so I make 'em.

Angeles Machado, also a moderately high-achieving senior who in a previous chapter admitted to putting up a front of someone strong and independent, maintained her ambivalence regarding her expectations of guidance from counselors: "It's their job, right, but I don't think they *should*, you know what I mean? It's completely up to them." Asked whether they have tried to reach out to her, she commented: "Well, yeah, they've called me in and that sort of thing, but then they call everybody else in, too." Angeles found the impersonality of typical sessions in the counselor's office too much to bear. Like Sandra, she wondered whether the counselors really knew students well enough to provide sound advice. Here, again, the perceived absence of close caring relations undermined the legitimacy of a counselor's ministrations, even when the guidance may have been sound. Angeles admitted to learning of college opportunities on her own, through reading brochures and other material available in the library and in the counseling center.

The theme of self-reliance and independence was evident throughout many of our interviews, both with the more acculturated youth and with recent immigrants. The challenge, of course, is to understand what these statements of self-reliance really mean, both in terms of students' perceptions and in terms of structural relations between students and school personnel.

Dolores Villanueva, a mid-achieving 11th-grader with 3 years in the United States, similarly embraced an identity of independence. Asked whether she sought assistance on her homework from friends and teachers, Dolores stated that she knew some girls in her class who could help her, but felt that presently, there wasn't sufficient mutual trust or *confianza* built up in their relations to warrant seeking help from them. She knew her close male friend Agustín would help her if she asked, but stated that his jealous girlfriend kept tight reins on him, so she decided to withdraw from him for a while. Dolores rarely sought out teachers for help, preferring to do her homework on her own. Her clear assertion of self-reliance leaves no room for doubt; in her own words: "*I'm pretty independent. I almost never talk to them* [teachers]. *I always try to do things myself.*"

Lourdes Acuña, an immigrant high-achiever and senior who had recently dealt with the loss of both her parents, demonstrated a similar orientation, in this case in reference to counselors. "*I've never needed them. I know what I want to do; I'm going to college.*" Lourdes stated confidently that she always enrolled in the courses she wanted, and hadn't felt the need to seek advice from counselors. Low or minimalist expectations of teachers and counselors as sources of help with academic assignments were common, and for some students, such expectations were associated with feelings of discomfort that were sometimes subtle, sometimes explicit.

For some students, the idea of approaching teachers and counselors for assistance was downright distressing. María Toledo, a mid- to low-achieving 11th-grader with 9 years in the United States, conveyed this discomfort when asked about seeking help from teachers. "Well, I don't really talk that much with my teachers. Um, I don't like to!" María admitted to having had problems with her grades, but stated, "Now they're up. They're improving. I'm studying a lot. Robert [a friend of the family] is helping me with geometry." When queried about her interactions with the school's guidance counselors, María revealed a similar aversion: "I should go to them [counselors] when I need help, but I don't. It feels weird." María admitted that her counselor, Ms. Whitlock, had helped her with her course schedule for next year, adding that "she is nice." Yet such an assessment seemed overshadowed by cognitions that frame Ms. Whitlock's office as a busy and uncomfortable place, a place one must go when there is no other recourse. "If I knew that I really had to talk to her, I would go. Sometimes it feels weird 'cause there are always people in there and you can't talk. No privacy. Every time I go she seems busy."

Sometimes students' aversion was clearly tied to an incident that was painful or humiliating. Héctor Ordaz, a low-achiever in the 11th grade, failed to mention any teacher at Auxilio High as a likely source of support, stating, "I don't know. I just don't feel comfortable." With probing, we came to learn that Héctor had on several occasions gone into mediation for talking back defiantly to teachers in the classroom.[1] Héctor felt his attitude toward teachers was justified. "Some of the teachers try to get smart. Some teachers, like, they put you down; and the whole class starts laughing . . . I don't like that." Héctor's disputes with a few teachers have clearly colored his perceptions, highlighting both teachers' status as authority figures and their power to publicly humiliate, while overshadowing their simultaneous capacity as sources of support and protection. His perceptions of counselors were similar; he revealed that past summons to his counselor's office have mainly been about his disputes with teachers. Héctor associated counselors with "being in trouble"; the idea that one can approach counselors as sources of social and institutional support emerged as a curious one for Héctor.

FEARS, ANXIETIES, AND SERIOUS CONCERNS: STRATEGIES OF SELF-PROTECTION

Researchers have shown us that the decision path to seeking help can be fraught with risks considered too ominous, particularly when the individual's self-esteem is diminished (e.g., Warren, 1981). Doubts over whether one is recognizable or—alas—invisible to a former teacher can be quite disconcerting, particularly when the student previously experienced many positive interactions with the teacher.

Luz María Loza, a moderately high-achieving 11th-grader in the United States since infancy, spoke of Ms. Armendáriz as a gifted teacher she had during the previous year. Not only did Luz María thoroughly enjoy the class in Spanish literature, but the strong rapport between teacher and students was something she sorely missed when the class ended. Yet the fear that Ms. Armendariz might no longer recognize her as a former student was too great for Luz María to risk a social visit and a request for minor academic assistance. For her, the idea of waving hello in the school quad raised the risk of a possible curious look on the face of this esteemed teacher.

Felipe Martínez, a native-born low-achiever who had recently fathered a child, conveyed his sense of invisibility with respect to the various coaches he had come to know as teachers during the past couple of years. Felipe, never involved in sports, was aware of the special status coaches enjoyed by way of their close relations with athletes and with students well integrated into the school's social scene. Although he spoke of one teacher-coach who was particularly attentive to him, Felipe spoke of the others with disdain, charging that they walk around campus thinking that they were "big shits." Without intervention, Felipe's perceptions probably functioned to obliterate any possibility of his seeking support from coaches or experiencing what others had learned so well—that coaches could be quite sensitive and responsive to students' feelings of marginality.

Face-saving and selective avoidance emerged as major strategies among adolescents for negotiating daily interactions with school personnel. At times, such strategies involved the careful withdrawal from potentially or actually humiliating experiences. In this imagined scenario, attempts by agents to provide support carried the risk of further undermining students' already low self-esteem.

Rosario Zárate, the senior we visited in Chapter 8, spoke of a number of instances in which teachers had sought to provide her with special tutoring outside of class, most notably her science teacher, Ms. Grossman, and her math teacher, Ms. Carlton. Yet Rosario feared taxing their patience, and claimed in a strong assertion that by continuing these tutorial sessions, she would be "wasting their time." In an exasperated voice, Rosario's anxieties come tumbling out: "Things don't really sink into my mind very easily, very quickly." Rosario eventually withdrew from these teachers' tutorial efforts, thereby avoiding what she feared most, the mortifying possibility that these teachers, in utter frustration, would withdraw first.

THE ART OF DEFENSIVE AVOIDANCE

For some students, avoidance became a way to prevent a potentially humiliating interaction that could confirm a sense of invisibility in the eyes of an esteemed or attractive teacher or coach, as was the case with Luz María and Felipe. Others feared the possible withdrawal of or rejection by an esteemed agent due to their (the students') presumed incompetence, as was the case with Rosario. For still other students, avoidance had to do with an agent deemed either a poor source of support or a source of grief and disappointment.

Gloria Hidalgo, a mid-achieving 11th-grader born in the United States, spoke confidently in Spanish, and revealed her aggravation when questioned whether she would seek help from Mr. Jacobs, her French teacher. Gloria stated that she had tried to seek help from Mr. Jacobs, but his frequent classroom displays of impatience and temper had rendered him an unattractive and unlikely source of help. She spelled out her displeasure quite clearly:

> *No es paciente con nosotros. ¡Es muy enojón!* [He isn't patient with us. He easily gets angry!] *If we ask him to explain a word or some activity, he never answers our question. If I don't understand something and I raise*

my hand to ask him, yeah he explains it to me; but if I still don't under-
stand him, he gets mad. He gets impatient. And there are times when I
need help and he's talking with another student and when he finishes, he
ignores me. He pretends that he doesn't see me and continues writing on
the chalkboard. It's like he doesn't care about what we need.

Although the reasons students gave for avoiding or not seeking help often focused on the aversive behavior of a particular teacher or staff person, the results of our network survey show that most of the adults with whom students had daily contact were never incorporated into students' school-based web of support. Most of these nonselections had little to do with conflictive relations or aversion, but rather had to do with the absence of close rapport and trust. Some students did, however, couch their nonselection of school personnel in terms of *generalized aversion,* as we see in the remarks by Mariana Zedillo, a native-born high-achieving senior. When asked what she would change at Auxilio High to make it a better school, Mariana declared: "What would I change? Um, about half the teachers [chuckle]. Most of the experiences that I've had, I guess, some are like I said before, they might not enjoy teaching and they're just doing it because they're getting paid for it."

The most emotionally charged and vociferous articulations by students were reserved for the school's guidance counselors. Here, students were able to speak more explicitly of their avoidance behavior mainly because they could exert more control over whether they entered the counseling center or a particular counselor's office. The following are best understood as illustrations of relational dynamics that prevented the establishment of rapport and trust, and therefore the transfer of social and institutional support.

Sara Barranca, a high-achieving senior with only 2½ years in the United States., would not go to Mr. Rocha, her official counselor. She perceived him as arrogant and demeaning. When originally asked whether she would call on him for help with school-related decisions, she strongly asserted her disdain:

INTERVIEWER: *And what's up with Mr. Rocha?*
SARA: *¡Ay, es bien sangrón, no me cae bien!* [Oh, he's such a jerk, I don't like him!]
INTERVIEWER: *You don't like him. Do you feel that you can't go to him? You don't trust him?*
SARA: *No, not for anything.*
INTERVIEWER: *Because he's such a jerk?*
SARA: *Yeah! And you can never tell, there are times when he's real nice to*

the girls, and with the guys he acts like a jerk. But there are times
when he's a jerk to the girls and to the guys.

Sara complained that Rocha didn't take into account students' opinions, preferences, and needs, and that he didn't treat students fairly or with respect. Even before Sara had contact with Rocha, she was informed by her peers to beware: "*. . . ya me habían dicho, ten cuidado con ese porque es insoportable* [they'd already told me to beware with this guy, that he's unbearable]." Marisol Urquilla, another recent immigrant, spoke of a confrontation with Mr. Rocha, saying she told him that he was not her officially assigned counselor and she preferred that he would stop calling her in. Marisol said she believed Rocha harbored prejudices toward recent-immigrant students.

Sara Barranca recounted that when she originally enrolled at Auxilio High, she found herself placed in a typing class; she subsequently informed Mr. Rocha that she had already taken 2 years of typing in Mexico, and that she was, "*hasta acá, harta,*" fed up with typing and desperately wanted another class. "And he told me, 'You know, I'm not going to change the class,' he said, 'because you're going to take this class no matter what!' Uy! I thanked him and I left." After this incident, Sara promised herself that she would avoid Mr. Rocha at all costs. Her friends' warning of Rocha being *insoportable* [unbearable] had been realized.

Soledad Arroyo, in the United States for 3 years, knew that Ms. Whitlock was her assigned counselor, but admitted that she didn't feel comfortable approaching her because Ms. Whitlock frequently yelled and frightened people. Soledad tells how Whitlock often scolded students in her office and did not seem to have much patience. She admitted to being fearful of her: "*Yes, I know her but she yells a lot, it's kinda scary. She's always scolding people, it's like she doesn't have any patience for anything. (¡Muy regañona!). She's always reprimanding you.*" Soledad indicated that she preferred to stay clear of Whitlock's office, stating that she somehow managed to get by without her aid.

FRACTURES OF TRUST, DISSATISFACTIONS WITH SUPPORT, AND LINGERING RESENTMENTS

Up to this point we have primarily dealt with relational dynamics that occurred early in students' interactions with various agents, dynamics that functioned to undermine the possibility for establishing relations of trust and rapport—a necessary vehicle for regular help seeking and for the fluid, recurrent, and tailored transfer of key institutional resources from agent to student.[2] The examples below, in contrast, involve the dynamics of on-going relations with school agents and negative appraisals of past instances of support. These relate less to appraisals of whether certain agents might become likely sources of help, and more with accumulated appraisals that finally function to fracture trust and to disqualify agents as future sources of social, emotional, and/or institutional support.

The fracturing of trust and the ensuing feelings of betrayal are evident in the account provided by Ernesto Arrevalo, a low-achieving immigrant senior with 7 years in the United States. Ernesto stated that his relationship with Mr. Robles, a history teacher at Auxilio High, originated in his junior high school where Robles was once employed. He admitted that at one time they were close, when he was a member of the cross-country team for several years at Auxilio High under Robles's direction. Ernesto enjoyed both multiplex and multistranded relations with Robles, until Robles apparently overstepped his boundaries as a professional educator and, according to Ernesto, began to meddle in the most defended arena of his private life. Ernesto charged that Robles told his girlfriend Eugenia that she was going to become a *"vaga"* if she remained with Ernesto (i.e., a person with a "bad" reputation; one who hangs with the wrong crowd, who exhibits loose morals). He also claimed that Robles went so far as to inform Eugenia's parents that Ernesto was a bad influence on their daughter's academic status. Whether such comments were made in calculated humor or as passing remarks, Ernesto saw them as evidence of betrayal. Ernesto withdrew from Robles, and continued to carry a good deal of resentment over the episode.

A perusal of this young man's network survey reveals his embeddedness in many peer and familial relations; yet Ernesto was becoming increasingly marginal to the school's mainstream academic networks, both to the more academically motivated students and to the teachers most dedicated to working with immigrants. His participation in athletics and his multiplex relationship with Robles had been his link to the school's mainstream, and now this link had been broken.

Many other instances emerged showing how relations between agents and students that were once close and highly supportive had later come to a crashing halt, with mixtures of resentment and disappointment lingering in the smoldering ashes. Dolores Villanueva, who earlier professed her self-reliance and disinterest in seeking support from teachers, spoke with animated disdain and disappointment about her past relations with Mr. Rocha. Dolores previously held him in high esteem, perceiving him as a good person and a caring counselor in whom she believed she could confide her problems and from whom she would receive good advice; but all that changed, as she now lamented: *"I'm a little disillusioned because I used to think he was a good person, someone that I could tell all my problems to and that he could give me better advice than the others."* She began to notice, however, that the classes he assigned her to weren't suited to what she believed were her true abilities, reflecting, instead, what she found most troubling—his low academic expectations for her.

> *He would tell me what classes to take, but I hadn't noticed that he was giving me the wrong classes. I think that Mr. Rocha could help me but I don't go to him because sometimes he tries to put things in my head, he wants to tell me things that aren't true. Well, I used to think he was a friend, but not this year.*

A minute later, as she continued her account, her anger and disappointment became most clear:

> *I go in hoping that he'll help me and he tells me that he wants to give me this [class], he looks at me like I'm stupid, he wants to treat me like any other student. It's okay if he wants to treat me like any other student, but at the same time I don't want him to think of me as stupid; like things like this, "This class is too advanced for you. You need to take this lower-level one." I know that is a lower-level class, and I know that I'd pass it easily, yet he insists that I take the class that he wants and doesn't give me the class that I really need.*

An esteemed teacher, Ms. Armendáriz, in a subsequent consultation with Dolores, warned her that Mr. Rocha had a history of assigning classes that were below students' true abilities. Armendáriz encouraged her to enroll in the more advanced courses Dolores had originally selected for herself. Although Mr. Rocha was not her assigned counselor, Dolores originally sought him out as someone who, because of their common ethnicity and his facility in Spanish, would be more sensitive to her needs and would provide her more individualized attention. As she put it: *"He isn't my counselor, but I went to him because he was Latino, so that we could talk more informally."* Yet Dolores's attempt at getting specialized attention backfired. She found herself wedged between counselors whom she assumed to be competent but who were not fluent in Spanish, and a counselor whom she originally found to be both fluent and culturally responsive, but whom she ultimately came to judge as both professionally incompetent and patronizing.

By no means was Dolores alone in her aggravation. Lilia Escarza, a high-achieving senior who in previous chapters gave evidence of her negative stance toward help-seeking, voiced sentiments shared by many others we interviewed. "My counselor is Mr. Rocha, but I don't think he's a good counselor. He'll go with the system, not what's good for you. I don't like him." Lilia explained that she found herself in a physics class she did not need, but apparently Rocha refused to let her drop it.

> I needed to get out of physics, 'cause I didn't need that class and he said I had to take it because, you know, it was part of some requirement, and here we are arguing. I said, "Why don't you just look at my credits?" So then he was, "Oh, well, you shouldn't even be in this school."

According to Lilia, Rocha refused to budge. In indignation, she took her case to Coach Shane, who subsequently intervened, making it possible for Lilia to be administratively removed from the class. Reconnecting with the frustration she experienced over this episode, Lilia offered her final indictment: "I think he sucks as a counselor. I feel he doesn't give anybody any support. I never go to him."

Luz María Loza likewise promised herself never to return to Mr. Rocha after an aggravating confrontation. She told of an incident where she was pulled out of Ms. Payne's algebra class and reassigned to a class taught by Coach Jefferson, evidently due to administrative efforts to distribute students more equitably across classrooms. Luz María very much wanted to return to Ms. Payne, finding that Coach Jefferson wasn't providing the extra assistance she needed and that she had enjoyed in Payne's class. Luz María indicated the way her request was handled: "*Well, he* [Mr. Rocha] *told me no, that I wasn't always going to be where I wanted to be, and that I was being capricious, and I don't know what else. So I said, 'OK, that's fine,' and I left. And yes, I passed the class, and no, he didn't do anything to help me, he just scolded me right then and there.*" That was the last time Luz María went to talk to Mr. Rocha.

For a good number of students we interviewed, disappointing or alienating encounters with counselors turned into justification for avoiding them at all costs; yet such withdrawal entailed a high price: their extrication from a network of agents who control key forms of institutional support. Although consultations with such agents have never guaranteed access to such support (Cicourel & Kitsuse, 1963; Cicourel & Mehan, 1983; Erickson & Shultz, 1982), social withdrawal—as a coping strategy—only lowers students' chances of access, particularly for those students similarly alienated from teachers and other school personnel.

Conscious withdrawal from the school's corps of counselors was accompanied by either intense antipathy and vocal resentment or a quiet and resigned estrangement. Though the latter mode was harder to detect in our interviews, in the end it appeared as the way most expressed their dissatisfaction. Yet the aggravated sentiments of the more vocal students give clues as to what the others felt, but could not or would not articulate. The sentiments of Aida Ponce, a U.S.-born, mid-achieving senior, are sufficiently representative of these more vocal students to warrant sharing here. When queried about whether she perceives school counselors as a viable resource, Aida responded in seething terms:

> I don't like them! They usually tend to tell you to do whatever they need you to do, not whatever you need them for. They're kind of just there. They're getting paid. They're not counselors. To me, they're not counselors. They're just there to tell you, "Oh, you're doing this wrong. Your teacher's been coming to me." Or they're just like, "What do you mean, you want to drop a class? No, you can't do this, you're at this point in the semester. You can't do this!" They're very negative!

Aida's encounters with her own assigned counselor, Ms. Whitlock, appear to parallel the accounts of others we've visited in this chapter. Asked to talk about Ms. Whitlock as a source of institutional support, Aida exclaimed with vociferous contempt: "She's a terrible counselor! I try to avoid her when she's in the counseling center. I don't want to see her!" Aida no longer sought help from Ms. Whitlock since she was forced to stay in a chemistry class she was failing.

Aida's contemptuous sentiments toward the counseling staff were tempered by her perception that at least one good counselor could be found in the counseling center. Yet Ms. Castañeda did not appear in Aida's network survey, nor do we find evidence that Aida had developed a supportive relationship with her. Her only supportive connections to school personnel were with the two male staff members who directed the ROTC program at the school, and with Coach Shane.

Calmer and more resigned sentiments of disappointment were also well represented in our interviews, as in the case of Miguel Angel Gonzales, a mid-achieving senior with 9 years in the United States. Note his lack of outward anger as well as his recognition that the support he has received from school agents is on a par with what he has received from his immigrant parents. Asked to talk about his experiences receiving help from both teachers and counselors pertaining to academic issues or to his post–high school plans, Miguel Angel mused:

> *The teachers don't help you much because they have too many students. No, they don't talk to you.* [Pauses] *My counselor could have helped me, I*

think [regarding post–high school plans]; *but since I was in a program called EOP that helps you with financial aid, he didn't help me. The truth is that I never got any support from them* [i.e., counselors]. [Long pause.] *Well yes, I did get support from them, just like from my parents: you know, that I stay in school and that I do well.*

GENDER DIFFERENCES IN COMMUNICATIVE COMPETENCE

Miguel Angel's views and mode of expression were similar to those heard from many of the boys we interviewed, regardless of generational status or acculturation. Girls tended to have been engaged with teachers and counselors as interactive participants and communicants; boys appeared to communicate less, which forced them to infer the meaning of an agent's words and actions, usually from a position of little trust. Among this group of boys, high-achievers did appear to have a slight advantage. Yet for the most part, boys tended to speak of their lack of satisfaction in almost emotionless, resigned tones; girls, in turn, tended to express their feelings in more elaborated and agitated ways. As the data in this chapter suggest, girls came to the interviews with a command of relational discourse, a working knowledge of how to articulate the dynamics of their relationships with various agents. Boys, more often than not, struggled to describe these very same dynamics, and to express their own feelings.

Rosario Zárate, detached and alone, yet never angry, demonstrated her communicative ability as well as the insights that many girls revealed in articulating the essence of students' withdrawal from school agents. Rosario felt that all counselors should be there for students, but that something important was lacking in their assistance:

Like Mr. Nielsen, I can go to him, and he'll do what he has to do, so I can graduate, but it's just to get me by, you know, so I can graduate and get it over with; but he's not somebody that, who is *really, really* interested, and really cares. I mean, maybe he does care, but, it's just to get me by, you know.

Rosario does consider the problem is that counselors have too many students to work with; but left without an acknowledgment by counselors of their difficult circumstances, Rosario's negative feelings predominate, as does her quiet estrangement from teachers and counselors.

ORGANIZATIONAL CONSTRAINTS ON HELP SEEKING

Many other students made direct references to constraints on help seeking rooted in the organizational arrangements of the school. Seeking help often required students to make extraordinary efforts to track down noticeably overburdened teachers. The most exasperated students were usually the ones most in need of help; they were also the ones with the lowest level of tolerance for organizational impediments.

Natividad Fernández, a low-achieving senior in the United States since infancy, found that teachers were not easily accessible for help with her schoolwork. She commented on her efforts to seek teachers outside of their regular class time: "No, there's nobody available. I think the teachers should be there. [They're there] only in class, but they're usually talking. I've gone after school and flopped. There's nobody there. They just leave." It is important to note that Natividad had not named one teacher in her network survey.

Crowded classrooms and a high teacher-student ratio were common complaints. Getting attention and assistance from teachers meant competing with other students in the classroom, and required aggressive and persistent efforts. Marisol Urquilla, a high-achieving senior with 2 years in the United States, explained that when she had Mr. Torres for math in the 10th grade, there had been only nine students in the room. Mr. Torres frequently told these nine students that it was his favorite class, and Marisol remembered him as being very attentive and very helpful to her and to her classmates. Later Marisol heard students enrolled in Torres's other classes complain that he was an impatient teacher, and that he was frequently in bad humor in the classroom, complaints she found hard to believe. When she subsequently enrolled in his physics class, she found it full to capacity. Marisol saw that Mr. Torres, under crowded conditions, used teaching methods that were largely didactic and poorly suited to his natural inclinations. This was a different Mr. Torres, an ill-humored and impatient teacher, distressed over the necessity of dealing with disciplinary disturbances and of attending to the special needs of too many students.

Marisol's previous experience with Mr. Torres, however, had already laid the groundwork for a close and supportive relationship that endured during the course of the semester. Although she found it difficult to gain individual attention in the classroom, her already well-established relations permitted her to engage Mr. Torres more informally, and during better moments after class she chatted with him about going to college and the related prerequisites. Marisol lamented, however, that once the semester was over, she hardly saw or talked to Mr. Torres.

Here emerged a prime obstacle students faced in incorporating caring teachers into their social networks. Students often took an entire semester to establish relations of trust and rapport with teachers, only to find that when they began to feel confident enough to approach teachers for emotional, social, and institutional support, the semester ended, and with it, daily interactions between teacher and student. In so many cases we studied, the end of the semester, as with the end of the year, brought the collapse of the structures on which nascent social capital formation had been sustained.[3]

The case of Luz María Loza, featured earlier, is one telling example of this organizational phenomenon. Recall that Luz María feared that Ms. Armendáriz might no longer recognize her as a former student, and thus, Luz María never approached her. She had also identified Ms. Payne as having been a trusted teacher who was always willing to help her with math or with other academic assignments. Yet, as we saw earlier, Luz María's connection to Payne was prematurely severed when she was suddenly transferred to Coach Jefferson's class. Asked whether her relationship with Ms. Payne had changed, she said: *"Well yeah, because I never saw her again [pauses] I never talked to her like I used to. Before if I had a problem in math or something like that, I'd go see her and she'd help me."*

Students get administratively transferred from one class into another, the semester terminates and teacher and students part company, the school year comes to an end, a well-liked teacher is transferred to a new school—such events weaken or sever relationships between students and agents, and seen together, essentially function as subterranean currents that interrupt the continuity necessary for the development of adolescent social capital.

And here we see what the school social structure really means in the lives of our urban, working-class, Latino high schoolers: Relationships between school agents and students seldom have an opportunity to develop beyond a superficial, ephemeral, transitory state; in the end, students' social webs remain perilously anemic. Enduring relations of support and informal mentorship always arise as exceptional cases. Such relations survive as long as agent and student remain steadfast against the institutionalized social order; but students grow weary of the turbulence in their social webs, weary of the strain of incorporating new and promising links, only to have them suddenly broken.

Luz María wondered whether Ms. Armendáriz would still recognize her. Marisol reminisced about her "special relationship" with Mr. Torres. Soledad Arroyo contemplated revisiting Ms. McKinney, perhaps to rekindle for a moment what had been a special blessing, a close relationship with a caring teacher who refused to distinguish between her academic life and her personal life. Yet even the most dedicated agents must conform to the established organizational order—and as they bid farewell to their students at semester's end, a new crop of students is already walking in the door.

SETTING COUNSELORS UP FOR REPUDIATION

The organizational order also infuses itself into the developing links between counselors and students. Counselor caseloads do not permit much individualized attention, except for the most persistent and assertive of students. With four full-time certified counselors and a student body of 1,500 students or more, the ratio between counselor and students leveled at around 375 students per counselor. There were about 400 Spanish-dominant or limited-English-proficient students, and only two of the four counselors were Spanish-proficient, so the ratio here translates into 200 students per Spanish-speaking counselor. These two counselors had to contend with their regular grade-level assignments as well as with the Spanish-speaking students who sought them out for assistance.

Lilia Escarza, a moderately high-achieving senior with little tolerance for the routine busyness of teachers and counselors, believed her detached manner was justified given the status quo at school. Lilia's dictum, "I live in my own world. I'm more comfortable," illustrates this adolescent's tenaciousness and ability to persist in school in spite of a weak network. On the other hand, her statement is an emblem of student alienation. Her position on visiting counselors is consonant with this guarded disposition: "The counselors should be there; they're there, but only if you come to them; they'll never come to you. It's like you've got to be bugging them all the time in order for them to listen to you." Although Lilia has done fairly well academically, by February of her senior year she had not taken steps to plan for the following year.

> There was this one lady here that came from some SOAP thing, I don't know. She was talking about financial aid, but she never gave me the application and I think the deadline was a couple of weeks ago. I never filled it out. We should get the applications for junior colleges at the end of the year.

Coach Shane and Coach Jesse were the only agents who appeared in Lilia's network survey. When asked about seeking their assistance, Lilia answered: "I'm pretty sure that Coach Shane would [help], if I get him like on his spare time. He's always busy."

Although some of the students we studied sought counselors other than the ones to whom they were officially assigned, other students interpreted their formal assignments as a prohibition on shopping around. When asked whether she ever thought about seeking help from Ms. Castañeda, Natividad Fernández, who was often described by school agents as shy and withdrawn, indicated: "Not really, she's not, she's only a counselor for the seniors; so I can't really talk to her." When students' already negative help-seeking orientations combine with the absence of organizational features that could ensure regular and meaningful access to the school's human and institutional resources, the stage is set for the alienated embeddedness of a high proportion of the school's student body.

Charges can be made that students must take responsibility for making the most of the school's available resources, that schools cannot be expected to spoon-feed "lazy" students. This widespread view, however, fails to take into account that throughout the most privileged sectors of society, as well as within the upper echelons of most organizations and businesses, many of the most valued resources, privileges, and opportunities flow (informally) through relationships and networks. Relationships and resource networks, of course, are not dispensing machines; rather they are entities lodged within relations of power and hierarchy; they embody dynamics that reach deeply into the human psyche, unearthing and agitating fears, prejudices, cultural preferences, and emotional commitments, each of which is inextricably entangled in society's social tensions and group solidarities.

Furthermore, from classical sociology, we know that sustained difficulty in participating in an institution's most resourceful networks and relationships spells *alienation*,[4] a state of consciousness that leaves young people looking "withdrawn and lazy." However, this state or "look" is better understood in terms of accumulated disillusionment, demoralization, and estrangement from adult sources of support. Of course, such alienation further reduces young people's chances of accessing psychological and mobility-related resources and support. At the level of the individual, alienation is the accumulated effect of past relational experiences and, simultaneously, a persistent factor in future difficulties with network-building.

The link between students' help-seeking orientations and the degree of alienation can be represented in the following proposition: The students who show the least signs of alienation in school, who have been able to cultivate a positive network or help-seeking orientation, are the most likely to be engaged in help-seeking behavior and social-capital formation. In other words, they are likely to be the most positively embedded within the school and to enjoy the greatest access to institutional support. This perspective follows the dictum that the rich get richer, the psychologically empowered are further empowered, and those most in need of social support are usually the least likely to get it.

Understanding help seeking, network-building, and persistence in school among low-status youth requires that we not shy away from the complexities of how resources flow within educational institutions—particularly, how they systematically flow away from those individuals most in need of them. Again, the visible flow of resources from agents to students is largely governed by the invisible flow of subterranean institutional currents.

ETHNICITY AND LANGUAGE ISSUES IN AGENT-STUDENT RELATIONS: CULTURAL CONFLICTS, BIASES, AND PREJUDICES

Do race and ethnicity matter in the formation of social capital within urban high schools? We wanted to know how and to what extent ethnic preferences and issues of cultural sensitivity play a part in students' perceptions of school agents as sources of institutional support. These questions can be answered in several ways and by examining the different evidence at hand.

The most obvious evidence came from immigrant students, who voiced a strong preference for teachers and counselors they could converse with in Spanish. Similar preferences were expressed by students who, although U.S.-born, spoke of a strong desire for Spanish-speaking school agents with whom to discuss their personal or academic problems. For many Latino students at Auxilio High, speaking in Spanish served as a means of establishing trust and rapport.

Gloria Hildalgo, a U.S.-born 11th-grader, said she trusted her teachers but admitted that she was shy, even embarrassed, about sharing her personal and academic concerns with them in English: "*Sí, pero me da vergüenza* [Yes, but I get embarrassed]. *Yeah I'm sure of myself, but I get embarrassed if I have to talk to them in English.*" The logic of establishing trust and rapport in one's home language appears to have been especially prevalent among Spanish-dominant immigrant students; yet basic structural access seems at times the more salient factor. For these students, lack of English proficiency combined with the lack of bilingualism among most of the staff at Auxilio High severely narrowed the pool of eligible sources of support.

Again we are faced with the task of delineating how the school's structure and students' social-psychological orientation interact to shape help seeking and the distribution of supportive ties within the school. As we shall see in Chapter 10, Spanish-dominant Latinos were the least likely to report mobilizing either of the two forms of academic support. Our statistical findings also showed that Spanish-dominant immigrants were the least open to sharing their problems with others (*Interpersonal Openness*), a finding representing a key aspect of their help-seeking orientation. Thus, it seems that for Spanish-dominant students, their language status not only narrowed the pool of eligible helpers at school, but also served as a proxy for these students' social-psychological orientation as newcomers: a help-seeking orientation that judged school agents as highly "supportive," but that also reflected these students' timidity and anxiety over making explicit demands on teachers and counselors—even those who were most accessible to them.

Identifying the principal motivation or reasoning underlying individual preferences for Spanish-speaking school agents was quite difficult. For bilingual adolescents, preferences for Spanish-speaking personnel seemed to be less about language proficiency and more about establishing relations of *confianza* (i.e., of trust and rapport). Little evidence emerged to show that bilingual students had any aversion to agents merely based on their being White or English-monolingual.

Miguel Angel Gonzales, a bilingual immigrant with 9 years in the United States, spoke about his difficulty in both classifying and establishing rapport with Mr. Cervántez, an English and journalism teacher at Auxilio High and a U.S.-born Chicano with minimal proficiency in Spanish.

> *Well, he's a man that appears to be Latino, but he's really like a "white boy." He's like any other teacher. Sí, es, es, como mixtiado [Yeah, he's, like mixed]. He was born somewhere in Arizona or Texas, somewhere around there, and he was raised with white kids and he doesn't know how to speak Spanish;* [pauses] *he doesn't know Spanish!*

Miguel Angel said he found Mr. Cervántez to be a compassionate and competent teacher and one very willing to help students in class, but the perceived contradiction between having close contact with a Latino teacher yet not being able to communicate or even banter in Spanish created a schism too great for Miguel Angel to cross. His neutral feelings toward Mr. Cervántez are quite evident: "*I don't really feel any attachment to him. Honestly, he's someone who is nothing more than my teacher.*"

The issue of acculturation and Spanish proficiency among Latino teachers at Auxilio High appeared elsewhere in our interviews, with respondents describing scenarios that were at times comical. Dolores Villanueva said she knew Ms. Castañeda was her assigned counselor, but had decided to seek out Mr. Rocha because of his public and visible exchanges and bantering with immigrant students in Spanish. She stated that at least with Rocha she had been able to express herself, and even argue with him, in her native language, "but with Ms. Castañeda I'm not really able to express myself. It's not that I don't trust her, but you know, with a Latino . . ." The interviewer interjects, informing Dolores that Ms. Castañeda is Latina, of Mexican descent. Dolores is surprised by what she hears. *"She's Latina? Really, I didn't know; the time that I went to see her, she talked to me in English, she even scolded me in English. I didn't understand anything she said. So, I never went back."* Although Ms. Castañeda was bilingual, her preference for English and her tendency to use English with immigrant students served to undercut the possibility of incorporating herself into the support networks of the very students she was sincerely committed to serving.

Although the school carries the public charge of developing immigrant students' English proficiency, and English is widely viewed as the "language of opportunity," the language of help seeking and social support, and certainly of most network and exchange relations in society, is none other than the language of trust. Needless to say, for almost all immigrant students, the language of trust—the idiom of *confianza*—is their native language. When the school's mission of English assimilation is pitted against the fragile process of building up immigrant students' social capital, the latter process always yields, especially when the development of students' support networks is never overtly assumed among the school's official mission and objectives.

Spanish-dominant students expected Latino teachers to be fluently bilingual—and were surprised or annoyed when they discovered otherwise. Evidence also emerged suggesting that the more acculturated sector of the Latino student body, particularly the native-born, likewise held Latino teachers and counselors to a higher standard. This standard, however, was not about professional or language competencies in the usual sense, but rather about these agents' degree of ideological and emotional commitment to Latino students, and their willingness to extend themselves beyond the usual boundaries of their professional roles. Salvador Baca, visited in the last chapter, captures the essence of this special standard by differentiating between what he sees as two kinds of Latino teachers:

> OK, there's the "stick-up-the-ass" Latino teachers, who look down upon Mexicans, who blame Mexican students who misbehave for all their problems, and then there's the kind that sees you fucking up and tries to help you out, instead of pushing you aside, which, if he is a Chicano, he should do it.

Although Latino teachers were expected to be more caring, this higher standard did not translate, for most students, into ethnic or racial preferences regarding classroom teachers. Apart from those immigrant and Spanish-dominant students who preferred Spanish-speakers as sources of academic and institutional support, few students, immigrant or native-born, explicitly stated that they preferred a Latino instructor over an Anglo instructor. The high-achieving acculturated students did, however, express this nonpreferential view more emphatically. In Chapter 8, we assessed the qualities students found most appealing in those agents with whom they had established close and supportive relationships. Racial preferences did not emerge as a prominent characteristic. The feelings expressed by Sandra Jacobo, a high-achiever who has spent most of her life in the United States, are representative, particularly among those students doing at least moderately well academically. "I don't think it matters much. It wouldn't matter their ethnic background or anything. It would matter how they taught, what they taught, their qualifications."

A careful analysis of our interview data on this issue reveals a somewhat overlapping, yet still independent set of factors implicated in students' assessment of school agents. In the realm of instruction, students emphasized the person's training, expertise, and pedagogical ability to teach the subject matter, his or her enthusiasm for the material, efforts to assist students with academic matters (patiently), and willingness and ability to transcend the instructor role and to establish authentically caring relations with students. Students saw these traits as transcending race and ethnicity, their past experiences having proven to them that these qualities could, indeed, be embodied in teachers of all backgrounds. They had also realized that ethnic co-membership was never a guarantee of finding these highly valued traits in school agents, as has been evident in the ethnographic accounts provided in these chapters.

Yet our data on help seeking suggest an ever more complex picture. The more guarded the adolescent, the lower his or her self-esteem and self-efficacy, and the more defensiveness and diminished trust marked his or her help-seeking orientation, the more the adolescent valued qualities normally associated with *familial agents* (i.e., kin). Here, a teacher's or counselor's language, ethnicity, class background, gender, and age functioned as status cues students used to determine which agents posed the least risk to their self-esteem, and the highest likelihood of demonstrating a caring or familial orientation toward students.

Other, nonascriptive status characteristics of school agents held salience as well: reputation among Latino students above all, but also curricular strand and subject material, whether teachers were athletic coaches or whether they taught IB English literature or regular history, or whether they oversaw the various remedial programs (e.g., NOVANET). Teachers in non–college oriented or remedial classes were generally seen as more accessible to those students whose academic performance was low to moderate. Thus, the adolescents we studied, particularly the most guarded, availed themselves of as many cues as possible, with ethnicity and language certainly included in these criteria, but not by any means always the most important.

CLOSING ANALYSIS AND REFLECTIONS

As we have seen over a number of chapters, the likelihood for the transmission of social and institutional support from agent to student largely depends on regular interactions that create a base of trust and rapport. Such a base, or relationship, can be understood as a conduit through which many of the school's most important resources flow. Furthermore, the less students are socially embedded in the school's patchwork of extracurricular activities, the more important becomes this basic establishment of trust.

Indicators of bureaucratic structure, organizational culture, and students' help-seeking orientation emerged as principal factors accounting for a student's likelihood of establishing trusting relations with school agents and of mobilizing different forms of support. I will summarize the findings on students' psychological orientation first.

From high-achievers to low-achievers, among both the recent immigrants and the native-born, the majority of the adolescents in our study revealed that, within the realm of the school, orientations were quite frequently more about self-protection and the guarding of self-esteem than about network-building and the necessity of accessing key forms of social and institutional support. As our interview data repeatedly revealed, the decision on the part of the student to seek help from agents entailed considerable psychological risks. Fears of rejection by or indifference from school personnel, as well as feelings of invisibility, ranked high as inhibitors. Low academic self-esteem also played a definitive role, as when students felt that their past academic performance or behavior might have branded them as undeserving of special attention or informal mentorship. This does not suggest that they believed themselves to be undeserving or unentitled; rather, the fear was that they might be made to feel undeserving by an insensitive agent or a disastrous encounter. Under conditions where "impression management" and "saving face" are the order of the day, the seeking of assistance from significant others appears as a rather troublesome coping strategy.[5] For those who find themselves in these problematic domains over long periods of time, the development of a negative or a defensive network orientation seems a high probability.

Disappointing or alienating encounters with school personnel who were approached as potential sources of support also ranked high as inhibitors, and turned into justification for long-term and even permanent avoidance. Students' *falta de confianza* (literally, the absence of trust), the subtle antagonisms between students and agents, and students' avoidance strategies were pervasive in almost all our discussions with students. On a broader scale, the overall consequence of these various inhibitors was the social estrangement of low-status students from the school system's agents of institutional support.

A number of distinctive and commonly shared traits emerged to characterize students' largely defensive help-seeking orientation, although the salience of such traits varied across individuals. As already mentioned, a generalized lack of trust or *confianza* in school personnel as sources of support was one key trait of this orientation. A "connection" to a particular agent at the school was experienced in the context of students' general wariness. This lack of trust produced, in turn, students' sense of physical and psychological estrangement, the former manifested through various avoidance strategies, and the latter through students' inability to envision particular teachers and counselors as approachable or as viable sources of support. Persistent wariness and estrangement commonly went along with investments in unsponsored self-reliance and independence. The most vocal adolescents couched their lack of help-seeking initiative as a value and a preference for resolving their problems on their own. Among the most alienated students, investment in this mode of adaptation revealed a visible sense of resignation and disillusionment.

As we discussed in Chapter 6, developmental psychologists seem to concur that the development of *individuation* and independence among adolescents is necessary mainly for the purpose of reconfiguring attachments with parents and adult significant others into more status-equitable terms (e.g., Grotevant & Cooper, 1986; Youniss & Smollar, 1985). Under the most propitious circumstances, early adolescents move from being considerably dependent on caretakers to becoming mature participants in family and community social networks.

However, in my view, optimal self-reliance occurs not merely to the extent that adolescents learn to take considerably more responsibility for accomplishing important tasks and resolving personal problems, but also and more importantly, that they do so in large part by mobilizing—on their own—the supportive capacities of various network members, including the "friends of friends" (Boissevain, 1974). Consistent and long-term socialization toward independence outside the realm of network-building spells alienation, characterized here in large part by social estrangement from the human and institutional resources necessary for reaching developmental milestones and for accomplishing socially valued goals. The push toward individualism in the urban school system appears to accomplish only the malintegration of the student body—in other words, large-scale alienated embeddedness and the psychological correlates of alienation.

Mistrust of adults by adolescents may be a widespread cultural phenomenon in contemporary capitalist societies; that is, it may be a phenomenon that transcends class and racial boundaries. The difference is that middle-class, majority-group adolescents are situated within structural relations where institutional support is tacitly provided through routine interactions with significant others, and where social capital formation exists as a built-in function of the schools and organizations they participate in. Distrust of adults and a lack of help-seeking initiative do not easily undermine the networks within which they participate, including the flow of resources and privileges. Social-capital formation among middle-class youth maintains a certain degree of resistance to the corrosive effects of adult-aversive subcultures. In contrast, for working-class youth, particularly those of racial-minority status, a defensive help-seeking orientation, especially when fully manifested within the realm of the school, is a consequence of past and ongoing institutional treatments, as well as a catalyst for the further decapitalization of the adolescent's adult social network.

The Organizational Culture of the School

The findings in this chapter on students' help-seeking orientation also suggest the significance of the school's organizational culture, in which students interact with potential adult providers of support. Especially important is the manner in which institutional resources (e.g., academic support, preparation for college, counseling, access to state-of-the-art curriculum) are tacitly organized and distributed, whether on a *competitive* or a more *communitarian* basis. Also critical within the school's organizational culture is how social support is defined and interpreted, and how the patterned distribution of supportive resources is legitimated—issues that are fundamentally ideological, and interpreted subtly by students as forms of inclusion or exclusion.

Auxilio High may not differ from many other urban or semi-urban schools characterized by a majority of low-income minority youth. Access to the school's most prized resources as well as personalized access to school personnel is tacitly organized to give advantage to those students with the following orientations: first, those who arrive with competitive and highly efficacious network and help-seeking orientations, who feel entitled, and who can make demands in an assertive yet nonthreatening manner; and second, those students—particularly immigrants—who are motivated to disassociate themselves from the stigma carried by more aversive and alienated students, and who display signs of conformity, cultural accommodation, optimism, and faith in the legitimacy of the institution. In short, access to an institution's human resources is reserved for students who have learned to *decode the system,* even when the "codes" appear arbitrary or as fetishes of those in charge. Of course, such decoding and accommodation can occur uncritically, outside of rational awareness. For many students, however, genuine faith in the legitimacy of the institution is *not* a basis for their scholastic efforts; for them, learning to decode the system means learning to manage one's critical penetrations into exclusionary structures of the school, particularly in ways that do not alienate those key gatekeepers highly invested in the institution's dominant ideologies and myths.

Why does the burden of social-capital formation within the school fall so heavily on minority students? A good part of the answer is that Auxilio High, like other urban schools throughout the country, is both noncommittal and ill-equipped to provide the various social supports geared toward meeting students' emotional and psychological needs; nor is it geared, in any authentic way, toward maximizing students' intellectual and multilinguistic strengths. I especially have in mind those developing forms of resiliency and resource needs so closely associated with class- and race-based residential segregation, discrimination, poverty or economic stresses, family stresses, and continuous cultural adaptation. For this population, the generous provision of various types of social support by multiple parties, combined with a commitment to foster prosocial forms of resiliency, appears to be essential for academic learning and network-building to take place (Stanton-Salazar & Spina, 2000). And yet, the school system continues to reserve its best resources for those who are relatively advantaged by their family and community networks.

A fundamental reason for distributing the best resources to the least alienated and the most resource-advantaged students is ideological and systemic. The allocation of school resources, including the investment of teachers' and counselors' time, has historically been founded on a number of troublesome properties inherent in the school's Anglo-Protestant ideological system: the primacy of individual choice, the mythology of competition and meritocracy, and a stubborn belief regarding the limited distribution of talent within the student body. Schools are thus charged with reserving their best resources, including social capital, for those who are deemed "most deserving." By way of the most medieval of motives, at the deepest ideological level, and through innumerable tacit policies and public dictates, the urban school system is charged with the task of sorting the "saved" from the "the damned," and with channeling the best of its institutional resources to the former.

NOVANET versus AVID

Besides identifying the "saved," the school traditionally has also been charged with the task of providing minimal services to the "damned," framed in the historical guises of "separate but equal," "equal educational opportunity," and compensatory education. Poor academic performance is normally handled by the urban school through "compensatory" instructional treatments, and only rarely through programmatic efforts designed to weave a web of supportive resources around poorly performing students. At Auxilio High, these two alternatives were embodied in the NOVANET program and AVID. NOVANET was a computer-based curriculum designed to remediate students' weak skills in math and reading. Low-achieving students assigned to NOVANET come to class, sit in front of a computer terminal, and dutifully proceed through a series of computer tasks that are matched to their individually assessed skill levels. The teacher in the classroom is charged with facilitating students' progress through the different exercises and skill levels and with maintaining order, yet the principal pedagogical relationship in this classroom is between student and computer. In this classroom, the teacher is made to serve technology, not the other way around.

As we saw in Chapter 8, AVID's approach to underperforming pupils is galactically different. First of all, selected underachieving pupils recruited into the AVID program are subsequently sanctioned as having considerable "academic potential." During the course of the year, extraordinary efforts are made by the AVID teacher and the school to enhance the students' social network, to saturate them in institutional and academic support, to train them in collaborative learning strategies, to alter their self-concepts and academic identities, and to attend to their emotional and psychological needs. AVID at Auxilio High embodied the organizational and pedagogical principles that the rest of the urban school system refuses to seriously entertain. Of course, to actualize these principles throughout urban schools would require restructuring and retraining on a massive and transformative scale. To operate at an optimal level, such radical restructuring would also require adequate funding.

Given current political realities, it seems unlikely that public schools will become environments designed to reconstruct and enhance minority students' social networks in ways that would saturate them with institutional support. Doing so would ultimately lead to a degree of equality of educational outcome that would threaten the hold of the middle class on existing privileges and benefits (e.g., access to good universities; lucrative employment opportunities). To alter drastically the urban school system's subterranean currents would no doubt rock the foundations of society's racialized class system—thus undercutting its preferential distribution of privileges and network resources.

10

School Personnel as Sources of Social and Institutional Support: Prevalence and Predictors

with Robert H. Tai[1]

The previous two chapters provided views of both the great supportive possibilities that inhere in relations with school personnel and the often hidden barriers to students' fully realizing that support. This chapter begins with the following two questions: First, just how prevalent are school personnel as sources of emotional, personal, and informational support? Second, who are those adolescents most and least likely to engage in network-building behavior and help seeking? In the course of the following pages, we report on a series of statistical analyses designed to address these two questions. In addressing the second question, we explore some of the more probable factors associated with actual help-seeking behavior within the school, including gender, achievement status, language proficiency, and help-seeking orientation. We also explore a number of factors hypothesized to predict positive help-seeking orientations among Latino adolescents, including a number of factors drawn from the literature on adult help-seeking behavior.

DESCRIPTIVE FINDINGS FROM SIX BAY/PENINSULA AREA SCHOOLS

The answer to the first question above lies in various surveys we conducted across several sites and in different periods. The first set of data reported below comes from our original network survey, administered during the 1987–1988 academic year, to 205 Mexican-origin students from six high schools in the San Francisco–San Jose Peninsula area.[2] All six schools were located within middle- and high-income areas; students from lower-income neighborhoods walked or were transported to these schools as part of district-wide desegregation plans. Latinos represented from

11.3% to 33.4% of the student body in each school, with Mexican-origin students forming slightly less than half of the Latino student population. The proportion of non-Latino White students ranged from 35.4% to 59.4%. Descriptive statistics are provided only for adolescents who were immigrant or second-generation (N = 145); third-generation students were excluded from this descriptive analysis. Statistics are provided by acculturation level, as indicated by language proficiencies and use (Highly Bilingual, n = 44; Limited English Proficient, n = 58; and English Dominant, n = 43). Details on this sample and the other samples used here, and of the methodology used, are found in Appendix B.

The second set of data comes from a replication of the original Bay/Peninsula network survey administered at Auxilio High School during the spring of 1991 (N = 75). For this data set, the sample is divided by gender and by immigration status. Students who had been in the United States 7 years or less were differentiated from everyone else (gender *x* acculturation level). Finally, the third set of data comes from a questionnaire survey administered to the entire student body of Auxilio High toward the end of the 1991–1992 academic year (N = 1,187).

We begin with our support network data from the six Bay/Peninsula area schools. Our initial inquiry sought to specify in some way the average number of school personnel indicated by students as likely sources for any of the forms of support identified in our network survey (*emotional*, *personal*, and *informational support*, with forms of "academic support" distributed across *personal* and *informational support*). Table 10.1 presents our calculations.

Immediately noteworthy is that between a fifth and a quarter of the students surveyed (22.5%) did not name any staff person as a likely source of support. This statistic is even more telling if we keep in mind that respondents had 14 distinct opportunities to name a school agent as a source of aid. A bit more than a third of the sample, 35.9%, indicated only one staff person as a likely source of support. Another 35.9% indicated between two and four staff members. Only five students, or 3.5% of the sample, indicated five or more staff members as sources. Thus, at least 60% of the sample appeared disinclined to actively seek social support from the network of adults at their school.

We proceeded by closely examining the kinds of support students who were so inclined sought from teachers, counselors, and other staff people.

Emotional Support

Let's look first at the extent to which students indicated school personnel as either likely or actual sources of emotional support.[3] Table 10.1

TABLE 10.1. School Personnel as Elected Sources of Support (Bay Area/Peninsula Data, N = 145, Statistics shown for First- and Second-generation Adolescents Only)

	One or More Elected	*No One Elected*	N
School Staff Person as an Elected Source of either *Personal*, *Emotional*, or *Informational Support*	74.5% (*n* = 108)	25.5% (*n* = 37)	145
School Staff Person as an Elected Source of *Emotional Support*	6.2% (*n* = 9)	93.8% (*n* = 136)	
Highly Bilingual (students)	4.5% (*n* = 2)	95.5% (*n* = 42)	44
Spanish-dominant	3.4% (*n* = 2)	96.6% (*n* = 56)	58
English-dominant	11.6% (*n* = 5)	88.4% (*n* = 38)	43
School Staff Person as an Elected Source of *Personal Support*	26.2% (*n* = 38)	73.8% (*n* = 107)	
Highly Bilingual	25% (*n* = 11)	75% (*n* = 33)	44
Spanish-dominant	29.3% (*n* = 17)	70.7% (*n* = 41)	58
English-dominant	23.3% (*n* = 10)	76.7% (*n* = 33)	43
School Staff Person as an Elected Source of *Informational Support*	71% (*n* = 103)	29% (*n* = 42)	
Highly Bilingual	72.7% (*n* = 32)	27.3% (*n* = 12)	44
Spanish-dominant	72.4% (*n* = 42)	27.6% (*n* = 16)	58
English-dominant	67.4% (*n* = 29)	32.6% (*n* = 14)	43

again displays these results. It appears that in these six schools, school personnel very seldom emerged as likely sources of emotional support; in fact only 6.2%, or 9 out of 145 students, indicated school personnel as viable sources. No sizable differences by acculturation level were apparent. This is not to say that students never shared with school personnel what was going on in their lives, or that school agents were never responsive to the students' distress signals. Much of the emotional support people provide each other occurs at the tacit level, in the context of routine interactions. As we saw in Chapter 8, school personnel can and do act as important sources of emotional support and intimate counsel. What the data show here, however, is that students seldom identified school personnel as people they would consciously seek out and *ask* for emotional support. As we also saw in Chapters 8 and 9, a good deal of trust and rapport have to be developed in a relationship for adolescents to perceive a school agent, in a conscious or deliberate way, as an approachable and safe source of emotional support.

Personal Support

The data on personal support indicate slightly more trust and more help seeking. The category of personal support included *material support* (which includes money), *personal favors, help with schoolwork,* and *advice regarding personal-private matters (i.e., "intimate counsel").* Electing a school staff member as a likely or actual source of at least one of the four forms of personal support constituted *personal support* from school personnel. Although it is significantly higher, we see that only a quarter of the students indicated school personnel as a likely source of personal support (26.2%). Put differently, three-fourths, or 73.8% of students, did not and would not deliberately seek out anyone on the school staff for this type of support. Of those who indicated at least one staff person, 79% reported either one or two people. Again, no significant differences by acculturation level were apparent.

Informational Support

The data on seeking *informational support,* which includes academic advice and guidance, indicate the highest level of engagement. Seven constituent forms of informational support were included in our measure:

1. Personal Advice on Academic Decisions;
2. Personal Advice and Guidance Regarding Future Educational and Occupational Plans;

3. Technical Information Related to Educational/Occupational Future;
4. Information Regarding Current Job Opportunities;
5. Legal Assistance;
6. Health Crisis Services (e.g., issues of substance abuse);
7. Psychological Services/Professional Crisis Management.

Close to three-quarters of the students surveyed, or 71%, indicated at least one staff member as a likely source of informational support, and nearly half, 49.7%, indicated actually seeking this type of assistance during the last 3 months. Of those students who named at least one staff person, 82.5% named either one or two people. Another 14.5% named between three and four people.

Although it is reasonable to expect that a student's gender would be a decisive factor in predicting the seeking of emotional and personal support, multiple regression analyses of school personnel as sources of informational support (as dependent variable) showed gender to have no independent effect. Similar findings surfaced in our Auxilio High School survey when we looked at a student's gender as a predictor of seeking academic support. A student's gender did, however, show signs of operating indirectly, through its influence on adolescents' help-seeking orientation. These findings on gender and orientation are reported in detail below. In sum, school personnel emerged as likely sources of informational support for most students, yet only a minority of students appear to have had relations with school agents that enabled them to confidently seek personal and emotional support from those agents.

DESCRIPTIVE FINDINGS FROM AUXILIO HIGH SCHOOL

We turn now to our data from Auxilio High School where we replicated our original network survey with 75 students (complete data). Table 10.2 displays the results of our calculations. With this sample we again sought to find out the average number of school personnel indicated as likely sources for any of the forms of support identified in our network survey (emotional, personal, and informational support).

In every category except for immigrant boys, only one person did not indicate at least one staff member. For immigrant boys, 4 out of 39 did not indicate at least one person. These statistics, across two different regions and school types, reveal an important and probable influence of school context on help seeking among Latino students. Our six Bay Area schools were predominantly White, and for the most part situated in

TABLE 10.2. School Personnel as Elected Sources of Support (Auxilio High School Data, N = 75)

School Staff Person as an Elected Source of Personal, Emotional, *or* Informational Support	*No One Elected*	*2–4 Elected*	*5 or More Elected*	*2 or More Elected*	N
Recent-immigrant girls*	10%	70%	20%	90%	
	($n = 1$)	($n = 7$)	($n = 2$)	($n = 9$)	10
Recent-immigrant boys	28.6%	57%	7%	64.3%	
	($n = 4$) ·	($n = 8$)	($n = 1$)	($n = 9$)	14
Acculturated girls	3.8%	53.8%	26.9%	80.8%	
	($n = 1$)	($n = 14$)	($n = 7$)	($n = 21$)	26
Acculturated boys	4%	44%	28%	72.8%	
	($n = 1$)	($n = 11$)	($n = 7$)	($n = 18$)	25

*Recent immigrants are those who have resided in the United States for 7 years or less

middle-class and upper-middle-class neighborhoods. Recall that for the entire Bay/Peninsula Area sample (N = 145), 25.5% did not name a staff member as a source of social support. In contrast, for our Auxilio High School sample (N = 75), only 9.3% did not name a staff person. The fact that Auxilio High School had a 61% Latino student majority, and an identity as a predominantly "Mexican school," certainly appears to have played a decisive role. Later in this chapter we will deal with the complex relations between *perceived support* and electing school agents as potential sources of help, on the one hand, and actual help seeking on the other.

Our Auxilio High students, as a group, also tended to name significantly more school personnel as potential sources of support. Whereas about 40% of the Bay/Peninsula Area sample named two or more adults, of the four subgroups of students at Auxilio High, the strong majority of three subgroups named two or more adults (90%, 80.8%, & 72.8%). Even the acculturated boys' group, where the percentage drops to 64.3%, registered significantly higher than each of the three language groups in the Bay/Peninsula Area sample (43.2%, 39.7%, & 34.9%). For both boys and girls, the mean number of ties to Auxilio High School personnel hovered around three adults.

GAUGING STUDENTS' SCHOOL-BASED SOCIAL CAPITAL:
USE OF MULTIPLE INDICATORS

Although the majority of our respondents at Auxilio High reported a likelihood of seeking help from two to three adults at the school, several questions emerge. The first question has do to with whether our sample of 51 students, selected to produce diversification, was truly representative of Latino students at Auxilio High and other similar schools. As we shall see later in this chapter, our questionnaire survey measures of seeking help from school personnel on academic matters showed a sizable percentage of students not seeking help (refer to Table 10.7). The second question has to do with whether any of the elected ties reported above approached a sufficient level of trust and intensity to actually allow for authentically supportive interactions (i.e., the actual mobilization of staff identified as likely sources). As we shall see, election of particular school agents as *likely* or *imaginable* sources of support didn't always translate into active help seeking, particularly among Spanish-dominant students. Of course, election of school personnel as likely or imaginable sources of support may have social-psychological or integrative benefits for students, apart from whether they actually seek them out for help. Our measures here may be serving as indices of "social integration," classically defined, rather than as indicators of social capital. For the moment, however, we shall focus on elected ties to school agents as relations that reflect a strong likelihood of being mobilized for social support.

This discussion also leads us to the challenges faced by any researcher interested in measuring social capital, particularly when surveying low-status respondents. How do we know whether the ties we've measured or documented constitute authentic social capital, or merely *fool's gold*? Conventional statistical/quantitative measures of help seeking and supportive ties tend to be poor and at times unreliable indicators of social capital, mainly because they provide little information regarding the intensity and dynamics of a relationship or about the quality of the resources and support.[4] A more reliable or perhaps more informative indicator is survey measures that indicate a multiplex relationship, that is, when a particular relationship or tie either provides or is seen as a promising source of multiple forms of support. When a friend provides counsel on intimate matters, has recently helped with a short-term loan, and is willing, on occasion, to drive you to work or school, such a relationship is multiplex. Multiplex relations tend to be associated with a high level of attachment and positive affect on the part of ego (i.e., the receiver). Still, unless we invest large amounts of time querying the respondent about his or her relationships, or directly observing the dynamics and interactions of a particular tie over time, we are forced to trust our tenuous methodological assumptions.

Multiplex Relations with Institutional Agents as an Indicator of Social Capital

In our study based at Auxilio High School we were fortunate enough to spend the necessary hours with respondents, surveying their network relationships and talking to them about the various people and sources of support in their lives, including different school agents. We even inquired about staff people they did not mention in the original network survey, particularly those we knew they had routine contact with. In this way, we were able to establish whether identified and likely sources of support were weak or strong, uniplex or multiplex, intimate or casual, and perhaps even ambivalent or conflictive. We were also able to investigate the dynamics underlying those interactions with agents not elected.

Identifying multiplex relations with institutional agents is a somewhat more informative (although still imprecise) way to measure adolescent social capital. Multiplex relations imply an above average level of inter-action and some significant foundation of trust. What is conveyed is an acknowledgement, on the part of the adolescent, that a certain adult is viewed as a source of multiple forms of support, for different problems and across different situations. Multiplex relations with school-based institutional agents are also associated with the provision of forms of support outside the person's official list of professional duties; they connote informal helping relations, motivated by a personal concern for, and an emotional investment in, the individual.

Our network survey data gave us basic numerical indicators of multiplex relationships with school personnel. Follow-up interview data on relations with identified supportive ties with school personnel, once partially transcribed and completely summarized, were coded and used to characterize the various ways students talked about their relationships with school personnel; for example, students might indicate that a particular agent knew how to inspire trust (*confianza*), and that the adult frequently recognized the student's achievements. Ties were also coded as CR ("caring") when the data suggested a high degree of involvement and affective attachment. Our findings on multiplex ties are displayed in Table 10.3.

How prevalent were multiplex relations between our respondents and school personnel? Our findings were derived from our sample of 75 students who participated in the network survey. Our calculations revealed that from one-quarter to about half of students' identified supportive ties were multiplex, with multiplexity in this instance defined as a relationship

TABLE 10.3. School Personnel as Multiplex Ties (Auxilio High School Data, N = 75)

School Staff Person Elected as a Source of:	MULTIPLEXITY		
	2 or More Forms of Support	3 or More Forms of Support	N
Percentage of Students Reporting at Least One Multiplex Relationship			
Recent-immigrant girls*	80% (n = 8)	70% (n = 7)	10
Recent-immigrant boys	57% (n = 8)	36% (n = 5	14
Acculturated girls	62% (n = 16)	50% (n = 13)	26
Acculturated boys	72% (n = 18)	52% (n = 13)	25

*Recent immigrants are those who have resided in the United States. for 7 years or less

serving as a perceived source of two or more types of support (i.e., school agent elected as potential/likely or actual/past source of more than one form of support).[5] At least 57% of each of our four groups reported at least one multiplex relationship. For those students who named at least one multiplex tie, the average number reported was between one and two people. When we define multiplexity in terms of three or more forms of support, we see that immigrant girls were most consistent (70%) in reporting highly multiplex relations with a school staff member.

What percentage of students showed evidence of close, affective attachments to school personnel? Our findings here were derived from complete data on 39 students, drawn from the sample of 51 students who underwent our intensive interviews. For all groups within this sample, close "caring" attachments, when they did occur, typically involved only one staff person. Keep in mind here that students, through their assigned courses, engage on average between six and eight teachers during the academic year.[6] Our calculations revealed that while only about a third of each group of girls demonstrated at least one close attachment (Recent-immigrant girls, 37.5%; Acculturated girls, 31.3%), about two-thirds of each group of boys reported close attachments to at least one adult (66.6% for both male groups).[7]

These findings parallel what we saw in our analysis of adolescent-parent relations, where adolescent girls were more emotionally invested and involved in their relationships with parents and, therefore, experienced more conflictive or ambivalent relations. Also, with close engagement comes a greater awareness of potentials and limits of relationships. Relative to boys, adolescent girls may very well have more stringent criteria for articulating a relationship as "close." It is very possible that close and affective relations between female students and school personnel were more developed and emotionally more involved that those between male students and personnel. Adolescent girls may be less likely to cite close and highly affective attachments to school personnel than boys, but those relations that are articulated as highly affective may be much more intimate than the close relationships identified and articulated by boys.

Our indicators of multiplexity and caring relations, as tenuous as they were, do provide us some sense of the likelihood of different Latino student groups' being engaged in supportive relations with school personnel. These indicators, however, do not tell us conclusively whether these relations were in fact conduits of authentic institutional support, or merely indicators of social-psychological integration in the classical sense. However, there is reason to suggest that a student's lack of multiplex relationships with school personnel does not bode well for either their integration into the institution or their access to vital forms of institutional support.

PREDICTING TIES TO SCHOOL-BASED AGENTS: FINDINGS FROM SIX BAY AREA/PENINSULA SCHOOLS

We shift here to a presentation of our statistical findings from our two research sites, and return to the second question posed at the beginning of this chapter: Who are those most and least likely to incorporate school personnel into their social support networks? Similarly, who are those most and least likely to engage in help-seeking behavior? These questions are addressed here through statistical analyses based on network and survey data collected during the San Francisco–San Jose Peninsula study, and originally published in 1995 (Stanton-Salazar & Dornbusch, 1995).

Our findings derive from analyses conducted on all 205 Mexican-origin students who participated in the survey, and focus exclusively on the number of ties to school personnel as likely sources of seven forms of information support. Table C.1 in Appendix C provides the means for the variables in the study, as well as correlations. Table C.2 in Appendix C presents the results of our multiple regression analyses. We examined a number of independent variables we believed were theoretically linked with the variation in social capital among ethnic and racial minority adolescents. We expected that students with the following attributes would report the highest number of ties to school-based sources of informational support: students reporting relatively higher SES, English proficiency, academic grades, and educational and occupational expectations.

Although family SES showed a small significant independent effect on reported school-based ties, our language variables proved to have the most consistent influence. In accordance with our original hypothesis, reported access to school personnel as sources of support is significantly enhanced by a student's reported proficiency in English. More interesting, however, is that controlling for English proficiency and SES, Spanish use by the student proved to have a positive and significant effect on supportive ties to school agents. Both English proficiency and Spanish use retained significant positive effects, net of other variables. Thus, not only do these analyses provide support for the hypothesized relation between language status and social capital, they also suggest that a highly developed bilingualism (and biculturalism) may play a prominent role in determining access to social capital (see Stanton-Salazar, 1997).

Grades failed to register a consistent independent effect on supportive ties to school personnel. The lack of an effect was puzzling. In separate stepwise analyses, we first introduced grades and a selected status expectation variable, then we added SES, followed by our two language variables, to complete the regression analyses. In the series of regressions run for the lower SES subsample (n = 152), grades retained a significant and independent effect on ties to school personnel until the introduction of the English proficiency index. The problem of colinearity does not appear to be the explanation, given that grades and English proficiency are not correlated (r = .08, p < .22).

Grade level was used as both a proxy for age and a control variable. In our regression analyses, grade level proved to have a significant and independent influence on our measure of social capital. Our descriptive analyses showed that the sophomores in our study reported the least access to school personnel as sources of "institutional support." We return to this issue a bit later.

We also expected students with higher status expectations (i.e., educational and occupational expectations) to report information networks characterized by significantly more ties to school personnel. Status expectations did not, however, register any independent effect on such ties. Auxiliary analyses did show that students with high educational expectations did tend to be slightly more actively engaged in seeking help for academic matters (beta = .18, p < .05), though it is somewhat perplexing that this relation did not extend to those with relatively higher occupational expectations or college plans.

The Special Role of Language Status

The acculturation differences in our sample make these analyses both perplexing and informative. The perplexity arises from trying to interpret the relation between socioeconomic status and social capital, as this relation may not be linear for this population. Other studies of Mexican-origin student populations have shown that the most significant challenge is interpreting the apparent educational advantages enjoyed by those who are bilingual and bicultural, in spite of low SES (e.g., Buriel, 1984). Although lack of English proficiency may inhibit contact with school-based agents, continued language competency in Spanish may reveal its own independent positive effect, once students attain a threshold level of English proficiency.[8]

One problem related to the issue of bilingualism is that our measures of language proficiency and use may be serving two simultaneous functions: as an indicator of cultural adaptation and as an indicator of second-language acquisition. In this sample, with our inclusion of lower-income, immigrant, or first-generation students, measures of language proficiency and use became a powerful differentiating device, overshadowing any possible effects of other measures on access to social capital. However, only one-third of our sample was first-generation, and among the 59 immigrant students who provided information on length of residence, only 34% had been in the country for 6 years or less (≤ 6 yrs = recent immigrants); 55.2% had been in the United States for 9 years or more (≥ 9 yrs = well-acculturated immigrants)—plenty of time for this latter group to become proficient in English. In fact, when we look at those who scored on or below the mean in English proficiency (n = 96), 81.2% reported speaking English "moderately well" to "very well." This further suggests that our measure of English proficiency, far from just accounting for language proficiency, evidently served as a proxy for acculturation and more consequential social-status markers, such as sociolinguistic cues and modes of self-presentation, that label one as a member of a low-status immigrant group. In majority-dominant middle-class domains in which these youth participated (e.g., the school), such markers may have had a stifling effect on intergroup relations—even when the students were functionally fluent in English. Figure 10.1 summarizes the findings of the study.

PREDICTING ADOLESCENTS' HELP-SEEKING ORIENTATION: REGRESSION RESULTS FROM AUXILIO HIGH SCHOOL SURVEY

Our interest in the social-psychological orientations of Auxilio High students focuses on their perceptions of support from teachers and counselors and on their generalized help-seeking orientations. These social-psychological orientations are viewed as the subjective dimension of social embeddedness, and referred to here as *social-psychological embeddedness*. Its complement, *behavioral embeddedness*, reflects the degree to which the individual is positioned within the flow, exchange, and transmission of institutional resources. A high degree of behavioral embeddedness implies a moderate to high degree of active help seeking on the part of the individual, relative to those who embrace more self-reliant coping strategies and who withdraw from institutional agents as sources of social support.

High degrees of behavioral embeddedness are seen as correlating with high degrees of social-psychological embeddedness, particularly, a positive help-seeking orientation. Such an orientation becomes evident, in part, in terms of the degree of confidence an individual has regarding the ability of others (in the environment) to provide quality support; also important is the individual's ability and willingness to share his or her problems with others. Thus, people with highly positive help-seeking orientations ex-

FIGURE 10.1. Factors Statistically Associated with Reporting Ties to School Personnel as Sources of Informational Support and Academic Support (Bay Area/Peninsula Sample, N = 205)

Proficiency in English

Spanish Usage (controlling for English

 Proficiency) ....*High Levels of Bilingualism*

Not being a Sophomore

 (i.e., Junior or Senior)

High Educational Expectations

hibit both confidence in the support process (*confianza en confianza* [trusting mutual trust]) and facility with self-disclosure (interpersonal openness).

In an auxiliary study based on data from our questionnaire survey of Auxilio High (Stanton-Salazar et al., in press), we examined three measures of help-seeking orientation, as well as a set of antecedent variables known to have a predictive value among adult populations: socioeconomic status (SES), gender, age, English-language proficiency, academic performance (self-reported grades), and self-esteem. The three separate measures of help-seeking orientation were labeled as follows: *Confidence* in the support process, Interpersonal *Openness*, and *Desire* for Academic Support). Our measure of *Confidence* represents the adolescent's confidence (or faith) in the process by which others could provide them with quality social support. This measure taps into a belief in "the support process"—in other words, that seeking support is an effective and appropriate coping strategy; it also reflects a belief (or faith) that known others could be adequately supportive in a time of need. Our measure of *Openness* represents the adolescent's ability and willingness to share personal problems with others. Our measure of *Desire* was designed to gauge whether or not the student desired pertinent information and guidance (from teachers or counselors) in making important educational and academic decisions.

Details as to the construction of these three measures are summarized briefly below.

- *Desire for Academic Support (Desire)*. Dichotomous variable originated from a 7-item scale used to gauge in what areas the students would have liked pertinent information and guidance. This scale was adapted from Hymovich (1983). The measure used here was based on the instruction, "Please indicate if you would or would not like to have help with or to discuss any of the following." We used one of the seven items, "Advice and guidance from teachers and counselors in making important educational and academic decisions," as a measure of the desire for academic support. The response format in the survey relied on the choices, "Would Not" and "Not Sure," which were assigned the value 0, and "Would Like," which was assigned the value 1.

The second and third help-seeking orientation measures relied on a 20-item scale developed and tested by Vaux, Burda, and Stewart (1986) and originally designed for adult respondents. Possible responses to items were set up in a 4-point agree-disagree format. Although Vaux, Burda, and Stewart (1986) conducted their validation using a unifactorial measure, our use of principal component analysis suggested two interpretable dimensions. Careful analysis produced two orthogonal factors:

- *Confidence in the Support Process* (*Confidence*). This first factor represents the respondent's confidence in the support process and in the ability of others to provide support. Items for this factor included, "Sometimes it is necessary to talk to someone about your problems."
- *Interpersonal Openness* (*Openness*). This second factor represents the respondent's ability and willingness to share personal problems with others. Items for this factor include, "Other people never understand my problems," and "If you confide in other people, they'll take advantage of you." The resulting scales showed reasonably good internal consistency, with Cronbach alphas of .76 for *Confidence*, and .61 for *Openness*.

Regression analyses were conducted using data from all students at the school who participated in the survey (those with complete data, N = 1,047). Analyses were also organized to test for differential effects of antecedent variables across three groups: Spanish-dominant Latinos, English-proficient Latinos, and non-Latinos.

Overall, the independent effect of socioeconomic status did not display a paramount role in our models, although some significant findings did occur. Family socioeconomic status did register significant positive effects on *Interpersonal Openness* among non-Latinos at this school. In accordance with published studies, non-Latino students from higher-income families tended to report a greater willingness to share problems with others. The findings for *Interpersonal Openness* among Latinos are difficult to decipher. As mentioned earlier, analyses of SES within Latino student populations are conventionally difficult due to the typically restricted socioeconomic variation (due in part to segregated schools).[9,10]

In accordance with published studies, gender displayed its prominent role in the help-seeking orientations of our high school sample, registering significant effects in each of our three principal regression models. Taken together, these findings appear quite unequivocal: Boys, relative to girls, consistently report lower *Confidence* in the support process, less willingness to share personal problems with others (i.e., less *Openness*), and less *Desire* for personalized academic support or assistance from school personnel.

Measures of English proficiency typically act as a particularly key variable differentiating Latino student samples. Although English proficiency showed no effect on *Confidence*, it showed itself to be a strong predictor of *Openness*. The findings connecting English proficiency with *Desire* were varied, with this relation apparently operative only among Spanish-dominant Latinos, and in the expected positive direction. Immigrants with the lowest levels of English proficiency seem quite unlikely to report a desire for academic support or assistance from school personnel.

Although age did not register any significant independent effect, preliminary descriptive analyses by grade level did show that 10th-graders (the youngest group) were, overall, less likely to be interested in academic support. Approximately 61% of all 11th-graders and 60% of 12th-graders desired academic support, while only 46.5% of 10th-graders desired support. This trend is accentuated when examining Latinos exclusively (only 37% of Latino sophomores desired academic support).

Our indicator of academic achievement appeared here to consistently substantiate its expected association with the help-seeking orientations of students, with effects significant across groups. As expected, students with good grades appear to have the most *Confidence* in the support process and to exhibit the most *Openness*; likewise, relative to low-achievers, high-achievers show greater *Desire* or interest in receiving advice and guidance on academic matters. Low-achievers—those most in need of academic help—appeared least inclined or prepared to engage the human resources of the school. Low-achieving males were especially disengaged.

Our findings for self-esteem were mixed and somewhat complex, given that our measure registered negative as well as positive effects on our dependent variables. Although reporting high self-esteem was associated with greater *interpersonal openness*, as would normally be hypothesized, high self-esteem was also associated with lower *confidence in the support process* and lower *desire for support*. Auxiliary bivariate correlations using the Spanish-dominant student subsample did show, however, a positive relationship between self-esteem and confidence in the support process. These auxiliary findings raise the possibility that the effects of self-esteem may be tied to distinctive perceptions of the help-seeking process, depending on cultural background and level of acculturation.

In summary, the strongest and most consistent effects across models came from our gender variable, followed by self-reported measures of academic performance. It appears that Latino males, low achievers, and recent immigrants tend to exhibit help-seeking orientations that would normally function to impede supportive interactions within and across social contexts, and perhaps most importantly, to impede supportive relations with school personnel.

We argue here that adolescents' help-seeking orientation, when manifested as a generalized coping strategy, is a crucial indicator of their social embeddedness within the school, and carries important and direct consequences for adolescents' access to forms of support that underlie educational mobility and developmental resiliency. In the analyses just reported, we see evidence suggesting that particular groups within the Latino high school population may be especially prone to social estrangement from vital sources of support in the school, home, and community. The findings here show that low-achieving males may be exhibiting a form of alienation describable as unsponsored self-reliance, characterized in part by a low degree of help-seeking initiative and a distrust of potentially supportive others. Within the high school setting, sophomores within this self-reliant group may be particularly at risk, at a time when their integration and *membership* within the school may be vital to their prospects for high school graduation and long-term academic success (Croninger & Lee, 1999; Wehlage et al., 1989). Recent-immigrant students may also be particularly at risk for remaining marginal to the school's resource networks. Only a fifth of the Spanish-dominant students reported a desire for more academic support, distinguishing themselves in this way from the other groups. Recent immigrants also reported significantly lower levels of *interpersonal openness*, again, relative to the other groups. Figure 10.2 summarizes our findings.

As we shall show in the following section, both of these orientation measures are quite predictive of actual help-seeking behavior and, potentially, of social-capital formation within the school environment. We see, then, that Spanish-dominant immigrants may be particularly prone to regulating their own marginality within the school, despite their well-documented optimism and scholastic motivation. Below we report on another parallel study that looked at the association between measures of help-seeking orientation and measures of actual help-seeking behavior—with such behavior cast as a key indicator of positive embeddedness within the school.

PREDICTING STUDENTS' BEHAVIORAL EMBEDDEDNESS
AT AUXILIO HIGH

In this section, we report on our investigation of the social embeddedness experiences of the Latino student body at Auxilio High School. We explore two help-seeking measures of behavioral embeddedness. We also explore four measures of social-psychological embeddedness, all derived from items taken from our questionnaire survey of Auxilio High. For our multivariate logistical analyses, we employed our measures of social-psychological embeddedness (including our three measures of help-seeking orientation) to predict positive behavioral embeddedness (i.e., actual help seeking). Like the analyses and findings reported above, statistics are also reported for the other major social groupings at the school. Below we sum-

FIGURE 10.2. Factors Statistically Associated with Positive Help-seeking Orientation (Auxilio High School-wide Survey)

	Confidence	Openness	Desire
Being female (Gender)	*Confidence*	*Openness*	*Desire*
Older adolescents (Spanish-dominant students only)			*Desire*
Not being a Sophomore (i.e., Junior or Senior)			*Desire*
High Grades	*Confidence*	*Openness*	*Desire*
Proficiency in English		*Openness*	*Desire*
High Self-esteem (Spanish-dominant students only)	*Confidence*	*Openness*	
* * *			
High Self-esteem (English-proficient Latinos; negative relationship)	**Low** *Confidence*		

marize the construction of our two measures of behavioral embeddedness and a fourth measure of social-psychological embeddedness, i.e., perceived support.

- *Sought Assistance from a Teacher or Counselor Regarding Academic Issues (Issues).* Based on the following item, "What have you done this semester [since January—a six-month period] when you needed to make an important academic or school-related decision? Examples of such decisions are taking or dropping certain courses, such as advanced academic courses or vocational courses, dropping out of school, or entering a tutorial program." There were seven possible responses, including "Spoke to a teacher" and "Spoke to no one; I figured it out alone." For purposes of analysis, a dichotomous variable was constructed based on whether or not the student reported speaking to either a teacher or a counselor. Following the

convention dictating the assignment of values to dependent variables in logistic regression, responses were coded yes = 1, no = 0.

- *Sought Assistance from a Teacher or Counselor Regarding Post–High
  School Plans (Plans).* Based on the following item, "What have you
  done this school year to plan for your future after high school?" A
  total of thirteen possible responses were available, including "I have
  not gotten around to doing anything about my plans after high
  school." Of the thirteen possible responses, eight pertained to different sources of advice and guidance. For purposes of analysis, a
  dichotomous variable was constructed based on whether or not the
  student reported seeking assistance from either a teacher or a counselor. Again, responses were coded yes = 1, no = 0.
- *Perceived Support.* Derived from an inventory composed of 11 items
  pertaining to perceptions of support from teachers and guidance
  counselors. Inventory adapted from an assessment scale developed
  and tested by Procidano and Heller (1983). Through factor analysis, a measure of perceived support of teachers was constructed.
  Items for this factor include "My teachers give me the moral support I need to do well in school" and "I rely on my teachers for
  advise and guidance in making important school related decisions."
  There were four possible responses to these items, from Strongly
  Agree to Strongly Disagree. A test of interconsistency produced a
  Cronbach's alpha of .74.

Table 10.4 displays the racial/ethnic group percentages for each measure of behavioral embeddedness, including language-group differences
within the Latino population. Although the majority of each group reported
seeking assistance, between one-third and two-fifths of each group did not
report seeking help.

Although Euro-Americans (Whites) appear to have the most seekers of
academic support (67.9%), the only statistically significant differences involving this group were those relative to Spanish-dominant Latinos (59.4%). The
differences between English-proficient and Spanish-dominant Latinos were
not statistically significant. When we look at support sought regarding
post–high school plans, we see that for each group, nearly half to two-thirds
did not seek such support. Latinos appear to be the least engaged in this
form of help-seeking. Looking at those who didn't seek help, differences
between Euro-Americans (47.4%) and both English-proficient (56.8%) and
Spanish-dominant Latinos (63.5%) were statistically significant. In this case,
the differences between English-proficient and Spanish-dominant Latinos
were statistically significant. Spanish-dominant Latinos appear most at risk
of not receiving both forms of institutional support.

TABLE 10.4. Two Measures of *Behavioral Embeddedness:* Sophomores vs. Upper-level students (Percentage of each group who spoke to a teacher or a counselor)

Spoke to School Personnel Regarding:	ETHNO-LINGUISTIC GROUPS				
	Latino (English-proficient)	Latino (Spanish-dominant)	African American	Asian	European American (White)
School Problems					
Entire Ethnic Group	66.0% (*n* = 309)	59.4% (*n* = 389)	59.7% (*n* = 114)	60.0% (*n* = 55)	67.9% (*n* = 215)
Juniors and Seniors	67.3% (*n* = 205)	68.6% (*n* = 204)	58.3% (*n* = 72)	56.8% (*n* = 37)	70.4% (*n* = 142)
Sophomores	63.5 % (*n* = 104)	49.2 % (*n* = 185)	61.9% (*n* = 42)	66.7% (*n* = 18)	63.0% (*n* = 73)
Post–high school Plans					
Entire Ethnic Group	43.2% (*n* = 308)	36.5% (*n* = 386)	54.55 (*n* = 112)	45.5% (*n* = 55)	52.6% (*n* = 213)
Juniors and Seniors	47.1% (*n* = 204)	47.6% (*n* = 204)	53.5% (*n* = 71)	48.7% (*n* = 37)	56.3% (*n* = 142)
Sophomores	35.6% (*n* = 104)	24.2% (*n* = 182)	56.1% (*n* = 41)	38.9% (*n* = 18)	45.1% (*n* = 71)

The influence of grade level may have contributed to the low mobilization of support among Spanish-dominant Latinos, given that this group had the largest proportion of sophomores—48.3% compared with an average of 34% in the other groups. Table 10.4 shows the differences in mobilization of support across ethnolinguistic group and grade level. We see that 50.8% of Spanish-dominant Latino sophomores did not seek assistance from a teacher or a counselor regarding academic issues; similarly, 75.8% of this group did not seek assistance with post–high school plans.

With the exception of African American students, sophomore status appears to have a consistent negative effect on the mobilization of support across ethnolinguistic groups. Sophomores tend to have the largest percentage of students not seeking support from either teachers or counselors. In auxiliary analyses at the aggregate level, looking only at teachers as sources of academic support, we found the trend accentuated, with 63.9% of all sophomores not seeking support from teachers, compared with 49.8% of all seniors not seeking out teachers. These findings mirror those in our Bay Area/Peninsula study (N = 205).

Logistic Regression Analyses and Findings

We move now to our regression results. Tables 10.5 and 10.6 display the logistic regression models for the two outcome measures of behavioral embeddedness.[11,12] To reiterate, we interpret students' positive help-seeking orientations and perceived support as two key indicators of positive social-psychological embeddedness. As stated earlier, *perceived support* speaks to the individual's past, cumulative, and current assessments of the support derived from school agents and the institution. Thus, we expected students reporting a high level of *Perceived Support* and positive help-seeking orientations (i.e., *Confidence* in the support process, interpersonal *Openness, Desire* for support) to be the most likely to report actively mobilizing academic support from teachers and counselors. Our results were mixed for the two outcome measures of behavioral embeddedness.

We begin with the outcome *Sought Support for Academic Issues* (please refer to Table 10.5). We discovered that *Perceived Support* and two of the three help-seeking orientations (*Desire* and *Openness*) were significant predictors of help-seeking behavior (Issues), while *Confidence* proved to be nonsignificant. Students registering a strong *Desire for Academic Support* were nearly twice as likely to seek support for academic issues as students with low *Desire*, net of the other factors.[13] Similarly, students registering high on *Openness* were more than twice as likely to seek support for academic issues as were students low on *Openness*.[14]

Our analysis also revealed differential effects for *Perceived Support* across our ethnolinguistic groups (Non-Latinos, Spanish-dominant Latinos, and English-proficient Latinos). In general, students registering high on *Perceived Support* were 10 times more likely to seek support for academic issues than were students with low levels of *Perceived Support*, net of the other factors.[15] However, comparing two students, one an English-proficient Latino and the second a Spanish-dominant Latino, with all variables set to averages, we discovered that the English-proficient Latino student was nearly twice as likely as the Spanish-dominant student to seek support for academic issues, even when both report the same level of *Perceived Support*. These analyses suggest that the mobilizing force normally behind

TABLE 10.5. Logistic regression models predicting *Seeking Support for "Academic Issues,"* one of three outcome measures of social embeddedness, with the four predictors of psychological embeddedness: *Perceived Support, Desire, Confidence,* and *Openness*

Predictors[†]		Intercept Only	MAIN EFFECTS MODELS						INTERACTIONS
			AI1	AI2	AI3	AI4	AI5	AI6	AI7
Student Background Predictors									
Intercept	PE	-.04	-.14		-2.14***	-2.42***	-2.96***	3.26***	3.83**
Grades (Self-report)	PE		.25***	.26***	.17***	.14*	.13*	.12~	.12~
	s.e.		.06	.06	.06	.06	.06	.06	.07
	SE		.14	.15	.10	.08	.08	.73	.07
Sophomore Status	PE		-.33*	-.30*	-.42**	-.36**	-.35*	-.35*	-.35*
	s.e.		.13	.13	.14	.14	.14	.14	.13
	SE		.08	-.08	-.11	-.10	-.09	-.09	-.09
English-proficient Latinos	PE			.23					.39
	s.e.			.17					.85
	SE			.06					.10
Spanish-dominant Latinos	PE			-.05					1.6~
	s.e.			.15					.86
	SE			-.01					.41
Psychological Embeddedness Predictors									
Perceived Support	PE				.17***	.18***	.17***	.18***	.23***
	s.e.				.03	.03	.03	.03	.04
	SE				.27	.27	.26	.27	.36
Desire	PE					.65***	.62***	.63***	.55***
	s.e.					.14	.14	.13	.14
	SE					.18	.17	.17	.15
Confidence	PE						.03		
	s.e.						.02		
	SE						.05		
Openness	PE							.06*	.05*
	s.e.							.02	.02
	SE							.09	.08
Significant Interactions									
English-prof. Latinos *Perceived Support	PE								-.02
	s.e.								.07
	SE								-.08
Spanish-dom.Latinos *Perceived Support	PE								.13*
	s.e.								.06
	SE								-.49
² Statistic		1432.37	1404.53	1401.33	1351.72	1328.02	1326.29	1322.62	1315.82
Deg. of freedom			2	4	3	4	5	5	9
²Test			27.84***	3.20	49.61***	23.70***	1.73	5.40**	6.8
(Nested Models)			(IntOnly,AI1)	(AI1,AI2)	(AI1,AI3)	(AI3,AI4)	(AI4,AI5)	(AI4,AI6)	(AI6,AI7)
Deg. of freedom			2	2	1	1	1	1	4
Pseudo-R² Statistic			.02	.02	.06	.07	.07	.08	.08

[†]Please note that *SES, Female,* and *English Proficiency* were included in the analyses to develop the control model, AI1. However, these three control variables were found to be not significant and thus not included in this table (*n* = 1,087).

***p < .001, **p < .01, *p < .05, ~p < .1

Table 10.6. Logistic regression models predicting *Seeking Support for "Post–High School Plans,"* one of three outcome measures of social embeddedness using the four predictors of psychological embeddedness: *Perceived Support, Desire, Confidence,* and *Openness*

Predictors[†]		Intercept Only	MAIN EFFECTS MODELS				
			PL1	PL2	PL3	PL4	PL5
Student Background Predictors							
Intercept	PE		-1.71^{***}	-4.98^{***}	-4.90^{***}	-6.19^{***}	-6.32^{**}
Grades (Self-report)	PE		$.29^{***}$	$.19^{***}$	$.17^{***}$	$.16^{*}$	$.16^{*}$
	s.e.		.06	.06	.07	.07	.07
	SE		.17	.11	.10	.10	.10
Sophomore Status	PE		$-.46^{***}$	$-.56^{**}$	$-.51^{***}$	$-.51^{***}$	$-.51^{***}$
	s.e.		.13	.14	.14	.14	.14
	SE		-.12	-.15	-.14	-.14	-.14
English Proficiency	PE		$.22^{***}$	$.36^{***}$	$.28^{***}$	$.27^{***}$	$.27^{***}$
	s.e.		.05	.06	.06	.06	.06
	SE		.15	.24	.19	.18	.18
Psychological Embeddedness Predictors							
Perceived Support	PE			$.23^{***}$	$.22^{***}$	$.20^{***}$	$.20^{***}$
	s.e.			.03	.03	.03	.03
	SE			.34	.33	.31	.31
Desire	PE				$.64^{***}$	$.59^{***}$	$.59^{***}$
	s.e.				.14	.14	.14
	SE				.18	.16	.16
Confidence	PE					$.07^{**}$	$.07^{**}$
	s.e.					.02	.02
	SE					.12	.12
Openness	PE						.01
	s.e.						.02
	SE						.02
χ^2 Statistic		1479.87	1410.19	1333.05	1311.72	1302.12	1301.85
Deg. of freedom			3	4	5	6	7
$\Delta\chi^2$ Test			69.68^{***}	77.14^{***}	21.33^{***}	9.60^{***}	.27
(Nested Models)			(Int.Only, PL1)	(PL1, PL2)	(PL2, PL3)	(PL3, PL4)	(PL4, PL5)
ΔDeg. of freedom			3	1	1	1	1
Pseudo-R^2 Statistic			.05	.10	.11	.12	.12

[†]Please note that *SES* and *Female* were included in the analyses to develop the control model, PL1. However, these two control variables were found to be not significant and thus not included in this table ($n = 1,079$).

***p< .001, **p<.01, *p<.05, ⁻p<.1

Perceived Support may not be as operative for Spanish-dominant immigrant students, relative to their English-proficient peers.

Next, we turn to the outcome *Sought Support for Post–High School Plans* (Plans) (please see Table 10.6). Controlling for the other factors, students registering high on *Perceived Support* were nine times more likely to seek support regarding post–high school plans than were students with low levels of *Perceived Support*.[16] Similarly, students registering a strong *Desire for Academic Support,* as well as those registering high on *Confidence,* were nearly twice as likely to seek support regarding post–high school plans as students with low *Desire* and low *Confidence.*[17] Interpersonal *Openness* did not register a significant effect.

We also expected that students who report high academic grades are significantly more likely to access important school-based sources of institutional support. With regard to seeking support for academic issues, grades appear to be a significant predictor of behavioral embeddedness. We see here that students with high grades (i.e., As) are a bit more likely to seek both forms of support (Issues and Plans) than are students with low grades (i.e., Cs), net of the other factors.[18]

With respect to our two help-seeking behavior measures, family SES did not register any significant effect. Once again, educational research studies have commonly revealed the muted or mixed effects of socioeconomic status among Latino student populations, and concomitantly, the more salient effects of linguistic and psychocultural variables within this population (e.g., Buriel, 1984).

Behavioral Embeddedness and English Proficiency

Our Bay Area/Peninsula study showed that students' level of positive behavioral embeddedness is positively associated with English proficiency. In contrast, the Auxilio High results for English proficiency are mixed; while they do register a significant positive influence on the likelihood of seeking help pertinent to post–high school plans, no independent effect surfaced with regard to seeking support for academic issues. Students registering the highest levels of English proficiency (i.e., 5) were nearly three times as likely to seek support regarding post–high school plans as students with very low levels of proficiency.

The Special Case of Spanish-dominant Latino Students

Explaining why *Perceived Support* showed itself to be less predictive of help-seeking behavior among Spanish-dominant Latinos provides an interesting theoretical challenge. Although methodological issues may have played a role here, based on existing research the psychocultural composition of non- or low-acculturated immigrant students suggests a far more productive avenue to explore. There are reasons to expect that among recent immigrants, the relation between perceived support and actual supportive experiences is weak. Perceptions of support among recent immigrants may be founded on their *dual frame of reference* (e.g., U.S. schools in contrast to Mexican schools) (Ogbu, 1991) and not on their assessment of their embeddedness in the school's existing support networks. Research by Ogbu and Gibson and associates (1991) and others (e.g., Suarez-Orozco & Suarez-Orozco, 1995) has extensively explored the distinctive frames of reference exhibited among different student immigrant groups.[19]

In spite of registering the highest *Perceived Support* scores, Spanish-dominants were the only group without a majority reporting firm *Desire* for more academic support. Close to two-thirds of this group did not report a desire for such support. Multiple t-tests also showed that the mean score for *Interpersonal Openness* for this group was significantly lower than was the mean score for their English-proficient Latino counterparts and for Euro-American students. Figure 10.3 summarizes our overall findings.

FIGURE 10.3. Factors Statistically Associated with Positive Behavioral Embeddedness (Seeking Help from School Personnel, Auxilio High School-wide Survey)

Sought Support for Academic Issues

   Perceived Support (stronger effects for English-proficient students)

   Desire for Support

   Interpersonal Openness

   High Grades

Sought Support for Post–high school Plans

   Perceived Support

   Desire for Support

   Confidence in the Support Process ("Confianza en confianza")

   High Grades

   English Proficiency

In sum, although our findings might suggest that Spanish-dominant Latino students maintain relatively high levels of (positive) social-psychological embeddedness—as measured here by *Perceived Support*—other findings cast a troubling light on their behavioral embeddedness. Spanish-dominant Latinos were the least open to sharing their problems with others and to seeking help, and the least desirous of more academic support. Perhaps most consequential was that this group was also the least likely to report mobilizing either of the two forms of school-related support. Overall, these findings demonstrate this group's persistent and positive appraisal of their circumstances within the school, even when our view of the empirical data indicates their tendency toward problematic embeddedness, particularly their probable exclusion from core networks of institutional support within the school. The next and final section expands on the overall theoretical significance of social embeddedness in the schooling experiences of working-class and minority youth.

DISCUSSION OF FINDINGS FROM THREE STUDIES

We have tried to press the point that integrative processes within the school can and should be understood within a critical network-analytic perspective. This perspective views school success as fostered by (positive) embeddedness in a social web of institutional agents oriented toward providing students with key forms of social and institutional support (including emotional support). In this scenario, existing structural and ideological constraints on help seeking and relationship-building are overcome. Although our empirical study did not feature achievement indicators as a dependent variable, our analyses did show some evidence that high-achievers are relatively more actively engaged in supportive relations with school-based agents. Furthermore, while we have suggested that school personnel play a direct role in facilitating a student's degree of positive embeddedness in supportive school networks, the presentation of our findings serves to focus on the probable reality that adolescents' network-specific orientations play a key role in the development of supportive relations with agents. As expected, our network-based measures of social-psychological embeddedness had strong associations with the mobilization of institutional support (via help-seeking practices). Furthermore, the relative absence or weakness of an association between social-psychological embeddedness and help-seeking among Spanish-dominant immigrant Latino students confirms our suspicions, that is, that measures that may indicate classical forms of "integration" do not always spell embeddedness in the school's resource-rich networks.

Methodological Issues in Measuring Adolescent Social Embeddedness and Social Capital

The social embeddedness of minority students is undeniably a complex issue, both theoretically and methodologically. Although a student may reveal a positive orientation toward the supportive potential of school agents, understood here as a fundamental dimension of positive social embeddedness, this doesn't necessarily guarantee that the student is enjoying the benefits of "social capital"—in other words, that he or she is embedded in secure relations with adults oriented toward ensuring the provision of quality social support (i.e., access to institutional resources, personal academic assistance, intimate counsel, and emotional support).

Certainly we can claim that those students who exhibit negative help-seeking orientations are the most "at-risk" of negative embeddedness, of social estrangement, and of experiencing minimal access to key resources and opportunities. But adolescent orientations alone cannot account for the variance in behavioral embeddedness. The influence of the school's organizational structures and the efforts of individual school personnel are fundamental and crucial (e.g., as we saw in the AVID classroom in Chapter 8).

Earlier in the chapter, we saw mixed findings regarding the propensity of students to elect school personnel as likely or promising sources of different forms of support. Using our semistructured network survey, we saw the strong majority of our Auxilio High sample (N = 75) electing two or more adults as likely sources of social support (90%, 64.3%, 80.8%, 72.8%, from Table 10.2). We also saw a small majority of students indicating at least one multiplex relationship with a school agent (a *likely* source of two or more forms of support) (80%, 57%, 62%, and 72%, from Table 8.3). From our school-wide survey of Auxilio High, we saw two-thirds or 68% of Latino students reporting having a "friendly and trusting relationship with a number of teachers" (from Table C.3, in Appendix C). Although such reports seem to increase the likelihood of actual help-seeking and of positive embeddedness overall, such indicators could also be tapping into positive feelings toward individual teachers and counselors, or into aspects of psychological integration in the classical sense (Wehlage et al., 1989). Serious questions arise as to whether such measures actually indicate that individuals are authentically linked to the flow and exchange of institutional resources, information, and opportunities.

Positive orientations toward individual school personnel as sources of institutional support are indeed important, but such orientations do not always lead to help seeking and to positive and enriching forms of behavioral embeddedness. It seems quite clear that we are much better able to measure social-psychological embeddedness than its behavioral or conductive counterpart. We must also admit that the theoretical link between social-psychological embeddedness and behavioral embeddedness remains to be adequately elaborated; disjunctions between the two may, in fact, be quite pervasive. Although this disjunction appears more readily visible in the case of Spanish-dominant immigrants, similar processes may be operating for the entire Latino student population. It may very well be the norm: positive help-seeking orientations and moderate to high levels of *perceived support* that never quite translate into ties to school personnel that function as conduits for key forms of social and institutional support (i.e., social capital).

From our measures of actual instances of seeking help from school personnel, we saw that from one-third to one-half of Latino students were not actively seeking academic help; and it is feasible that a significant proportion of these students may have had moderate to high levels of positive help-seeking orientation and perceived support. To complicate matters even more, even if we were to concentrate on reported ties to school personnel as recently mobilized sources of support, this would still leave the problem of *fool's gold*—that relations perceived to be "supportive" may not necessarily function as sources of authentic institutional support (e.g., reliable and high-quality forms of academically related information expertly tailored to the needs and aspirations of the student).

The distinctive circumstances of recent immigrants, we believe, deserve special attention. Our finding of high *perceived support* among Spanish-dominant students raises the issue of whether existing ethnographic and anecdotal evidence showing positive levels of social-psychological embeddedness among Latino immigrants may be obscuring what is really happening, leaving educators and policymakers to wrongly assume that all is well with this sector of the Latino student population. Much of the anthropological research on immigrants and schooling has not focused on differential access to institutional resources, nor has the field aggressively explored instances of malintegration and alienation within this sizable Latino subgroup.[20] Although many immigrant students may report positive appraisals of the supportive potential of their U.S. school and its personnel, as emphasized above, such assessments do not appear to easily translate into positive *behavioral* embeddedness. Spanish-dominant Latino students may strongly identify with their schools, while experiencing a form of network marginality that threatens short- and long-term success within the school system.[21]

In the final analysis, we must concede that network survey and questionnaire measures of "social capital" and "social support," regularly used across disciplines and fields, are quite imprecise measures of embeddedness, social capital, and concrete social support. On the other hand, our own network survey measures, together with our measures of *help-seeking orientation* and *perceived support,* may be telling us a number of important things. First, such measures can help us identify which adolescents are the best prepared to facilitate social-capital formation, that is, if institutional agents— those actually able to affect organizational practice—do their part. Second, these measures also may be informing us which students have lost faith that institutional contexts (in this case, the school) would or could ever operate in any systematic fashion to tend to their multiple needs and, ultimately, to infuse social wealth into their egocentric networks.

CLOSING ANALYSIS AND REFLECTIONS

In general, the students in our study who exhibited positive help-seeking orientations and who perceived themselves to be well supported may very well represent that sector of the student population best prepared to manage the stresses inherent in our contemporary society and to maximize their access to the mainstream arena, where institutional resources, privileges, and opportunities for leisure, recreation, career mobility, social advancement, and political empowerment are abundant, yet exhaustively distributed across many social contexts throughout society. In the final analysis, differential conditions and opportunities for learning to mobilize institutional support effectively may represent another key dimension of the school's *hidden curriculum.*

The development of self-empowering networks and help-seeking orientations among low-status minority children and adolescents must not be underestimated. Although supportive relations with school agents and positive help-seeking orientations do not guarantee school success among minority youth, such integrative processes would be expected to foster academic persistence and developmental resiliency; most certainly, negative embeddedness spells disaster for too many minority youth.

For low-status children, negative embeddedness during the elementary school years, especially the early development of negative help-seeking orientations, could greatly increase the likelihood of negative embeddedness in junior and senior high school. In turn, negative embeddedness, especially an aversion to help seeking during adolescence, might not only spell future social death in key adult institutional arenas (e.g., the labor market), but could also position low-status individuals to experience the worst possible effects of class and racial forces (i.e., poverty, segregation, discrimination, exposure to racist myths). This is an evolutionary institutional process that can be termed *internalized oppression,* whereby exclusionary forces operating within mainstream institutions tacitly function to deny young individuals the conditions for the development of self-empowering orientations; such individuals then go on to develop social-psychological and behavioral defense mechanisms that only exacerbate their dire structural circumstances. Institutional exclusion works through processes that tacitly function to get the excluded and dispossessed to regulate and reinforce their own marginality. It also permits us to "blame the victim" (Ryan, 1976).

11

Alienated Embeddedness and Internalized Oppression: Concluding Analysis and Reflections

I'm ready now to tell you my secret.
                    —Cole, in the movie "The Sixth Sense"[1]

Who knows but that, on the lower frequencies, I speak for you?
                    —Ralph Ellison

Throughout these chapters we've heard many adolescents speak of estranged relations with various constituents of their interpersonal networks, frayed relations that lose or never attain the functional capacity to act as lifelines of social, institutional, or emotional support. In these scenarios, we see emotional detachment and dissipated trust becoming the rule. Sometimes, other resourceful ties emerge or are sought to replace the loss. At other times, however, estranged relations serve only to accelerate either the quiet withdrawal into self or the escape into partnerships with disaffected others. The specter of contemporary youth alienation and despondency comes to mind through the many accounts of conflictive and broken relationships, or of relations with institutional agents that never crossed the affective threshold to permit genuine social support, perhaps due to preexisting distress patterns of both adolescent and agent.

And yet, this has not been the whole story in *Manufacturing Hope and Despair*; instances of social and institutional support are found throughout these chapters. Many cases did emerge in our interviews where parents, older siblings, aunts, teachers, and counselors—in relationship with the adolescent—reveal some of the intrinsic social elements of life that Marx, Dewey, Freire, and others see as constituting full "humanness" in the most authentic sense. Here, at least momentarily, life's challenges are solved in fellowship, not in painful isolation.

According to Marx, life becomes genuinely human not only through a particular kind of productive activity or labor, but also through fellow-

248

ship with others (see Schacht, 1970). Such fellowship, of course, is played out through collective problem-solving, the exchange of support, and the communal enjoyment of the fruits of network relations. Töennies's (1887/ 1963) well-known work on *gemeinschaft* and *gesellschaft* vividly captures how communal relations faltered with the rise of modern industrial capitalism. Yet we know too that modern cultural adaptations to the challenges and afflictions of capitalism and urbanism continue to depend on network-based strategies of mutual support (see Fischer, 1982; Keefe & Padilla, 1987; Wellman, 1981).

As already discussed, the principles of full humanness and *gemeinschaft* are richly embodied in the normative aspects of Mexican communalism, particularly in the concept of *confianza en confianza*. In community life, they act as the organic substance that creates the social webs within which children and youth are embedded, protected, and nurtured. Yet these normative aspects of *Mexicano* communities in the United States are set within the overlapping arenas of Anglo individualism and coercive assimilation, of class relations set within an advanced capitalist global economy, and of continuing segregation and institutionalized racism. Maintaining communal webs within such overlapping arenas is not impossible, but the empirical literature on immigrant settlement, for example, shows us that strong collective resistance and considerable organizational resources must be continually mobilized (e.g., Gibson & Ogbu, 1991; Portes & Bach, 1985; Zhou & Bankston, 1996).

The many instances visited in the book that reflect the full power of *confianza en confianza*, and that reveal to us the buffering potential of protective webs and relations, however plentiful, ultimately carry the haunting aura of exceptionality. The pleasing accounts we saw in Chapters 4, 6, and 8 are to be appreciated only in the context of our bitter recognition of the too-often-silent majority, those adolescents from working-class immigrant households locked in perilous webs socially organized to generate isolation, alienation, and repressed adolescent rage. However uplifting and pleasing we find the instances of social support, and however crucial they were in the lives of our informants, in many low-income urban communities across the United States, these occasions of support do not define the overall social embeddedness of low-income urban youth; and it is this problem, the one of perilous webs to which I shall speak first.

ALIENATION: TOWARD A NEW ARTICULATION OF AN OVERLOOKED DIMENSION

Marx saw alienation as rooted in social structures under industrial capitalism, structures that denied people the ability to experience those intrinsic aspects of their human nature that were psychologically empowering. In this study, the task has been to articulate the alienation of urban minority youth as rooted in social structures that in the end deny these young people the relationships and resources that would ensure healthy development and the expression of their vast human potential as aspiring young people. The point argued here is that this alienation is not merely some arduous developmental stage that youth must go through as a test of their resiliency and character, but rather a systematic process of dehumanization built into our social system that prepares the majority of low-status youth for their future as alienated labor.

The painful accounts that fill this book serve to put us in touch with these adolescents' individual feelings of estrangement, anxiety, and anger; yet our critical network-analytic approach prevents us from viewing this issue as one that merely provokes our compassion and moral outrage. Rather, our network approach provides sociological insight, and a look at the human consequences of our deep investment in the status quo. The youthful cries of estrangement that fill this book are rooted in continually recreated dynamics between low-status youth and the principal constituents of their social networks, which in turn are set within the dominant structures of power and privilege in society. My approach in *Manufacturing Hope and Despair* has been to take the circumstantial and psychological aspects of adolescent life and use them to reveal key structural features and constitutive practices of American life.

In Chapter 7, Angeles Machado revealed to us the real person hidden behind the otherwise publicly resilient young woman. Interested in national and international politics, determined to go to college, well-respected by her teachers, she appeared self-sustaining; no one saw, however, the panic attacks, her bouts with minor depression, the painful isolation she suffered, her need for support. Is Angeles an exceptional case, or is she revealing how Latino working-class adolescent life is socially structured in the United States? Is she merely revealing to us her own personal tribulations associated with the classical *storm and stress* accounts of adolescence, or do we see a window into our national culture, with its deep historical and fetishistic roots in utilitarian individualism? Here we move from the *micro*, to the *meso*, to the *macro*, then back again. It is precisely this bridging between key levels of analysis that has been so lamentably neglected in American mainstream sociology—including sociological studies of adult networks.

The challenge, then, is to listen attentively to these youths from the *emic* perspective, while simultaneously considering social structure at the *meso* and *macro* levels, investigating the networks, institutions, political economy, and subcultural forces within which these adolescents are daily embedded. In this way, we hear the exasperated young Latina woman who avoids her immigrant mother in the morning, then later storms out of the school's counseling office in the afternoon, and then finally eschews her peer group in the early evening, and interpret these events as interrelated incidents that carry deep sociological significance. Her painful secret, carried from one perilous web to another, remains eclipsed only by our collective investment in mainstream mythologies and conventional frameworks and theories. Only through a disciplined and critical framework that integrates the *micro*, the *meso*, and the *macro* can her secret be revealed and our understanding of social inequality be substantially broadened.

This framework has drawn attention to various institutional conditions and forms of social organization that systematically operate to thwart the development of authentic social capital. I speak specifically here of the dehumanizing yet often hidden aspects of class, race, and gender—the inhibiting of cooperative social activity and exchange, shared meaning-making, and assessment of common interests; the undermining of trust in the context of hierarchical power relations; and the inability of both familial and school agents to provide developmentally empowering resources. This represents the objective dimension of alienation, the reality of *alienated embeddedness*, with the *social* and *relational* remaining as primary as ever. Just as Marx's industrial workers remained socially engaged in labor, production, and community interactions with similar others, alienated youth remain highly engaged in social interaction, deeply embedded in social relationships with a diverse cast of agents and significant others. In both cases, however, network relations with *resource*-ful agents are fundamentally reconfigured such that *social capital* (i.e., ties that transmit "institutional support") cannot easily emerge and accumulate. Consequently, those caught in such relations are never able to truly realize their human potential for creativity and intellectual empowerment.

In many instances such objective alienation has little to do with the intentions and conscious value commitments of agents. Interactions with significant others and agents are usually plentiful, often *caring* (even pleasant), although such interactions rarely rise to the level of master-and-apprentice or the dialogic transfer of institutional support, including cultural knowledge funds and critical insight. As a whole, these interactions are not fundamentally organized (or are unable to organize) to ensure that low-status children and adolescents receive the social, emotional, and institutional resources necessary for optimal development and mobility; nor are they organized to ensure that these young people truly master the greater institutional matrix, including the overlapping hierarchies and subordinating forces that socially structure it. However, interactions are usually organized, within each site, to inculcate a particular moral and normative order (Figure 2.1 in Chapter 2). Even within the immigrant household (Chapter 5), parents with quite restricted levels of formal schooling tried to heighten their children's chances of educational success by exhaustive attempts to shape their moral character. Yet, across sites (home *and* school), attempts to shape the moral character of low-status minority youth usually occur *without* the adequate and effective provision of institutional support (i.e., institutional resources typically possessed by middle-class agents and their institutions, *and* those resources necessary to overcome stratification forces).

THE INTERNALIZED OPPRESSION OF AGENTS AND ADOLESCENTS: THE SUBJECTIVE DIMENSION OF ALIENATED EMBEDDEDNESS

The effects of alienated embeddedness on minority youth are felt on multiple levels, not only directly diminishing the pool of eligible sources of institutional support through segregation and urban isolation, but also working, in the most insidious of ways, through the distress patterns of those agents most devoted to the welfare of these youth. This is to say that working-class and resource-strapped families, schools, and communities are regularly forced into regulating, unwittingly, the social oppression of their young people. Outside of normal awareness, agents at each particular site collectively *play host to the system* (Bowles & Gintis, 1976; Fine, 1991; Freire, 1973/1993, 1973/1990; Willis, 1981), legitimating mainstream ideologies and enacting patterns of social interaction, labor, resource allocation, goal-striving, and problem-solving that serve in hidden ways to reproduce the unequal, hierarchical relations of our racialized, patriarchal, capitalist society.

The distress patterns of adult agents (e.g., parents, school personnel) also manifest themselves by actions and pronouncements that either neglect or invalidate the routine *border* reality of oppressed youth.[2] Quiet shame, confusion, and feelings of powerlessness are the accompanying sentiments of many low-status adolescents, often masked by youthful bravado or stoicism. Such feelings are rooted in the individual's difficulty in reconciling his or her perceptive penetrations into society's social structures with the mythologies and deceptions of adults (cf. Willis, 1981). These feelings are aggravated by adolescents' clumsy attempts to "decode the system," to demystify the many challenges inherent in successful social development—as occupants of the social bottom—with very little systematic guidance and adult honesty. Complicated by society's obsession with the myths of self-reliance, fair competition, and meritocracy, assertive help-seeking in nonfamilial arenas carries the risk of exposing one's feelings of shame, powerlessness, and confusion; it also carries the risk of subtle rejection and invalidation.

The ignorance and invalidating messages that underlie the distress patterns of both protective and institutional agents can also serve to inadvertently fuel the development of cognitive orientations that express distress, frustration, resentment, and rage. Ultimately, these result in coping strategies that are not founded on help seeking, network-building, and social support (Stanton-Salazar, 2000). Such youthful cognitive orientations toward school and authority figures are often associated with individual and collective efforts to demonstrate contempt for, and adaptability to, the surrounding forces of stratification. In many cases, however, such "resistance" and defense are expressed primarily by creating subcultural forms and collectively shared coping strategies that only exacerbate already oppressive circumstances (Brake, 1985; Freire, 1973/1990, 1973/1993; Willis, 1981).

As we saw in different segments of the book, the structuring or social decapitalization of adolescent-agent relations is accomplished in distinctive ways across institutional arenas and social contexts. In Chapters 5, 6, and 7, having to do with parent-adolescent relations, we see this decapitalization manifesting itself in terms of parents not possessing the knowledge forms, resources, and middle-class cultural capital that would socially and academically empower their children and ensure their mobility. Perhaps more sociologically important, we see parents experiencing difficulty in generating the personal connections to those familial and nonfamilial agents and webs that could provide key forms of institutional support. As discussed in Chapter 6, such connections, however tacit, are the founding matrix of middle-class suburban life in the United States.

In Chapters 9 and 10, we see a different set of structural constraints on another key pool of eligibles, in this case, teachers and counselors. The evidence suggests that for about half the Latino students at Auxilio High, relations with school personnel were socially organized in ways that obstructed the formation of supportive relations and active help seeking. Although cases emerged where an adolescent experienced good rapport and supportive relations with one or two teachers, the evidence also suggests that most adolescents were not embedded in a tightly knit and coordinated web of teachers, counselors, and staff, either at the level of ego or at the *meso* level.

Help-seeking orientations and behavior by a large sector of Latino students at this school were largely characterized by some significant degree of ambivalence and avoidance, even when one or two school agents were named as likely sources of support. Much of the research on adult help seeking focuses on this problem of *ambivalence*—that people in need of help often do not ask for it. Many individuals are willing to forgo help when they perceive that the act of seeking or obtaining assistance may be too psychologically costly. Here again, we see the *shame factor* at play. Reminiscent of what happens in the fable *The Emperor Has No Clothes*, many here are forced to pretend that teachers and counselors are fulfilling their roles in a rational and proper way; part of this drama also has to do with students pretending they need no help; no one dares to reveal the secret—the sheer nakedness of the oppression they routinely experience.

A good deal of the ambivalence around help seeking at Auxilio High is associated with the manner in which institutional resources within urban schools are socially organized and distributed (e.g., counseling, mentorship, preparation for college, help with schoolwork, access to state-of-the-art curriculum). This particular urban school, as perhaps most, continued to cast achievement and success through a mainly individualistic, competitive, and sorting paradigm, rather than through a *communitarian* one, an organizational/cultural imperative oriented toward fulfilling the human potential of every student. Also critical within this school's organizational culture was how the social support process and help seeking were collectively interpreted—issues that are fundamentally ideological, and too often interpreted by students mainly in terms of hyperselection and exclusion. The cooperative or communitarian ideal, also manifested in terms of students' acting as skillful providers of support to other students (emotional as well as academic), was likewise not an intrinsic feature of the school's organizational culture, in spite of the fact that the school was officially undergoing "restructuring."

The full weight of class, gender, and racial oppression on the Latino adolescents I studied occurred when *each* of the arenas and social webs comprising their social universe was structured either to undermine relations of trust and social support or to prevent the transmission of key resources for optimal development and mobility. It should not be surprising that such adolescents in my study were the most difficult to pin down for scheduled interviews. Their level of distrust of and aversion to authority figures and to prosocial age-mates played itself out in our researcher-informant relations. Maintaining their active participation during our year-long study required considerably more of our time and energy than was typically the case with our other informants.

Adolescents' aversion and ambivalence in their network relations was not always easy to see, however; alienated embeddedness often existed alongside cordial social interaction and participation in routine activities. Outwardly raging adolescents who signified their subjective alienation in attention-getting ways were the exception. The network and help-seeking orientations of most alienated adolescents we encountered were much more subtle, perhaps invisible to most; in our interviews, social estrangement emerged in adolescents' self-reported lack of trust and confidence in significant others and in key agents, in their lack of help-seeking initiative, and in their overall resignation to, or investment in, unsponsored self-reliance. Again, the lack of trust and confidence in parents, agents, and peers often coexisted with positive sentiments toward, and pleasant interactions with, these "significant others." In the case of relations with immigrant parents, feelings of estrangement could very well coexist with feelings of respect, love, and duty—though conflictive relations between adolescent and immigrant parent were pervasive (Chapter 7). In other words, while there were many instances when the basis of their distrust was attributed to the crass unreliability or uncaringness or shameful incompetency of particular individuals in their network, many adolescents, without the formal tools of sociological discourse, attributed the situation to ubiquitous social patterns and dynamics beyond their control (or the control of agents), sometimes articulating this situation as "well that's just the way things are, I don't know!"

For some adolescents, alienated embeddedness in one sphere or arena was offset by compensating relations in another, at least in terms of emotional and basic forms of social support. For some, peer friendship and social cliques did provide the safety net during times of crisis when family or schools could not meet their emotional needs. For many adolescents, specific instances of caring and support emerged at key moments of distress or need. These instances, however, never reflected the general pattern of their daily lives. For most minority adolescents from disfranchised urban communities, stratification forces indeed operate to socially organize school, family, neighborhood, and peer networks—at both the ego and *meso* levels—in ways that leave youth alienated from each. Relationships with significant others, agents, and neighbors may involve considerable interaction and activity, yet seldom act as vital conduits for the flow of key developmental resources and institutional support.

Stratification forces also operate at the *meso* level to undermine cooperation and coordination between institutional arenas. Thus, while adolescents may regularly participate in these multiple institutional spheres, the agents in these spheres (school personnel, recreation center leaders, parents, adult neighbors, older siblings) are not socially organizing with agents in other spheres for the purpose of ensuring that the community's youth develop the necessary connections and receive the necessary social, emotional, and institutional support. This is not to say that relations between webs and institutional contexts are "disorganized," but rather that they are socially organized, at the subterranean level, to perpetuate the status quo.

It is precisely this simultaneous participation in disparate and un-coordinated social worlds and arenas that distinguishes the unique character of urban minority socialization (Ianni, 1989; Phelan et al., 1998). Multiple participation also translates into partial integration in a number of social worlds divided by class-, ethnic-, and gender-based borders that have historically evolved in ways that make these worlds inherently conflictive, incompatible, and contradictory (Boykin, 1986; Boykin & Toms, 1985; Stanton-Salazar, 1997). Conflict and the lack of coordination are the rule. Intergenerational closure across institutional sites rarely occurs (Coleman, 1988, p. S105).

EXCEPTIONAL AND CELEBRATED CASES

Exceptional adolescent cases where simultaneous participation across disparate and conflictive social worlds is successful become synonymous with the development of an interpersonal (egocentric) network with structural features that reveal numerous social ties across overlapping but still largely uncoordinated social networks. In contrast to the situation of middle-class youth, the burden of participation in multiple (uncoordinated) webs, and of accessing various forms of social and institutional support, largely falls on the adolescent. Exceptional low-status minority youth painstakingly earn their stripe of individual exceptionality, although this exceptionality is usually generated in key counterstratification initiatives rooted in one or more institutional contexts in the adolescent's universe (Jarrett, 1995; Levine & Nidiffer, 1996; Williams & Kornblum, 1985).

Such effective networks appear at first to share much in common with the cosmopolitan egocentric networks of middle-class adults (Fischer, 1982), in that minority individuals similarly experience self and society through the kaleidoscope of their own egocentric networks, rather than as members of a densely-knit, closed ethnic community. Yet, while middle-class Euro-American adults experience this kaleidoscope within the confines of their own dominant culture, for minority members, their cosmopolitan situation is experienced through the lens of multiple marginality, and is circumscribed by cultural conflict and the subterranean forces of *institutionalized exclusion* (Bourdieu, 1977b; Lamont & Lareau, 1988). Remember, too, that many middle-class adults come out of middle-class suburban communities where, as children and adolescents, they were embedded in multiple social webs characterized by some substantial degree of (tacit and explicit) coordination and adult monitoring (Ianni, 1989).[3]

ADOLESCENT AGENCY AND THE COUNTERSTRATIFICATION BLUES

A more accurate picture of the role of adolescent networks in both social reproduction and individual mobility requires sustained attention to forces beyond stratification. Low-status youth are socially embedded in multiple spheres and networks that are subject to the push and pull of both stratification and counterstratification forces. Many low-status youth do find themselves involved in academic programs similar to Auxilio High's AVID (Chapter 8), and some adolescents are fortunate enough to be befriended by a deeply committed institutional agent acting as a human bridge to a new social system of resources and opportunities. In sum, many low-status youth do experience membership within one or more social and institutional webs that provide the resources and support to propel them, as individuals, into higher strata in the social hierarchy—or at least to prevent them from falling into the nether world of adult poverty and despair (see Maeroff, 1998).

Many of the counterstratification efforts of family, community, and school appear as forms of socialization that foster social skills, attitudes, and problem-solving styles. These, in turn, are particularly conducive to survival in the *borderlands* of our society: to network-building and maintenance, to the development of multiple identities and cultural competencies, as well as to the mobilization of social and institutional support across multiple sites (Clark, 1983; Cochran et al., 1990; Jarrett, 1995; Maeroff, 1998; Stanton-Salazar, Vásquez, & Mehan, 2000).

However, as is so often the case, stratification forces can also infect organized efforts at counterstratification. Often, valiant efforts by families, schools, and communities are contaminated with ideological messages that serve not only to dismiss or minimize attention to the structural realities and borders their youth are embedded in, but to give credence to mainstream mythologies (e.g., meritocracy and the myth of self-reliance; bilingualism as a deficiency). Michelle Fine (1991) writes of teachers' regular practice of *silencing* students' attempts to process their common experiences with racism and class oppression, for fear that students will end up feeling demoralized (pp. 8–9, 31–34). Rather than being able to articulate and discharge their common experiences of distress around race, class, and sexual orientation, and feel empowered in the process, these young people were ultimately demoralized by the routine practice of silencing.

For most lower-working-class minority youth, counterstratification forces, in the form of institutional mediations or family- and community-based cultural strategies, operate principally as a buffer against the full burden of class and racial oppression. This is their primary function, regardless of institutionally-coded goals. For most youth, counterstratification forces play themselves out in their *buffering* function, not in their promise to significantly compensate low-status youth for the accident of not being born middle-class. Counterstratification processes, when directed toward impacting the dynamics inhering in adolescents' social webs, provide developmental opportunities that enable adolescents to experience fellowship, moments of hope for the future, and some modicum of academic accomplishment. However, simultaneous participation in other webs and arenas reminds them that instances of distress, distrust, isolation, and aggravated alienation still abound. Counterstratification initiatives across the domains of family, school, and community do not eliminate adolescents' generalized estrangement, but rather temper or moderate it, enough for these youth to survive the trek through adolescence and into the acquiescent and alienated ranks of the adult working class. It is rare when counterstratification initiatives orient themselves toward refining working-class adolescents' *penetrations* into the structural trinity of society's stratification system. Most public high schools, for example, don't formally include the sociological study of race, class, and gender inequality in their core curriculum—at least not in the way it is approached in college courses.[4]

It is important that we remind ourselves again and again that counterstratification forces are not ideologically neutral. Although such forces may prevent low-status adolescents from experiencing the full or crushing weight of alienated embeddedness and subjective estrangement across multiple sites, without clear political commitments, such mitigating forces may just pave the way for a smoother process of social reproduction—a "gentler and kinder" social oppression. The ongoing maintenance of racialized and gendered class relations in society requires that most low-status youth be nurtured to the extent that they not become criminal, politically defiant, or long-term dependents of the state. The social networks of low-status minority youth cannot be left to become wastelands of despair, although for a sizable segment of inner-city youth, this continues to be the case. Still, school-based networks and agents, for example, do provide some measure of access to institutional resources and support in order to replay the school system's supposed commitment to democracy and equality of opportunity. Furthermore, a certain small minority of low-status youth must be selected, nurtured, and exalted to demonstrate that meritocracy remains alive and well, and that public institutions remain committed to the heralded tradition of (individual) social mobility in America.

The mediating processes of counterstratification work in tandem with opportunities created by the upward pull of the economy. The social embeddedness of working-class minority youth is ultimately set within the greater logic of Western global capitalism; positive embeddedness in supportive webs spells individual mobility and social reproduction. As Willis (1977) tells us, "The whole nature of Western capitalism is . . . such that classes are structured and persistent so that even high rates of individual mobility make no difference to the existence or position of the working class" (p. 127). However, the situation is more complex in the United States.

Counterstratification efforts, when too successful, wide-scale, and cumulative, do in fact serve to jostle class, race, and gender relations. This happens when the pipeline is widened and the outflow and mobility of working-class persons, non-Whites, and women are substantially increased, inevitably generating competition and precipitating a backlash by the suburban middle-class, particularly when the economy fails to maintain its guarantee of prosperity and privilege to all dominant-group, middle-class youth. The recent demise of affirmative action policies, of course, is a perfect example of this attempt to stifle class, racial, and gender competition for middle-class privileges. Then again, even when the middle class is forced to accommodate the new entrants, ideological forces come into play to minimize loyalties between these new entrants and their social webs of origin. The ideological assimilation of new entrants has always been a fundamental feature of our mobility system in the United States.[5]

VARIATIONS IN THE ADAPTIVE RESPONSES OF LATINO YOUTH

The crucial role of adolescent subcultures must also be addressed. The complex interplay between stratification forces and counterstratification initiatives is usually mediated by adolescent subcultures, of which there may be many in any one particular school and urban community (see Matute-Bianchi, 1986). The stratification forces of class, race, and patriarchy have their impact not only by shaping young people's material existence and social networks, but also by generating forms of group consciousness and coping strategies that, while born out of resistance to the system, too often function to regulate young people's own oppression.

The mode of adaptation among nonimmigrant minority youth in low-income urban communities is usually the most visible, audible, and distressing (see Stanton-Salazar, 2000). Yet the current attention paid to these youth is due not merely to their rebellious or defiant character and apparent rejection of mainstream standards of morality, features that have been historically present, but to the sights and sounds of violence and increasing destructiveness. Even within community boundaries, the oppositional and sometimes violent character of youth behavior is perceived as disruptive to those community members pursuing more conventional or traditional means of survival. This was made quite evident in Chapter 3. With the increase of violence and gang involvement in urban communities has come another round of heightened attention in the public arena, followed usually by new policy initiatives and calls for law and order. In the scholarly realm, attention is focused on how low-income, disenfranchised minority communities embody alternative, often competing, youth *subcultures*, each reflecting distinctive modes of adaptation to social oppression and marginalization (e.g., Gibson & Ogbu, 1991; Heath & McLaughlin, 1993).

The adaptive responses and defiant behavior of a growing segment of inner-city Latino youth and young adults appear to stem from a *social character* that rejects the accommodation and conformity of immigrants, while adopting the most excessive and corrupted aspects of utilitarian individualism. The causes and meaning of their defiant behavior are typically portrayed by the mainstream using the logic of deviance, individual pathology, and learned helplessness. In doing so, the mainstream ignores the fact that the marginalization of many minority youth is rooted in class and racial inequalities and antagonisms that characterize our society. In reality, what we find is a continuum whereby low-income urban youth can be distinguished by the degree to which they embody what Sánchez-Jankowski (1991) terms a *defiant individualist* character. The greater the experience of extreme multiple marginality among youth, and the more it is shared by similar and significant others who also lack institutional support, the greater the probability that youth will assume and express such a character.

The point here is that institutionalized and community-generated counterstratification initiatives must contend not only with the material ravages and media-hyped mythologies of class, racial, and gender exclusion, but also with the defensive and oftentimes skeptical and rebellious character of low-status adolescent youth cultures. It is important to emphasize that most alienated youth are not located on the extreme end of the defiant individualist continuum; nonetheless, counterstratification initiatives usually must contend with negative adolescent network orientations born of long-standing embeddedness in alienating, accommodationist, and resource-poor social webs.

Due to the segregation and concentration of poor families in low-income neighborhoods and housing projects, the prospect of their obtaining support and assistance is often restricted either to similar others coping with the same resource-poor conditions, or to overly distressed and resource-strapped institutional agents (e.g., teachers, social workers). Although reciprocal and communitarian relations are clearly visible in these communities, such relations or networks are usually organized around survival and accommodation rather than optimal well-being or politically informed resistance. These networks take many forms, from kinship networks (Chapter 4), to female-centered neighborhood networks (Eames & Goode, 1973; Lomnitz, 1977), to highly selective school-based interventions (Chapter 8), to church-based or neighborhood-based outreach programs (Maeroff, 1998; Williams & Kornblum, 1985). Along with the humanness, mercy, and support generated within many of these webs, participation may exact many psychic and relational costs (e.g., overinsulation, over-dependence on uniplex relations or on overprotective cliques and informal mentors, cultural assimilation and deculturation, the further ingestion of mainstream myths, identity detachment from family and community).

Some theorists have, in fact, written about the downsides of social capital (Portes, 1998), circumstances that may be exacerbated among adolescents from low-income immigrant families and enclaves. Submission to counterstratification initiatives in the school and community often requires deference to institutional mythologies and adult prejudices, a negation of one's own "penetrations" into the established social order (Fine, 1991, pp. 132–137; Willis, 1977, p. 119; see also note 1), and a coerced detachment from more disaffected peers. For many youth, then, a generalized peer-based cultural consensus may dictate more cautious, skeptical, and individualistic network and help-seeking orientations, a loosely knit consensus that views the more collectivist and cooperative orientations in the school and community with some suspicion or cynicism.

Furthermore, although young people observe many adults struggling to survive through participation in reciprocal support networks, they also "observe, confront, and negotiate with people" whose mode of survival, although predatory, often reaps greater material benefits (Sánchez-Jankowski, 1991, p. 24).[6] Some adolescents may, in fact, express more appreciation for the latter strategy. This may be twisted thinking, but we must remind ourselves of how the media and commercial industry promulgate the view that the acquisition of commercial goods is a viable route to higher social status, self-esteem, and individual happiness.

It is also important to point out that predatory modes of survival usually require continued identification and integration in the neighborhood and community. Drug addicts, drug dealers, pimps, gang members, those engaged in armed robberies and burglaries, and those working within the underground street economy usually depend on the community's tolerance (Sánchez-Jankowski, 1991; Sullivan, 1989). Their underground subculture and life-style become recognized features of the community's cultural mosaic. Under conditions of scarcity, marginalization from the mainstream, and predatory-type danger, coping and surviving for these participants becomes a principal life activity—"the goal is to fight, to survive, to overcome," usually against great odds (Sánchez-Jankowski, 1991, p. 25). Although most of the adolescents in our two research sites were not engaged in these illicit networks, they understood the fear and awe these subcultures generated in the community and in the larger society. They also saw the hidden heroic and defiant elements of these subcultures. Without directly participating in these networks, many adolescents understood, if not identified with, the rage and resistance these subcultures reflected, all the while simultaneously fearing their own potential victimization. Such fearful and defensive orientations were made evident in Chapter 3.

Persistent calculations and wariness, embodied in the network orientations of many low-status urban adolescents, pave the road to firmer and firmer commitments to affective detachment from community adults and institutional agents, traits not only dramatized in the coping styles of the most dispossessed and disaffected youth groups in the community, but also regularly romanticized within the mainstream media where *self-reliance* and *rugged individualism* are dutifully portrayed as core American values. And here we see the hidden scourge of mindless cultural assimilation. Self-reliance among resource-rich middle-class Americans, of course, is categorically and qualitatively different than the same trait under conditions of scarcity, segregation, and poverty. This is particularly the case when entire urban communities become isolated from members of the mainstream, including members of the stable labor force (Wilson, 1987). Middle-class *self-reliance*, of course, is supported by embeddedness in highly structured middle-class networks of exchange and support (De Sola Pool & Kochen, 1978; Fischer, 1982). Thus, while counterstratification initiatives generated by the family, school, government agencies, and community offer protections and benefits that frequently are unpalatable to many low-status youth, mainstream mythologies further inoculate low-status adolescents from coming to know the possibilities entailed in communitarian forms of social embeddedness.

Without some critical-sociological consciousness on the part of well-meaning institutional agents, mainstream ideological currents, legitimations, and invalidating impulses within school, family, government bodies, and community too often work together to sabotage the best of intervention efforts, thus undercutting the possibility of adolescents' investment in those social webs and institutional sites dedicated to the provision of key resources and support. Given this scenario, unsponsored self-reliance remains a highly likely outcome for many urban youth, an orientation reinforced by collectively shared peer perceptions conveying that "this is the way it is," or that the "price" for receiving adult support is much too high. Affective detachment and estrangement from significant others, committed agents, and resilient, prosocial peers becomes the rule, in spite of the counterstratification initiatives at work in the school and community.

It is important to emphasize that the adoption and maintenance of negative network and help-seeking orientations, while founded on accumulated personal experiences with alienated embeddedness, may get played out not in terms of some rational "cost-benefit decision" or "choice," but rather as an adaptational strategy collectively created among those who share similar social biographies and life experiences. Many youth articulate their resignation to unsponsored self-reliance as merely part of the status quo of their adolescence, as was shown in past chapters:

> I'm pretty independent. I almost never talk to them [teachers]. I always try to do things myself. [Dolores, Chapter 9]

> That's what I'm saying, I don't think anyone has the responsibility. Well [laughing], I would say my parents should be there for me. I say it'd be nice, but I can't say they *should*. [long pause] I feel fine because I know that not every family is like perfect, not everybody's Ozzie and Harriet and that sort of thing; I just feel that I've got what I've got and I've just got to learn to accept it, so. [Angeles, Chapter 7]

Unsponsored self-reliance (across contexts) emerges as the norm, although often subtle, sometimes crafty; protective, validating, and highly supportive family webs are dismissed as "Ozzie and Harriet" TV mythology. Similarly, long-standing and highly supportive ties to teachers and school personnel are seen as exceptions to the rule. One rides the bus one is already in. Full-blown defiant individualism is one such bus, while the adoption of a moderately negative network orientation is another. Leaving either bus to board another more socially acceptable or productive one usually requires a radical and transformational experience—clearly possible, but highly improbable without major outside social intervention. The question remains whether the institutions serving the residents of Harrison Heights, Augusta Heights, Southview, and Vista possess the social capital, the resources, and the sociological insights to successfully engineer such a transformational experience for a sizable segment of the youth community. The answer is, unequivocally, no.

Counterstratification initiatives work when they win the ideological battle, or when they insulate youth from the contradictions inhering in the provision of support. As argued here, such initiatives are mediated by the adolescent cultures that permeate the school and community. The adoption of positive network and help-seeking orientations among low-status youth depends on some respectable degree of ideological hegemony and intergenerational closure across institutional arenas (Coleman, 1988), as well as on a history of embeddedness that has ensured protection and the generous provision of support. The individual comes to recognize his or her exceptional experience, relative to similar—though *not-as-fortunate*—others; identification with the dispossessed and most alienated is gradually and systematically weakened.

For low-status adolescents as a class, social embeddedness in their principal overlapping networks is defined, in the final analysis, by the complex interplay between the greater political economy, counterstratification efforts at the level of the school and community, and adolescent subcultures. Counterstratification and the mediations of youth subcultures are, indeed, key dimensions of the social embeddedness of low-status adolescent youth, and must remain central to our continued scholarly elaborations of social inequality. It is my contention, however, that counterstratification efforts under current macro-structures and the ever-growing prosperity gap will never be sufficient to alter the social embeddedness of low-status minority youth so that it approximates the social embeddedness of middle- and upper-class youth. The hierarchically privileged in society will never permit it. Many exceptional cases will continue to emerge, and will be celebrated in the usual American way, yet the network templates and configurations for each group will remain distinctively different in terms of social capital and power. And yet, let us at last consider, without the innumerable honest efforts across the country to socially embed low-status youth in humanizing and fortifying webs, what untold ravages of stratification would befall us all.

APPENDIX A

Defining Social Capital and "Institutional Support"

One of the most widely discussed and influential constructs in American sociology has been the notion of social capital. However, there has been little consistency across studies in the way social capital is conceived or measured. Part of the problem is that the researchers who use this construct draw on formulations that are rooted in quite different theoretical frameworks and traditions. This is not the place for a detailed and critical review of the scholarly work on social capital; I do, however, provide a brief overview of how I have defined and employed this concept in *Manufacturing Hope and Despair*, and how I've drawn from the work of both James Coleman (1988, 1990) and Pierre Bourdieu (1977, 1986).

Social capital is a set of properties existing within socially patterned associations among people that, when activated, enable them to accomplish their goals or to empower themselves in some meaningful way. Such associations can occur in various ways: between two individuals (e.g., teacher and student), between individuals in a group (e.g., parents in a neighborhood), and between groups within a community (e.g., parents, school personnel, police).

Social capital can be said to have three fundamental properties. First, it is a dynamic process founded on reciprocal investments in a relationship or set of relations. Following Homans (1950), such investments have to do with the very substances of social life—that is, with social interaction, cooperative activity and exchange, shared meaning-making, and continual assessments of common interests. To have social capital is to be in relationship where both parties, or all parties, make reciprocal investments and commitments, although not always to the same degree—power differences between parties play a key role.

The processual nature of help seeking and exchange depends on the relative (hierarchical) status and power of the *seeker* vis-à-vis the intended *provider* (Boissevain, 1974). The party who is more powerful than the one occupying the *provider role* makes "investments" and asks for assistance one way, while the party with less power than the one in the provider role makes investments and asks for help in another way. Under the proper conditions, including the effective management of power differentials, such reciprocal investments lead to trust as well as to enforceable expectations and obligations (in Coleman's terms [1988, 1990], a "credit slip"). These *cultural rules and resulting obligations and expectations*, set within contextualized power relations, represent the second property of social capital. Coleman (1988, 1990), in his landmark contribution to the literature on social capital, calls attention to the obligations (social debts), expectations, and trustworthiness that can inhere in sustained relationships and that make possible the flow and exchange of resources and support.

This leads to the third property of social capital, that is, its *resource-generating* capacity. Here, valued resources flow back and forth between individuals engaged in these relationships of trust and mutual (and enforceable) expectations. Enjoyment of such resources (including the various forms of social support) can occur as a direct result of activating particular relationships or ties (e.g., help seeking), or as a natural by-product of social interaction and cooperative activity. During times of need, tailored access to valued resources and forms of support, in the context of trusting and binding relations, allows actors to achieve their objectives and to experience a degree of individual or collective empowerment (e.g., enhanced scholastic performance; protection from the worst psychological consequences of a life crisis or trauma; economic stability or mobility). Such empowering resources can be emotional, social (e.g., giving of one's labor), material (e.g., money), and institutional (e.g., "connections" to gatekeepers). Following Coleman (1988), "resources" can take other key forms as well, in the enforcement of community norms and identity forms, and in the execution of social sanctions (i.e., social pressure to conform; refer to Figure 2.1 in Chapter 2).

SOCIAL CAPITAL AS A CONCEPT LODGED WITHIN A POLITICAL-ECONOMY FRAMEWORK

My own rendition of social capital is rooted much more in Bourdieu's elaboration of cultural and social capital (1986), than in Coleman's (1988, 1990) important contributions. Coleman's model remains decontextualized, lacking attention to unequal power relations in society, and to the political economy overall (A. Lareau [in press] offers similar criticisms). Social capital is fundamentally an economic concept; thus, it is a form of capital subject to laws that regulate its conversion from one form into another, almost always within an economy that is socially stratified in a hierarchical manner (Bourdieu & Wacquant, 1992). Thus, Coleman's definition, "Social capital is productive, making possible the achievement of certain ends that in its absence would not be possible" (1988, p. S98), is recontextualized in the present work. The mobilization of social relations for instrumental purposes always occurs within the context of power relations, and within an economy that unequally distributes socially valued resources, as well as ready access to such resources through proximal ties and networks.

Of all the different kinds of valued network-related resources in society, I have emphasized those institutional resources most associated with what it means to be middle class, or to be privileged, or to "participate in power." This is to say that my use of the concept of social capital, like Bourdieu's, is lodged within a class-economic framework. In my 1997 essay on social capital and minority youth socialization, I intentionally confine the characterization of social capital to the degree and quality of *middle-class* forms of social support inherent in a young person's interpersonal network. I also emphasize those forms of support that represent authentic *counterstratification*—including forms of support that foster coping strategies (among low-status individuals) characterized "in terms of the problem-solving capacities, network orientations, and instrumental behaviors that are directed toward [successfully] dealing with stressful borders and institutional barriers" (Stanton-Salazar, 1997, p. 26). These forms of support would not normally be found within middle-class relational contexts; rather, they are forms that are distinctly created in order to help low-status individuals cope effectively with marginalizing forces in society and to enable them to socially advance in spite of these forces. The AVID classroom in Chapter 8 is an example of how such support becomes partially institutionalized within a school; other noted works do a good job of illustrating these processes in the neighborhood and community (Maeroff, 1988; Williams & Kornblum, 1985).

I have conceptualized these forms of support in terms of *institutional support*, and have highlighted six specific forms. The list is not exhaustive; rather, I focus on those forms of support I see as particularly necessary for success within the school system and in other mainstream institutional arenas (e.g., occupational sector). The six forms of institutional support are outlined in Figure A.1. Note that I include in my conception of institutional support the act of *bridging*, defined as the process of acting as a human bridge to gatekeepers and to important social networks. The first form of institutional support in my list, conceived in terms of *the provision of various funds of knowledge*, is viewed here as closely associated with ascension within the educational system. These funds of knowledge are outlined in Figure A.2. Among the various funds of knowledge originally outlined in my 1997 essay, I call particular attention to one fund described as *problem-*

FIGURE A.1. Six Forms of Institutional Support

1. *Funds of knowledge*	Those funds most associated with ascension within the educational system; such funds also underlie the process of *implicit and explicit socialization into institutional discourses*—those which regulate communication, interaction, and exchange within mainstream institutional spheres.
2. *Bridging*	The process of acting as a human bridge to gate-keepers, to social networks, and to opportunities for exploring various mainstream institutions--e.g., university campuses.
3. *Advocacy*	The process of intervening on behalf of another for the purpose of protecting or promoting their interests.
4. *Role modeling*	Modeling behaviors associated with (1) effective participation in mainstream domains, and (2) effective coping with stratification forces via help-seeking behaviors, rational problem-solving strategies.
5. *Emotional and moral support*	Provided in the context of other forms of support geared toward promoting effective participation in mainstream domains and effective coping with stratification forces.
6. Personalized and soundly-based *evaluative feedback advice* and *guidance*	Incorporates the provision of institutional funds of knowledge as well as genuine emotional and moral support.

FIGURE A.2. Seven Forms of Institutionally Based Funds of Knowledge

1. *Institutionally sanctioned discourses*	Socially acceptable ways of using language and of communicating.
2. *Academic task-specific knowledge*	Subject area knowledge: math, science, etc.
3. *Organizational/bureaucratic funds of knowledge*	Knowledge of how bureaucracies operate--chains of command, resource competition among various branches of bureaucracy.
4. *Network development*	Networking skills: knowledge of how to negotiate with various gatekeepers and agents, build supportive/cooperative ties with peers well integrated in the school, and seek out instrumental ties with informal mentors outside the school.
5. *Technical funds of knowledge*	Computer literacy; study skills, test-taking skills; time-management skills; decision-making skills.
6. *Knowledge of labor and educational markets*	Job and educational opportunities; knowledge of how to fulfill requisites and how to overcome barriers.
7. *Problem-solving knowledge*	How to integrate the first six knowledge forms above in order to solve school-related problems, make sound decisions, and reach personal or collective goals.

solving knowledge, which refers to the insights gained about how to use these different knowledge funds both for effective coping and for reaching personal or collective goals (e.g., going to college; bringing a class-action lawsuit against the school district or police department).

Let me emphasize here that my conceptualization of resources as "social support" (or institutional support) serves the purpose of accounting for both the process-related *and* the concrete (resource) properties of social capital. In other words, social support covers both "the process" of serving another (the relational dynamics that facilitate support) and any concrete or tangible entity that is transferred in the process; for example, knowledge funds, money, ties to people in key bureaucratic positions whose service can be activated, and so forth. Thus, social capital is the value inhering in an individual's relationships when those relations are capable of, as well as socially organized for the purpose of, transmitting to the individual forms of institutional support—particularly in times of greatest need.

APPENDIX B

Overview of Samples, Methods, and Research Sites

Below I present an overview of the two research sites from which data were collected and analyzed for this book. Included are the details of sampling procedures, the social groupings that were most important to us, the methods of data collection and organization, and the methods of data analysis. We begin with the Bay Area/Peninsula study, followed by the one conducted in San Diego.

THE SAN FRANCISCO–SAN JOSE PENINSULA AREA STUDY

Over the course of 3 months, a close colleague and I surveyed 205 Latino high school students from six high schools distributed throughout the San Francisco–San Jose Peninsula area. Subjects were selected from 744 Mexican-origin sophomores, juniors, and seniors who had participated in two school-wide questionnaire surveys administered during the 1987–1988 academic year by a related Stanford University project. All six schools were located within middle- and high-income areas; students from lower-income neighborhoods walked or were transported to these schools as part of district-wide desegregation plans. Latinos represented from 11.3% (N = 136) to 33.4% (N = 387) of the student body in each school, with Mexican-origin students forming slightly less than half of the Latino student population. The proportion of non-Latino White students ranged from 35.4% (N = 589) to 59.4% (N = 742).

Collection of Egocentric Network Data

Semistructured interviews were conducted to determine the students' social support networks, their familistic orientations and practices, and their future plans regarding college, work, and marriage. We inquired about four principal classes of social support: (1) Social/Material Support,

271

(2) Emotional/Crisis Support, (3) Peer Interaction and Recreation, and (4) Informational Support. Informational Support included: (1) Personal Advice on Academic Decisions, (2) Personal Advice and Guidance Regarding Future Educational and Occupational Plans, (3) Personal Advice on Personal Nonacademic Matters, (4) Technical Information Related to Educational/Occupational Future, (5) Information Regarding Current Job Opportunities, (6) Legal Assistance, (7) Health Crisis Services (e.g., issues of substance abuse), and (8) Psychological Services/Professional Crisis Management.

Respondents were asked to elect those people they would seek out with confidence if they needed specific forms of support. The criterion of *confidence* or *confianza* was emphasized. After each question, respondents were asked to specify which people, among those elected, they had actually gone to in the past for this type of support, in a time frame ranging from the "last three or four months of the past school year" to the "past year." Students were asked to provide detailed demographic information on each person identified, including occupational status and ethnicity. We also obtained the names and demographic characteristics of friends, identified as those nonadult persons with whom the adolescent shared leisure activities.

Besides detailed data on both the structure and the composition of the adolescents' networks, extensive data were also collected on each student's peer network and social cliques, as well as on his or her level of participation in school-based and community-based organizations. Careful estimates of the size of the student's kinship network in the geographic area were also taken, with information regarding the frequency of contact with different relatives also recorded. In attempting to further document and map their networks, we queried our adolescent participants about various family responsibilities they undertook, as well as the extent to which they filled the role of cultural broker in their families, an important role that many minority youth commonly assume in assisting various immigrant family and community members. For the Bay Area/Peninsula study, much of this network data was converted into quantifiable form and then merged electronically with the questionnaire data derived from the larger Stanford study of the six schools; this data treatment subsequently allowed for statistical analysis. For the San Diego study, the data derived from the network survey instrument (used with Auxilio High students) were subsequently coded, and tabulations and descriptive statistics were done by hand and by calculator and organized into data sheets.

Our Peninsula Area sample is represented here in different ways as *Sample 1*, *Sample 2*, and *Sample 3*. In *Sample 1*, displayed in Table B.1, generational status was measured using nativity of adolescents and of parents and grandparents. As with the San Diego sample, some first-gen-

Table B.1. *Sample 1.* San Francisco-Peninsula Area Sample (*N* = 205) by Generational Status

First Generation	*Second Generation*	*Third Generation*
(*n* = 67)	(*n* = 78)	(*n* = 60)
32.7% of sample	38% of sample	29.3% of sample

eration students (non–U.S. born) came to the United States at a very early age. Among these non-U.S.-born adolescents, 59 students provided information on length of residence in the United States: 34% had been in the United States for 6 or fewer years; 55.2% had been here for 9 years or more. Thus, only about a third of our first-generation adolescents were really recent immigrants. As we can see in *Sample 2,* displayed in Table B.2, most of these first-generation adolescents, even those with some years in the United States, continued to rate their English-language competencies low. Many of these adolescents may have been conversationally proficient in English, but still rated themselves low in English ability. *Sample 3,* displayed in Table B.3, shows how the three language groups were distributed, with third-generation students excluded. Most of the tables in this book that display data drawn from our Peninsula study rely on this truncated sample, mainly for the purpose of making it compatible with our San Diego sample, comprised of immigrant and second-generation adolescents.

Table B.2. *Sample 2.* San Francisco-Peninsula Area Sample by Language Group

	N = 205
Spanish-dominant	61
Bilinguals	54
English-dominant	90

Table B.3. *Sample 3.* San Francisco-Peninsula Area Sample by Language Group

	N = 145
Spanish-dominant	58
Bilinguals	44
English-dominant	43

THE SAN DIEGO STUDY

The San Diego study began in the spring of 1991 with a survey of 98 students at Auxilio High School. At the time of this survey, students were either sophomores or juniors. Since I planned to return in the fall to conduct follow-up interviews, no seniors were selected in the original sample. Students were all Mexican-origin and, as a whole, were selected to provide variations of immigration and generation status, in gender, and in academic performance.

Replication of Original Network Survey

Complete network data were eventually collected from 75 students. This particular high school was selected for two principal reasons: (1) it was a school that I found to be representative of many inner-city schools serving a mainly low-income minority student population; and (2) the school had a high proportion of Mexican-origin students—my target population (62% of the student body was Latino; about 92% of these Latino students were of Mexican-origin). Most of the initial (quantitative) network survey data were obtained using the instrument a colleague and I originally designed for the Peninsula Area study described above. Tables B.4 and B.5 show the break-

Table B.4. San Diego Network Survey Sample, Auxilio High

	N = 75	
Recent-immigrant girls	10	
Recent-immigrant boys	14	
Acculturated girls	26	50% U.S.- born
Acculturated boys	25	76% U.S.- born

Table B.5. Intensive Interview Sample (N = 51) (High-achievers, Mid-achievers, Low-achievers)

		High-	Mid-	Low-
			Achievers[*]	
Recent-immigrant girls	9	66.6%	33.3%	
(7 years or less in U.S.)		($n = 6$)	($n = 3$)	($n = 0$)
Recent-immigrant boys	6	16.7%	50%	33.3%
(7 years or less in U.S.)		($n = 1$)	($n = 3$)	($n = 2$)
Acculturated girls				
1.5 Generation[**]	10		70%	30%
		($n = 0$)	($n = 7$)	($n = 3$)
U.S.-born	10	10%	60%	30%
		($n = 1$)	($n = 6$)	($n = 3$)
Acculturated boys				
1.5 Generation[**]	7	28.6%	28.6%	42.9%
		($n = 2$)	($n = 2$)	($n = 3$)
U.S.-born	9	22.2%	66.6%	11.1%
		($n = 2$)	($n = 6$)	($n = 1$)
	$N = 51$	$N = 12$	$N = 27$	$N = 12$

[*]Adolescents designated as "high-achievers" were identified in terms of GPA (3.0 and above—without PE) and guidance counselor reports; students designated as "mid-achievers" showed high performance in some classes, but performance was not consistent. (See relevant endnote for Chapter 1.)
[**]Arrived as either young children or infants.

down of adolescents selected for the network survey and interview portions of the San Diego study. Students designated "recent immigrants" were those who had resided in the United States for 7 years or less (≥ 7 yrs); "acculturated" students were either U.S.-born or immigrants with more than 7 years in the United States.

Interviews with Adolescents, Parents,
and Institutional Agents (San Diego)

Intensive semistructured interviews with adolescents and parents were conducted during the course of the 1991–1992 school year. This series of intensive interviews followed "ethnographic" principles and methodologies in the preparation of our interview questions, in the process of interviewing (with prompts), and in the subsequent analysis of the interview data. Methodological guidelines were drawn primarily from James P. Spradley's (1979) *The Ethnographic Interview*.

Four interviewers worked together as a team to complete the series of intensive ethnographic interviews with our sample of 51 adolescents (drawn from the original spring 1991 sample, N = 75). Sample distribution is displayed in Table B.5. At the time of these intensive interviews, all adolescents were either juniors or seniors at Auxilio High. Interviewers consisted of myself, two bilingual women, and one other bilingual man. All three interviewers hired to assist me were college-educated, in their 20s, and concurrently working in the fields of social services and education. I, as principal investigator, conducted about one-fourth of the interviews with our adolescent female subjects, and a bit more than one-third of the interviews with the adolescent males (N = 51). I also conducted about a one-third of the interviews with parents. Depending on circumstances and the student's preference and schedule, interviews were conducted in various places: at the school, in the student's home, somewhere in the neighborhood.

The principal motivation for conducting the San Diego study was to incorporate an ethnographic and intensive interview component into my research on Latino adolescents' social and information networks. Two types of intensive interviews were conducted at the San Diego site. The first type entailed open-ended questions directly related to the adults verbally identified as sources of support in the 1991 spring survey; queries were also made regarding those not identified or elected (e.g., counselors, parents). All interviews (N = 51) were recorded on audiotape. Rather than transcribe these interviews verbatim, my research assistants and I listened to each recorded interview and took extensive notes and quotations, closely following a detailed and thematic note-taking scheme. Training procedures were followed to ensure reliability across note-takers.

The second type of interview entailed open-ended questions about a range of issues having to do with academic achievement and the influence of various social domains in the school, community, and the greater society. Included in the interview schedule were questions pertaining to folk theories of "success" and social mobility, perceptions of discrimination in the school and in the greater society, peer influences on achievement, the student's academic orientation, role models, and parent-school relations. These interviews (N = 51) were transcribed verbatim and subsequently coded, using a series of codes founded on a review of the literature and on the findings and field experiences derived from the Peninsula study. Coded interview data were eventually entered into *File Maker Pro*, a software program that was adapted for our purposes.

Another important component of the San Diego study entailed home visitations and interviews with a subset of parents of those adolescents participating in the intensive interview component of the project (N = 51). Interviews with parents (almost always with the mother, sometimes with the father present) entailed questions and prompts similar to those posed to students; however, the focus was on the parents' own perception of the support process, including the obstacles they perceived that inhibited their children's access to various sources of social and institutional support. Special attention was also devoted to parents' own strategies for dealing with these obstacles. By the end of June 1992, although many more families were interviewed, we had complete interview data from 18 parents. These interviews were also transcribed verbatim and coded, and entered into a *File Maker Pro* data set.

During the 1991–1992 academic year, I also personally conducted interviews with adults identified by my adolescent informants as important and reliable sources of social support, particularly those identified as institutional agents working in various domains within the school (e.g., instruction, counseling, administration, extracurriculum) and in the community (e.g., federally sponsored programs, churches, voluntary civic and political associations, social clubs, and other small-scale institutions within and outside the residential colonies). These adults were asked to provide their own perceptions regarding the social conditions and circumstances that allowed them to be supportive, as well as the problems that existed in their own institutional domains that restricted their supportive capabilities. Most of these interviews were similarly transcribed and analyzed. Although most of the data featured in *Manufacturing Hope and Despair* come from the interviews with adolescent participants (N = 51), the interviews with institutional agents in the school and community figured prominently in my analysis of adolescent interviews, and in the eventual arguments I make in this book.

While conducting interviews with adolescents, parents, and selected institutional agents, I undertook participant observation within the school and the community, visiting classrooms, school sporting events, neighborhood recreation centers, church events, family parties, and park festivals. These observations generated ethnographic fieldnotes that provided a critical store of information about how different adolescent groups experienced their relations with different significant others in those contexts that together constituted their overall social universe.

SOCIOECONOMIC DISTRIBUTION OF LATINO STUDENTS AT AUXILIO HIGH

An occupational prestige scale employed in Blau and Duncan's seminal 1967 book was used as a measure of family socioeconomic status. Measures relied on students' reports of each parent's occupational status. The score used in the regressions presented in the book represents the average of mother's and father's occupational prestige ratings. In the case of single-parent households, the sole parent's score was used.

Table B.6 displays the five categories used to get one perspective of how Latino students were distributed by socioeconomic status, using both

TABLE B.6. Socioeconomic Distribution of Latino Students' Families (Data from Auxilio High School Questionnaire/school-wide survey)

FATHER'S OCCUPATIONAL PRESTIGE SCORES

SES	Frequency	Percent	Cumulative Frequency	Cumulative Percent
0	90	11.7	90	11.7
1	372	54.5	372	54.5
2	189	27.7	561	82.3
3	115	16.9	676	99.1
4	6	0.9	682	100.0

MOTHER'S OCCUPATIONAL PRESTIGE SCORES

HLSES4Z	Frequency	Percent	Cumulative Frequency	Cumulative Percent
0	90	11.7	90	11.7
1	472	69.2	472	69.2
2	91	13.3	563	82.6
3	116	17.0	679	99.6
4	3	0.4	682	100.0

Social Class Breakdown: 0 = missing data, 1 = 20 or less, 2 = 31 to 39, 3 = 40 to 74, 4 = 75 or above.

father's and mother's occupational prestige scores (if data for mother were missing, we used father's score; if data for father were missing, mother's score was used; the "0" in the table represents those students who did not provide data on either parent—that is, missing data). Number 1, indicating 20 or less, signifies people who fill the lowest rungs of the occupational sector. Number 2, indicating 31 to 39, represents the classic *blue-collar* category. Number 3, indicating 40 to 74 on the Duncan scale, signifies people who are lower middle class to middle class; number 4, indicating 75 or higher on the scale, signifies high-status professionals. Among all students who provided information on mother's occupational status, 82.6% came from "blue-collar" or "working-class" households; a nearly identical statistic was produced using father's score. A bit more than half of Latino students had fathers who worked in the lowest-status sector of the San Diego economy, and close to 70% had mothers who worked in the lowest-status sector. Only about 17% of students reported a parent who held a job that could be designated a middle-class occupation. Table B.7 displays the statistics for mother's level of education. Three-quarters of Latino mothers had less than a high school diploma or equivalent.

TABLE B.7. Mother's Level of Formal Education

Level	Frequency	Percent	Cumulative Frequency	Cumulative Percent
1	273	35.4	273	35.4
2	155	20.0	428	55.4
3	149	19.3	577	74.7
4	112	14.5	689	89.2
5	83	10.8	772	100.0

Breakdown of levels: 1 = Some grade school, 2 = Finished grade school, 3 = Some high school, 4 = Finished high school, 5 = Some college or more.

APPENDIX C

Miscellaneous Tables

FIGURE C.1. Logistics regression analysis revealed a significant interaction for the outcome of *Issues* between the racial/linguistic background variables (Spanish-dominant Latino, English-proficient Latino, and non-Latinos) and *Perceived Support*. This interaction is displayed in this figure, and shows estimated probabilities for prototypical values of Model AI7 for three ethno/linguistic groups.

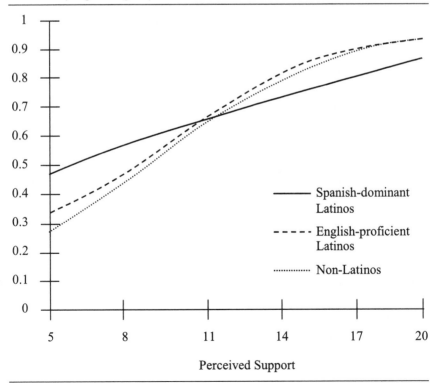

Table C.1. Means, Standard Deviations, and Zero-order Correlations for Variables Examined in Study (*N* = 205) Bay Area/Peninsula

	Mean	*2*	*3*	*4*	*5*	*6*
1. Total Number of Information Contacts (Network Size)	6.52 (2.49)	.42[c]	.27[c]	.28[c]	-.03	-.02
2. Non-family Weak Ties	1.78 (1.42)		.75[c]	.67[c]	.35[c]	-.01
3. School-based Weak Ties	1.12 (1.17)			.79[c]	.45[c]	-.03
4. High-status Ties (High SES)	1.60 (1.37)				.65[c]	.06
5. Socioeconomic Index of *Information Network*	44.17 (14.76)					.14[a]
6. Socioeconomic Index of *Peer Network*	33.06 (14.98)					
7. Activated Academic Support	3.15 (1.96)					
8. Proportion of Non–Mexican origin Friends	0.46 (0.36)					
9. Socioeconomic Status (SES)	54 34.12					
10. Household Size	4.8 (2.18)					
11. English-proficiency Index	4.24 (0.86)					
12. Spanish-proficiency Index	3.21 (1.12)					
13. Spanish Usage in Context	13.27 (4.94)					
14. Grades (Self-reports)	2.80 (0.98)					
15. Educational Expectations	-0.18 (16.32)					
16. Occupational Expectations	6.23 (2.33)					

[+]p < .10, [a]p < .05, [b]p < .01, [c]p < .001

7	8	9	10	11	12	13	14	15	16
.57^c	.06	.05	-.01	.25^c	-.03	.14$^+$	.10	.09	.11
.14^a	-.01	.06	-.09	.18^a	.15^a	.13$^+$	.17^a	.15^a	.11
.09	-.01	.10	-.03	.16^a	.11	.13$^+$	.13$^+$	.20^b	.16^a
.22^a	.08	.18	-.14	.21^b	.03	-.00	.09	.21^b	.18^b
.06	.12$^+$	.33^c	-.21^b	.19^b	-.05	-.10	.03	.2^b	.17^a
.11	.26^c	.31^c	-.27^c	.22^b	-.14^a	-.24^c	-.10	.02	.19^b
	.07	.17^b	-.09	.20^b	-.06	-.05	.04	.21^b	.18^b
		.25^c	-.10	.27^c	-.20^b	-.29^c	.06	.11	.21^b
			-.20^b	.22^c	-.24^c	-.31^c	-.15^a	.16^a	.20^b
				-.17^b	.25^c	.30^c	.20^b	.03	-.08
					-.19^b	-.33^c	.09	.21^b	.14^a
						.84^c	.25^c	.19^b	-.02
							.22^c	.12$^+$	-.02
								.33^c	.18^b
									.32^c

TABLE C.2. *Regressions:* Measures of Social Capital on Social Class, Language Variables, Grades, Grade Level, and Status Expectations (N = 205; Bay Area/Peninsula Study)

		DEPENDENT VARIABLES					
		School-based Weak Ties			Non-Family Weak Ties		
Friends							
Independent Variables		Ed	Occ	CP	Ed	Occ	CP
Socioeconomic Status	*B*	*.008*[+]	*.008*[+]	*.010*[*]	*.008*	*.008*	*.008*
	s.e.	.005	.005	.005	.007	.007	.007
	beta	.114	.117	.143	.196	.097	.101
English Proficiency	*B*	*.092*[*]	*.101*[*]	*.107*[**]	*.158*[**]	*.161*[**]	*.159*[**]
	s.e.	.050	.049	.051	.061	.060	.062
	beta	.139	.152	.162	.195	.199	.200
Spanish Usage	*B*	*.024*[*]	*.028*[*]	*.027*[*]	*.034*[*]	*.035*[*]	*.034*[*]
	s.e.	.015	.014	.015	.018	.018	.018
	beta	.139	.159	.158	.159	.165	.161
Grades (Self-reports)	*B*	*.109*	*.128*[+]	*.150*[*]	*.193*[*]	*.201*[**]	*.200*[*]
	s.e.	.087	.085	.088	.107	.104	.107
	beta	.094	.110	.129	.136	.142	.14
Juniors	*B*	*.488*[**]	*.496*[**]	*.464*[**]	*.491*[**]	*.493*[**]	*.494*[**]
	s.e.	.184	.185	.188	.225	.226	.228
	beta	.200	.202	.189	.163	.164	.164
Seniors	*B*	*.547*[**]	*.531*[**]	*.565*[***]	*.729*[***]	*.724*[***]	*.747*[***]
	s.e.	.198	.199	.201	.242	.243	.244
	beta	.209	.203	.216	.228	.226	.233
Status Expectations	*B*	*.100*[+]	*.054*	*.004*	*.037*	*.019*	*.074*
	s.e.	.062	.036	.192	.076	.044	.233
	beta	.122	.110	.002	.037	.032	.024
$R^2 =$		.135	.133	.123	.138	.138	.137

Unstandardized coefficients in italics.
Key: Ed, Educational Expectations; Occ, Occupational Expectations; CP, College Plans.
[+]p < .10, [*]p < .05, [**]p < .01, [***]p < .001

			DEPENDENT VARIABLES					
Socioeconomic Index of Information Network			Proportion of Non-Mexican-Origin Friends			Socioeconomic Index of Peer Network		
Ed	Occ	CP	Ed	Occ	CP	Ed	Occ	CP
.229***	.235***	.235***	.002	.002	.002	.184***	.153**	.172***
.068	.069	.068	.002	.002	.002	.070	.069	.069
.263	.269	.270	.112	.080	.083	.208	.173	.194
.914	1.032+	.878	.031*	.029*	.022	1.208*	1.060*	1.091*
.634	.627	.640	.016	.015	.012	.647	.634	.653
.106	.120	.102	.146	.137	.104	.138	.121	.125
-.010	.030	-.009	-.012**	-.012**	-.014**	-.405**	-.417**	-.428**
.184	.183	.184	.005	.004	.004	.188	.185	.188
-.004	.0134	-.004	-.222	-.215	-.248	.177	-.182	-.187
.349	.634	.356	.035**	.028	.016	-.730	-1.200	-1.027
1.106	1.076	1.108	.027	.026	.027	1.128	1.088	1.131
.023	.042	.024	.196	.077	.044	-.048	-.078	-.067
3.229	3.245	3.540	-.070	-.058	-.045	.225	.740	.475
2.333	2.347	2.362	.058	-.057	.057	2.380	2.375	2.409
.101	.102	.111	-.091	-.074	-.058	.007	.023	.015
7.063**	6.952**	7.825**	-.073	-.087+	-.046	1.324	.827	1.387
2.503	2.521	2.529	.062	-.062	.062	2.553	2.551	2.580
.208	.205	.231	-.089	-.106	-.056	.038	.024	.040
1.196	.527	3.567	.009	.026**	.164***	-.421	.705	.871
.786	.460	2.418	.020	.011	.059	.802	.466	2.467
.113	.082	.110	.033	.164	.207	-.039	.108	.0264
.174	.170	.173	.147	.169	.180	.166	.175	.165

TABLE C.3. *Perceived Support* Indicators, Associated with Relations with School Personnel, Auxilio High School (*N* = 1,087)

	Latinos (N = 698)	English proficient Latinos (N = 309)	Spanish dominant Latinos (N = 389)	Non-Latinos (N = 389)
1. My *teachers* give me the moral support I need to do well in school.	84.3% (n = 588)	74.8% (n = 231)	91.7% (n = 357)	69.7% (n = 271)
2. Most other students at this school are closer to their *teachers* than I am.	39.6% (n = 277)	42.4% (n = 131)	37.6% (n = 146)	35.7% (n = 139)
3. I rely on my *teachers* for advice and guidance in making important school-related decisions.	59.6% (n = 416)	51.7% (n = 160)	65.8% (n = 256)	47.9% (n = 186)
4. I rely on our *school counselors* for advice and guidance in making important school-related decisions.	61.9% (n = 432)	51.4% (n = 159)	70.2% (n = 273)	45.0% (n = 175)
5. My *teachers* are sensitive to my personal needs.	49.3% (n = 344)	47.9% (n = 148)	50.4% (n = 196)	45.0% (n = 175)
6. My *teachers* are good at helping me solve *school-related or academic* problems.	78.4% (n = 547)	70.9% (n = 219)	84.3% (n = 328)	68.7% (n = 267)
7. My *teachers* are good in helping me solve *personal* problems.	34.9% (n = 244)	34.6% (n = 107)	35.2% (n = 137)	19.6% (n = 76)
8. My *school counselors* are good at helping me solve *school-related or academic* problems.	70.8% (n = 494)	57.9% (n = 179)	81.0% (n = 315)	54.0% (n = 210)
9. My *school counselors* are good at helping me solve *personal* problems.	36.7% (n = 256)	33.3% (n = 103)	39.3% (n = 153)	22.9% (n = 89)
10. I have a friendly and trusting relationship with a number of *teachers*.	67.6% (n = 472)	66.0% (n = 204)	68.9% (n = 268)	65.6% (n = 255)
11. I have a friendly and trusting relationship with at least one of the *school counselors*.	48.0% (n = 335)	44.6% (n = 138)	50.5% (n = 197)	43.5% (n = 169)

Questionnaire items featured the following scale: 1 = Strongly disagree, 2 = Disagree, 3 = Agree, 4 = Strongly agree. Percentages represent the combination of "Agree" and "Strongly Agree" responses in the survey.

Notes

Chapter 1

1. From editorial article entitled "Kids Get Tough Love Without the Love" (Goodman, 2000).

2. In a forthcoming work, I show that peer-group dynamics reveal still another set of distinctive obstacles.

3. Angela Valenzuela was my team partner in the field; at the time, she was a doctoral student working toward her degree in the Department of Sociology at Stanford University. Her work on social capital and *subtractive schooling* is cited in the References (Valenzuela, 1999).

4. See Appendix B for relevant statistics on the range of family socioeconomic status in our sample.

5. *auxilio* [aek-sí-ljo] [Spanish] *m.* aid, help; sometimes used in exclamatory fashion, as when someone is experiencing great distress and seeking immediate aid.

6. I place the term "high-achieving" in quotation marks because I found very few Latino students (from working-class or low-income households) who were taking a full college preparatory curriculum and doing well. What I found were students who showed some evidence of high scholastic performance, who seemed very motivated to do well in school and to attend college, but who experienced high degrees of emotional stress due to a variety of personal burdens and who, in the final analysis, lacked the academic support system to enable them to perform at their full potential.

Chapter 2

1. *Writings of the Young Marx on Philosophy and Science*, translated and edited by Lloyd D. Easton and Kurt H. Guddat, p. 429.

2. My own critique of functionalist thought in contemporary studies of youth and schooling centers on what I see as the emphasis on processes of social control, conformity to norms, and group identity (see Table 2.1), usually without attention to widespread instances of discrimination and social conflict linked to the societal hierarchies of class, race, and gender. The functionalist theoretical current is usually seen as reaching its height in sociology in the late 1930s with the

work of Talcott Parsons, yet it continues to find expression in dominant branches of mainstream sociology, economics, and psychology. Functionalist thought in the social sciences has usually been linked to 17th- and 18th-century Anglo-Protestant utilitarian individualism, which is widely understood as providing the ideological foundation for modern industrial capitalism (Watt, 1989; Weber, 1904/1958). Functionalist frameworks, as expressed within the social and behavioral sciences, have deep ideological traditions oriented toward the preservation of the status quo in society. Most important for our purposes, functionalist frameworks have been responsible for generating simplistic and extremely ethnocentric accounts of social inequality (Ryan, 1976; Howitt & Owusu-Bempah, 1994).

3. Such a perspective is wonderfully brought to cinema in the motion picture *The Matrix*.

4. Such adverse effects may include the internalization of racist myths, feelings of inferiority, rejection of native language and culture, and heightened feelings of shame. Speaking to the socialization effects experienced by colonialized Blacks in the Caribbean, Frantz Fanon (1967) begins his book *Black Skin, White Masks* with a quotation from Aimé Césaire (from *Discours sur le Colonialsme*): "I am talking of millions of men who have been skillfully injected with fear, inferiority complexes, trepidation, servility, despair, abasement."

5. Cochran and his associates (1990) call attention to genetic predispositions that combine in complex ways with sociocultural and environmental influences to shape an individual's network orientation (i.e., network-building and help-seeking dispositions and skills).

6. See p. 24 of Baca Zinn and Eitzen (1999) for their definition of *human agency*.

7. Social stratification can be defined as the hierarchical organization of social inequalities. Key to this organization is how scarce resources and social rewards are allocated to different groups, based on their place in the hierarchy. The three principal hierarchies in society are social class, race, and gender. As used here, social stratification includes those forms of power employed by dominant groups to maintain each group's position in the hierarchy.

8. This particular part of my argument was aided by Carnoy and Levin's *Schooling and Work in the Democratic State* (1985), particularly Chap. 6, "Contradictions in Education."

9. Looking at a study that examines the buffering potential of low-status adolescent social networks may help clarify my points. Frank Furstenberg and Mary E. Hughes (1995) report on their insightful study of 252 children of teenage mothers, showing how indicators of social capital do play an important role differentiating the low-status youth population. Specifically, these researchers asked the following question: Does the availability of social capital in 1984 influence the outcomes of the youth even after accounting for the youth's trajectory through 1984? Their statistical findings strongly suggest that some of their indicators of social capital do "appear to improve the odds of socioeconomic success in early adulthood, even when we take into account how the youth were doing 3 years earlier" (p. 588). The three indicators of social capital responsible for these youth's advantaged status were: "support to and from own mother, the number of the

child's friends the mother knows, and whether the mother has a strong help network or sees a close friend weekly" (p. 589). Note here that the emergent indicators are largely interpreted as having to do with coping resources and activities that function to buffer mother and child from the worst emotional and material consequences associated with their life condition. For the most part, the kind of social capital associated with access to influential institutional agents, to monetary resources, and to expert knowledge funds is rarely in the purview of the disenfranchised. For this sector of society—the social bottom—effective network-based forms of defense are the most they can hope for; another form is family networks that push forms of conformity that may heighten the chances of institutional sponsorship, which in turn paves the way for regular and informal access to mobility-related resources.

10. My use of the concept of personal initiatives (in lieu of the more familiar concept of "choices") is modeled after the conceptual work of Moncrieff Cochran (1990). Cochran uses the term *initiatives* (rather than choices) "because it conveys action without necessarily assuming that alternatives exist" (p. 279).

11. Erickson and Shultz, in their book entitled *The Counselor as Gatekeeper* (1982), do a superb job of demonstrating how class and other status differences can inadvertently sabotage the supportive potential of counselor-student relations. Annett Lareau, in her insightful book *Home Advantage* (1989), shows how relations between working-class parents and school personnel are regularly characterized by social distance, mutual suspicion, and distrust.

12. Drawing from Barth's (1969) and Erickson's (1993) studies on inter-ethnic group relations, Phelan and associates (1998) make an important distinction between "boundaries" and "borders." Boundaries are defined as real or perceived lines that demarcate one social world or setting from others; they function to alert people to the rules and requirements necessary for effective participation within the respective world or social setting. The *requirements* essentially entail the acquisition of a distinctive repertoire of both sociocultural and institutionally based knowledge and behaviors necessary for effective social relations and problem-solving. When boundaries are neutral, "movement between worlds occurs with relative ease—social and psychological costs are minimal" (Phelan, Davidson, & Yu, 1993, p. 53). Boundaries, however, are transformed into "borders" when the participation becomes stressful and obstructive—as when minority children and youth find participation and movement within school settings difficult and overly stressful.

13. Based on the work of Suzanne Lipsky (1987), I use the term *distress pattern* to mean "some form of rigid, destructive, and ineffective feeling and behavior" that has its origins in some earlier psychological injury (p. 2). A particular distress pattern, when "restimulated, will tend to push the victim through a reenactment of the original distress experience." Sometimes the distress pattern is played out with someone else in the victim role, as in the classic case of an adult who was physically abused by a parent and who now victimizes his or her own child (Lipsky, 1987, p. 2). Lipsky views forms of oppression such as racism and classism as founded and "powerfully reinforced by the distress patterns of indi-

vidual members of the majority culture and their institutions" (p. 2). This mistreatment, in turn, installs heavy chronic distress patterns on subordinate members of society, usually forcing them to regulate their own oppression.

14. I highly recommend Moncrieff Cochran's (1990a) figures on pages 278 and 298 of *Extending Families*. These two figures were instrumental in my own understanding of the literature on network development.

15. Considering its cultural importance within immigrant communities as a key basis for self-reference and meaning making, the deterioration of *confianza* in a person's most significant network relations might very well prompt aspects of classic social-psychological alienation (see Berry, 1980; Schacht, 1970). See Stanton-Salazar (2000) for an elaborated discussion of this issue.

16. The appraisals made by adolescents, and their decisions whether or not to seek help from a parent, are always influenced by their own respective attitudes and beliefs regarding whether certain people are appropriate sources of help, the risks involved, and the effectiveness of seeking help within different domains—in this case, the family.

17. Regarding "defiant individualism," see also my discussion in Stanton-Salazar, 2000; the term originated in Sánchez-Jankowski's (1991) work on gangs.

Chapter 3

1. Taken from Miller's book entitled *The Drama of the Gifted Child: The Search for the True Self.*

2. Tijuana is known for its abundant commerce, which includes 500-plus "maquiladora" assembly plants. Tijuana accounts for about 34% of the Mexican population living along the country's 2,000 miles of border with the United States.

3. The Latino population in the county continues to be substantially younger than the region's total population. While the median age for Latinos in 1990 was 24.3 years, for the general population it was 30.9. Latinos also accounted for 29.3% of the region's population under 5 years of age, and 29.1% of the school-age population (ages 5–17). This youthful trend within the Latino population parallels the trend throughout the state (Hayes-Bautista, Schink, & Chapa, 1988).

4. The school system has had to respond to the growing presence of LEP students. For example, in 1990, San Diego County employed 875 teachers with bilingual credentials, yet this number accounted for only a bit less than half of the region's need for bilingual and credentialed educators (United Way of San Diego County, 1991).

5. On June 2, 1998, California voters passed Proposition 227, the anti-bilingual education measure; 61% of the voters were in favor, compared with 39% who were opposed. Civil rights organizations filed for injunctions the following day. In July, a federal district court denied the petitions. Proposition 227 became law on August 3, 1998. The law calls for a return to pedagogical methods similar to those used before the development of bilingual education programs in the 1970s. Specifically, the new law called for a one-year "sheltered English immersion" program and the development and implementation of curricula designed for

English language learners. The measure was intended to put a stop to bilingual education's principal methodology: the development of primary literacy skills in non-English-speaking children's native language (e.g., Spanish).

6. I present here the demographic compositions of Augusta Heights and Southview together as one profile. Augusta Heights is situated on the northwestern corner of Southeast San Diego; Southview is positioned directly east of it. At the turn of the century, both neighborhoods featured stately homes strategically positioned to take in the beautiful views of the city and the harbor. Compared with Harrison Heights, Augusta Heights and Southview had slightly higher concentrations of Latinos, with a combined percentage of 87.1%. African Americans double their numbers in Southview, but overall represent only 6.3% of the population. Whites, Asians, and Pacific Islanders (many Filipinos) represent another 6.3%. Almost all of each neighborhood remains residential; only a small portion of the area is reserved for industrial (4% and 5%, respectively) and commercial (5% and 10%) uses. The income distribution in these two neighborhoods is quite similar to that of Harrison Heights. Here we also find many people living in poverty, with about 47% of the total number of residents and about 60% of children living below the official poverty line. Nearly 83% of all occupied housing units were rented at the time of the study. These two neighborhoods were benefiting from a couple of community service agencies located within their boundaries. Yet, apart from Southview Park—which is quite small and unsupervised—places for supervised recreation were virtually nonexistent. Youth looking to participate in city-funded recreation centers had to travel to Harrison Heights or to Vista. The city did provide a city recreation staff person at Southview Elementary School who checked out balls and play equipment in the afternoons.

7. Before we proceeded with our prepared list of questions regarding the neighborhood, we asked adolescents to look at a photocopy of a map of the area and to outline, using a colored marker, the area they considered to be "their neighborhood." In most cases, these areas were smaller than the areas we have already identified in our demographic profiles. They constituted the area or turf that surrounded their homes and that constituted the familiar spaces they socially and physically negotiated on a regular basis.

8. By the end of the 1990s, the site had been turned into a police substation.

9. Spivak (1987).

10. Statistics for San Diego County (Blumstein, 1996) for the period 1990–1994 do show an increase in violent crime among youth of about 22% (San Diego Association of Governments, 1995). We also know that beginning in 1985, murder by and of people under 24 began to increase; by 1992, the homicide rate for this group had doubled. Arrest rates for youth homicide skyrocketed, with the arrest rate for White juveniles climbing 80%, and for non-Whites rising about 120%. Four causal factors are hypothesized: First, during this period we see a significant rise in the number of juveniles recruited to sell crack and other drugs on the street (or to serve as "scouts"); second, carrying a gun was increasingly seen as an effective mode of protection when transporting valuables, whether money or drugs. As more young people felt threatened by the existence of fire-

arms around them, including those not in the drug trade, they too obtained guns. This situation was combined with a third factor, that possession of a firearm not only promised "protection," but also symbolized status and power. And finally, disputes and rivalries among juveniles (and between territorial gangs) once settled by fistfights now are frequently resolved through firearms (e.g., drive-by shootings).

11. It is important to mention here that despite the dramatic increase in gang-involved cocaine sales (from 9% in 1983 to almost 25% in 1985), there exists little or no evidence showing that gangs are principally responsible for the ongoing development of the drug market, or for the often-presumed relationship between drug marketing, gangs, and violence (Blumstein, 1996; Blumstein, Cohen, & Farrington, 1996). One study of three U.S. cities showed that while some gangs are involved in drug sales and distribution, others are not (Blumstein et al., 1996). Such studies suggest that most gangs are not intimately involved in the drug trade, although individual members of any gang may casually participate, at some level, from time to time (see also Centers & Weist, 1998).

12. A review of existing literature by Centers and Weist (1998) found that "around one in six urban adolescents [16.6%] have had some involvement in drug dealing, with rates even higher for African-Americans males over 16" (p. 395). They go on to outline the various problems usually associated with drug dealing, "including juvenile arrest, involvement in violence (as victims and perpetrators), substance abuse, behavioral and emotional difficulties, academic failure and drop-out" (p. 395).

13. Spivak (1987).

14. The 1980s saw crack cocaine devastating the Black community in South-east; the evidence regarding the devastating impact of *crack* across Black urban communities appears overwhelming. Some social service and youth workers in Southeast believed that the use of phencyclidine or PCP also became popularized during this period (and into the early 90s), particularly among Chicano gangs, quickly bringing a hyper-aggressive mentality that resulted in violent confrontations and death. Studies on the relationship between phencyclidine intoxication and violent behavior, however, do not support this claim (Brecher, Wang, Wong, & Morgan, 1988; Khajawall, Erickson, & Simpson, 1982; Wish, 1986). Khajawall and associates (1982) state that PCP-induced "aggression appears to be a rare phenomenon, if it occurs at all" (p. 1604). What role PCP plays in the overall distressed situation of Southeast has yet to be clearly and conclusively articulated.

15. Other studies provide the necessary perspective of those actually involved in the drug economy. Izabel Ricardo (1994), in her study of 22 youth interviewed through semi-circular, open-ended interviews, quotes a 15-year-old who tells of his involvement with drug sales: "Well I was just thinking, I didn't ever get what I wanted to get, than I finally had a chance to, that was my fast move. I knew I couldn't get a job because I wasn't old enough, so you know it wasn't like I wasn't willing to work, cause I was willing to work, so my best bet was to do what I could while I had a chance, to get the things I wanted to get in life. All of us who were selling drugs, we didn't sell drugs because we wanted to, we sold drugs cause we didn't have any other choice. When your parents,

when grown people don't have jobs to take care of their sons and daughters, how do they expect their sons and daughters to get things they want out of life? It's not like I want to see drugs, it's just that things people get nowadays is just not good enough" (p. 1057).

16. *Negros* (literally, "Blacks"); the Spanish colloquial term used to refer to Black people, in this case, for African Americans; *cholos* usually refers to Chicano youth who adopt certain working-class stylistic conventions in dress and language use that reflect urban Chicano identities and neighborhood loyalties; these subcultural traits are also associated with normal adolescent involvement in social cliques.

17. *Gente* roughly translates here into community members (literally, "the people"). *Quinceañeras* are traditional Mexican right-of-passage celebrations that occur at a young woman's 15th birthday; a highly adorned Catholic mass is typically incorporated into the festivities.

18. The percentage of housing units that were owner-occupied in 1990 for three of the four neighborhoods is as follows: Harrison Heights: 22.77%—average across three tracts; Augusta Heights: 15.9%; Southview: 18.4%.

Chapter 4

1. Recreational centers in the neighborhood tended to serve older children and early adolescents, particularly those in junior high school.

2. The survey was administered to 205 students, comprising immigrant and second- and third-generation adolescents. For purposes of comparability, we eliminated the 60 third-generation adolescents for this report.

3. See also the study conducted by the anthropologist Carlos Vélez-Ibáñez (1997, p. 144), which examined kinship network size and structure among predominantly U.S.-born (working-class) Mexicans in Tucson, Arizona. Similar to the research findings reported by Keefe and Padilla (1987), Vélez-Ibáñez found that the familial networks in Tucson were dynamic in composition, and increased in size with each generation (see also Valenzuela & Dornbusch, 1996).

4. Valenzuela and Dornbusch (1994) define *familism* in terms of three dimensions that operate within the extended family system: "The structural dimension marks the spatial and social boundaries within which behaviors occur and attitudes acquire meaning. These boundaries are delineated by the presence or absence of nuclear and extended family members. The attitudinal dimension refers to the expressed identification with the interests and welfare of the family. The behavioral dimension involves different degrees of attachment and affinity during contact with family members" (pp. 18–19).

5. It is evident that we need to reconcile this less-than-resourceful embeddedness in the kin network with what we know about adult kin relations in Mexican communities in the United States. Keefe et al. (1979), in their study of Mexican American and Anglo kinship relations conducted from 1975 through 1977 in three Southern Californian cities, found that (non–recent immigrant) Mexican Americans are more likely than Anglos to rely on kin for emotional and social support. They write that "Mexican Americans are much more likely than Anglos to have

large numbers of relatives living in the community" (p. 151). These Mexican-American kin groups "are well integrated and encompass three or more genera-tions. Anglos, on the other hand, tend to live apart from their extended family or have only a few related households nearby" [note: social class not statistically controlled for in these comparative analyses]. While the evidence does suggest that Mexican Americans (adults and youth) tend to be more "familistic" than Anglos (see Valenzuela & Dornbusch, 1996; Vélez-Ibáñez, 1997), such familism does not necessarily translate into positive embeddedness among adolescents, as defined here (i.e., plentiful ties to a network of relatives engaged in parent-like/mentor-like behaviors). This relates to a key dimension of adolescent embedded-ness as delineated in Chapter 2 (i.e., that proximity and exposure to sources of support do not automatically translate into actual support).

6. Our surveys and interviews in the Bay Area study and in San Diego also investigated involvement in church-based youth groups. In both studies, such involvement was rare. Exceptional cases, however, did emerge. One indicator of church-based support was the election of a priest or clergy as a source of per-sonal, emotional, or informational support. In our Bay Area study (N = 145), approximately 98% of the sample did not elect a minister or priest; similar find-ings emerged in our San Diego study.

Chapter 5

1. An important issue is raised by Sra. Barrera's remarks: Youngsters in many Mexican-origin communities have immigrant parents who provide moral support, but who are not equipped to assist in the career decision-making process. Ado-lescents are really on their own. Parents do not have the education, nor are they familiar with the intricate relation between the different careers and their corre-sponding educational requirements—especially, that college is a necessity for even beginning to consider what kind of good job one wants. In Mexico, people speak of selecting careers during adolescence—that is, working people make decisions fairly early on. "Carrera" (career) often means technical training for a trade. In Mexico, the notion of a liberal education for the general masses is foreign. Par-ents are not fully aware that privileged people usually pick school first (a univer-sity), then choose a professional career fairly late in the game. The role of college and university training in differentiating people is not well understood. Nor is it understood that, at this time in economic history, people are differentiated by whether they go on to college. Sra. Barrera may not truly realize that going to a 4-year university is a rarity for working-class people, and that in her family, she has a daughter who has already passed this critical threshold and that she has a son who will very likely distinguish himself by going to college. She also may not realize that given their economic status and their racialized status, the fact that her son Antonio could easily qualify to go to higher-status universities is remarkable.

2. Parents received three formal progress reports during a semester. In total, parents receive six reports during the course of the academic year, including two final grade reports.

3. When we look solely at the parents of U.S.-born students, the percentage climbs to 51%; in general, the statistics are similar to those reported for the larger group.

4. For three important sources that examine how working-class parents are treated by schools, see Michelle Fine's *Framing Dropouts* (1991), Annette Lareau's *Home Advantage* (1989), and Lareau and Horvat's (1999) "Moments of Social Inclusion and Exclusion: Race, Class, and Cultural Capital in Family-school Relationships."

5. Such alienation is also evident within the immigrant parent community, although it is not as pervasive as that found in more established Chicano working-class communities (such as in Texas). A few immigrant parents in my study did in fact exhibit attitudes consonant with John Ogbu's (1991) "involuntary minorities."

6. Catsambis and Garland (1997) rely on statistical data drawn from *The National Educational Longitudinal Study* (NELS:88); they examined differences across four ethnic groups: Whites, African Americans, Latinos, and Asians.

7. See Eames and Goode, 1973.

Chapter 6

1. See Rosaldo's (1989; p. 198) discussion of cultural visibility and invisibility, about how mainstream members of society who see themselves as "full citizens" also see themselves as lacking "culture."

2. A good place to begin is James Youniss's (1983a) review article entitled "Mutuality in Parent-adolescent Relationship: Social Capital for Impending Adulthood"; also useful is Cooper et al. (1983). The other articles cited in this chapter on parent-adolescent conflict and individuation are similarly useful, particularly Grotevant and Cooper (1986) and Montemayor (1983).

3. The past 20 years have witnessed many calls within the academy for an antiracist, antisexist, and anticlassist psychology; this new psychology would include a commitment to theories of child and adolescent development that, as a matter of design, would address cultural and group variations in an informed sociological manner. See, for example, Boykin and Toms (1985) and Henwood (1994); see also Berry, Poortinga, Segall, and Dasen (1994) for an overview of the field of cross-cultural psychology. For a critical historical view of European and American psychology and its treatment of race, see Robert Guthrie (1998).

4. Cited in the *Los Angeles Times*, 5/27/96, p. A16.

5. Examples of *macro-structural currents* would be the growing "prosperity gap" between wage earners and those working in the middle and upper echelons of high-tech industries; we can also include here the national backlash against affirmation action policies seen throughout the 1990s.

6. See Jarrett (1995).

7. For a more elaborate discussion of apolitical *antagonistic acculturation* styles, see text and citations in Stanton-Salazar (2000).

8. The CILS is the largest survey study of its kind to date in the United States. The survey included a total of 5,266 eighth- and ninth-graders in 42 schools in California (San Diego) and South Florida (Miami and Fort Lauderdale); this sizable sample of teenage "second-generation" youth represents 77 nationalities. See López and Stanton-Salazar (in press) for analyses focusing on Mexican American teens drawn from the CILS data set.

9. The measure of parent-adolescent conflict was constructed using a 3-item inventory, as was the outcome variable in Rumbaut's multiple regression analyses.

10. It is important to note that included in these standards are restrictive dating policies that young women must adhere to.

11. In a study of outpatient clients, Barrera and Baca (1990) found, among other things, a significant and positive association between positive help-seeking orientation and support satisfaction. Translated in reverse, this means that persons with a negative disposition toward seeking and receiving aid are less likely to benefit from social support when experiencing distress.

12. There were four possible responses to these items, from to Strongly Agree to Strongly Disagree.

13. Tests of interconsistency produced Cronbach's alphas of .90 and .70, respectively.

14. One possibility is that recent immigrants may feel disinclined to give true indications of *perceived familial support* owing to feelings of familial loyalty and/ or cultural prohibitions against making negative comments about one's family.

15. Blau and Duncan (1967).

16. Based on findings from our intensive interviews showing adolescent-parent relations more conflictive among girls, we hypothesized that boys would be slightly more motivated than girls to elect their parents.

17. 1.5–generation youth are those children of immigrant parents who arrived in the United States at an early age. Although technically "immigrants," these youth are often indistinguishable from children of immigrants who are U.S.-born.

Chapter 7

1. One incident of attempted sexual abuse or harassment (by a stepfather) emerged in our data; due to space limitations, I did not discuss this case in the chapter. A parent's failure to protect her children from the sexually abusive behavior of the other parent (or stepparent) would most likely precipitate emotional detachment by the adolescent from the unprotecting parent. Thus, defensive detachment from the abusive parent (or stepparent) becomes coupled with alienation from the unprotecting parent. Sexual and other forms of abuse among children and youth is a national problem deserving wider recognition. In one survey, half of all Americans believe child abuse and neglect is the most important public health issue facing this country. Although the nation's crime rate fell 22% from 1993 to 1997, reports of child abuse and neglect grew by 8% and confirmed cases increased 4%. Poverty and economic problems in the home are significantly related to incidence rates in nearly every category of maltreatment (statistics taken from Third National Incidence Study [NIS-3] of child maltreatment released by

the National Center on Child Abuse [NCCAN] in the fall of 1996). One study (Kercher & McShane, 1984) found that incestuous victimization for Latina women is about 1 in 5, only slightly higher than for other groups. Studies on high-risk early adolescent females show that those who experience social isolation or parental absence or unavailability, and those who report poor relationships between their parents, are all at higher risk. The presence of a nonbiologically related father (i.e., stepfather) is cited as another risk factor (Finkelhor & Baron, 1986).

2. *Ni de aqui, ni de alla,* translates literally into, "Neither from here, nor from there."

3. For a thorough discussion of Mexican and Latino religiosity in the United States, see Gonzales and La Velle (1985).

4. In the course of this study, it has become clear to me that there is a need for a *theory of appraisals* applicable to minority adolescents from low-SES immigrant households. In the interpretation of my interview findings, I've drawn insights from the extensive theoretical and empirical work on appraisals by Lazarus and Folkman (1984). As employed here, this theory alerts us to adolescents' tendency to make a number of risk assessments before seeking support—for example, assessing whether a person is a viable source of support or whether someone can be trusted with confidences.

5. The term *consejos* carries many layers of meaning in Mexican Spanish, connoting guidance and counsel buttressed by a good deal of trust and evidence of genuine caring.

6. This at first may appear a universal phenomenon: a father arriving home late and feeling exhausted, a child reluctant to approach the parent in this condition. However, the adolescents we studied were frequently having to broker for or assist their immigrant parents with tasks that better-educated and English-proficient parents usually do on their own. Because of this, I suspect that many of my adolescent informants had become quite sensitive to their parents' feelings of frustration and of incompetency regarding bureaucratic and/or school-related tasks and problems. Many adolescents were thus prone to manage delicately those situations where they were forced to burden their parents with such tasks and problems.

7. The AVID academic program at Auxilio High is described in some detail in Chapter 8; also see endnote on AVID at end of that chapter.

8. See our discussion of the psychological literature on emotional "attachments" to caregivers in Stanton-Salazar and Spina (2000), which includes a critique of Ainsworth (1978) and of Bowlby's (1969) theory of attachment.

9. The issue of role reversal in immigrant and working-class Latino families has been understudied; furthermore, it is not always discussed in studies of immigrant families. Specifically, I am referring to the situation where immigrant parents are regularly forced to defer to, and to depend on, their adolescent children when interfacing with bureaucracies and institutional agents and when working through household economic matters (e.g., bill statements). Adolescents, in turn, are placed in the position of caretakers and agents for their parents, assuming a good deal of power and influence in the process. Parental authority, in these cases, is usually renegotiated in the adolescent's favor.

Chapter 8

1. This 4-to-1 ratio is compared to about 2-to-1 in California and less than 2-to-1 for Los Angeles or the Miami metropolitan area (Rumbaut, 1997, p. 4).

2. Statistics drawn from documents provided by Community Relations and Integration Services Division of the San Diego City Schools (February 5, 1991).

3. Some of this enrollment change reflects the fact that a number of Latino/a students move with their parents when the latter find better jobs in other cities.

4. These statistics are based on those students who were surveyed, and only 78% of the students at the school participated in the survey. It is possible that students fully participating in the IB curriculum (especially Euro-American students) were undersampled.

5. After a number of years at San Diego City College, Salvador Baca successfully transferred to a University of California campus, where he completed his bachelor's degree in 1999. In the fall of 1999, he entered a Ph.D. program in public policy at an East Coast Ivy League college.

6. Actually, during most of the school day, the counseling office required students to check in when they walked in the door. Informal interactions with counselors occurred mainly after school. Also, few teachers ever entered the counseling office; thus informal interactions, when they did occur, were with guidance counselors and with a small group of paraprofessionals who took on various duties throughout the school.

7. California has a history of educating undocumented students. In 1998, in the Supreme Court decision *Plyer v. Doe*, the high court found it unconstitutional to deny young undocumented immigrants access to public education through the high school level. The decision, however, did not include access to state institutions of higher education. In 1985, an Alameda County Superior Court (California) made it possible for undocumented immigrants to attend a California state university without having to pay out-of-state fees. This ruling, known as *Leticia A*, permitted undocumented students to establish residency by demonstrating intent to reside in the state for more than a year. In 1990, in a Supreme Court ruling known as *Bradford*, the high court held that all higher education systems in California must require proof of students' U.S. residency; also, undocumented students would be required to pay out-of-state tuition. For a while, the California State University (CSU) system found a way to avoid *Bradford* through its adherence to *Leticia A*. However, in 1995 a Los Angeles appellate court required the CSU to align itself with the UC system and the community college system, which require both a screening device and out-of-state tuition charges (normally between $7,000 and $8,000 a year) for those identified as undocumented. Of course, the final legal victory of Proposition 187 would make these decisions moot, while still preventing many talented undocumented students from pursuing a higher education degree.

8. Youniss and Smollar (1985) also found that 25% of the interactions specified *conversation* (i.e., about common interests or practical matters), vs. 42% with mothers; 17% involved shared *recreational* or *work activities*.

9. This analysis of the special position of coaches within the school was greatly informed by a conversation with Professor Patricia McDonough of UCLA (March 25, 1998).

10. Please refer to Betty Harragan's *Games Mother Never Taught You* (1977) and Warren Farrell's *The Liberated Man* (1974/1993). Both books discuss the values, orientations, and gender perspectives inculcated in male children and youth through competitive sports.

11. Mehan, Villanueva, Hubbard, and Lintz (1996) provide a comprehensive analysis and assessment of AVID's operation in San Diego, focusing on high school graduates who had participated in the program for 3 years. A total of 1,053 such AVID students graduated between 1990 and 1992 from 14 high schools in the San Diego City Schools system. Mehan and associates were able to interview 288 of these students. Although statistics are not readily available on the ethnic breakdown in AVID classrooms (in these 14 schools), 41% of the Mehan sample was Latino, and 30% was African American. Yet only four of the eight schools studied extensively had Latino student bodies of 25% or more.

Chapter 9

1. Mediation is an extensively employed method at Auxilio High for dealing with disputes between pupils as well as between pupils and teachers. Pupils and school personnel trained in mediation are called in to help resolve disputes and to find appropriate courses of action.

2. Although relations of trust and rapport are certainly a necessary vehicle for the regular transfer of institutional support, such relations do not guarantee the transfer of high-quality institutional support. Such transfer ultimately depends on the competency and commitment of the agent, on whether the agent actually possesses the knowledge and resources in question, and on the ability of the adolescent to draw such support from the agent. I have made this statement elsewhere in this book, but it merits repeating.

3. Many courses at Auxilio High were sequenced across two semesters; thus, students had opportunities to engage teachers over two terms. The other possibility, however, was also frequent. In some cases, the second sequence of a course (or an area of study) was taught by a different teacher.

4. The concept of alienation is often discussed in terms of both anomie and anomia. Anomie and anomia, in turn, are closely related but conceptually distinct concepts. *Anomie* refers to a property of a social system, whereas *anomia* is used to designate the psychological state of the individual. Although Leo Srole (1956) proposed the term *anomia* to refer to individual manifestations of a systemic phenomenon, I use the term *alienation* in order to place myself in the tradition of researchers working within classical Marxist and neo-Marxist frameworks. As used here, alienation is an individual manifestation, shared with similar others, rooted in the systemic conditions of the school and of the stratification system in society.

5. The notion of "impression management" is lodged in Erving Goffman's (1971) dramaturgical theory. Goffman stressed how we judge ourselves and are

judged by others "in terms of how well we perform in the roles we are given or have adopted. A good performance gains us status or respect with ourselves and our audience" (Kerbo, 1989, p. 183). However we act in the public realm, our behavior carries important consequences. Applied here, this logic translates into low-status persons' having to control impressions gatekeepers have of them. As Lamont and Lareau (1988) have written in their extension of Bourdieu's theory of cultural capital, gatekeepers are quite sensitive to the *cultural signals* transmitted by low-status persons in social interactions (e.g., language use and behavior), and use these signals to exclude lower-ranked persons from participation in institutional arenas deemed the exclusive privilege of "the qualified and deserving" (i.e., members of the dominant group in society and those *deserving outsiders* willing to pledge alliance to this group).

Chapter 10

1. Robert H. Tai is co-author of the articles where our regression and logistic analyses were originally reported (Stanton-Salazar, Chávez, & Tai, in press; Stanton-Salazar, Tai, & Bressler, 1999). Given our collaborative efforts, we are both responsible for the analyses and reporting of the data pertaining to the social embeddedness and help-seeking orientation studies.

2. The survey was administered to 205 students, comprising immigrant, second-, and third-generation adolescents. For purposes of comparability, we eliminated the 60 third-generation adolescents for this report.

3. We followed with a question as to whether they had actually relied on the people indicated: "During the last 3 or 4 months, which of these people have actually provided you with some form of emotional support?"

4. It is important to point out, however, that relational data obtained from semistructured surveys, such as those used by Barrera (1986), Cochran et al. (1990), and Fischer (1982), are far superior to measures in large-scale questionnaires. See also Methodological Note in Stanton-Salazar and Dornbusch (1995, p. 132).

5. We counted both the election of a school agent as a likely source of support *and* the indication of a school agent who had actually been sought out for help.

6. Students usually had six teachers during the fall semester; since most classes are stretched over an academic year at Auxilio High, most students tended to return to most of their teachers during the winter-spring semester.

7. Recent immigrants are those who have resided in the United States for 7 years or less (≤ 7 yrs); percentages are based on cases with complete data.

8. In Stanton-Salazar and Dornbusch (1995, p. 129), we provide auxiliary analyses that further explore the influence of Spanish use and bilingualism on various school and network outcomes.

9. Approximately 82.3% of Latino fathers at this school were found to be blue-collar workers, and three-quarters of Latino mothers had not finished high school (or the equivalent). See Appendix B for complete information on parental socio-economic status.

10. Particularly perplexing was the reverse relationship among Spanish-dominant immigrant Latinos, with higher SES associated with lower interpersonal openness—opposite of the finding for non-Latinos.

11. We began each of our logistic regression analyses by establishing a baseline model with the student background variables. In different terms, for our three separate outcome measures of behavioral embeddedness, we established three respective baseline models.

12. See Stanton-Salazar, Tai, and Bressler (1999) for analyses on organizational participation as a third indicator of behavioral embeddedness.

13. The results show that given two prototypical students, the student with *Desire* = 1 was 1.8 times more likely to seek support than a student with *Desire* = 0. (Unless otherwise stated, we define prototypical as two students similar in all respects except for the variable under consideration in the analysis.)

14. For *Openness*, the results indicate that given two prototypical students, the student with high levels of *Openness* was 2.3 times more likely to seek support for academic issues than a student with low levels of *Openness*. (Please note that we distinguish "high" to be two standard deviations above the average for a variable and "low" to be two standard deviations below the average.)

15. For *Perceived Support*, given two prototypical students, the student with a high level of *Perceived Support* was 10.1 times more likely to seek support for academic issues than a student with low levels of *Perceived Support*.

16. Given two prototypical students, the student with a high level of *Perceived Support* was 9.2 times more likely to seek support for post–high school plans than the student with a low level of *Perceived Support*.

17. Given two prototypical students, the student with *Desire* = 1 (high desire) was 1.8 times more likely to seek support with post–high school plans than the student with *Desire* = 0 (low desire). Given two prototypical students, the student with a high level of *Confidence* was 2.4 times more likely to seek support for post–high school plans than his counterpart with a low level of *Confidence*.

18. A prototypical student with an average grade of A was 1.3 times more likely to seek support with academic issues than his or her counterpart with an average grade of C. Similarly, a prototypical student with a grade of A was 1.4 times more likely to seek support for post–high school plans than his or her counterpart with an average grade of C.

19. See Stanton-Salazar, Tai, and Bressler (1999) for auxiliary analyses focusing on our Spanish-dominant subsample.

20. The work of Patricia Phelan and associates (1998) is an important exception.

21. The exception here appears to be Spanish-dominant students with high grades. Although grades registered the hypothesized effect on seeking academic support for all students, high grades may be particularly relevant for Spanish-dominant students. Besides English proficiency, high grades may be the factor—at the individual level—that generates the onslaught of authentically empowering embeddedness. This, of course, is fortunate for individual students, but it spells disaster for the group as a whole, and for low achievers in particular.

Chapter 11

1. Motion picture (1999), directed by M. Night Shyamalan, about a doleful little boy who sees dead people all around him and a wobbly child psychologist who tries to help him. The little boy resigns himself to keeping his secret to himself because he perceives that the living adults in his life aren't predisposed to believing and validating his experience, and thus lack what would be necessary to help him. The child psychologist passes this threshold and genuinely validates the boy's experience, and in the process earns the boy's trust; the psychologist is now able to deeply comprehend the boy's ghostly reality and, perhaps more important, finally comes to see his past illusive perceptions of self, and to comprehend his own new reality.

2. For an elaboration of how the notion of "borders" is used in the social sciences and youth studies, see Anzaldua (1987), Phelan et al. (1998, p. 11), and Stanton-Salazar (1997, p. 22).

3. Of course, exceptions to this middle-class rule abound (see Hewlett, 1991, chap. 3: "Mainstream Kids and the Time Deficit").

4. See Gene Maeroff's (1998) description of an exceptional youth intervention called *El Puente Academy for Peace and Justice*, located in Brooklyn's Williamsburg section.

5. The concept of *vendido* in Spanish is an emotionally sensitive if not explosive one, roughly translated as "sellout," or one who betrays his original loyalties for personal gain and thus loses his or her integrity in the community of origin. The concept is somewhat synonymous with the colloquial term *Uncle Tom* or *Tom* originating in the African American political lexicon.

6. Occasional exposure to the predatory machinations of *Wall Street* may also reinforce what they see in the streets.

References

Ainsworth, M. D. (1978). *Patterns of attachment: A psychological study of the strange situation*. NJ: Lawrence Erlbaum.

Ames, R. (1983). Help-seeking and achievement orientation: Perspectives from attribution theory. In B. M. DePaulo, A. Nadler, & J. Fisher (Eds.), *New directions in helping: Vol. 2. Help-seeking* (pp. 165–186). New York: Academic Press.

Anthony, E., & Cohler, B. (Eds.). (1987). *The invulnerable child*. New York: Guilford Press.

Anzaldua, G. (1987). *Borderlands, la frontera: The new mestiza*. San Francisco: Spinsters.

Arbona, C., & Novy, D. M. (1991). Career aspirations and expectations of black, Mexican American, and white students. *The Career Development Quarterly, 39*, 231–239.

Baca Zinn, M., & Eitzen, D. S. (1999). *Diversity in families* (5th ed.). New York: Longman.

Bandura, A. (1969). *Principles of behavior modification*. New York: Holt, Reinhart and Winston.

Barnes, J. A. (1972). *Social networks*. Reading, MA: Addison-Wesley.

Barrera, M., Jr. (1981). Social support in the adjustment of pregnant adolescents: Assessment issues. In B. H. Gottlieb (Ed.), *Social networks and social support* (pp. 69–96). Beverly Hills: Sage Publications.

Barrera, M., Jr. (1986). Distinctions between social support concepts, measures, and models. *American Journal of Community Psychology, 14*(4), 413–445.

Barrera, M., Jr., & Baca, L. M. (1990). Recipient reactions to social support: Contributions of enacted support, conflicted support, and network orientation. *Journal of Social and Personal Relationships, 7*, 541–551.

Barth, F. (1969). *Ethnic groups and boundaries: The social organization of cultural difference*. London: Allen & Unwin.

Bellah, R. N., Madsen, R., Sullivan, W., Swidler, A., & Tipton, S. (1985). *Habits of the heart: Individualism and commitment in American life*. Berkeley: University of California Press.

Belle, D., Dill, D., & Burr, R. (1991). Children's network orientations. *Journal of Community Psychology, 19*, 362–372.

Berliner, D. C., & Biddle, B. J. (1995). *The manufactured crisis: Myths, frauds, and the attack on America's public schools*. Reading, MA: Addison-Wesley.

Berndt, T. J. (1979). Developmental changes in conformity to peers and parents. *Developmental Psychology, 15,* 608–616.

Berry, J. W. (1980). Acculturation as varieties of adaptation. In A. Padilla (Ed.), *Acculturation: Theory, models and some new findings* (pp. 9–25). Colorado: Westview Press.

Berry, J. W., Poortinga, Y. H., Segall, M. H., & Dasen, P. R. (1994). *Cross-cultural psychology: Research and applications.* New York: Cambridge University Press.

Blau, P. M. (1964). *Exchange and power in social life.* New York, J. Wiley.

Blau, P. M., & Duncan, O. D. (1967). *The American occupational structure.* New York: Free Press.

Blood, L., & D'Angelo, R. (1974). A progress research report on value issues in conflict between runaways and their parents. *Journal of Marriage and the Family, 36,* 486–491.

Blos, P. (1979). The second individuation process of adolescence: The adolescent passage. In P. Blos (Ed.), *The adolescent passage: Developmental issues* (pp. 141–170). New York: International University Press.

Blumstein, A. (1996). Youth violence, guns, and illicit drug markets: A summary of a presentation (Report presented at the H. John Heinz III School of Public Policy Management, Carnegie Mellon University.) Govt Doc. No.: J 28.24/7:Y 8/996. Washington, DC: U.S. Department of Justice, Office of Justice Programs, National Institute of Justice. [Available on-line: http://www.ncjrs.org/txtfiles/drugmark.txt]

Blumstein, A., Cohen, J., & Farrington, D. P. (1996). Criminal career research: Its value for criminology. In D. F. Greenberg (Ed.), *Criminal careers; Vol. 1* (pp. 391–425). Aldershot, England: Dartmouth Publishing Company Limited.

Boissevain, J. (1974). *Friends of friends: Networks, manipulators and coalitions.* Oxford, England: Basil Blackwell.

Bourdieu, P. (1977a). *Outline of a theory of practice.* Cambridge: Cambridge University Press.

Bourdieu, P. (1977b). Cultural reproduction and social reproduction. In J. Karabel & A. H. Halsey (Eds.), *Power and ideology in education* (pp. 487–511). New York: Oxford University Press.

Bourdieu, P. (1986). The forms of capital. In J. G. Richardson (Ed.), *Handbook of theory and research for the sociology of education* (pp. 241–258). New York: Greenwood Press.

Bourdieu, P., & Wacquant, L. J. D. (1992). *An invitation to reflexive sociology.* Chicago: University of Chicago Press.

Bowlby, J. (1969). *Attachment and loss: Vol. 1. Attachment.* New York: Basic Books.

Bowles, S., & Gintis, H. (1976). *Schooling in capitalist America.* New York: Basic Books.

Boykin, A. W. (1986). The triple quandary and the schooling of Afro-American children. In U. Neisser (Ed.), *School achievement of minority children: New perspectives* (pp. 57–92). London: Lawrence Erlbaum Associates.

Boykin, A. W., & Toms, F. (1985). Black child socialization: A conceptual framework. In H. McAdoo & J. McAdoo (Eds.), *Black children* (pp. 33–51). Beverly Hills, CA: Sage Publications.

Brake, M. (1985). *Comparative youth culture: The sociology of youth culture and youth subcultures in America, Britain, and Canada*. London and New York: Routledge.

Brecher, M., Wang, B., Wong, H., & Morgan, J. P. (1988). Phencyclidine and violence: Clinical and legal issues. *Journal of Clinical Psychopharmacology, 8*(6), 397–401.

Bronfenbrenner, U. (1979). *The ecology of human development: Experiments by nature and design*. Cambridge, MA: Harvard University Press.

Brown, T. F. (1999, August 24). *Theoretical perspectives on social capital*. Unpublished manuscript. [On-line.] Available: http://jhunix.hcf.jhu.edu/~tombrown/Econsoc/soccap.html

Buriel, R. (1984). Integration within traditional Mexican American culture and sociocultural adjustment. In J. L. Martinez & R. Mendoza (Eds.), *Chicano psychology* (2nd ed.) (pp. 95–130). New York: Academic Press.

Burr, W., Leigh, G., Day R., & Constantine, J. (1979). *Symbolic interaction and the family: Contemporary theories about the family*. New York: Free Press.

Carnoy, M., & Levin, H. M. (1985) *Schooling and work in the democratic state*. Stanford, CA: Stanford University Press.

Catsambis, S., & Garland, J. F. (1997). *Parental involvement in students' education during middle school and high school* [Microform]. (No. 18) (December). New York: Center for Research on the Education of Students Placed at Risk.

Centers, N. L., & Weist, M. D. (1998). Inner city youth and drug dealing: A review of the problem. *Journal of Youth Adolescence, 27*, 395–411.

Cicourel, A. V., & Kitsuse, J. I. (1963). *Decision-makers*. Indianapolis: Bobbs-Merrill.

Cicourel, A. V., & Mehan, H. (1983). Universal development, stratifying practices, and status attainment. *Research in Social Stratification and Mobility, 4*, 3–27.

Claes, M. (1994). Friendship characteristics of adolescents referred for psychiatric care. *Journal of Adolescent Research, 9*(2), 180–192.

Clark, R. (1983). *Family life and school achievement: Why poor black children succeed or fail*. Chicago: University of Chicago Press.

Cochran, M. (1990a). The network as an environment for human development. In M. Cochran, M. Larner, D. Riley, L. Gunnarsson, & R. H. Charles (co-authors), *Extending families: The social networks of parents and their children* (pp. 265–276). New York: Cambridge University Press.

Cochran, M. (1990b). Environmental factors constraining network development. In M. Cochran, M. Larner, D. Riley, L. Gunnarsson, & R. H. Charles (co-authors), *Extending families: The social networks of parents and their children* (pp. 277–296). New York: Cambridge University Press.

Cochran, M., Larner, M., Riley, D., Gunnarsson, L., & Charles, R. H. (1990). *Extending families: The social networks of parents and their children*. New York: Cambridge University Press.

Cohen, J. (1996). Characterizing criminal careers. *Crime and Society: Readings in Crime, 1*, 386–393.

Coleman, J. S. (1988). Social capital in the creation of human capital. *American Journal of Sociology, 94*, S95–S120.

Coleman, J. S. (1990). *Foundations of social theory*. Cambridge, MA: Belknap Press of Harvard University Press.

Coleman, J. S., & Hoffer, T. (1987). *Public and private high schools: The impact of communities*. New York: Basic Books.

Colletta, N. D. (1987). Correlates of young mother's network orientations. *Journal of Community Psychology, 15*, 149–160.

Comer, J. P. (1980). *School power: Implications of an intervention project*. New York: Free Press.

Connell, W. F., Stroobant, R. E., Sinclair, K. E., Connell, R. W., & Rogers, K. W. (1975). *12 to 20: Studies of city youth*. Sydney: Hicks, Smith.

Cooper, C., Grotevant, H. D., & Condon, S. M. (1983). Individuality and connectedness in the family as a context for adolescent identity formation and role-taking skill. *New Directions for Child Development, 22*, 43–59.

Costa, F. M., Jessor, R., & Turbin, M. S. (1999). Transition into adolescent problem drinking: The role of psychosocial risk and protective factors. *Journal of Studies on Alcohol, 60*(4), 480–490.

Croninger, R. G., & Lee, V. (1999). *Social capital and dropping out of school: Benefits to at-risk students of teachers' support and guidance*. Unpublished manuscript.

Darder, A. (1991). *Culture and power in the classroom: A critical foundation for bicultural education*. New York: Bergin and Garvey.

De Sola Pool, I., & Kochen, M. (1978). Contacts & influence. *Social Networks, 1*, 5–51.

Demo, D., Small, S., & Savin-William, R. (1987). Family relations and the self-esteem of adolescents and their parents. *Journal of Marriage and the Family, 49*(4), 705–715.

DeSena, J. N. (1990). *Protecting one's turf: Social strategies for maintaining urban neighborhoods*. Lanham, MD: University Press of America.

Dryfoos, J. (1990). *Adolescents at risk: Prevalence and prevention*. New York: Oxford University Press.

Eames, E., & Goode, J. G. (1973). *Urban poverty in a cross-cultural context*. New York: Free Press.

Eckert, P. (1989). *Jocks and burnouts: Social categories and identity in the high school*. New York: Teachers College Press.

Ellison, R. (1994). *Invisible man*. New York: Modern Library. (Original work published 1947)

Ellwood, D. T. (1988). *Poor support: Poverty in the American family*. New York: Basic Books.

Erickson, B. (1996). Culture, class, and connections. *American Journal of Sociology, 102*(1), 217–251.

Erickson, F. D. (1993). Transformation and school success: The politics and culture of educational achievement. In E. Jacob & C. Jordan (Eds.), *Minority education: Anthropological perspectives* (pp. 27–52). Norwood, NJ: Ablex.

Erickson, F. D., & Shultz, J. (1982). *The counselor as gatekeeper: Social interaction in interviews*. New York: Academic Press.

Fanon, F. (1967). *Black skin, white masks*. New York: Grove Press, Inc.

Farrell, W. (1993). *The liberated man; beyond masculinity: Freeing men and their relationship with women*. New York: Berkley Books. (Original work published 1974 by Random House.)

Fine, M. (1991). *Framing dropouts: Notes on the politics of an urban public high school.* Albany: State University of New York Press.

Finkelhor, D., & Baron, L. (1986). Risk factors for child sexual abuse. *Journal of Interpersonal Violence, 1,* 43–71.

Fischer, C. S. (1982). *To dwell among friends.* Chicago: University of Chicago Press.

Freire, P. (1990). *Education for critical consciousness.* New York: Continuum. (Original work published 1973.)

Freire, P. (1993). *Pedagogy of the oppressed.* New York: Continuum. (Original work published 1973.)

Frydenberg, E. (1997). *Adolescent coping: Theoretical and research perspectives.* London and New York: Routledge.

Furstenberg, F., & Hughes, M. (1995). Social capital and successful development among at-risk youth. *Journal of Marriage and the Family, 57,* 580–592.

Garbarino, J., Dubrow, N., Kostelny, K., & Pardo, C. (1992). *Children in danger: Coping with the consequences of community violence.* San Francisco: Jossey-Bass.

Garbarino, J., Kostelny, K., & Dubrow, N. (1991). *No place to be a child: Growing up in a war zone.* Lexington, MA: Lexington Books.

Garbarino, J., & Sherman, D. (1980). High-risk neighborhoods and high-risk families: The human ecology of child maltreatment. *Child Development, 51*(1), 188–198.

Gibson, M. A., & Ogbu, J. U. (1991). *Minority status & schooling: A comparative study of immigrant and involuntary minorities.* New York: Garland Press.

Goffman, E. (1971). *Relations in public.* New York: Basic Books.

Gonzáles, R. O., & La Velle, M. (1985). *The Hispanic Catholic in the United States.* New York: Northeast Catholic Pastoral Center for Hispanics.

Goodman, E. (2000, January 4). Kids get tough love without the love. *Los Angeles Times,* p. B7.

Gordon, M. M. (1964). *Assimilation in American life: The role of race, religion, and national origins.* New York: Oxford University Press.

Gorman-Smith, D., & Tolan, P. (1998). The role of exposure to community violence and developmental problems among inner-city youth. *Development and Psychopathology, 10,* 101–116.

Granovetter, M. S. (1985). Economic action and social structure: The problem of embeddedness. *American Journal of Sociology, 91,* 481–510.

Greene, E. E. (1986, June). A brief introduction to the International Baccalaureate Program. *International Quarterly,* 16–17.

Gross, A. E., & McMullen, P. A. (1983). Models of the help-seeking process. In B. M. DePaulo, A. Nadler, & J. D. Fisher (Eds.), *New directions in helping: Vol. 2. Help-seeking* (pp. 47–70). New York and London: Academic Press.

Grotevant, H. D., & Cooper, C. R. (1986). Individuation in family relationships: A perspective on individual differences in the development of identity and role-taking skill in adolescence. *Human Development, 29,* 82–100.

Grubb, W., & Laserson, M. (1988). *Broken promises: How Americans fail their children.* New York: Basic Books.

Gurin, P., & Epps, E. (1975). *Black consciousness, identity, and achievement.* New York: John Wiley & Sons.

Guthrie, R. V. (1998). *Even the rat was white: A historical view of psychology* (2nd ed.). Boston: Allyn and Bacon.

Harragan, B. L. (1977). *Games mother never taught you*. New York: Warner Books.

Hayes-Bautista, D. E., Schink, W. O., & Chapa, J. (1988). *The burden of support: Young Latinos in an aging society*. Stanford, CA: Stanford University Press.

Heath, S. B., & McLaughlin, M. W. (1993). *Identity & inner city youth: Beyond ethnicity and gender*. New York: Teachers College Press.

Henwood, K. L. (1994). Resisting racism and sexism in academic psychology: A personal/political view. *Feminism and Psychology, 4*, 41–62.

Hewlett, S. A. (1991). *When the bough breaks: The cost of neglecting our children*. New York: Basic Books.

Hill, J. P. (1980). The early adolescent and the family. In M. Johnson (Ed.), *Toward adolescence, the middle school years* (The Seventy-Ninth Yearbook of the National Society for the Study of Education) (pp. 32–55). Chicago: University of Chicago Press.

Hochschild, A. R. (1989). *The second shift*. New York: Viking Penguin.

Homans, G. (1950). *The human group*. New York: Harcourt Brace.

Hondagneu-Sotelo, P. (1994). *Gendered transitions: Mexican experiences of immigration*. Berkeley: University of California Press.

Howitt, D., & Owusu-Bempah, J. (1994). *The racism of psychology: Time for a change*. New York: Harvester Wheatsheaf.

Hughes, D., Galinsky, E., & Morris, A. (1992). The effect of job characteristics on marital quality: Specifying linking mechanisms. *Journal of Marriage and the Family, 54*, 31–42.

Hunter, F. T., & Youniss, J. (1982). Changes in functions of three relations during adolescence. *Developmental Psychology, 18*(6), 806–811.

Hymovich, D. P. (1983). The chronicity impact and coping instrument: Parent questionnaire. *Nursing Research, 32*(5), 275–281.

Ianni, F. (1989). *The search for structure: A report on American youth today*. New York: Free Press.

Jarrett, R. L. (1995). Growing up poor: The family experiences of socially mobile youth in low-income African American neighborhoods. *Journal of Adolescent Research, 10*, 111–135.

Kandel, D., & Lesser, G. S. (1969). Parent-adolescent relationships and adolescent independence in the United States and Denmark. *Journal of Marriage & the Family, 31*(2), 348–358.

Keefe, S. E., & Padilla, A. M. (1987). *Chicano ethnicity*. Albuquerque: University of New Mexico Press.

Keefe, S. E., Padilla, A. M., & Carlos, M. L. (1979). The Mexican American extended family as an emotional support system. *Human Organization, 38*(2), 144–152.

Kerbo, H. R. (1989). *Sociology: Social structure and social conflict*. New York: Macmillan.

Kercher, G. A., & McShane, M. (1984). The prevalence of child sexual abuse victimization in an adult sample of Texas residents. *Child Abuse and Neglect, 8*(4), 495–501.

Khajawall, A. M., Erickson, T. B., & Simpson, G. M. (1982). Chronic phencyclidine and physical assault. *American Journal of Psychiatry, 139*(12), 1604–1606.

Koenig, M., & Zelnik, M. (1982). The risk of premarital first pregnancy among metropolitan-area teenagers: 1976–1979. *Family Planning Perspectives, 14*, 239–248.

Lamont, M., & Lareau, A. (1988). Cultural capital: Allusions, gaps, and glissandos in recent theoretical developments. *Sociological theory, 6*, 153–168.

Lareau, A. (1987). Social class differences in family-school relationships: The importance of cultural capital. *Sociology of Education, 60*(2), 73–85.

Lareau, A. (1989). *Home advantage: Social class and parental intervention in elementary education.* New York: Falmer Press.

Lareau, A. (in press). Linking Bourdieu's concept of capital to the broader field: The case of family-school relationships. In B. Biddle (Ed.), *Social class, poverty, and educational policy* (Vol. 3). New York: Garland Press.

Lareau, A., & Horvat, E. M. (1999). Moments of social inclusion and exclusion: Race, class, and cultural capital in family-school relationships. *Sociology of Education, 72*, 37–53.

Lazarus, R. S., & Folkman, S. (1984). *Stress, appraisal and coping.* New York: Springer.

Levine, A., & Nidiffer, J. (1996). *Beating the odds: How the poor get to college.* San Francisco: Jossey-Bass.

Lin, N., Dean, A., & Ensel, W. (1986). *Social support, life events, and depression.* Orlando: Academic Press.

Lipsitz, J. (1977). *Growing up forgotten: A review of research and programs concerning early adolescence.* Lexington, MA: D. C. Heath.

Lipsitz, G. (1998). *The possessive investment in whiteness: How white people profit from identity politics.* Philadelphia: Temple University Press.

Lipsky, S. (1987). *Internalized racism.* Seattle, WA: Rational Island Publishers.

Lofland, L. H. (1973). *A world of strangers: Order and action in urban public space.* New York: Basic Books.

Lomnitz, L. A. (1977). *Networks and marginality: Life in a Mexican shantytown.* New York: Academic Press.

Lopata, H. Z. (1979). *Women as widows: Support systems.* New York: Elsevier.

López, D., & Stanton-Salazar, R. (in press). The Mexican American second generation: Yesterday, today, and tomorrow. In R. Rumbaut & A. Portes (Eds.), *Ethnicities: Children of immigrants in America.* Berkeley and New York: University of California Press and Russell Sage Foundation.

Lyman, S. M., & Douglass, W. A. (1973). Ethnicity: Strategies of collective and individual impression management. *Social Research, 40*, 344–365.

MacLeod, J. (1987). *Ain't no makin' it: Aspirations and attainment in a low-income neighborhood.* Boulder: Westview Press.

Maeroff, G. I. (1998). *Altered destinies: Making life better for schoolchildren in need.* New York: St. Martin's Press.

Martin, J. M., & Martin, E. P. (1985). *The helping tradition in the black family and community.* Silver Spring, Md.: National Association of Social Workers.

Marx, K. (1967). *Writings of the young Marx on philosohpy and science* (L. D. Easton & K. H. Guddat, Eds. & Trans.). New York: Doubleday & Co., Inc.

Matute-Bianchi, E. (1986). Ethnic identities and patterns of school success and failure among Mexican-descent and Japanese-American students in a California school. *American Journal of Education*, 95, 233–255.

Mehan, H. (1978). Structuring school structure. *Harvard Educational Review*, 48(1), 32–64.

Mehan, H. (1992). Understanding inequality in schools: The contribution of interpretive studies. *Sociology of Education*, 65, 1–20.

Mehan, H., Villanueva, I., Hubbard, L., & Lintz, A. (1996). *Constructing school success: The consequences of untracking low-achieving students.* New York: Cambridge University Press.

Messner, M. (1992). *Power at play.* Boston, MA: Beacon Press.

Miller, A. (1997). The drama of the gifted child: The search for the true self. New York: Basic Books. (Original work published 1979)

Montemayor, R. (1983). Parents and adolescents in conflict: All families some of the time and some families most of the time. *Journal of Early Adolescence*, 3(1–2), 83–103.

Montemayor, R., & Hanson, E. (1985). A naturalistic view of conflict between adolescents and their parents and siblings. *Journal of Early Adolescence*, 5(1), 23–30.

Moore, J. (1994). The chola life course: Chicana heroin users and the barrio gang. *The International Journal of the Addictions*, 29(9), 1115–1126.

Nelson-Le Gall, S. (1985). Help-seeking behavior in learning. In E. W. Gordon (Ed.), *Review of Research in Education*, 12 (pp. 55–90). Washington, DC: American Educational Research Association.

Newmann, F. M. (1992). Introduction. In F. M. Newmann (Ed.), *Student engagement and achievement in American secondary schools.* New York: Teachers College Press.

Newmann, F. M., Wehlage, G., & Lamborn, S. D. (1992). *Student engagement and achievement in American secondary schools.* New York: Teachers College Press.

Ogbu, J. U. (1991). Immigrant and involuntary minorities in comparative perspective. In M. A. Gibson, & J. U. Ogbu (Eds.), *Minority status & schooling: A comparative study of immigrant and involuntary minorities* (pp. 3–33). New York: Garland Press.

Orfield, G. (1994). The growth of segregation in American schools: Changing patterns of segregation and poverty since 1968. *Equity and Excellence in Education*, 27, 5–8.

Park, R. (1967). *The city: Suggestions for the investigation of human behavior in the urban environment.* Chicago: University of Chicago Press.

Patterson, O. (1998). Affirmative action: Opening up workplace networks to Afro-Americans. *Brookings Review*, 16(2), 17.

Paxton, P. (1999). Is social capital declining in the United States?: A multiple indicator assessment. *American Journal of Sociology*, 105(1), 88–127.

Pescosolido, B. A. (1992). Beyond rational choice: The social dynamics of how people seek help. *American Journal of Sociology*, 4(97), 1096–1138.

Phelan, P., Davidson, A. L., & Yu, H. C. (1993). Students' multiple worlds: Navigating the borders of family, peer, and school cultures. In P. Phelan & A. L.

Davidson (Eds.), *Renegotiating cultural diversity in American schools* (pp. 52–88). New York: Teachers College Press.

Phelan, P., Davidson, A. L., & Yu, H. C. (1998). *Adolescents' worlds: Negotiating family, peers, and school.* New York: Teachers College Press.

Portes, A. (1996). *The new second generation.* New York: Russell Sage Foundation.

Portes, A. (1998). Social capital: Its origins and applications in modern sociology. *Annual Review of Sociology, 24,* 1–24.

Portes, A., & Bach, R. L. (1985). *Latin journey: Cuban and Mexican immigrants in the United States.* Los Angeles: University of California Press.

Portes, A., & Rumbaut, R. G. (1996). *Immigrant America: A portrait.* 2nd Edition. Berkeley: University of California Press.

Procidano, M. E., & Heller, K. (1983). Measures of perceived social support from friends and from family: Three validation studies. *American Journal of Community Psychology, 11*(1), 1–25.

Pynoos, R., & Eth, S. (1985). Children traumatized by witnessing personal violence: Homocide, rape or suicide behavior. In S. Eth & R. Pynoos (Eds.), *Posttraumatic stress disorder in children* (pp. 19–43). Washington, DC.

Pynoos, R. S., & Nader, K. (1988). Psychological first aid and treatment approach to children exposed to community violence: Research implications. *Journal of Traumatic Stress, 1*(4), 445–473.

Ramírez, M., & Castañeda, A. (1974). *Cultural democracy, bicognitive development, and education.* New York: Academic Press.

Ricardo, I. (1994). Life choices of African-American youth living in public housing: Perspectives on drug trafficking. *Pediatrics, 93*(6), 1055–1059.

Richardson, R. A., Galambos, N. L., Schulenberg, J. E., & Petersen, A. C. (1984). Young adolescents' perceptions of the family environment. *Journal of Early Adolescence, 4*(2), 131–153.

Rodman, H. (1964). Middle-class misconceptions about lower class families. In A. B. Shostak & W. Gomberg (Eds.), *Blue collar world: Studies of the American worker* (pp. 59–69). Englewood Cliffs, NJ: Prentice Hall.

Rogers, E. M., & Kincaid, D. L. (1981). *Communication networks: Toward a new paradigm for research.* New York: Free Press.

Romo, H. D. (1986). Contrasting perceptions of schooling among the Mexican-origin population. In H. L. Browning & R. O. de la Garza (Eds.), *Mexican immigrants and Mexican Americans: An evolving relation* (pp. 175–193). Austin: CMAS Publications, The University of Texas, Austin.

Romo, H. D., & Falbo, T. (1996). *Latino high school graduation: Defying the odds.* Austin: University of Texas Press.

Rosaldo, R. (1989). *Culture and truth: The remaking of social analysis.* Boston: Beacon Press.

Rumbaut, R. G. (1996). The crucible within: Ethnic identity, self-esteem, and segmented assimilation among children of immigrants. In A. Portes (Ed.), *The new second generation* (pp. 119–170). New York: Russell Sage Foundation.

Rumbaut, R. G. (1997). *Passages to adulthood: The adaptation of children of immigrants in Southern California* (A Report to the Russell Sage Foundation). East Lansing: Michigan State University.

Rumbaut, R. G. (1998). Coming of age in immigrant America. *Research Perspectives on Migration, 1*(6), 1–14.

Rutter, M., Graham, P., Chadwick, O., & Yule, W. (1976). Adolescent turmoil: Fact or fiction? *Journal of Child Psychology and Psychiatry, 17*, 35–36.

Ryan, W. (1976). *Blaming the victim.* New York: Vintage Books. (First published in 1971.)

Sampson, R. J., Raudenbush, S. W., & Earls, F. (1997). Neighborhoods and violent crime: A multilevel study of collective efficacy. *Science, 277*(N5328), 918–924.

Sánchez-Jankowski, M. (1991). *Islands in the street: Gangs and American urban society.* Berkeley: University of California Press.

San Diego Association of Governments (SANDAG). (1995). *Juvenile arrests for violence, San Diego region, 1990, 1991, 1992, 1993, and 1994.* San Diego, CA. [On-line], Available: http://www.sandag.cog.ca.us/data_services/criminal_justice/cj_publications.html

Schacht, R. (1970). *Alienation.* New York: Doubleday & Company, Inc.

Sebald, H. (1986). Adolescents' shifting orientation toward parents and peers: A curvilinear trend over recent decades. *Journal of Marriage & the Family, 48*(1), 5–13.

Shannon, S. M. (1990). English in the barrio: The quality of contact among immigrant children. *Hispanic Journal of Behavioral Sciences, 12*(3), 256.

Simpson, C. H., & Rosenholtz, S. J. (1986). Classroom structure and the social construction of ability. In J. G. Richardson (Ed.), *Handbook of theory and research for the sociology of education* (pp. 113–138). New York: Greenwood Press.

Smetana, J. (1988). Adolescents' and parents' conceptions of parental authority. *Child Development, 59*, 321–335.

Smetana, J. G. (1989). Adolescents' and parents' reasoning about actual family conflict. *Child Development, 60*(5), 1052–1067.

Spivak, S. (1987, July 22). Despair, crime woes face aspirants in the 4th district. *San Diego Tribune*, pp. A1, A-8.

Spradley, J. P. (1979). *The ethnographic interview.* New York: Holt, Rinehart, and Winston.

Srole, L. (1956). Social integration and certain corollaries: An exploratory study. *American Sociological Review, 21*, 709–716.

Stack, C. B. (1974). *All our kin: Struggles for survival in a black community.* New York: Harper and Row.

Stanton-Salazar, R. D. (1997). A social capital framework for understanding the socialization of racial minority children and youth. *Harvard Educational Review, 67*(1), 1–40.

Stanton-Salazar, R. D. (in press). Defensive network orientations as internalized oppression: How schools mediate the influence of social class on adolescent development. In B. Biddle (Ed.), *Social class, poverty, and educational policy* (Vol. 3). New York: Garland Press.

Stanton-Salazar, R. D. (2000). The development of coping strategies among urban Latino youth: A focus on help-seeking orientation and network-related behavior. In M. Montero-Sieburth & F. A. Villarruel (Eds.), *Making invisible Latino adolescents visible: A critical approach to Latino diversity* (pp. 203–238). New York: Falmer.

Stanton-Salazar, R. D., Chávez, L. F., & Tai, R. H. (in press). *The help-seeking orientations of white and Latino high school students: A critical-sociological investigation. Social Psychology of Education: An International Journal.*

Stanton-Salazar, R. D., & Dornbusch, S. M. (1995). Social capital and the social reproduction of inequality: The formation of informational networks among Mexican-origin high school students. *Sociology of Education, 68*(2), 116–135.

Stanton-Salazar, R. D., Tai, R. H., & Bressler, M. (1999). *Social embeddedness: How social networks facilitate academic persistence among high school students.* Unpublished manuscript.

Stanton-Salazar, R. D., & Spina, S. Urso (2000). The network orientations of highly resilient urban minority youth. *The Urban Review: Issues and Ideas in Public Education, 32*(3), 227–261.

Stanton-Salazar, R. D., Vásquez, O., & Mehan, H. (2000). Reengineering success through institutional support. In S. T. Gregory (Ed.), *The academic achievement of minority students: Comparative perspectives, practices, and prescriptions* (pp. 213–247). Lanham, Maryland: University Press of America.

Suárez-Orozco, C., & Suárez-Orozco, M. (1995). *Transformations: Migration, family life, and achievement motivation among Latino adolescents.* Stanford, CA: Stanford University Press.

Sullivan, M. L. (1989). *Getting paid: Youth, crime and work in the inner city.* Ithaca, NY: Cornell University Press.

Suttles, G. D. (1972). *The social construction of communities.* Chicago: University of Chicago Press.

Tinto, V. (1993). *Leaving college.* Chicago: University of Chicago Press. (Original work published 1987)

Töennies, F. (1963). *Community and society.* New York: Harper and Row. (Original work published 1887)

United Way of San Diego County. (1991, December). *Herencia y futuro: Latino future scan.* San Diego, CA: Author.

Valencia, R. R. (1991). *Conclusions: Towards Chicano school success.* In R. R. Valencia (Ed.), *Chicano school failure and success: Research and policy agendas for the 1990's* (pp. 321–325). New York: Falmer Press.

Valencia, R. R., & Aburto, S. (1991). The uses and abuses of educational testing: Chicanos as a case in point. In R. R. Valencia (Ed.), *Chicano school failure and success: Research and policy agendas for the 1990's* (pp. 203–251). New York: Falmer Press.

Valenzuela, A. (1999). *Subtractive schooling: U.S.–Mexican youth and the politics of caring.* New York: State University of New York Press.

Valenzuela, A., & Dornbusch, S. (1994). Familism and social capital in the academic achievement of Mexican-origin and Anglo high school adolescents. *Social Science Quarterly, 75*(1), 18–36.

Valenzuela, A., & Dornbusch, S. (1996). Familism and assimilation among Mexican-origin and Anglo high school adolescents. In R. M. De Anda (Ed.),

Chicanas and Chicanos in contemporary society (pp. 53–62). Boston: Allyn & Bacon.

Valle, R., & Vega, W. (1980). *A natural resource system for health-mental health promotion to Latino/Hispano populations.* Sacramento, CA: Department of Mental Health.

Vaux, A., Burda, P., & Stewart, D. (1986). Orientation toward utilization of support resources. *Journal of Community Psychology, 14*, 159–170.

Vélez-Ibáñez, C. G. (1980). Mexicano/Hispano support systems and confianza: Theoretical issues of cultural adaptation. In R. Valle & W. Vega (Eds.), *A natural resource system for health-mental health promotion to Latino/Hispano Populations* (pp. 45–54). Sacramento, CA: Department of Mental Health.

Vélez-Ibáñez, C. G. (1983). *Bonds of mutual trust: The cultural systems of Mexican/ Chicano rotating credit associations.* New Brunswick, NJ: Rutgers University Press.

Vélez-Ibáñez, C. G. (1997). *Border visions: Mexican cultures of the Southwest United States.* Tucson: University of Arizona Press.

Vigil, J. D. (1988). *Barrio gangs: Street life and identity in Southern California.* Austin: University of Texas Press.

Voydanoff, P. (1987). *Work and family life.* Beverly Hills, CA: Sage.

Wallerstein, J. S., & Kelly, J. B. (1980). *Surviving the breakup: How children and parents cope with divorce.* New York: Basic Books.

Warren, D. I. (1981). *Helping networks: How people cope with problems in the urban community.* Notre Dame, IN: University of Notre Dame Press.

Watt, J. (1989). *Individualism and educational theory.* London: Kluwer.

Weber, M. (1958). *The Protestant ethic and the spirit of capitalism.* New York: Charles Scribner's & Sons. (Original work published 1904)

Wehlage, G. G., Rutter, R. A., Smith, G. A., Lesko, N., & Fernandez, R. R. (1989). *Reducing the risk: Schools as communities of support.* Philadelphia: Falmer Press.

Wellman, B. (1981). *The application of network analysis to the study of social support* (Resource Paper No. 3). Centre for Urban and Community Studies, University of Toronto.

Wellman, B. (1983). Network analysis: Some basic principles. In R. Collins (Ed.), *Sociological Theory* (pp. 155–200). San Francisco: Jossey-Bass.

Williams, T., & Kornblum, W. (1985). *Growing up poor.* New York: Lexington Books.

Willis, P. (1981). *Learning to labor: How working class kids get working class jobs.* New York: Columbia University Press.

Wilson, W. J. (1987). *The truly disadvantaged: The inner city, the underclass, and public policy.* Chicago: University of Chicago Press.

Wish, E. D. (1986). *PCP and crime: Just another illicit drug?* (Research Monograph Series). Bethesda, Maryland: National Institute on Drug Abuse (NIH).

Wynn, J., Richman, H., Rubinstein, R. A., & Littell, J. (1987). *Communities and adolescents: An exploration of reciprocal supports* (A Report to the William T. Grant Foundation Commission on Work, Family and Citizenship: Youth and America's Future). Chicago: University of Chicago, Chapin Hall Center for Children.

Youniss, J. (1980). *Parents and peers in social development*. Chicago: University of Chicago Press.

Youniss, J. (1983a). *Mutuality in parent-adolescent relationship: Social capital for impending adulthood*. Washington, DC: William T. Grant Foundation, Commission on Youth and America's Future.

Youniss, J. (1983b). *Social construction of adolescence by adolescents and parents*. San Francisco: Jossey-Bass.

Youniss, J., & Smollar, J. (1985). *Adolescent relations with mothers, fathers, and friends*. Chicago: University of Chicago Press.

Zavella, P. (1987). *Women's work and Chicano families: Cannery workers of the Santa Clara Valley*. Ithaca, NY: Cornell University Press.

Zhou, M. (1997). Growing up American: The challenge confronting immigrant children and children of immigrants. *Annual Review of Sociology, 23*, 63–95.

Zhou, M., & Bankston III, C. L. (1996). *Growing up American: How Vietnamese children adapt to life in the United States*. New York: Russell Sage Foundation.

Zill, N., Morrison, D. R., & Coiro, M. J. (1993). Long-term effects of parental divorce on parent-child relationships, adjustment, and achievement in young adulthood. *Journal of Family Psychology, 7*(1), 91–103.

Index

Abuse, physical, 110, 138–40
Academic achievement, 3, 10, 13, 14, 113, 122, 233, 243, 258. *See also* Grades
Academic support, 2, 31
  and constraints on immigrant parent–adolescent relations, 154
  and constraints on school personnel–student relations, 209, 211, 214, 216
  and empowering school personnel–student relations, 166, 168, 170, 172, 177, 181, 184, 187
  and school personnel as sources of support, 221–22, 224, 231, 232, 233, 234, 235–36, 243
Acculturation, 22, 29, 123
  and adolescents' perceptions of parental support, 121, 131
  and cases of gratifying adolescent–parent relations, 130
  and constraints on immigrant parent–adolescent relations, 142–47, 156–57
  and constraints on parent-adolescent relations, 116, 118, 121, 122, 123, 126, 131
  and constraints on school personnel–student relations, 209–10, 211
  and generational dissonance, 143, 145, 146
  immigrant parents' concerns about, 100–103
  and immigrant parents' involvement in children's education, 90
  and Mexican parents' model of social mobility and achievement, 99, 100–103
  and parents as sources of support, 126
  and school personnel as sources of support, 221, 223, 229, 242

  styles of, 116
  and ways children are encouraged to do well in school, 95–96
  See also Assimilation
Achievement
  Mexican parents' model of, 98–105
  See also Academic achievement
Acuña, Lourdes, 178–79, 194
Adolescents
  cases of gratifying support between immigrant parents and, 128–31
  characteristics of, 55, 155–57
  emic view of, 4, 5, 6, 7
  importance of help-seeking initiatives from, 122–24
  interviews with, 68–76
  perceptions of parental support by, 117, 119–22
  perceptions of support capabilities of immigrant parents by, 147–52, 153–55
  perspectives of ecological dangers of neighborhoods of, 40–52
  See also Students; *specific topic*
African Americans, 38, 39, 40, 53, 61, 75, 164–65, 166, 237
Age/grade level, and school personnel as sources of support, 230, 233, 235, 237–38, 239, 240
Alienated embeddedness
  characteristics of, 251
  and internalized oppression, 248–64
  and sociological significance of networks, 21
  and stratification and counterstratification, 258–64
  and variations in adaptive response of Latino youth, 259–64

About the Author

Ricardo D. Stanton-Salazar is Associate Professor of Education at the Rossier School of Education, University of Southern California. Dr. Stanton-Salazar received his B.A. in Sociology from the University of California, San Diego (1979). After working as a bilingual elementary school teacher in National City, California, he left to pursue graduate studies at Stanford University in 1983. He earned his M.A. in 1984, and his Ph.D. in Education in 1990. After his doctoral studies, Dr. Stanton-Salazar received a U.C. President's Fellowship and commenced a new research project on Mexican-origin adolescents in San Diego, California. He served on the faculty in the Department of Sociology at UC San Diego from 1992 to 2000. Dr. Stanton-Salazar has served on the editorial board of *Sociology of Education*. His main fields of interest are sociology of education, social stratification, youth culture, race and ethnic relations, and family studies.